The Lives of the Wise in an Anti-God World

The Lives of the Wise in an Anti-God World

Daniel 1–6

MICHAEL KENNETH WILSON

Foreword by Paul R. Williamson

RESOURCE *Publications* · Eugene, Oregon

THE LIVES OF THE WISE IN AN ANTI-GOD WORLD
Daniel 1–6

Resource Publications
An Imprint of Wipf and Stock Publishers
199 W. 8th Ave., Suite 3
Eugene, OR 97401

www.wipfandstock.com

PAPERBACK ISBN: 978-1-7252-8814-0
HARDCOVER ISBN: 978-1-7252-8815-7
EBOOK ISBN: 978-1-7252-8816-4

11/30/20

For Barbara

"Wisdom without power would be pathetic, a broken reed; power without wisdom would be merely frightening; but in God boundless wisdom and endless power are united, and this makes him utterly worthy of our fullest trust."

—J. I. PACKER, *KNOWING GOD*

"History is not open to rational comprehension and mastery, but becomes comprehensible only in so far as God reveals his purposes and fulfils them."

—RICHARD BAUCKHAM, *BIBLE AND MISSION*

"Experience, it is said, makes a man wise. That is silly talk. If there were nothing beyond experience it would simply drive him mad."

—SØREN KIERKEGAARD, *THE JOURNALS OF KIERKEGAARD* 1834–1854

Contents

Foreword

When Mike casually mentioned his work on Daniel a few years back, I had no idea that he was writing such a detailed study. However, I quickly realized that it deserved a much wider audience. I am thus delighted that this first volume has now been published.

"Not seeing the forest for the trees" is something those studying Daniel must certainly avoid. For a relatively short Old Testament book, Daniel contains more than its fair share of interpretative issues and challenges. Moreover, the question of its date, authorship, and genre has been a decisive factor in the hermeneutical stance adopted by most biblical scholars. Consequently, while there is broad agreement on its theological message, there is much debate over many of its details.

It is thus an understandable but unfortunate fact that numerous commentaries on Daniel tend to focus primarily on the latter—the book's interpretative problems—rather than on how its theological truths are artfully woven and communicated through the literary details of the text. The few exceptions to this generally reflect a fairly negative approach to the text's historical value, understanding it mostly—if not entirely—in terms of creative *fiction*.

However, *The Lives of the Wise in an Anti-God World* bucks both these trends. It pays careful attention to how literary devices, including satire, are employed to enhance the book's theological message, without seriously undermining its historical significance. The result is a critically-informed and insightful interpretation of Daniel 1–6 which takes the literary artistry, historical credibility, and theological message of the text most seriously.

I am confident that all who read this book will grow not only in their understanding of the book of Daniel, but also, and more importantly, in their appreciation of the God of Daniel *"whose kingdom"*—as Nebuchadnezzar discovered—*"is an eternal kingdom, and whose dominion endures from generation to generation"* (Dan 4:3).

PAUL R. WILLIAMSON
Moore College, Sydney

Preface

This study of Daniel 1–6 is not a stand-alone. It is my hope and intention to produce a companion analysis of Daniel 7–12.

Many commentaries adopt an atomistic approach, which involves a verse-by-verse analysis of the text. While this is foundational for understanding a passage it is but preparatory. For, as readers, what we need to do is understand the main ideas and major points that are being conveyed in a passage of Scripture. Consequently, I have tried to set out my analysis in a way that, hopefully, enhances the impact of God's Word upon the minds and hearts of readers. Any feedback on how I can do this better would be appreciated.

My bibliography, while extensive, will indicate the extent and limits of my research. I fully expect that there may be key contributions I've missed. I welcome all the help I can get in identifying "must read" books and articles.

It would take a separate volume to deal with the myriad of historical, literary and theological issues that are raised by this book. I have deliberately limited the scope of this particular volume to an exegesis of the text itself, though inevitably my own presuppositions about historical, literary and theological matters clearly impact this. Of course, exegesis is massively affected by one's decisions concerning the dating of this book, especially given the undoubted major attention devoted to Antiochus IV Epiphanes and the detailed predictive material which many consider to be *ex eventu*. My own position is this: allowing for some later touch-ups, this book was predominantly a sixth century BC work. In my exegesis of the text it will become evident that if this position is jettisoned then the basic theology of the book is fundamentally undermined. God is no longer a God who truly controls history. Instead, it becomes a case of "Let's pretend God controls history."

There are strong satirical elements in Daniel's often highly entertaining re-telling of history. This approach to history certainly does not equate with modern historiographical techniques, but it is nonetheless essentially reliable. For example, Nebuchadnezzar is not mistaken with Nabonidus. The purpose is not to recall historical events in a manner that will "set the record straight," but to communicate major theological truths. Not least of these is that God is sovereign over all expressions of human rule and that he alone is in control of the historical process and, though this will continue to involve immense expressions of evil and suffering for God's people, he will ensure the ultimate success of his "kingdom" and the exaltation and glorification of his people.

Daniel is a book that stands in awe of the sovereignty of God. But this sovereignty is not just viewed *by* the book but extends to the very composition *of* the book. I entertain no doubt that this is God-breathed Scripture. Yes, it is simultaneously a 100 percent human product and, therefore, it is right and proper for us to apply the same methods of analysis and interpretation we apply to literature in general. But remember "Daniel" means "God is my judge." We insult God himself when we treat the book of Daniel as if its authority and standing depend on our assessment and fail to let our sovereign God use this wonderfully constructed book to judge us. If we would stand in awe of our sovereign Lord then we must stand in awe of his sovereign Word.

May studying Daniel be for you a truly "awesome" experience.

Introducing Daniel

THE MESSAGE OF DANIEL

Notwithstanding the disasters and sufferings experienced by God's people, and the desolation of their sacred city and temple, they must understand it is not oppressive foreign rulers who control the course of history. Rather, God the Creator is Lord of the nations and the Lord of history as he has demonstrated in his dealings with the foreign rulers known personally to Daniel, judging and humiliating them in their pride, and using them to bring glory to himself.

Nevertheless, this is no excuse for political conspiracies or acts of sedition, responses conspicuously absent from the lives of Daniel and his friends. Barring the kinds of crises faced by Daniel and his friends, God's people, like them, must be faithful servants of the foreign ruler concerned, in recognition of the fact that God has granted him his right to rule. Yet their service must be sharply discriminated from the servile, obsequious service rendered by those motivated by fear, ambition, and jealousy. Daniel and his friends exemplified the allegiance of God's people that is first and foremost to God and not to the foreign power. God's people must not compromise on this point, but, like Daniel and his friends, be prepared to forfeit their own lives if so required, and, in fact, many will lose their lives in latter days when human rule will blasphemously defy God and endeavour to blot out his people.

Ultimately all human reigns will be displaced and succeeded by the everlasting reign of God expressed in the vindication of his people, the re-building of Jerusalem, and the climactic coming of the messianic ruler to whom God has given all authority, glory, and power. But until that time comes, God's people, like Daniel and his friends, can expect to be sorely tried and unjustly treated. God's people will continue to live and suffer under oppressive foreign rule, their sacred sanctuary will again be treated with utter contempt by blasphemous human authority, and even their long-awaited messianic ruler will die. But terrifying as the future might seem, their covenant-keeping God is able to sustain them, and, should he so choose, to prosper them, as he amply demonstrated in the lives of Daniel and his friends. Regardless, he will most certainly and most gloriously deliver his people, even if from death itself, as he already foreshadowed in his miraculous deliverances of Daniel and his friends.

Daniel and his friends provided a model of the covenant-faithfulness and covenant-distinctiveness that must characterize God's suffering people, and of the proper stance to adopt with respect to foreign rule. Like them, God's people need to draw upon God's wisdom, a wisdom which is enabled by God alone and which, in its understanding of the future, cannot be matched by the wisdom available to human rulers. This too was demonstrated in Daniel's lifetime and experiences, with the mightiest of foreign rulers, in their God-created confusion, being at times forced to acknowledge that the God of Daniel is the source of the wisdom they desperately need. Indeed, just as through the Book of Daniel, Daniel and his friends teach God's suffering people how to remain faithful to God, so all who are truly wise will teach many to share their understanding of God's over-arching sovereignty and his ultimate purposes, and in so doing, will lead many to live, like them, a life of covenant-faithfulness.

Deity is inaccessible to the elite wise men of this world, but for those, like Daniel, who fear and know God, and who refuse to compromise their ultimate allegiance to God, God is not distant, as indicated by the acknowledged presence of his Spirit in Daniel, and his angelic presence with his servants in times of crisis.

THE HISTORICAL CONTEXT

In the seventh century BC the Aramean inhabitants of Mesopotamia viewed the Assyrians as their most dangerous enemy. Therefore, they championed the Babylonian cause against Assyrian domination and successfully led a liberation movement that resulted in the establishment of the Chaldean dynasty under Nabopolassar and his son, Nebuchadnezzar II.[1]

---

1. Oppenheim, *Ancient Mesopotamia*, 60.

Nabopolassar began to revolt against Assyrian rule in 626 BC when Sinsharishkun was king of Assyria. Nabopolassar's name means "Oh, Nabu, protect my son." As the Nabopolassar Cylinder[2] reveals, Nabopolassar regarded both Marduk and Nabu, the son of Marduk, as his patrons.[3] It was Nabopolassar who founded the Neo-Babylonian, that is, Chaldean empire, ruling it from 625 to 605 BC. He established his empire after conquering Assyria, though the Medes under Cyaxares had also been attacking Assyria, capturing Ashur, the religious center of Assyria. It was under the ruined walls of Ashur that Nabopolassar and Cyaxares formed an alliance sealed by marriage between Nebuchadnezzar ("Oh, Nabu, protect my offspring"), Nabopolassar's son, and Amytis, Cyaxares's granddaughter. The Scythians joined the coalition and in 612 BC these three allies destroyed Nineveh, the administrative center of Assyria, following a three-month siege. Sinsharishkun was possibly killed at this time for he now disappears from the historical scene. At this point the Neo-Assyrian empire, which commenced in 911 BC, came to its end. The Neo-Babylonian empire that replaced it, the eleventh Dynasty of Babylon[4], was of much shorter duration.

Following the fall of Nineveh the Assyrians, now led by Ashur-uballit II (possibly Sinsharishkun's brother), moved their capital to Harran. However, this too fell to the Babylonians in 609 BC and it is possible that Ashur-uballit himself was killed at this time. The Assyrians were thus forced to move their capital yet again, this time to Carchemish, an important city on the upper Euphrates.

Ashur-uballit had formed an alliance with Egypt in order to repel the Babylonian invaders. Prior to this, an earlier victory of Neco II of Egypt over the Assyrians at Carchemish resulted in Egypt occupying the Phoenician provinces of the Neo-Assyrian empire. However, in 605 BC, Nebuchadnezzar defeated the Egyptians at the famous Battle of Carchemish.

2. Unearthed in Baghdad around 1921 and dated at late 7th century BC. The text is 102 lines long and written in Akkadian.

3. Nabopolassar states: "When I was young, although the son of a nobody, I constantly sought out the temples of Nabu and Marduk, my patrons. My mind was preoccupied with the establishment of their orders and the complete performance of their rites." Translation presented by K. C. Hanson adapted from Al-Rawi and Beaulieu. "K. C. Hanson's Collection of Mesopotamian Documents." http://www.kchanson.com/ANCDOCS/meso/nabo.html Downloaded 20/2/07

4. 1st Dynasty: c.1894–1595 BC; 2nd Dynasty (involving no rule over Babylon itself, but over Sumerian areas to the south): c.1732–1460 BC; 3rd Dynasty: c.1570–1153 BC; 4th Dynasty: c.1155–1025 BC; 5th Dynasty: c.1025–1004 BC; 6th Dynasty: c.1004–985 BC; 7th Dynasty: c.985–979 BC; 8th Dynasty: c.979–943 BC; 9th Dynasty: c.943–732 BC; 10th Dynasty: c.732–620 BC; 11th Dynasty: 626–522 BC.

The Chaldean empire now controlled all Assyrian provinces, including the Phoenician ones.

It is worth noting that in the process of coming to Carchemish to meet the Babylonian threat, the Egyptian army was delayed at Megiddo by King Josiah. In the ensuing battle Josiah was killed and his army defeated. Still, delays like this meant that by the time the Egyptians got to Carchemish and joined their forces with those of the Assyrians they found themselves facing a Babylonian army that had had time to build its own formidable forces to full strength.

The Chaldean victory at Carchemish ensured Egypt would not block Babylonian access to the Mediterranean. Conquest and control of Judah was thus deemed a necessary part of ensuring a flourishing Babylonian economy.

Nabopolassar died in 605 BC while his son Nebuchadnezzar was leading the Chaldean army in Syria. On hearing the news Nebuchadnezzar speedily returned to Babylon to secure his power. The Medes and Scythians had withdrawn leaving most of the Assyrian empire for Nebuchadnezzar II ("Nebuchadnezzar the Great") and his successors to rule. Like the Assyrians before him, Nebuchadnezzar made it an annual practice to send his army to each conquered territory to collect tribute. The Chaldean army would conquer and punish recalcitrant cities, as it did with Jerusalem in 597 and 586 BC.[5]

The book of Daniel is set early in Nebuchadnezzar's rule. Nebuchadnezzar was actually born about 630 BC and died around 562 BC at the age of 68. Nebuchadnezzar made Babylon the largest city of the world, a status it had once had before from around 1770 to 1670 BC and was now to have again until about 320 BC. Indeed, many believe that Babylon was the first city in the world to attain a population exceeding 200,000. According to estimates Babylon covered an area over 2,500 acres (10,000 hectares). The Euphrates River flowed through Babylon with the name of this great city symbolizing the entire empire.

In 601 BC the forces of Nebuchadnezzar and of Egypt's Pharaoh Neco clashed in an inconclusive battle with both sides suffering heavy losses. Nebuchadnezzar returned to Babylon to reorganize his army. Like many other states controlled by Babylon at this time, Jehoiakim committed a serious error of judgment, believing this turn of events indicated the time was right to rebel against Babylon with Egyptian assistance.[6] But Egyptian aid was not forthcoming (2 Kings 24:7). Babylon was poised to crush this revolt but

---

5. Oppenheim, *Ancient Mesopotamia*, 163.

6. Bright, *A History of Israel*, 327.

Jehoiakim died in 598 BC, probably assassinated (see Jer 22:18–23; 36:30), leaving his 18 year old son to face the Chaldean onslaught. After reigning for but three months Jehoiachin lost Jerusalem to the Babylonian army and he himself, along with other high officials and leading citizens, was taken to Babylon. Daniel had already been in Babylon for a number of years by this time.

2 Kings 24:10–17 describes what happened in 597 BC, when the temple was stripped of all its treasures and Nebuchadnezzar carried into exile "all Jerusalem," including "all the officers and fighting men, and all the craftsmen and artisans—a total of ten thousand," which included "the entire force of seven thousand fighting men . . . and a thousand craftsmen and artisans." From Jeremiah 52:28 it would appear that an additional 3,023 prominent Jews were deported (presumably, a much greater number when women and children are included). We are informed: "Only the poorest people of the land were left" (2 Kings 24:14).

After Jehoiachin's removal Babylon appointed a Jew, Zedekiah, Jehoiachin's uncle, to represent Babylonian interests as the King of Judah. In 589 BC Pharaoh Apries mounted another attempted invasion of the Levant. Once again various states mistakenly believed the time was opportune to rebel against Babylon. Judah was one such state. Babylon decided it was time to prevent anything like this recurring and in 588 BC laid siege to Jerusalem, destroying both it and the temple in 587 BC. This was followed by a relocation of the bulk of the population to Babylon. Jeremiah notes that 832 people, apparently eminent Jews, were carried into exile at this time (Jer 52:29).

Following their defeat at Carchemish in 605 BC, the Egyptians never again became a major power in the Middle East. As we have seen this was not for want of trying. In 570 BC yet another attempt to establish a presence in the area was thwarted when Pharaoh Apries was defeated by the Greeks at Cyrene. This situation became all the more embarrassing because it was followed by a revolt among the Egyptian troops. Amasis, the general Apries sent to deal with this crisis actually joined the revolt and made himself Pharaoh. Ironically, the ensuing clashes between Apries and Amasis resulted in a defeated Apries seeking refuge in Nebuchadnezzar's court. In 568 BC Apries invaded Egypt with Nebuchadnezzar's support. However, he was defeated and imprisoned and later put to death by Amasis (Ahmose II), who then had him buried with full military honors.

The last king of the neo-Babylonian period was Nabonidus ("Nabu has exalted the king") (555–539 BC) from Harran, a king not mentioned in the book of Daniel. Nabonidus usurped the throne, replacing the weak Labashi-Marduk. The cuneiform texts reveal that, like Nebuchadnezzar, Nabonidus was responsible for extensive building projects throughout Babylon.

Nabonidus spent ten years of his seventeen-year reign in Tema in a desert area. The supreme deity of Babylonia was Marduk and Nabonidus angered the Babylonian priests when he sought, with his mother, to promote the cult of Sin, the moon god. His contemporaries regarded him as the "mad" king of Babylon.[7] Nabonidus had left his son Belshazzar in Babylon to rule in his stead.

There were a further three obscure kings between Nebuchadnezzar and Nabonidus who are also not mentioned in Daniel: Amel-Marduk (562–560 BC; called Evil-Merodach in 2 Kings 25:27–30, the king who released Jehoiachin and treated him with honor), Nebuchadnezzar's son Neriglissar (560–556 BC), and the son of Neriglissar, Labashi-Marduk (556 BC).

Cyrus the Great began to extend the Persian empire from around 550 BC onwards, after revolting against the Median emperor, Astyages (585–550 BC). He took the Median Empire. From 547–546 BC he took Upper Mesopotamia and Lydia in Asia Minor. Then, in the east, he took Hyrcania and Parthia and campaigned in Afghanistan. In 539 BC Cyrus conquered the province of Elam. The Babylonian empire came to an end in the same year when the Persian emperor, half Median himself, conquered Babylon through the instrumentality of the former governor of Elam, Gobryas (Gubaru).[8] In 538 BC Cyrus issued his famous decree, permitting Judeans to return to Jerusalem.

7. Oppenheim, *Ancient Mesopotamia*, 152.

8. Redditt, *Daniel 7*.

HISTORICAL PERIOD RELEVANT TO DANIEL

BC		BC
605	Nebuchadnezzar (605/4–652), as crown prince, defeats Egyptians at Carchemish	626–585 Cyaxeres
601	Nebuchadnezzar is repulsed by Pharaoh Neco	
586	Babylon defeats Jerusalem: walls demolished and temple destroyed	585–550 Astyages
	Babylonian Rulers: Amel-Marduk/Evil-Merodach (562–560); Neriglissar (560–556); Labash-Marduk (556); Nabonidus (556–539) + Belshazzar co-regent (549–539)	
539	Cyrus captures Babylon	550–530 Cyrus
	Edict of Restoration (Ezra 1:1–4)	530–522 Cambyses (Media)
520	Rebuilding of temple beings	522–486 Darius I (Hystaspes)
490	Persians defeated at Marathon by Greeks	486–465 Xerxes I (Ahaseurus)
	Persian rulers: Artaxerxes I Longimanus (465–424); Xerxes II (423); Darius II Nothus (423–404); Artaxerxes II Mnemon (404–358); Artaxerxes III Ochus (358–338); Arses (338–336); Darius III Codamannus (336–331)	
	Alexander the Great (336–323) defeats Persians at: River Granicus (334); Issus (333); Guagamela (331)	
332	Alexander conquers Palestine	
	WARS OF SUCCESSION (332–301)	

Ptolemaic Kingdom:	Seleucid Kingdom:
Ptolemy I Lagi/Soter (323-285) = Dan 11:5; Ptolemy III Philadelphus (285-246) = Dan 11:6; Ptolemy III Euergetes I (246-222) = Dan 11:7-8; Ptolemy IV Philopater (222-204) m. Arsinoe III = Dan 11:11,12,14; Ptolemy V Epiphanes (204-180) m. Cleopatra I = Dan 11:17	Seleucus I (312/11-280); Antiochus I Soter (280-261); Antiochus II Theos (261-246); Seleucus II Callinicus (246-226); Seleucus III Ceraunus (226-223); Antiochus III the Great (223-187); Seleucus IV Philopator (187-175)
	Battle of Magnesia (190): Seleucids routed by Romans

	Antiochus IV Epiphanes (175–164/3)
174	Polis founded in Jerusalem. Jason usurps high priesthood. Onias deposed
172	Jason deposed. Menelaus is High Priest
170	Onias murdered
169	Antiochus invades Egypt. Loots Jerusalem temple with Menelaus
168	Second war with Egypt. Apollonius founds citadel in Jerusalem
	Persecution and Jewish Revolt begin
167	(15 Kislev—Dec 6): Antiochus sacrifices pigs on the temple altar
164	Temple captured by Judas Maccabeus. On 25 Kislev (Dec 14) temple cleansed

Daniel 1

Drawing the Line

The Establishment of the Distinctiveness of Daniel and his Friends: God's Sovereignty Veiled, and the Superior Wisdom of the Jews Explained

INTRODUCTION

Scholars generally agree that Daniel 1 not only introduces the stories of Daniel 2–6 —as the time frame from Nebuchadnezzar to Cyrus indicates— but also the book as a whole, as indicated by such themes as temple desecration, the contrast between divine and human sovereignty, and wisdom.[1]

---

1. Hamilton contends that Daniel 1 corresponds to Daniel 10–12. He maintains that the book begins with exile and ends with return from exile. However, at no point does he demonstrate that Chapters 10–12 bear this reading, other than to make much of 12:2, the significance of resurrection from the dead. Hamilton interprets this in the light of Ezekiel 37 and Hosea 5:14–15, which treat exile from the land as a departure from the realm of life and therefore as a state of death. This is certainly not evident in Hosea 5:14–15. Hamilton then takes Ezekiel 37 and Hosea 6:1–3 as likening return from exile to resurrection from the dead. Along these lines he supposes that Daniel 12:2 therefore implies return from exile. But without a fuller exegesis of Daniel 10–12 (especially Daniel 12) that will demonstrate such a motif, this remains highly speculative. (Hamilton, *Clouds of Heaven*, 77.) Subsequently, I note that Philpot has also noted the lack of data to support Hamilton's claim that chapters 10–12 form an inclusio with

STRUCTURE

To describe Daniel 1 as a *tale* is problematic.[2] But the pattern characteristic of tales identified by Coats, while somewhat artificial, roughly fits Daniel 1: Exposition (vv. 1–2); Complication (vv. 3–7); Resolution (vv. 8–16); Denouement (vv. 17–20); Conclusion (v. 21). Coats observes that often "the resolution of the complication will mark the critical insight into the goals of the story, or at least it will provide some signpost toward that end."[3] This indicates that verses 8–16 have special structural significance.

Unlike Coats, Milne, applying Vladimir Propp's model, does not see verses 1–7 performing the functions of a "tale" but rather describing "the initial situation."[4] Goldingay, structuring the chapter on the basis of content alone, uses the word "resolution" differently.[5] He observes that verses 1–14 create "tension" while verses 15–21 involve "resolution." The chiastic structure shown below represents a modification of Goldingay's:

Tension: The Implications of Defeat (1–14)

1–2 Nebuchadnezzar defeats Israel

3–7 Nebuchadnezzar requires certain Israelites to undergo training

8 Daniel (representatively) resolves to avoid defilement

9–14 The setting up of a test for Daniel and his friends

Resolution: Triumph (15–21)

15 Daniel (and friends) triumph in the test

16 Daniel and his friends triumph in avoiding defilement

17–20 Daniel and his friends triumph in the training

21 Daniel outlasts Nebuchadnezzar

It is difficult from this analysis to determine whether any particular part of the chapter should be accorded especial significance relative to the rest. Many understand the center of a chiasm to hold this status and if this

---

chapter 1: Philpot, "Review of Hamilton," 813.

2. John J. Collins, who is typical of the kind of literary criticism which disparages the historicity of Daniel, uses the label "court tale" in describing Daniel 1. See "The Court Tales," 218–34.

3. "Tale" in *Saga, Legend, Tale*, 65.

4. She recognizes, though discounts the possibility, that verses 1–7 may accomplish two Proppian functions: (1) Villainy—Nebuchadnezzar's conquest of Jerusalem? (2) Departure—the deportation of Daniel and his friends. Milne, *Vladimir Propp*, 207. Milne notes that the issue of whether verses 1–7 operate as an initial situation or as a tale function depends on whether the actions of Nebuchadnezzar described here set a specific plot in motion or not. *Vladimir Propp*, 208.

5. Goldingay, *Daniel*, 8.

is so then presumably verses 9–15 perform this function. This substantially overlaps with Coats' identification of verses 8–16 as holding the key to the chapter.

Also worthy of note is John Sweigart's proposal of a more detailed chiastic structure for Daniel 1:[6]

A (1:1)The beginning of Daniel's career.

  B (1:2) Articles taken from the house of God (to demonstrate the inferiority of Israel's God).

    C (1:3) Master of the eunuchs brings young men to Babylon (at the end of the siege).

      D (1:4) Young men are shown to be capable of learning Chaldean language and literature.

        E (1:5) The king chooses their diet and training.

          F (1:6) Daniel and his three friends among the sons of Judah chosen

            G (1:7) New names are given to the four.

              H (1:8) Daniel fears God and chooses not to be defiled.

                X (1:9) God had granted Daniel favor with the master of eunuchs.

              H' (1:10) Chief of eunuchs fears the king.

            G' (1:11–14) New diet of clean food given to the four.

          F' (1:15) Daniel and his three friends compared to their peers—better health.

        E' (1:16) King's diet discarded.

      D' (1:17) God gives the young men ability in all literature and knowledge.

    C' (1:18,19) Master of eunuchs brought Daniel and friends to the king at the end of days.

  B' (1:20) Daniel and friends shown to be superior to Babylonian worship leaders.

A' (1:21) The end of Daniel's career.

This analysis suitably places central focus on the role of God in this situation. But in biblical narrative it is typical for narration to be subordinate to direct speech. Alter comments:

---

6. Downloaded from www.inthebeginning.org 8/6/2009. This analysis serves to highlight the role played by God behind the scenes.

> In any given narrative event, and especially, at the beginning of any new story, the point at which dialogue first emerges will be worthy of special attention, and in most instances, the initial words spoken by a personage will be revelatory, perhaps more in manner than in matter, constituting an important moment in the exposition of character.[7]

If we accept the above then verses 10–13 assume particular significance in the exegesis:

Narrative: vv. 1–9	Prepares for direct speech
Direct Speech: vv. 10–13	Central ideas in chapter
Narrative: vv. 14–21	Confirmation of direct speech

As the above analyses indicate there is no one way of understanding the structure of Daniel 1, though in all three of the options above the central portion—resolution/center of chiasmus/direct speech—emerges as being of particular importance.

Another helpful way of looking at Daniel 1 is provided by Rata,[8] who sees Daniel 1 as conveying the following message to God's people: "Heavy times call us to show faithfulness and provide pathways to wonderful opportunities of service."

He grounds this in what he sees as three movements involving trial and a call to faithfulness:

1. "Sometimes God allows us to face heavy trials to accomplish His holy purposes." This reflects the way God allowed (1) Judah to be conquered; (2) temple articles to be carried off and placed in Marduk's treasure house; and (3) the taking captive of some of the finest young Israelites to be trained to serve Nebuchadnezzar.

2. "Sometimes God tests us, then helps us successfully face those tests when we determine to be faithful." This reflects (1) the superior health of Daniel and his friends after they determined not to be defiled and then prospered following the ten-day test in which they are only vegetables and water; and (2) the giving by God of unusual abilities to the four men, with Daniel receiving special ability to understand visions and dreams.

3. "At all times, God gives us wonderful opportunities of service when we have determined to be faithful." This reflects (1) the exaltation of the

---

7. Alter, *The Art of Biblical Narrative*, 74.
8. Downloaded from www.fgbc.org/equip/ 8/6/2009.

four men to be part of the king's regular staff of advisors due to their faithfulness to God and the excellence displayed in the training program; (2) their greatly superior ability when compared with their peers; and (3) the longevity with which Daniel served at the highest level.

> This analysis is helpful in highlighting the way in which Daniel 1 can be applied to the lives of readers in all ages. In particular, it links together such themes as suffering, testing, God's sovereignty, faithfulness, and service.

HISTORICAL MOORINGS

Given the demise of the northern tribes it becomes increasingly the case that "Judah" stands for "Israel."[9] Historical research has shown that Judeans "integrated to various degrees into the life of their new home" and that some "even gravitated around the royal court."[10] At the beginning of the twentieth century administrative documents were discovered in the storeroom of the Babylonian royal palace, datable to the thirteenth year of Nebuchadnezzar's reign, which were published by Ernst Weidner in 1939. A group of Judeans appeared in these cuneiform tablets.

Beaulieu summarizes the evidence gleaned from a group of cuneiform contract tablets which originated mainly from two localities in the Babylonian region of Nippur. Most of those named in these documents have West Semitic and Judean names. Evidently, then, it was recent Jewish exiles who founded one of the above two localities, which they called Al Yahudu/Yahudayu ("city of Judah/of the Judeans")—the Babylonian name of Jerusalem.

In these tablets we learn of rations being delivered to groups of foreigners of whom some were clearly state prisoners. These include none other than Jehoiachin himself, plus a number of unnamed Judean men and princes. It would appear that they were part of Jehoiachin's retinue. As Beaulieu concludes:

> . . . the story of Daniel and his three companions being taken to the court of Babylon, given rations from the king's table, and educated in the lore and manners of the Chaldeans, fits remarkably well with the evidence available from contemporary documents.[11]

9. Meadowcroft and Irwin, *The Book of Daniel*, 28.
10. Beaulieu, "Babylonian Background," 274.
11. "Babylonian Background," 275.

FROM TEMPLE DESECRATION TO THE PROSPECT
OF TEMPLE RESTORATION (1:1–2, 21)

At the commencement and near the very close of the book of Daniel stands an act of temple desecration. Daniel begins with Nebuchadnezzar taking vessels from the house of God and placing them in the treasury of his own god.[12] The siege of Jerusalem, the surrendering of the king of Judah, and the desecration mark the beginning not merely of this literary work but of a new era. The book of Daniel takes us from the opening of this new era to its close. The book finishes with Daniel and the true people of God, the wise, still being immersed in a world controlled by blasphemous anti-God rule. Indeed, worse is yet to come. For beyond the hope of returning from captivity and rebuilding the temple lies the prospect of yet further temple desecration. The wise know that human nature will not change. The wicked will continue to act wickedly (12:10). Inevitably, there will come the time when "the regular burnt offering is taken away and the abomination that makes desolate is set up" (12:11).

The book begins by indicating that the catastrophe which envelops God's people via Nebuchadnezzar is not outside, but subject to the sovereignty of God. In the same way, the book ends by indicating that God is sovereign over the terrible history that will culminate in the ultimate act of temple desecration. For God himself has pre-determined when this evil act will occur: after "1290 days" (12:11). Following this God's people will only need to endure a little while, till the end of "1335 days," and then they will experience the blessing of God. "The end" lies well beyond the lifetime of Daniel. He must go his way, "rest" in death and then bodily rise to receive his inheritance "at the end of the days" (12:13).

Daniel 1:1–2 and 1:21 provide the historical framework for the chapter and these statements are evidently drawn from 2 Chronicles 36 (see chart below).[13] Once this connection is recognized then we are able to understand the implication of 1:21. That is, we first encounter Daniel in connection with the desecration of the temple (and the loss of Jerusalem). But this

---

12. A parallel is provided by what the king of Moab, Mesha, once reported: "At that time, Chemosh said to me, 'Go! Take Mt. Nebo from Israel.' So I deployed my soldiers at night and attacked Nebo from dawn until noon. I won a great victory and I sacrificed seven thousand men, women, and children from Nebo to Chemosh. I brought sacred vessels from the sanctuary of Yahweh and laid them before Chemosh." Matthews and Benjamin, "Annals of Mesha," 169.

13. See particularly 2 Chronicles 36:5–7, 18, 22–23 (and cf. Daniel 1:3 with 2 Chron 36:20). Daniel 1:1–7 may well also involve a deliberate echo of Isaiah 39:5–7, especially if, as Grillo contends, the book of Daniel as a whole gives evidence of interaction with the book of Isaiah, as a whole. See Grillo, "From a Far Country," 363–380.

same Daniel is still present when Cyrus issued his decree that the Jerusalem temple be rebuilt and the Jewish people be allowed to return to Jerusalem to achieve this.

		In the first year of Cyrus king of Persia, in order to fulfill the word of the Lord spoken by Jeremiah, the Lord moved the heart of Cyrus king of Persia to make a proclamation throughout his realm and to put it in writing:
In the third year of the reign of Jehoiakim king of Judah . . . (Dan 1:1a)	And Daniel remained there until the first year of King Cyrus (Dan 1:21)	
Nebuchadnezzar king of Babylon came to Jerusalem and besieged it. (Dan 1:1b)	Nebuchadnezzar king of Babylon attacked [Jehoiakim] and bound him with bronze shackles to take him to Babylon. Nebuchadnezzar also took to Babylon articles from the temple of the Lord and put them in his temple there. (2 Chron 36:6–7)	
And the Lord gave Jehoiakim king of Judah into his hand, along with some of the articles from the temple of God. These he carried off to the temple of his god in Babylonia and put in the treasure house of his god." (Dan 1:2)	He carried to Babylon all the articles from the temple of God, both large and small. (2 Chron 36:18a)	"This is what Cyrus king of Persia says: 'The Lord, the God of heaven, has given me all the kingdoms of the earth and he has appointed me to build a temple for him at Jerusalem in Judah. Anyone of his people among you—may the Lord his God be with him, and let him go up.'" (2 Chron 36: 22–3)
TEMPLE DESECRATION	TEMPLE RESTORATION	

TWO HUMAN KINGS CONTRASTED (1:1–2)

On verses 1–2 Fewell comments, "The book of Daniel begins with an ending."[14] That is, verse 1 ends the story of life in the Judean homeland. The new story is subordinated to the old story. The native, weak king is succeeded by the strong, foreign one. For Nebuchadnezzar the conflict involves himself and Jehoiakim. Nebuchadnezzar is denoted "*king of Babylon*" and

14. Fewell, *Circle*, 13.

Jehoiakim is denoted "*king of Judah*" in verse 1. Given this we might expect that when his name is mentioned again in verse 2 there would be no need to add the words "*king of Judah*." But they are retained, presumably to draw attention to the fact that God now backs Babylonian kingship against the king of his own people. This is the only place in the entire book where the name of a Jewish king appears, which demonstrates that in Daniel there is limited interest in the concept of a national Israel.[15]

The irresistible nature of Nebuchadnezzar's kingship is implied by the language which stresses the consequence of Nebuchadnezzar's action: (1) he comes; (2) he takes; (3) he places.[16] However, putting the temple articles in the temple of his god[17] implies that the human conflict for Nebuchadnezzar mirrors a divine conflict. On the Ishtar Gate the inscription has Nebuchadnezzar representing himself as "the faithful prince appointed by the will of Marduk." Nebuchadnezzar's primary allegiance to Marduk, also named Bel, is indicated in the naming of his son as Amel-Marduk (or Evil-Merodach, Jer 52:31–34; 2 Kgs 25:27–30), that is, "man of Marduk."[18] As far as Nebuchadnezzar is concerned, his god has defeated the god of Jerusalem.[19] But, ironically, the real source of Nebuchadnezzar's victory is Adonai not Marduk. Nebuchadnezzar has a wrong concept of victory. For the words "*he gave . . . into his hand*" suggest that Jehoiakim did not submit but sought to resist Nebuchadnezzar. However, Nebuchadnezzar proved to be stronger, not because he was intrinsically stronger, as he himself would have taken for granted, but because God made him so.[20]

---

15. Dumbrell, *The Faith of Israel*, 259.

16. Indeed, the passivity and subjection of Israel is implied by the fact that Nebuchadnezzar and his chief official are the subjects of the verbs in verses 1–7. In addition to these three verbs we also have "commanded" (v. 3), "assigned" (v. 5) and "gave . . . names" (v. 7). Edlin, *Daniel*, 55.

17. The word can also be translated as "gods"—so TEV. If so, it is conceivable he distributed the temple articles in different temples: Harman, *Daniel*, 38. It is also possible to render this: "the place where he worshiped" or "the house of his religion." Péter-Contesse and Ellington, *Handbook*, 12–13.

18. "Nebuchadnezzar is categorically a henotheist, one believing in his own local deity; most likely the way that he would view any religious Judean, who worships the Hebrew god of Jerusalem, Yhwh." Hebbard, *Reading Daniel*, 59.

19. " . . . Nebuchadnezzar sees the conflict manifest in the material world is a reflection of a similar conflict in the spirit world . . . this cosmically dualistic perspective, which Nebuchadnezzar possesses so early in the narrative, is a view partially upheld by the implied author . . ." Hebbard, *Reading Daniel*, 60. In this respect, Daniel 10 takes on special importance by indicating that what happens politically on earth reflects transcendent conflict between angelic powers.

20. Cf. Goldingay, *Daniel*, 4n. As Hebbard, *Reading Daniel*, 60, rightly points out, because this is so there is no need for either Jehoiakim or Nebuchadnezzar's god to

On the dedicatory inscription on the Ishtar Gate Nebuchadnezzar also describes himself as "beloved of Nabu." Nabu was the patron god of scribes and it was customary for scribes to deposit, as votive offerings, beautifully written tablets in his *ezida*, that is, temple and chapels.[21] It has been suggested by van Selms[22] that the Hebrew form "Nebuchadnezzar" is intended to correspond with Nabu-kudanu-usur which means "Nabu protect(s) the mule," though it is more usual to see correspondence with Nabu-kudurru-usur which presumably means "Nabu protect(s) the eldest son." As such this may be construed as either a prayer to the god Nabu to provide protection, or a confession of the fact that he does. But if the former meaning proposed by van Selms is entertained, it is interesting to see how Nebuchadnezzar acts like a beast and eventually is even reduced to the level of a beast (Dan 4). It is certainly possible that "Nebuchadnezzar" is a deliberately corrupted form and represents the writer's riposte to the way Nebuchadnezzar had maliciously corrupted the names of Daniel and his friends (1:7). This is consistent with our identification of the genre of especially Daniel 1–6 as satire. The reader is encouraged to regard Nebuchadnezzar and pagan kings as buffoons, while at the same time there is emphasis upon the fact that Daniel himself never shows anything but the profoundest respect for Nebuchadnezzar.

If the siege of Jerusalem occurred before the battle of Carchemish then technically speaking Nebuchadnezzar was still not king. But, as Walvoord points out, the proleptic use of such a title was very common.[23]

THE IMMENSITY OF NEBUCHADNEZZAR'S ACT: A TALE OF TWO CITIES (1:1–2)

What was the major military conquest of Nebuchadnezzar during his entire reign? As far as the narrator is concerned it is the conquest of Jerusalem and its temple. The other conquests of Nebuchadnezzar are totally irrelevant. The most significant act performed by Nebuchadnezzar in history was the appropriation of articles from the Jerusalem temple.

As Thompson points out, the book of Daniel "very clearly is a story of two cities and two kings.[24] Each of the cities, in fact, is much more than a

---

receive any further attention throughout the Danielic narrative.

21. Oppenheim, *Ancient Mesopotamia*, 242.

22. Noted by Goldingay, *Daniel*, 4.

23. Walvoord, *Daniel*, 32.

24. So Ford, *Daniel*, 75.

city. In the pages of the Bible these cities represent a different outlook on the world, two different approaches to reality."[25]

THE DESECRATION OF THE TEMPLE AND
THE DEFIANCE OF GOD'S KINGSHIP (1:2)

We have already observed that just as the book has begun with an act of desecration, so the book ends with the ultimate act of temple desecration (cf. 12:11). Desecration of the temple sanctuary is a major motif in Daniel: 8:10–13; 9:16–19, 25–27; 11:31 (cf. vv. 36–37); cf. 5:2–4.[26] The central importance of the temple for Daniel is also underscored by his refusal in the face of death to discontinue his practice of praying to the temple three times a day (6:10). It is not hard to work out the content of Daniel's prayers concerning the temple at this time given the vocalization of his anguish in 9:16–19. The prayer of Daniel 9 presupposes the end of captivity after seventy years, as prophesied in Jeremiah 29:10–23. So it is additionally significant that in Jeremiah 27 the prophecy that Nebuchadnezzar would take the temple articles is not merely a sign of judgment but also of restoration (vv. 19–22).[27]

In fact in every chapter of the book of Daniel, with the solitary exception of chapter 10[28], major attention is devoted to description of a high-handed act of defying the Kingship of God (which either has occurred or is predicted to occur—see also 7:25). Consistently in Daniel the Supreme Kingship of God is revealed in the context of such blasphemous self-exaltations on the part of human kingship.

Verse 2 counter-poses "the house of *the* God" (the only true God?) and "the house of *his* god," indicating that conflict over worship is integral to the book of Daniel.[29] By taking the temple articles—some would include

---

25. "Living in Babylon—Daniel 1." Fyall similarly remarks, "The paralleling of the names of Babylon and Jerusalem symbolise not simply two states, but the conflict between the city of the world and the city of God in every generation." *Daniel*, 20.

26. Goswell also observes the pervasiveness of references and allusions to the temple in the book of Daniel. He prefers to view the temple as a leading "theme" rather than as a "motif." He understands motif to have "the more concrete sense of a recurrent image or object," but sees theme as broader with the possibility of various motifs contributing to the one theme. Goswell, "The Temple Theme," 510.

27. See Vogel, "Cultic Motifs," 30.

28. Daniel 10 begins the last unit of the book, Daniel 10–12, which is very much concerned with blasphemous anti-God rule.

29. Ford, *Daniel*, 75–76: "Chapter 1 reveals that those who worship idols are inferior in wisdom to the worshipers of the Creator . . . Chapter 2 describes how only a true

furniture, and other equipment along with utensils, but Ezra 1:7–11 speaks mainly of dishes, bowls and pans—and depositing them in the treasury of his god,[30] Nebuchadnezzar was effectively declaring that his god was mightier than *Adonai* (v. 2), (the God of Israel).[31] This explanation, however, only goes part of the way towards understanding the full significance of what we are being told here.

During a period when Assyria controlled Babylon, king of the realm, Ashurbanipal (668-626 BC) had himself represented in a demeaning manner, as a slave laborer who builds a temple for Marduk, the chief Mesopotamian deity. Daniel 1:2 probably expresses Nebuchadnezzar's similar desire to do something for the temple of Marduk which will secure his favor.

Keel, *Symbolism*, 270. Used with permission.

It is crucial to appreciate in this respect, that the temple is God's palace. Ostensibly its presence in Jerusalem indicates that God rules his people through his human regent, in this case Jehoiakim. It is therefore no accident that the subjection of Jehoiakim to Nebuchadnezzar and the transfer of temple vessels should be mentioned in the same breath. The two are inextricably linked. Not only has Nebuchadnezzar made a mockery of Davidic rule, but by taking vessels from the palace of the God-King he shows contempt for God, treating him as one of his vassal kings. Such blasphemy will be amplified by Belshazzar in his abuse of temple articles (Dan 5:1–4).

---

worshiper could understand the mysteries of the future . . . Chapter 3 tells how God can deliver from fiery ordeal those who refuse to submit to idolatrous worship . . . Chapter 4 . . . Self-worship is shown to be self-destructive. Chapter 5 . . . Man-made worship issues in a harvest of death. Chapter 6 . . . The theme remains that of conflict between true and false worship."

30. Evidently Marduk (also known as Bel)? So Young, *Daniel*, 38; Goldingay, *Daniel*, 15. Some confusion arises from the fact that Nebuchadnezzar's name involves association with the god Nabu who was presumably the god of his father.

31. A number of scholars have recognized this: Dumbrell, *Faith of Israel*, 259. Cf. the way the Philistines, after defeating the Israelites in Eli's time, took the ark and put it in the temple of Dagon (1 Sam 5:1–2).

At the very outset of the book a fundamental question is being raised: does history now reveal that God has been reduced to the status of being the vassal of Nebuchadnezzar?

THE ULTIMACY OF GOD'S RULE (1:2A)

The narrator is careful at the very outset to stress that this catastrophe has occurred because God has so ordered it. Nebuchadnezzar does not conquer Jerusalem or treat its king and temple as he does because he truly has irresistible power. His power and authority to perform these acts are given to him by God. The fact that Nebuchadnezzar places the temple articles in the treasury of Marduk shows that Nebuchadnezzar is completely unaware of the real significance of what he has done. He thinks that his conquest of this petty power has been enabled by his god Marduk.[32] He is blind to the fact that it is the God of Israel who has given him victory. He assumes that the carrying off of all Yahweh's earthly property, including Israelites from the royal family and nobility, stands as a symbol of how Yahweh has been humiliated and made subject to the rule of Marduk. As the book of Daniel will make clear, in reality "the transfer of Yahweh's property to Babylon ironically turns into a strategic invasion of Marduk's own god-space."[33] The hiddenness of God's rule is an integral feature of the book of Daniel.[34] Indeed, reference to "his [sc. Nebuchadnezzar's] god" occurs twice in the one verse, presumably to indicate that the ultimate conflict is between Marduk and Yahweh,[35] just as during the time of Israel's enslavement in Egypt the ultimate conflict was between Yahweh and the gods of Egypt (Ex 12:12).

32. For an intriguing study of Nebuchadnezzar's own thinking concerning his relationship to Marduk see Sheriffs, "Nebuchadnezzar's Theology and Ours."

33. de Bruyn, "A clash of gods," 5. See also Nel, "Function of space," 1–7.

34. The giving of Jehoiakim and the temple articles into the hands of Nebuchadnezzar does not mean, contra Venter, that "the space of Babylon is to be understood in terms of continuation of the life in Judah." Venter sees these events as connoting the following: "Life has come to an end in the Judean homeland and is now continued in the place where God sent them." Venter, "Space in Daniel 1," 994. This is not so. Rather, it is the rule of God that continues in the place where God sent them as stressed by the fact that it was he who caused these events to occur. However, Venter is quite correct in asserting the following: "The foreign space in Babylon is therefore an alternative space in which the relationship with the Lord can still be lived. The Diaspora space presents a challenge to these young Judeans to reconcile foreign circumstances with their born identity. They were in no position to distance themselves from their exilic situation. They had to live under a foreign king in a strange land. The challenge was, however, to accept the foreign space God led them to, while keeping their identity." "Space in Daniel," 994.

35. Gangel, Daniel, 17.

DOES GOD WANT TO BE MISUNDERSTOOD? (1:2)

In the ancient world the battlefield was understood to be the testing ground for deity. All peoples had their gods. When armies confronted each other then each looked to their respective gods to give them the victory. This meant that the god of the victor was more powerful than the god of the vanquished. Consequently God has permitted the impression to be conveyed that Marduk (Bel), the god of Nebuchadnezzar, is more powerful than himself. God has allowed the world to think that he is a lesser, and relatively inconsequential deity. This in turn means God has permitted the world to think that the Jewish people are not a special people. In actual fact God, not Marduk, is the one who gave victory to Nebuchadnezzar.

It is hard to read these verses without being reminded of the similar way in which God reveals himself in Christ. In the eyes of the Jewish people and Jesus' disciples, Jesus is shaping up to be the great king. But at the cross the impression is conveyed that Jesus, and his God, are weak and insubstantial.

In the case of Daniel 1 we must ask: why does God choose to allow the development of an historical situation which disguises his sovereignty?

We must allow the book of Daniel to answer this question, if it will. It is easy to jump the gun and to retort hastily that God is not trying to disguise his sovereignty, but that he is judging his people; that the confusion which results concerning God's ultimate sovereignty is but an unfortunate consequence of this judgment upon the Jews. But even to express the situation in these terms is to cast doubts upon the adequacy of such an interpretation. Could it be that the sovereignty of God is in some way advanced by its seeming obscurity?

BABEL REVISITED (1:2B)

In Daniel 1:2 Babylonia is called *"the land of Shinar."* It is a pity that translations often obscure this because it is a matter of exegetical importance. This phrase occurs only four times in the Old Testament, and three of these references are of particular importance:[36]

1. Genesis 10:10. Here the name is associated with the kingdom of Nimrod, the mighty hunter.[37]

---

36. See Kim, *Biblical Interpretation*, 52–72.

37. Kim, *Biblical Interpretation*, argues at length that Nebuchadnezzar is modeled on Nimrod ("the analogy between Nimrod and Nebuchadnezzar is central to our interpretation of allusion in Daniel 1 to Genesis 11–12") and that Daniel 1 presupposes a

2. Zechariah 5:11. Sin in the form of a woman in a measuring basket is consigned to the *"land of Shinar,"* where fittingly a "house," that is, a temple is built for it. Babylon is, then, the place where sin is deified.

3. Genesis 11:2. The *"land of Shinar"* becomes the center for realizing what has been the persistent humanistic dream of one world, one common set of social values, and one language. This attempt to order the world without reference to the Creator, this misplaced search for the center, was then rejected. And now in the *"land of Shinar"* (Dan 1:2) we find this common set of unities (one language, one social policy, one common bond of education, etc.) consciously revived as a tool of empire by Nebuchadnezzar. Since there is a remarkable degree of allusion in these early chapters of Daniel to the material of Genesis 1–11, we have probably in Daniel 1:2 a deliberate reference to the Babel incident and to Nebuchadnezzar as the humanistic reviver of these policies."[38]

The fact that "land of Shinar" is juxtaposed with "Babel" and "king" (cf. Gen 10:10) intensifies the allusion. To Daniel Babylon is a revival of Babel with all its humanistic self-sufficiency. Continuance of the Babel motif may be suggested by the reference to one language (v. 4), and is confirmed by the imposition by Nebuchadnezzar of one common social policy, namely eating at the same table.

As readers we are invited to view Nebuchadnezzar's treatment of the temple articles as analogous with the Babel builders' defiance of God's authority.[39] An air of expectancy is created. Will God respond in similar vein? How striking it is, then, that this revival of Babylon should begin with one language, yet end with a confusion of language (Dan 5:5–28)! Another way of viewing the fall of Babylon is to see it as involving the triumph of divine language. The prior accounts of the king being dependent on Daniel to interpret his troubling dreams highlights the transcendence of divine language over the Babel-like imposition of one language.[40]

---

conflation of Genesis 10:8–12 and 11:1–9, 60–65. Kim often seems to be over-reaching here, for example, when he speaks of Nimrod desiring "to dominate even the realm of God in heaven." *Biblical Interpretation,* 63.

38. Dumbrell, *Faith of Israel,* 259.

39. Kim, *Biblical Interpretation,* 59.

40. See *Biblical Interpretation,* 71.

A MAN ON THE TAKE (1:3-6)

The preceding narrative has carefully built up a picture of Nebuchadnezzar which stresses, from a Jewish perspective, the immensity of the acts he has performed. Does this king possess more power than even the God of Israel? After all, he has apparently scuttled all that the Davidic covenant had stood for and has even treated the palace of God as though God was one of his vassals. The apparently irresistible power of Nebuchadnezzar is accentuated by the reuse in verse 3 of the same verb "to take" which was used in verse 2:

> he *took* some of the articles from the house of God . . .
> The king told Ashpenaz . . . to *take* some of the Israelites . . .

Nebuchadnezzar assumes the right to treat God's people in the same imperious manner with which he has treated the temple articles. Over a twenty-three year period from 605 BC Nebuchadnezzar transported almost the entire population of Judah to Babylon in four stages. Among these captives were Daniel and his three friends.[41]

One way of understanding verse 3 is that Nebuchadnezzar had taken into captivity many "children of Israel" (Israelites) from the royal family and nobility and that certain "children of Judah" (v. 6), namely Daniel and his three friends, were specially selected from this wider group.[42] However, as Stone argues, it is more likely that Daniel and his friends are one and the same group as the "children of Israel" referred to in verse 3—the only Jews at the court of Nebuchadnezzar.[43]

WILL NEBUCHADNEZZAR DETERMINE THE FUTURE IDENTITY OF GOD'S PEOPLE? (1:3-6)

Nebuchadnezzar is not out to destroy God's people. They have a future—of sorts. But it is he who will determine what kind of people they will be. He

41. It is significant that these early verses do not dwell on the tragedy of the captivity. "The real concern is found in the lessons of the story; paradigms of interpreting Adonai and history must somehow shift to meet new circumstances. Rather than demonstrate the horrific conditions of life in captivity, the Narrator rather prefers to show the ability to overcome the religious, social, and moral oppression under which Daniel, Hananiah, Mishael, and Azariah are to live." Hebbard, *Reading Daniel*, 61.

42. Some have understood that the selection was made in Judah, i.e., the Israelites were "taken" from there. But Wooden argues that the "taking," the selection, is made from a larger group of new exiles in Babylon. Wooden, *The Book of Daniel*, 180. The same verb is used again at 1:18 with the sense of "bring to court," as opposed to "bring to Babylon"—Wooden, *The Book of Daniel*, 182.

43. Stone, "A Note on Daniel i.3," 69–71.

will determine Jewish identity. When he picks what he regards as being the cream of Jewish youth, he is selecting those who represent the future of God's people. He is seeking to control that future. By shaping these youths into the mould he has set he intends to shape the very future identity of God's people.

Paul points out that Daniel 1:3–5 involves a fascinating stage by stage correlation with a letter from Mari sent to Sibtu, the wife of king Zimrilim which describes the procedure of induction into court service[44]:

1. Candidates are selected from among captives taken as war booty and are brought to the capital city. In the Mari letter the captives are female and are brought to Mari.

2. The candidates already possess unique skills. The female captives are weavers.

3. Officials appointed to supervise them are named: Waradilisum and Mukannisum.

4. The purpose of selection is to instruct the youthful candidates in a new profession. The female captives are to be trained "to become adept at singing Subarean music."

5. Following training there is an official change of status. The weavers become singers.

6. Explicit mention is made of the specific food portions the women were to be given during their "residency" training period: "pay heed to their food allotment."

7. The stated purpose of this special food allotment is to enable the women to maintain their "healthy appearance": "so that their countenance does not change."

DID THE FOUR YOUTHS' SEXUALITY EXPRESS NEBUCHADNEZZAR'S SOVEREIGNTY? (1:3)

Jerome marks a tradition of interpretation that understood Daniel and his friends to be eunuchs.[45] In 1:3 Ashpenaz is described as being the chief of the *sarisim*. This word can be translated as "eunuch" and this appears to be the sense in which it is used in Isaiah 39:7: "And some of your descendants, your own flesh and blood who will be born to you, will be taken away, and

44. Paul, "Mesopotamian Background," 62–63.
45. Gammie, "A Journey," 150.

they will become eunuchs in the palace of the king of Babylon." It is doubt-
ful that Daniel 1:3 is intended as an allusion to this verse[46] since there is no
attempt to connect Daniel and his three friends with Hezekiah's lineage. The
meaning of the word as used in Isaiah 39:7 is determined by the context
which evidently intends to teach that castration will prevent at least some of
Hezekiah's descendants from perpetuating his line.

What about the meaning in Daniel 1:3? Is it being implied that Nebuchadnezzar had effected the castration of the four youths? It is impossible to
be certain on this point since:

1. The *sarisim* were not necessarily castrated even during Persian rule.[47]
   While the word might originally have applied to eunuchs (castrated
   males) it seems clear that it later became an official title, which did not
   necessarily carry such a connotation. In *The Testament of Joseph* 7, the
   "eunuch" Potiphar is married with children.[48]

2. The term pertains to Ashpenaz's position and does not necessarily
   imply that Daniel and his companions were themselves regarded as
   sarisim.

It is possible that Daniel and his friends were castrated. In verse 4 they
are indeed described as being "without any physical defect." From a traditional Israelite standpoint castration would certainly be a physical defect.
However, as Longman points out, this requirement is one made by Nebuchadnezzar for whom it would have been quite normal to have eunuchs in
the court around him.[49]

Quite apart from such considerations, Lucas[50] maintains that *sarisim*
corresponds to the Akkadian *sa resi*, meaning "he of the head (of the king),"
that is, a "confidant" of the king. The term denotes any palace official. While
such officials were often eunuchs this term is not restricted to them. In
short, the text simply does not tell us enough for us to be able to decide on
this matter. However, on balance it seems improbable that Daniel and his
friends were castrated because this would probably only have been required
of those eunuchs responsible for the king's harem,[51] for obvious reasons. By

---

46. Contra the proposal of Hartman and Di Lella, *The Book of Daniel,* 130.

47. Hartman and Di Lella, *The Book of Daniel,* 129.

48. Montgomery, *A Critical and Exegetical Commentary,* 125.

49. Longman, *Daniel,* 51.

50. *Daniel,* 47.

51. Miller, *Daniel,* 59.

contrast, they were intended to serve in the king's palace. Arguably, castration would be considered a physical defect in this context.[52]

NEBUCHADNEZZAR'S SOVEREIGN CHOICE (1:3)

The NIV translates: "Israelites from the royal family and the nobility" (v. 3) (lit. "of the seed of the kingdom"), thus recognizing two classes of Jewish exiles.[53] However, though less likely, the Hebrew can be construed as referring to three classes: (1) Israelites; (2) members of the Babylonian royal family; (3) members of the Babylonian nobility.[54] It is also possible that we should understand but one class: "Israelites from the royal family, *even* from the nobility . . . " If so, this would mean that Daniel and his friends were from the line of kings.[55] But verse 4 dwells on the excellencies of the youths chosen and, therefore, we can be confident that verse 3, in keeping with this, focuses upon the high rank of those chosen. In his *Antiquities* (10:188) Josephus speaks of Daniel's royal or noble descent.

The introduction of these Israelites as "the seed of the kingdom" may very well be loaded theological language. On the one hand, the words probably do imply that Daniel and his friends were "from the royal family and nobility." On the other hand, we have just had two verses underscoring the implicit demise of that which was considered to be the kingdom of God. At any rate, as we keep reading we discover that it is precisely through "the seed" comprised of Daniel and his three friends that God "sows" his kingdom in Babylon. Jerusalem may, for the moment, no longer serve as fertile soil for God's kingdom, but God's kingdom will continue to grow and flourish even in the hard clay soil of Babylon.

---

52. See Retief, Cilliers, and Riekert, "Eunuchs in the Bible," 247–58.

53. This is the understanding of almost every Bible version.

54. Porteous, *Daniel*, 27. Stone also takes the view that "the *seed royal* and *nobles* were non-Israelites." *A Note*, 71. The Murasu Archive from Nippur (464–404 BC) involves business documents showing exilic Jews involved in commerce. Coogan also finds them as agriculturalists, fishermen, sheep-herders, and co-creditors. Smith-Christopher, "Prayers and Dreams," 277–78.

55. So Slotki; as cited by Miller, *Daniel*, 60.

NEBUCHADNEZZAR'S SOVEREIGN
REQUIREMENTS (1:4)

Note the possible irony in verse 4: Nebuchadnezzar starts with malleable
"youths" (*yeladim*), presumably teenagers.[56] He requires these young nobles
to be "without blemish."[57] In the light of our discussion above concerning
eunuchs it is precarious to conclude from this expression that this indicates
Daniel and his friends had not been castrated.[58] This may imply a contrast
with God who also requires that sacrifices and those in divine service be
without blemish (Lev 22:17–25; 21:16–24).[59] If so, then the idea is reinforced that Nebuchadnezzar is usurping the throne of God.[60]

"Handsome" translates a word meaning "well favored," that is, "good
ones in appearance."[61] Nebuchadnezzar also required intellectual ability, an
academic pedigree—"skillful in all wisdom" ("showing aptitude for every
kind of learning"), "gifted in knowledge" (lit. "knowers of knowledge;"
while this could imply they were "well informed" the idea seems rather to
be that they were intelligent, that is, able to acquire knowledge),[62] "quick
to understand." Nothing but the best for this king! For he wanted to train
those who were "qualified to serve in [his] palace." The word "qualified"
is actually "power" in the sense of "ability." That is, Daniel and his friends
needed to learn the "proper manner, poise, confidence, and knowledge of

56. MacArthur, *An Uncompromising Life*, 19. MacArthur, evidently assuming Persian educational practice, assumes Daniel and his friends would have been between
thirteen and seventeen years of age. We don't know how closely Babylonian practice
conformed to this, though it seems likely they were teenagers.

57. Veiss cites a Babylonian text reported by Conenau in his book *Everyday Life
in Babylon and Assyria*: "the diviner whose father is impure and who himself has any
imperfection of limb or countenance, whose eyes are not sound, who has any teeth
missing, who has lost a finger, whose countenance has a sickly look or who is pimpled,
cannot be the keeper of the decrees of Shamash and Adad." Veiss, *Ideological Texture
Analysis*, 48.

58. So Charles; Walvoord, *Daniel*, 33.

59. Fewell, *Circle*, 15.

60. While the majority of OT uses of "blemish" are overwhelmingly cultic, there
are extra-biblical texts that list this characteristic for diviners, slaves, and scribes in the
ancient Near East. Wooden, *Daniel and Manticism*, 187.

61. Their looks must be such as not to detract "from the overall splendour of the
beautiful Babylonian palace. Personal attractiveness and perfection are looked upon
as characteristics belonging to the moral and intellectual nobility." Hebbard, *Reading
Daniel*, 62.

62. Miller, *Daniel*, 61.

social proprieties"[63] required for service in Nebuchadnezzar's court.[64] Wooden reasons that a later Jewish audience, reading this list religiously, would have understood these attributes to be "at their best when found in faithful Israelites such as Daniel and his three friends."[65]

All of the above does not merely indicate that Nebuchadnezzar chose the elite but serves to emphasize a primary point in the continuing narrative—*Babylonian wisdom was fundamentally elitist*. It should also be noted that Nebuchadnezzar regarded himself as a lover of wisdom. This is seen, for example, by the way he describes himself on the dedicatory inscription on the Ishtar Gate as "the faithful prince . . . who has learnt to embrace wisdom." This is consistent too with his name which links him with Nabu, his protective deity, the god of wisdom and knowledge.

NEBUCHADNEZZAR'S SOVEREIGN INDOCTRINATION PROGRAM (1:4)

Ashpenaz is ordered to teach those selected "the language and literature of the Chaldeans," that is, Akkadian, not Aramaic language and literature.[66] In verse 4 the term *Chaldean* (rendered "Babylonians" in the NIV) is ambiguous.[67] Baldwin explains,

> Kaldu is referred to by Assyrian kings as the country inhabited by the Kaldai, independent tribes who lived by farming and fishing in the swampy land to the north of the Persian Gulf. They were Semitic people who migrated from the Syrian desert and in due course they mingled with the old-established city-dwelling Babylonians, and the late Babylonian language, used before Aramaic, is largely characterized by Aramaic syntax with Babylonian words.[68]

The Chaldeans were the people who, under the leadership of Merodach-Baladan (Marduk-appal-iddina), harried the Assyrians in the late

---

63. Miller, *Daniel*, 61, citing Wood.

64. Wooden argues that because the word rendered "qualified" connotes strength, the idea is rather "the power of personality or the stamina that is required of one in a court context," that is, psychological strength. So the combined effect of all these attributes is that those selected are "the finest in their societal, religious, physical, intellectual and psychological attributes." "Changing Perceptions," 191–2.

65. *Daniel and Manticism*, 201.

66. Wooden, *Daniel and Manticism*, 192.

67. See Fewell, *Circle*, 16; Millard, "Daniel 1–6 and History," 69–71.

68. Baldwin, *Daniel*, 80.

eighth century BC. Indeed later, Nebuchadnezzar's father Nabopolassar (Nabium-apil-usur), together with the Medes, led the Chaldeans to destroy Nineveh. If in verse 4 these people are in mind (see 5:30; 9:1) then Nebuchadnezzar wants these youths to learn the culture of his people. While the term Chaldean can carry an ethnic connotation, as other verses in Daniel show (see 2:2–10; 3:8–12; 4:7; 5:7), it could also be applied to the class of professional sages. In fact "Chaldeans" was used in a non-ethnic sense to denote "astrologers" as early as Herodotus.[69] This appropriation of the name for such magicians, enchanters, and sorcerers presumably arose because of the internationally held view that the Chaldeans were experts in magic.[70] Robert D. Wilson proposed that the old Sumerian title *Gal.du* ("master builder") was later altered to the pronunciation *kas.du* (singular of *kasdim*), so that "Chaldeans" develops as a homonym.[71] It seems likely that the professional rather than the ethnic connotation is intended here.

Indeed, Lenzi observes that these Chaldeans assume the same role at the Babylonian court as the Assyrian *ummânū* did at the Assyrian court. These scholars are known to us by the letters they wrote to Assyrian kings. Parpola finds the terms used to describe the Chaldeans in the book of Daniel (1:20; 2:2, 27; 4:4; 5:11) are often similar to Akkadian terms for court scholars[72]:

Aramaic	Hebrew	Akkadian	
חכימין	חכמים	*ummânū*	Scholars
אשפין	אשפים	*āšipū*	Exorcists
כשדאין	כשדים	*tupšarrū*	Astrologers
חרטמין	חרטמים	*hartibī*	Interpreters of dreams

Porteous supposes that the Jewish youths are to be indoctrinated in astrology and the magical arts.[73] This was no doubt included but the very choice of the word "Chaldean" rather than "sage" or "magician," perhaps implies that the training would involve national (and thus political) as well as professional indoctrination.[74] Babylonian literature included omen texts and texts concerning "devils and evil spirits," magic incantations, copied sign lists, prayers, hymns, word lists, paradigms, myths, legends, "scientific"

69. Collins, *The Apocalyptic Vision of the Book of Daniel*, 32.

70. Baldwin, *Daniel*, 80.

71. Archer, "Modern Rationalism and the Book of Daniel," 136–37.

72. See Lenzi, "Secrecy," 335.

73. Porteous, *Daniel*, 28.

74. Fewell, *Circle*, 37.

formulae for skills such as glass-making, economic data, historical texts, mathematics and astrology,[75] law codes, etc.[76] But the very nature of ancient thought would prevent any of such studies being distinguishable from religious and magical conceptions. Calvin believed Daniel and his friends were kept from exposure to such material but there really is no foundation in the text or logical possibility that such was the case. No! Just as Moses was versed in the wisdom of Egypt so now Daniel and his friends studied the wisdom of Babylon, yet without compromising their faith.[77]

NEBUCHADNEZZAR'S SOVEREIGNTY AS EXPRESSED IN MAGICAL WISDOM (1:4B)

Wisdom in Babylon is elitist as indicated in verse 4 where Nebuchadnezzar's view of what makes a wise man is made manifest. To him wisdom is the preserve of those who have good birth and education. This concept of wisdom stands in contrast with the Jewish idea. In the Hebrew context wisdom has ethical and religious connotations, as exemplified in the devotion of Daniel in chapter 1 and in the consistent portrayal of his pious, faithful devotion to God. In verse 4 Daniel and his three compatriots are described as being *maskilim*, that is, "*showing aptitude* for every kind of learning" (NIV). It is notable that the book also closes by distinguishing the "*wicked*" and the "*wise*":

> Many will be purified, made spotless and refined, but the wicked
> will continue to be wicked. None of the wicked will understand,
> but those who are wise (*maskilim*) will understand.

Daniel, as the main representative of the *maskilim* in this book, is told in the very last verse: "As for you, go your way till the end. You will rest, and then at the end of the days you will rise to receive your allotted inheritance." Thus will the promise of 12:3 be fulfilled for Daniel: "Those who are wise (*maskilim*) will shine like the brightness of the heavens, and those who lead many to righteousness, like the stars for ever and ever."

The same root—*sakal*—is also used in 1:17: "God gave them knowledge and skill (*sakal*) in all learning and wisdom." In 9:13 Daniel confesses on behalf of the people:

75. Baldwin, *Daniel*, 80.
76. Miller, *Daniel*, 62.
77. See Walvoord, *Daniel*, 41.

Just as it is written in the Law of Moses, all this disaster has come
upon us, yet we have not sought the favour of the Lord our God
by turning from our sins and understanding (*sakal*) your truth.

We might say that the failure of the Israelites to be *maskilim* accounts
for the catastrophe that fell upon them. The word is used also in 9:22, 23,
25; 11:33, 35. The uses at 11:33, 35 bear a close correspondence to 12:3, 10
because in both cases the totality of "those who understand"/"the wise" is
in view:

> *Those who understand* will instruct many, though for a time
> they will fall by the sword or be burned or captured or plun-
> dered. When they fall, they will receive a little help, and many
> who are not sincere will join them. Some of *those who under-
> stand* will stumble, so that they may be refined, purified and
> made spotless until the time of the end, for it will still come at
> the appointed time.

Clearly this passage leads into chapter 12.

Babylonian literature was predominately religious with little interest in
history. So in exile the Hebrews were forced to enter a new thought world.
In Egypt there was enormous reverence for that which was banned in Israel—magic (Deut 18:10–12; 1 Sam 28:3). In fact except in Israel wisdom
and magic were inseparable in the ancient world. Major questions in Daniel
are: Who are the wise? What is true wisdom? Note the climax in Daniel
12:3, 10—the wise will be vindicated on the last day! In the book Daniel
exemplifies true wisdom.

Daniel's wisdom is God-given and is not derived from his Babylonian
context as is stressed in 1:17. Daniel refuses to be re-made as a Babylonian
wise man. His wisdom is superior to theirs—1:20. His wisdom is distinctly
Israelite, historically-oriented, and non-magical.

Many scholars are persuaded that the wise in chapter 11 are the pious
leaders of the *Hasidim* who resisted Antiochus IV Epiphanes,[78] and Towner
proposes that the writer(s) of Daniel is/are of the *hasidim*.[79] But it is of major importance to observe that Daniel does not oppose the learning of the
wisdom required by Nebuchadnezzar. Indeed he and his companions excel
in this very wisdom, though their wisdom outstrips that of their Babylonian peers because it is essentially not a magical, manipulative wisdom, but
wisdom endowed by God. This means that it is quite preposterous to think
(as many scholars do) of the author as being a pious Jew of the Maccabean

78. See Collins, *Apocalyptic Vision*, 55.
79. Towner, *Daniel.* 7–8.

period who was trying to incite Jews to take their stand against Hellenistic influences. It was utterly inconceivable to such Jews that they should study foreign literature and ideas in the way in which Daniel and his friends studied Babylonian literature. To even suggest such a thing to pious inter-testamental Jews would have outraged them. Indeed the attitude of inter-testamental Jews to foreign wisdom represents a serious departure from the biblical perspective reflected here in Daniel 1—"biblical" because it is fully consistent with the obvious biblical endorsement of the Egyptian learning of Joseph and Moses, and with the free borrowing of other ancient wisdom traditions in such books as Proverbs and Ecclesiastes.

Baldwin's application of this is particularly pertinent to culturally diverse societies, e.g., cities like Sydney and Melbourne in Australia:

> In order to witness to their God in the Babylonian court they had to understand the cultural presuppositions of those around them, just as the Christian today must work hard at the religions and cultures among which he lives, if different thought-worlds are ever to meet.[80]

NEBUCHADNEZZAR'S SOVEREIGN PROVISION (1:5)

The king requires them to eat from his own table. He "appointed" food, that is, "assigned it in the sense of numerical distribution."[81] What is provided is "a daily amount from the *pat-bag* of the king. The Hebrew term *pat-bag* . . . is derived from the Old Persian word *patibaga*, a technical term designating a government-supplied 'portion, ration' of food."[82] The expression does not mean that the amount of food given to the king would be reduced to feed these young Jews. The term rather indicates that they would receive the same kind of food given each day to the king and his family.[83] As this suggests the idea here is that the king displays his control by determining even what these men will eat. The notion is not that the king is displaying his generosity and high regard for these youths. Remember, they are still on probation.

In 11:26 rebellion against the king of the South will be unexpected and extreme, because the rebels are those who eat the king's provisions; they eat

---

80. *Daniel*, 80–81.

81. Walvoord, *Daniel*, 35.

82. Hartman and Di Lella, *The Book of Daniel*, 130. In 340 BC Deinon used the word patibaga to refer to barley bread and "mixed wine in a golden egg from which the king drinks." Farrar, *The Book of Daniel*, 128.

83. Péter-Contesse and Ellington, *Handbook*, 16.

from the king's table. In other words, eating from the king's table is symbolic of political covenant and compromise.[84] When David stops eating at Saul's table, Saul surmises that David has rebelled against him (1 Sam 20:30–34). Nebuchadnezzar is imposing political allegiance.

NEBUCHADNEZZAR'S SOVEREIGN IMPOSITION OF A RITE OF PASSAGE (1:5)

Nebuchadnezzar's policy implies that following completion of the training he has determined, he himself will take credit for the achievements of the youths concerned. His policy is an expression of his kingship and eating at table symbolizes their submission and dependence on his largesse. As we learn in verse 5 the purpose of this regime was to equip the trainees to "stand before the king"—a technical term for royal service.[85] Nebuchadnezzar is seeking to shape highly proficient sages who will be completely subservient to himself.[86] This also suggests that Nebuchadnezzar was keenly aware that the strength, security, and reality of his sovereignty must be anchored in wisdom. This is consistent with the fact that he associates himself with Nabu, the god of wisdom, whom he regarded as his primary source of protection.

Tragically, though, it was his conception that the wisdom he needed to consolidate and empower his kingship was a magical wisdom with which he would be enabled to manipulate the gods to promote his own megalomaniacal ends. Indeed the sovereignty of Nebuchadnezzar proves to be a "paper tiger" precisely because it rests upon an insubstantial, tissue-thin wisdom, and not upon the true wisdom which cannot be inveigled or manufactured, but can only be received as a sovereign gift of the transcendent God who rules in heaven.

Fewell sees in Nebuchadnezzar's imposed regime for the youths a classic model of a rite of passage, a ritual designed to facilitate a person's passing

84. Fewell, *Circle*, 19.

85. Baldwin, *Daniel*, 81.

86. Berquist points out, "An empire is not a static unit" and that such is the process of imperialization that "the empire exists only insofar as it continues to extract resources." "Postcolonialism," 16–7. Such resources include human capital. It became a matter of necessity to use the elite of other nations to supply the expertise it needed for continued imperialization. Longman, *Daniel*, 47–8, notes the Roman practice of taking the children of kings and important people in client states and holding them hostage: "This practice was not punishment as much as security against rebellion. As these hostages lived in Rome, a high-ranking Roman family became their patron and they became acclimated to Roman ways, with the idea that they would be friends of Rome when they returned to their native lands." Longman notes that in Daniel 11 there are predictive allusions to the way in which the Romans did just this with Antiochus IV and Demetrius.

from one phase of life into another.[87] There were three basic stages for such initiates:

1. *Separation.* They were separated from their community and put in seclusion (so v. 3).

2. *Training.* They were taught special knowledge to enable them to function in new roles. They were fed special food. They were urged to suppress their former allegiances (in this case political allegiance to Judah's royal house) and to elevate new allegiances (here to Nebuchadnezzar, king of Babylon). It is especially during this liminal stage that the induced experiences aim at effecting a change of being, a change of identity.[88]

3. *Reintegration.* They were then reintegrated into society.

Fewell finds irony in Nebuchadnezzar's policy: "In one sense their rite of passage is a promotion from prisoners to professionals. But in another sense, the passage is a demotion from 'royal seed' to servanthood."[89]

NEBUCHADNEZZAR'S SOVEREIGN DETERMINATION OF IDENTITY (1:6–7)

Porteous, noting that Joseph had a similar change of name (Gen 41:45) and even married into an Egyptian priestly family, does not think that acceptance of new Babylonian names indicated a tendency to apostatize.[90] This is fair enough, but the context of Daniel 1 is substantially different and the preceding verses have stressed Nebuchadnezzar's sovereignty. In giving these four Jews new names Nebuchadnezzar *is* expressing ownership rights and making claim to being the one who shapes their destiny.[91] There is, therefore, a real need for Daniel and his friends to assert their separate identity and preserve their distinctiveness and religious integrity that has been called in question by the allocation of new names (v. 6). In Genesis, Pharaoh's treatment of Joseph is not set in a context of trying to extinguish the distinctive identity of God's people and assimilate them into Egypt. Indeed Pharaoh actively cooperates with God's use of Joseph to preserve Israel, and he positively condones measures calculated to maintain the distinctiveness

87. *Circle*, 15–18.

88. See too Venter, "Space in Daniel 1," 995.

89. *Circle*, 18.

90. *Daniel*, 28. Accepted also by Baldwin, *Daniel*, 81.

91. Cf. Goldingay, *Daniel*, 17.

of God's people. Thus the name-giving of Daniel 1:9 belongs to a radically different context.[92]

Even though Nebuchadnezzar is concerned to shape the identity of these trainees it does not follow that the name change was intended to humiliate or degrade them.[93]

Daniel's name means "God is my judge" or "my judgment is God's" and it may well be that this anticipates Daniel's role as an interpreter.[94] He has been renamed "Bel (sc. Marduk) protect his life!"[95] This introduces a note of irony. No sooner has he been given this name than "Daniel" puts himself into a situation where he is expecting Yahweh, not Bel, to protect his life. Indeed there is a strong and persistent theme in Daniel of Yahweh protecting Daniel's life. The implied reader, of course, reads not of *Belteshazzar's* response, but of *Daniel's* response to what has preceded. This enables the reader to anticipate the outcome of Nebuchadnezzar's attempt to control the identity of this man. The reason the story exists at all is because this man retained his identity and integrity. Indeed, verse 21 may imply that Yahweh's ability to protect Daniel surpasses Bel's ability to protect and sustain Nebuchadnezzar. Daniel's life points to the truth that:

> . . . if Yahweh can operate within the profane world outside of his own original territory, the land of Israel, he can also protect his people within the profane world. In light of this assurance God's chosen people do not have to fear the profane world, neither other nations nor their gods who want to challenge Yahweh's rule on earth.[96]

As for the other names: *Hananiah* ("Yah is gracious" or "Yah has been gracious") becomes *Shadrach*; *Mishael* ("Who is he that is God?" or "Who is what God is?" or "Who is equal to God?") becomes *Meshach*; and *Azariah*

---

92. Thompson ("Living in Babylon—Daniel 1") observes the same dynamics at work in modern secular Australia, as expressed in new insertions in school curricula that are radically at odds with Christian values, and also in business and other social contexts where a person is effectively told that their future in this firm, in this industry, in this society depends on their acceptance of the new orthodoxy which will tolerate no dissent. In addition, he notes, we see human identity being reconstructed before our very eyes—"what it means to be a human being, what it means to be a family, what it means to be a man, what it means to be a woman." The issue facing us is the same as in Daniel, "How do we live in a world like this?"

93. Miller, *Daniel*, 64.

94. Proposed by Hebbard, *Reading Daniel*, 66.

95. Lucas, *Daniel*, 53, considers the possibility that the name may also mean "Lady, protect the king," that is, an address to the consort of Bel. Similarly, Millard, "Daniel 1–6," 72.

96. de Bruyn, "A Clash of Gods," 5.

("Yah helps" or "Yah has helped") becomes *Abednego*;[97] though the meaning of the Babylonian names is uncertain. Walvoord sets out options, e.g., for "Shadrach" proposals include "command of Aku"[98] [sc. the moon deity] or a perversion of "Marduk," the principal Babylonian god. Assyriologist Berger proposes "I am very fearful [of God]."[99] For "Meshach" consider "who is what Aku is?" as being a deliberate reformation of the name *Mishael* to replace the implicit reference to "God" (El = Yahweh) with Aku, though Berger proposes "I am of little account."[100] "Abed-nego" probably means "servant of Nebo (sc. the son of the Babylonian god Bel)" or, as Berger proposes, "Servant of the shining one" (still with Nebo in mind).[101] While, as indicated, there is some difficulty in pinning down the precise meaning of these names the overall thrust is clear—an attempt to change the essential identities of these men by radically aligning them with Babylonian kings and deities.[102] Significantly, while the names of the foursome reflect Israelite monotheism, their Babylonian names reflect a polytheistic worldview in which multiple deities are worshiped.[103]

NEBUCHADNEZZAR'S SOVEREIGNTY
MEETS RESISTANCE (1:8)

Verse 8 constitutes a major turning point in the narrative.[104] For the first time an Israelite becomes the subject of a main verb.[105] The initiative no longer

97. Walvoord, *Daniel*, 36.

98. Farrar, *Book of Daniel*, 129.

99. Millard, "Daniel 1–6," 72.

100. Millard, "Daniel 1–6," 72.

101. Millard, "Daniel 1–6," 72.

102. Valeta following Buchanan. Valeta, *Lions*, 69.

103. Kim, *Biblical Interpretation*, 70.

104. Milne, *Vladimir Propp*, 208, regards verse 8 as "the plot-initiating function." Applying Propp's model, she is not able to see in verse 9 Propp's function of the consent of the hero to counteraction since Daniel is not presented here as a seeker but as a victim. She suggests that the function of "villainy" or of "lack" may be implicit here, since "Daniel's action is necessitated by the lack of what he considers proper or acceptable food and drink." However, see my exegesis, where it is proposed that Daniel is reacting against a more profound level of "villainy" than merely improper food and drink. "Villainy" is a problematic term to employ here since the characterization of Nebuchadnezzar in Daniel is of a complex order. He is the agent of God yet also blasphemous in his actions. He threatens the identity of God's people and yet is respected as the king God himself has set in place. As such the story told in Daniel 1 is profoundly different from any of the fairy tales analyzed by Propp.

105. Goldingay, *Daniel*, 11.

lies with Nebuchadnezzar but with Daniel. From this point on God will use his servants to communicate (in various ways) the truth that he controls the course of history. From this point on it will become increasingly clear that pagan kings are but instruments God uses to fulfil his purposes. They will come and go, but God will control the historical process so as, ultimately, to benefit his saints who are now represented by Daniel and his friends.

Daniel and his friends are portrayed as ideal figures. On no occasion is attention drawn to any imperfection or flaw in their characters. The reader will see that my exegesis will involve a head-on collision with Fewell who relies on reading "between the lines" of the text, and arguments from silence, in order to charge Daniel with being manipulative and guilty of duplicity. In her Preface Fewell is up front about her methodology:

> Within a text, undercurrent meanings repeatedly disturb, if not displace, surface meanings. This meaning of Daniel, admittedly, looks for undercurrents, meanings that subvert many of the traditional readings of the book.[106]

No! There is not the hint of a slur on any of these four men's characters. Even in Daniel 9, when Daniel identifies himself with the sin of his people, there is no isolation of any particular sin committed by Daniel. The sheer blamelessness of the lives of these four individuals alone makes it evident they are presented as models for emulation. Thus, in this immediate context Daniel's actions are described in a manner that is of relevance to God's oppressed people in another historical and social setting.

Note the play on words in verses 7–8: "After the chief eunuch 'fixes upon' or 'sets for' them (*yasem*) Babylonian names, Daniel 'fixes' or 'sets' (*yasem*) upon his heart that he will not defile himself with the king's food or drink."[107] It is probable that this pun implies that the assignment of a new identity spurs Daniel to show resistance, "to limit in some way the all-consuming indoctrination process."[108]

Baldwin again summarizes the matter in a manner that is intensely relevant to culturally diverse areas of Australia:

> These godly men now have to decide how they will adjust to living in an environment unsympathetic to their religious convictions. Like everyone caught in cross-cultural change they had to

106. Fewell, *Circle*, 10.

107. Fewell, *Circle*, 18.

108. Fewell, *Circle*, 18. Nelson, *Daniel*, 64: "The former can choose names for the Jewish captives without resistance, but Daniel can choose to refuse the king's food and drink. Daniel will accept the imposition of a foreign name but will not acquiesce to defiling fare."

think through the principles involved in their actions, and begin as they meant to go on.[109]

In verse 8 why does Daniel decide to refrain from eating food at the king's table? We are told: "Daniel resolved not to defile himself." What kind of defilement is in view here? In answering this question it is critical to recognize, as we have indicated above, that the intended readers, presumably God's oppressed people, are expected to imitate Daniel in different historical and social circumstances.

The Book of Tobit describes the exile of the northern tribes and in 1:10–11 we read:

> When I was carried away captive to Nineveh, all my brethren and those that were of my kindred did eat the bread of the Gentiles: but I kept myself from eating, because I remembered God with all my soul (cf. Judith 10:5; 12:1–4; I Maccabees 1:63).

Is this passage analogous to Daniel 1:8? If so it would seem that avoidance of *cultic* defilement is the primary motive.[110]

Porteous finds three possible reasons why Daniel may have had an aversion to meat on ritual grounds: (1) the kind of meat involved (Lev 3:17; 11:1–47); (2) its method of preparation (Lev 17:10–14); (3) its association with idolatrous worship.[111] There are many scholars who believe Daniel was seeking to punctiliously obey the Jewish food laws. So Collins reasons,

> The thrust of the argument is not that one can have a successful career at a foreign court while remaining a loyal Jew, but that strict obedience to the Jewish law, even in its distinctive elements, is a necessary prerequisite of the wisdom which brings success.[112]

But if cultic defilement is in mind then Daniel's refusal of the wine appears to make no sense at all, assuming Levitical law as the assumed dietary guide.[113] Still, the possibility of cultic defilement is not altogether impossible, since in 5:4 Belshazzar uses wine in the context of idolatrous worship and it is conceivable that he is repeating a practice that had been previously observed by his father. Accordingly, some believe Daniel's decision

---

109. *Daniel*, 82.

110. So Walvoord, *Daniel*, 37–38.

111. *Daniel*, 29.

112. Collins, *Apocalyptic Vision*, 32–33.

113. Only Nazarites were required to abstain from wine (Num 6:1–4).

is based on opposition to idolatry.[114] However, the Babylonians offered up every kind of food to their gods so that it was virtually impossible for Jewish exiles to remain ritually clean.[115] Beaulieu summarizes inscriptions in which Nebuchadnezzar boasts of having established regular offerings of eggs, birds, and fish, collectively designated as "the pride of the marsh" for the gods of Babylon and Borsippa.[116] On these inscriptions delicacies such as honey, butter, milk, oil, wine, and beer are listed. Vegetarian food, for example, flour, was also evidently offered up to idols.[117] Consequently it is hard to see how Daniel, even by restricting himself to a vegetarian diet, could avoid partaking of food which had been previously used in idolatrous worship.[118] In addition to these considerations, it is notable that the issue of food offered to idols is not mentioned in other parallel stories, e.g. Joseph, Moses, and Esther.[119]

Actually, 10:3 tells against both the food law violation and the idolatrous worship explanations. Nor does it fit with the suggestion that pagan food and drink simply epitomized the pagan uncleanness associated with exile.[120] Daniel 10:3 also casts grave doubts on the view that in 1:8 Jews are being exhorted to maintain loyalty to the food laws even in the face of death at the hands of Antiochus Epiphanes.[121] Anyway, we have already noted such a view—that Daniel and his friends are champions of resistance against a hated pagan ruler—is untenable because it cannot be reconciled with the obvious readiness of Daniel and his friends to master Babylonian literature and thought.

In 10:3 Daniel remarks that during the three week period concerned: "I ate no choice food; no meat or wine touched my lips; and I used no lotions at all until the three weeks were over." The clear inference is that normally Daniel did eat "choice food" and that he ate meat and drank wine.[122]

114. Olyott, *Dare to Stand Alone*, 20.

115. Baldwin, *Daniel*, 82–83.

116. For example, we read: "Together with the gods of Esagil and the gods of Babylon, fish, birds, voles (and) eggs, the pride of the marsh (. . .), did I provide abundantly, like the countless waters of a river, for the table of Marduk and Zarpanitu my lords." Beaulieu, Babylonian Collection.

117. Goldingay, *Daniel*, 18.

118. Similarly, Fyall, *Daniel*, 24.

119. Fyall, *Daniel*, 24.

120. Considered by Goldingay, *Daniel*, 19.

121. So Porteous, *Daniel*, 29. Similarly, Nelson suggests that this incident presupposes second century readers: "The Seleucid soldiers were forcing Jews to eat pork that had been sacrificed to Zeus." *Daniel*, 28.

122. See Meadowcroft and Irwin, *Book of Daniel*, 34.

Also, apparently, Daniel regards this as normally an appropriate practice since there is not the slightest indication that he feels guilty about this. His abstinence from these things at this time was an expression of his dedication to the Lord—his resolve to prepare himself properly for divine revelation and its explanation.

From the above it would seem that in 1:8 the defilement Daniel shuns is not so much a ritual or cultic defilement but moral defilement.[123] But it must be noted the issue *is* explicitly one of defilement and this rules out the suggestion that Daniel refrains from meat and wine as festive foods inappropriate for one who is mourning in exile or that he is adopting ascetic practices in order to seek God.[124]

Given that such interpretations miss the mark, what then is the nature of the defilement Daniel seeks to avoid? The preceding context has stressed Nebuchadnezzar's implicit claim to be absolutely and unqualifiedly sovereign. We must recall that the purpose of this liminal "betwixt and between" phase of the rite of passage is to effect a change of being and identity. The crucial issue for Daniel is the source of the food,[125] for the food from which Daniel resolves to abstain is "*the king's* food." As 11:26 indicates: "those who shared the king's table also entered a covenant relationship with him. By eating his food they committed themselves to a friendship and so accepted that they had an obligation to be loyal to him."[126]

123. Isaiah 59:3 provides an example of moral defilement. Also adopting a moral explanation, Calvin reasons, "For Daniel not only wished to guard himself against the delicacies of the table, since he perceived a positive danger of being eaten up by such enticements; hence he simply determined in his heart not to taste the diet of the court, desiring by his very food perpetually to recall the remembrance of his country. He wished so to live in Chaldea, as to consider himself an exile and a captive, sprung from the sacred family of Abraham. We see, then, the intention of Daniel. He desired to refrain from too great an abundance and delicacy of diet, simply to escape those snares of Satan, by which he saw himself surrounded." Calvin, Daniel 1:8 in "Commentary on Daniel—Volume 1," (cf. his restatement of this same explanation in his comments on Daniel 1:10).

124. Contra Edlin, *Daniel*, 56. Edlin airs the possibility that "Daniel's intent was to identify with the poverty and loss of his people in exile." The idea here is that meat and wine were the food of the wealthy. Tertullian used Daniel 1 to justify his advice that Christians fast and eat only dry foods as the path to wisdom. Origen taught that the abstinence of Daniel and his supposedly simple diet of water and grain made him superior to pagan prophetic figures, e.g., Phythian priestess to Apollo at Delphi or those who delivered oracles at Dodona. Hippolytus commented on 1:12: "Not earthly meats that give to men their beauty and strength." Aquinas remarked: "abstinence and chastity dispose man very much to the perfection of the intellectual operation." Gammie, "A Journey," 146, 148, 149, 152.

125. Venter, "Space in Daniel 1," 997.

126. Reid, *Kingdoms in Conflict*, 33. Reid compares the situation here with the way

Later Jehoiachin's abject subservience to the king of Babylon was symbolized by his eating regularly at the king's table (2 Kings 25:27–30).[127] In this context food is the symbol of political patronage, and to eat is tantamount to declaring complete political allegiance.[128]

Hebbard astutely observes,

> The conflict over the mandatory diet speaks more about the establishment of the integrity of the main characters and the possibility of living a Yahwistically-devoted life in the midst of a pagan environment than it does about the resolution of a dietary debate.[129]

Daniel and his friends are prepared to enter the king's service and indeed are willing to serve the king wholeheartedly and not in a merely token fashion.[130] But while Daniel is ready to be the king's servant he is not prepared to be an obsequious, bootlicking lackey.[131] Proverbs 23:1–3 advises: "When you sit to dine with a ruler, note well what is before you, and put a knife to your throat if you are given to gluttony. Do not crave his delicacies, for that food is deceptive." The point is that the king's rich food comes with "strings attached."

---

a businessman might create a sense of obligation by paying for lunch. Reid wryly remarks, "There is no such thing as a free lunch!"

127. Reid, *Kingdoms in Conflict*, 34.

128. Compare Baldwin, *Daniel*, 83; Péter-Contesse and Ellington, *Handbook*, 18. See too Wooden, *Daniel and Manticism*, 194. Goswell: ". . .food and wine 'from the king's table' (1:5) has political connotations. It is a sign of political allegiance and subservience to eat from that table (see 2 Samuel 9; 2 Kings 25:27–30). *Daniel*, 12. Thompson, similarly thinking that Daniel's actions had little to do with Jewish food laws, states, "Food was just the presenting issue." "Living in Babylon."

129. *Reading Daniel*, 65–66.

130. Breed rightly states, "Daniel negotiates the space of royal bureaucracy without challenging God-given authority of the king or his bureaucrats." Breed, "A Divided Tongue," 119. Daniel does not have the same difficulty in accepting Babylonian higher education. Hebbard, following LaCocque, notes that the intrinsic worth of this education is never questioned in the book. Hebbard, *Reading Daniel*, 66, conjectures, "This may be the case since Daniel's godly wisdom is the filter through which all Babylonian training will pass."

131. Cf. Towner, *Daniel*, 25–26. Goldingay casts doubt on this interpretation. *Daniel*, 18–19. Because Daniel and his friends do in fact accept a position as the king's courtiers he finds it hard to see how the decision to avoid defilement has anything to do with serving the king. But this perhaps misses the point which is not one of role but of who is the ultimate master. Veiss (*Ideological Texture*, 49) cites Chia: "whether for cultural, religious, or nationalistic reasons, Daniel's resistance to the food from the king's table lends a strong support to a postcolonial reading of his act as a resistance to colonial power."

Daniel's action "is an attempt to express some modicum of personal control in a seemingly uncontrollable situation."[132] His refusal to comply at this point represents God's invisible providence, which ensures the preservation of the distinctive identity of his people. The fact that the commitment here is not purely the individual decision of Daniel, but is shared by the three other Jewish youths, expresses the failure of Nebuchadnezzar, notwithstanding his awesome sovereignty, to squeeze these people into the mould of his making. In keeping with the satirical tone of the narratives of Daniel 1–6 the cultic word "defiled" insinuates that there is something fundamentally "unclean" about blasphemous, idolatrous rule. Nebuchadnezzar must not be allowed to extinguish the essential identity of God's people. The direct speech that follows will underscore this point by describing a situation of which Nebuchadnezzar is totally ignorant, and which, therefore, he is completely unable to control. Further, as Longman argues, the policy adopted by these Jews keeps them "from believing that their physical appearance (and by consequence, perhaps, their intellectual gifts) were the gifts of the Babylonian culture."[133]

Arguably, this interpretation best meets the fundamental criterion we have identified: the readers, God's oppressed people, are expected to imitate Daniel. The precise dating of Daniel is open for debate. But presupposed is a situation where God's people are on the receiving end of harsh and overbearing pagan rule, a scenario that is envisaged as typifying the condition of God's people right through to "the end" of history. Many Jews in the Maccabean period could not have found Daniel and his friends very good role models, because Daniel and his friends were not insurrectionists in any sense of the word. Daniel and his friends were committed to excel in serving the pagan ruler and yet in their inner lives their ultimate allegiance was to God and not the foreign king. This veiled higher loyalty was no superficial, merely token acknowledgment of God's claim to ultimate authority. As the narratives will go on to show, Daniel and his friends were prepared if necessary to forfeit their lives rather than deny their God his role as their absolute lord.[134]

---

132. Fewell, *Circle*, 19.

133. *Daniel*, 53. Longman, however, questions the notion of political defilement, maintaining that the very eating of vegetables still involves eating the king's food. But this is not the point, which is that Daniel and his friends are refusing to eat the food and drink "assigned" by the king (v. 10). A combination of the political and faith motives seems the best way of explaining the policy of Daniel and his friends.

134. Wooden argues from the phrase "there were among them" (v. 6) that Daniel and his friends were not merely distinguished from the Chaldeans but also from other Israelites whom, it is implied, did fully succumb to Nebuchadnezzar's program of indoctrination. *Daniel and Manticism*, 194–195, 199.

No matter in what historical or social setting God's persecuted people might find themselves, it is imperative they maintain their identity as God's people while also, in recognition of God's sovereignty, being prepared to wholeheartedly serve the foreign authorities. Such service is not to be confused with servility because as God's people imitate Daniel and his friends, they will be careful to ensure their fundamental allegiance is to God. Consequently, if any conflict between these loyalties should arise, God's people will pay any price, even the price of their lives, to remain true to their God.

DANIEL AND ASHPENAZ (1:8-13)

Just as Yahweh showed *hesed* to Joseph and gave him *rahamim* in the sight of the chief jailer (Gen 39:21), so now God allows Daniel to receive *hesed* and *rahamim* from the palace master (v. 9). The words *hesed* ("covenant love," "favor") and *rahamim* ("compassion") are familiar markers of God's covenant faithfulness.[135]

Verses 10–13 constitute the only occurrence of direct speech in the chapter and there is good reason to see the preceding narrative as leading to this point in the chapter, and to view the succeeding narrative as confirming it. If this is a fair reading of the chapter then these verses constitute the core of the chapter.

> . . . the official told Daniel, "I am afraid of my lord the king, who has assigned your food and drink. Why should he see you looking worse than the other young men your age? The king would then have my head because of you." Daniel then said to the guard whom the chief official had appointed over Daniel, Hananiah, Mishael and Azariah, "Please test your servants for ten days: Give us nothing but vegetables to eat and water to drink. Then compare our appearance with that of the young men who eat the royal food, and treat your servants in accordance with what you see."

The following motifs are stressed in this central unit of thought:

1. Fear of Nebuchadnezzzar (1:10)

The official's[136] expression of fear serves to underscore the awesome, even frightening power and authority of Nebuchadnezzar. In verse 10 Ashpenaz

135. Pace, *Daniel*, 34.
136. The word probably means "guardian." Lucas, *Daniel*, 48.

speaks of Nebuchadnezzar as "my lord." He uses the word *adoni*. This appears to be a deliberate play on words which recalls Adonai in verse 2 and thus points to an implied contrast between Nebuchadnezzar and God. Who is truly the Lord? For the palace official "lordship belongs to the king; for the narrator, lordship belongs to God. The use of *adoni/Adonai*, then, reflects the crux of Daniel's dilemma—the acknowledgment of sovereignty."[137] Given the overwhelming authority of the king is there any possibility for these men to live a life of separation from all that would defile them?

The palace official's words are important: "the king has assigned your food and drink" (verse 10). This serves not merely to repeat what we have already been told by way of narrative in verse 5, but to underscore and highlight the sovereignty and control of Nebuchadnezzar.

"Why should he see you looking worse than the other young men your age?" (v. 10) alludes back to the narrative of verse 4. The king's choice and expectations are emphasized here.

Most take verse 10 as implying that in order to "look" as healthy as the other young men it is necessary for them to live the same way (eat the same food); i.e., they are expected to conform, to become the "clones" Nebuchadnezzar is trying to produce. Nebuchadnezzar sets the standards: he assigns the food and drink. Nebuchadnezzar treats these young men as though they were part of a factory process. He chose them because they were physically impressive (v. 4) and he wants them to continue to be so.

It is possible to read verse 10 as involving a different nuance: "I fear my lord the king . . . should view your expressions to be discontent [or even malcontent?] in comparison with the young men around you . . . " That is, "the chief eunuch" may not be thinking that they will look unhealthy and weak, but that there will be an outward expression of rebellion: "Refusing the king's food symbolizes political dissent and, in the opinion of the eunuch, such an attitude will eventually become more obvious. The official will take no responsibility for nonconformity."[138] In chapter 1 there is a persistent stress on conformity, on subordination to the king.

There is no great hiatus between these two alternate interpretations. If the Jewish youths had looked seedy and unhealthy when presented to the king then an inevitable train of questions would be set in motion: "Why has their health condition so deteriorated? Were they not fed with the same food as the others? They weren't! Why ever not? Why did you (sc. chief eunuch) and they defy my orders?" Thus a failure to match the Babylonian youths in

---

137. Fewell, *Circle*, 20. See too Venter, "Space in Daniel 1," 1002–3.
138. Fewell, *Circle*, 20.

physical robustness and health would inevitably be expressive of rebellion. From his perspective, the chief eunuch has every reason to be afraid.

2. The wisdom of Daniel (1:11–13; clearly implicit; the same idea is made explicit in 2:14)

It is highly significant that the first expression of Daniel's wisdom in the book concerns knowing how to relate to people in a skillful manner (verses 8, 11–13). Note how pragmatic Daniel's wisdom is. In Daniel we are not dealing with a wisdom which is altogether removed from traditional wisdom. In the book of Daniel it is wrong to drive a wedge between so-called apocalyptic wisdom and traditional wisdom. In verse 17 we see God giving wisdom to the four heroes that they might know and understand "all kinds of literature and learning," not merely to understand visions and dreams.

To the guardian[139] Daniel adopts a more subtle approach. He asks the guardian to allow their diet[140] and then to compare their appearance with their peers.[141] Fewell[142] sees Daniel's choice of the word "appearance" as an indication of his tact and diplomacy. The chief eunuch was worried that their facial expressions and demeanor, having had their own way, would somehow betray their underlying rebelliousness of spirit. Daniel has noted this fear, and so, in arguing his case with the guardian, he avoids use of the more ambiguous word "face" which can also connote expression or demeanor. Fewell reasons that by using the word "appearance" Daniel is lessening the impression that any fundamental rebellion is involved, though, in fact, it is, objectively speaking. While, had Nebuchadnezzar known of this

139. The word is probably related to an Akkadian word meaning "overseer." Péter-Contesse and Ellington, *Handbook*, 20–21.

140. Walton suggests that the term here indicates Daniel prefers "his own concoctions from the 'seeds.'" He notes that the Hebrew term for the king's food is understood in later Greek as a prepared dish. He proposes that Daniel's choice is "not usually food at all" and that "perhaps he is asking for the rations from which he would prepare his own meals." Walton, "The *Anzu* Myth," 69. Lucas, however, points out that all that can really be deduced from the term is that as "seed" it refers to "that which is sown," namely vegetables. Lucas, *Daniel*, 48. As Péter-Contesse and Ellington point out, the idea of the request is to avoid eating meat and drink: *Handbook*, 22. There is a possibility that the use of the word "seed" is intended to recall verse 3 and remind us of God's program to sow the seed of his kingdom in Babylon.

141. Given the prior assurance that God gave Daniel favor and compassion in the sight of the chief of the eunuchs it is probably incorrect to conclude that Daniel went behind his back in speaking to the steward or "guardian." Contra Hebbard, *Reading Daniel*, 71–72.

142. *Circle*, 21.

initiative, Daniel and his friends would have been considered rebels, it over-
states the situation to depict Daniel and his friends as acting with rebellious
hearts. Rather, they are simply wanting to ensure that their essential identity
is not lost. It is possible, as Fewell suggests, that the guardian's decision was
motivated by the realization that the food and wine not consumed by Daniel
and friends would be available for his private consumption.

3. The Sovereign Providence of God

It is a cynical misreading of the passage to cast Daniel as a cunning manipu-
lator. The sovereign hand of God is involved in the entire outworking of this
matter as verse 9 clearly indicates. Indeed there is an apparently deliberate
contrast between "the king ordered Ashpenaz . . . " (verse 3), and "God had
caused the official to show favour and sympathy to Daniel" (verse 9). God
undoes what Nebuchadnezzar ordains. The fear of the official is stressed, but
not even the terror of Nebuchadnezzar's cruel power and might can prevent
God from overruling Nebuchadnezzar.

In observing the adroitness with which Daniel manages the situation
we should also note the implicit impotence of Nebuchadnezzar to prevent
this development. Up to this point in the chapter the awesome dimensions of
Nebuchadnezzar's sovereignty have been indicated. God now demonstrates
his surpassing sovereignty by orchestrating a situation which involves fundamental non-compliance with Nebuchadnezzar, and thus implies the rejection of his claims to absolute sovereignty (which will be further checked
in chapter 2).

But the surpassing sovereignty of God is not merely revealed in the
fact that Daniel chooses to express devotion to God rather than obey Nebuchadnezzar. The point is that Nebuchadnezzar remains ignorant of the
act of non-compliance. In order to be the absolute sovereign that he thinks
himself to be it would be necessary for him to have complete knowledge of
his subjects' inner resolves and actions, so as to nip intended resistance in
the bud. Ironically, the chapter will end with Nebuchadnezzar not only failing to spot the latent rejection of his claim to absolute sovereignty, but even
rating the "rebels" as by far the best products of his training program. The
chapter will end with Nebuchadnezzar even thinking that he himself is responsible for producing such impressive results. He will not realize that his
claims to absolute sovereignty have actually been invalidated. The presentation of his autocratic, even despotic behavior in chapter 2 thus masterfully
follows on from chapter 1.

4. The Distinctiveness of the Four Jews (1:13–20; cf. v. 9)

The central concern of the chapter concerns the comparison of these four Jews with their peers (and with all the magicians and enchanters in Babylon).

In Daniel 1 there is considerable stress on testing.[143] Daniel asks Ashpenaz to test them (v. 12). Daniel's very name implies "testing": "God is my judge." The real issue is not what Nebuchadnezzar thinks of Daniel and his men—it is not the testing by the guard that matters. Daniel and his friends pass all tests because they are approved by God. Significantly, the chapter concludes with Nebuchadnezzar "testing" the four heroes (v. 20).

A study of the solitary occurrence of direct speech in the chapter at 1:10–13 highlights a major theme, not only of this chapter, but of the book this chapter introduces: the distinctiveness of these four Jews. They are without peer. In the first place they look healthier and better nourished, that is, "plumper," than their counterparts.[144] Indeed, in describing this language is used which deliberately forges a connection between Daniel and Joseph. All four Hebrews are said to be "fat of flesh," an expression which elsewhere is only used in Genesis 41 to describe the fat cows of Pharaoh's dream.[145]

Their primary devotion to God is stressed over and over again. Also emphasized is that God blesses them and is with them; that he invests them with supernatural wisdom which far outclasses their peers, and protects them. Insofar as these youths become thoroughly acquainted with Babylonian literature and yet remain faithful to God it is clear that the imparted wisdom of God has enabled them to discriminate between that which is true and that which is false in the wisdom tradition of Babylon.[146]

It is important to note in verse 17 that God gives Daniel a wisdom that is not attributable to the learning he has acquired through the study of Babylonian literature, even to the extent that this involved the study of Babylonian dreams and visions. There is no suggestion, either here or elsewhere

143. Milne, *Vladimir Propp*, 210, flounders here as she continues to try to read Daniel 1 in the light of Propp's model. She sees the contest described in verses 12–20 as resembling Propp's functions "struggle with the villain" (we have already noted major problems with this conception) and "victory." However, as Milne recognizes, there is no direct contact between the hero and the supposed "villain" (Milne, forced to modify Propp's model to make it fit, prefers to call him "opponent"), Nebuchadnezzar.

144. In ancient and many societies still today plumpness is regarded as a positive thing. Péter-Contesse and Ellington, *Handbook*, 23.

145. Widder, "The Court Stories of Joseph," 1123. Widder speculates that just as the fat cows in the Pharaoh's dream represented years of plenty, so the application of this imagery to the four Hebrews might hint that they will bring "years of plenty" to the Babylonian royal court (see note 29). See too Wooden, *Daniel and Manticism*, 235.

146. Compare Baldwin, *Daniel*, 84.

in the book, that the wisdom-ability of Daniel to understand dreams and visions was shared by his three friends. God gives Daniel a special, clearly supernormal wisdom. What is being said here is that God has chosen to make Daniel a special conduit for his self-revelation through dreams and visions. Daniel's success in keeping himself morally pure, and in avoiding the compromise of his faith, equips him to serve as a fit channel for the accomplishment of God's purposes.

It is also noteworthy that as God prepares to reveal himself in a Babylonian context he chooses media that constitute a close cultural fit. It is at this point that Daniel's prior study of Babylonian dreams and visions will prove most useful.

Oppenheim[147] identified three methods of dream interpretation in the ancient Near East:

1. Interpretation by intuition. Eligibility? Someone qualified by age, social status, or simply personal charisms.

2. Interpretation by precedent. Eligibility? Being a trained scholar learned in the collections of dream-omina.

3. Interpretation by a further revelation. "The interpreter could turn to the deity who was the source of the dream either for verification of a proposed interpretation or for an unequivocal message." Eligibility? Professional priests who had special skills and rituals which could be applied to the situation.

It was the purpose of the rite of passage that the Jewish youths and their peers should "stand before the king" (v. 5), that is, be equipped to serve the king. Now we are told that they have far surpassed their peers (v. 18) and that therefore "they stood before the king" (v. 19). There is some wry humor here:

> Irony of ironies—the four who disobey the king's orders are the four who show themselves to be exceptional. The four who refuse to align themselves politically with the king are the ones chosen for royal service. Moreover, the independence of the four is underscored by the narrator's use of their Hebrew names rather than their assigned Babylonian names. Thus, though they stand in royal service, they are not what they seem, in the king's eyes, to be. The illusion of political unanimity covers the reality of compromise and raises a question for the reader: What will

---

147. Summarized by Collins, *Apocalyptic Vision*, 31.

happen later, in the larger story, if these men are called upon to
prove their political fidelity?[148]

This context does not lead to a cynical evaluation of the loyalty of Daniel and his three friends (contra Fewell). Indeed, precisely because of their primary allegiance to God, these men prove to be the very best of servants that such a pagan king could have.[149]

Venter cites Humphreys who sagely observes that this story along with the other tales of court conflict and court contest . . .

> . . . present a style of life for the diaspora Jew which affirms most
> strongly that at one and the same time the Jew can remain loyal
> to his heritage and God and yet can live a creative, rewarding,
> and fulfilled life precisely within a foreign setting, and in inter-
> action with it.[150]

The four Jews top the class.[151] The idea that Daniel and his companions are vastly superior (lit. "ten hands" = "ten times better") to "all the magicians and enchanters"[152] in Nebuchadnezzar's kingdom involves a number of basic dimensions:

1. It corresponds to the central stress of the direct speech portion of the chapter. The issue brought out in that section is the imperative that Daniel and his companions, as "Israelites" (v. 3), be a distinctive

---

148. Fewell, *Circle*, 22.

149. As Hebbard points out, the "irony is that those who are found to be the best [sc. most suited to serve the king] are the very same who resisted total assimilation into Babylonian life and whose diets and talents stem from a source that is clearly not Babylonian." *Reading Daniel,* 74–75.

150. Venter, "Space in Daniel 1," 994. At the same time, as presented in the Daniel narratives, these exiles exhibit characteristics identified by Safran as typical of modern diasporas: 1) they, or their ancestors, have been dispersed from their homeland; 2) they hold a collective memory about their homeland—its physical location; 3) they are not fully accepted by their host society; 4) they consider their homeland an ideal home; 5) they believe collectively they should restore or maintain their homeland; 6) they relate to the homeland and have solidarity Veiss, *Ideological Texture,* 50. Veiss also goes on to recognize that Daniel provides a fine model of cultural intelligence through cultural strategic thinking, motivation and behavior. *Ideological Texture,* 52.

151. The *Instruction of 'Onchsheshonqy* tells of two children, both sons of priests of Re, namely 'Onchsheshonqy and Harsiese, who are raised together and go to the same school where they outshine their peers. Another text, *Setne II,* which speaks of a child prodigy, Si-Osire, son of Setne Khamwas, who ends up surpassing the scribe who was training him and by the age of 12 he also surpasses all scribes in Memphis in his ability to recite protective spells. Holm, *Courtiers,* 422.

152. Van der Toorn, "Scholars," 39, assuming an Akkadian root for this second term prefers "exorcists" to "enchanters."

people. Thus it is crucial that they be distinguishable from their Babylonian peers. The fact that the chapter ends with them being referred to, not by their recently assigned Babylonian names, but with their Hebrew names, underscores "that the attempt to eradicate their commitment to God had been unsuccessful."[153]

2. When in verse 20 it is said that Daniel and his friends were ten times better than "all the magicians and enchanters" the context indicates that we are to understand that the four Jews are excluded from this category. They are not classifiable as magicians and enchanters despite, ironically, their superior knowledge of the very literature studied by magicians and enchanters. The fact that Daniel and his friends are distinguished from their Babylonian peers will be developed further in the book by showing that the wisdom of Daniel is to be utterly differentiated from the magic-oriented wisdom of the Chaldeans.

3. It is likely that the motif of Daniel's superiority to the magicians and enchanters is intended to recall Joseph's similar superiority (Gen 41:8, 24). In this regard it is to be noted that the Hebrew word *hartummîm*, "occurs only in reference to the soothsayers of Egypt in the accounts of Joseph . . . and of Moses and Aaron at the court of Pharaoh (Ex 7:11, 22; etc.) . . . "[154]

GOD'S RULE OUTLASTS BABYLONIAN RULE (1:21)

Aside from summarizing the major thrust of the chapter, verses 17–21 also provide connective material, anticipating the plot development of chapter 2 and beyond.[155] We have already observed that the first year of King Cyrus's rule was the year when he issued his great decree to rebuild the temple. The chapter moves from temple desecration and the loss of Jerusalem to the prospect of temple rebuilding and return to Jerusalem. Dumbrell adds:

153. Goswell, *Daniel*, 14.

154. Hartman and Di Lella, *Book of Daniel*, 131.

155. Milne, *Vladimir Propp*, 210, fails to find any of Propp's functions in verses 17–21 and, therefore, incorrectly, does not treat them as being part of the story proper—a big mistake since these verses represent the climax to the story and encapsulate its essential thrust. Yet she is right in treating this material as "connective" for indeed it does communicate further information that will be developed in subsequent chapters: Daniel's ability to interpret visions and dreams, the completion of the process of training, a reminder that the heroes are still in exile and likely to remain so.

The laconic conclusion of the chapter (1:21) reports that Daniel outlives the Babylonian Empire and sees the ushering in of the Persian period. He has exhibited the uncompromising characteristics of the man of faith, whose life is able to sustain the effects of a changed world. He is thus the exemplary figure of the period.[156]

We have noted the strength of the deliberate parallels drawn between Daniel and Joseph. Given this, the fact that Daniel is said to have remained until the first year of King Cyrus may also carry the implication that Daniel, like Joseph, is the forerunner of a new exodus.[157]

GOD THE SOVEREIGN GIVER

The only verb associated with God in Daniel 1 is the verb "give." In verse 2 we read that God "gave" Jehoiakim into the hand of Nebuchadnezzar. In verse 9 that he "gave" Daniel favor and compassion in the sight of the official. In verse 17 we read that he "gave" the four Jewish youths knowledge and understanding, etc.

It is precisely these actions of giving which indicate that it is God, not Nebuchadnezzar, who is the supreme sovereign. It is most significant that all of these actions of sovereign giving are performed, as it were, behind the scenes. Nebuchadnezzar makes a big show of his kingship—a point which will become even more pronounced in the chapters which follow—but his sovereignty is hollow. Real sovereignty—the ultimate kingship of God—is hidden. Nebuchadnezzar is oblivious to the fact that his victory over Jehoiakim and his desecration of the temple are not due to his irresistible sovereign might (which would, after all, appear to be the natural and obvious interpretation of history), but in actual fact represent the outworking of God's purpose. The facade of sovereignty is assumed by Nebuchadnezzar, but real sovereignty belongs to God.

Similarly there is no suggestion that the official was aware that it was God who was making him well disposed towards Daniel. Certainly this action of God is completely unknown to the main rival, Nebuchadnezzar.

It is only the implied reader who is privy to the imparted knowledge that it was God who gave the four Jewish youths their outstanding ability, and thus demonstrated his sovereignty in making his chosen ones superior to their Babylonian peers.

156. Dumbrell, *Faith of Israel*, 259.
157. Hamilton, *Clouds of Heaven*, 231.

It cannot be overstressed that God gives these Jewish youths wisdom to understand Babylonian literature and thought, and enables them to understand such things better even than native Babylonians themselves. This means that the Book of Daniel stands completely at odds with the implacable attitude of pious inter-testamental Jews towards foreign wisdom. It is precisely because God gives wisdom and understanding to Daniel and his friends that they are safe as they study foreign wisdom. That is, God-endowed wisdom enables them to discern the difference between truth and falsehood, between right and wrong. Security against error is not attained by cutting oneself off from "foreign" influences, but in being able to evaluate such influences in the light of God-given wisdom. In this respect the Book of Daniel constitutes a major challenge to many Christians who in their fear lest they be tainted with the thinking of the world inure themselves to living in an artificial world of essentially "Christian" music, literature, conversation, and society.

SUMMARY

Daniel 1 introduces the book of Daniel in the following ways:

1. The Temple. Daniel 1 introduces the all-important motif of temple-desecration. The record of Daniel's life stretches from the time of the desecration of the Temple (explicit) to the time of its restoration (implicit). The conquest of Jerusalem was the most important military act of Nebuchadnezzar's reign. The most significant thing he ever did was to appropriate articles from the Temple.

2. Wisdom. Daniel 1 introduces the pervasive theme of wisdom: Babylonian wisdom was essentially elitist; God-given wisdom is profoundly ethical. Along with this goes the matter of the true identity of God's faithful and utterly distinctive people. Presumptuously, Nebuchadnezzar tries, unsuccessfully, to shape the identity of God's people. In line with this the Jewish youths were forced to immerse themselves in magic-suffused literature. But Daniel's diet expresses his refusal to be completely defined by Nebuchadnezzar. Daniel resolved to avoid moral, not cultic defilement. The identity of the Jewish youths essentially consists in their uncompromising but wise devotion to Yahweh. But this devotion to Yahweh and his rule does not mean that God's people rebel against human rule (contra Maccabeans). Ironically, it is those most faithful to Yahweh who are best fitted to genuinely serve the Babylonian king.

3. Kingship. Daniel 1 introduces the issue as to the real source of the Babylonian king's power and authority. Associated with this is the pervasive contrast between human self-sufficiency, epitomized by Babylon and its ruler, and the kingship of Yahweh. Nebuchadnezzar attributes his power to the wrong deity. In reality, God backs Babylonian kingship against the king of his own people. Daniel 1, therefore, introduces the true understanding of Yahweh's sovereignty in a world in which God's people are ruled by a seemingly irresistible foreign power. This includes indicating the hiddenness of God's rule. In Daniel 1 Yahweh demonstrates his kingship through three acts of sovereign giving.

POINTS OF CONTACT WITH THE NEW TESTAMENT AND WITH LIFE

1. God's power is made perfect in weakness (2 Cor 12:9). In Daniel's time Yahweh was still very much in control, notwithstanding the conquest of Jerusalem, the desecration of the Temple, and the subjugation of God's people. The death of Jesus on the cross was a seeming catastrophe for the rule of God which Jesus had proclaimed during his ministry. In reality, never was God's sovereignty more wonderfully in action. At a secondary level, it is worth remembering that it was in accordance with Jesus' prophecy that Jerusalem and the Temple were again destroyed. As in Daniel, but to an even more radical extent, it becomes necessary to conceive of God's rule as not contingent upon Zion and Temple.

2. Devotion to the Lord does not require physical separation from the world (1 Cor 5:9–10). God's people today do not live in a controlled theocratic society. Sometimes Christians must expose themselves and even immerse themselves in cultural forms that have potentially damaging aspects. Like Daniel and his three friends we are dependent on the Lord to protect us and ensure the preservation of our moral integrity. Fundamental to all true piety is a Daniel-like resolve not to be defiled.

POSSIBLE SERMON OUTLINE

Title: "All the King's Men"

1. *Relocation and Identity.* In the shaping of the identity of Daniel and his three friends what was the significance of being uprooted from the land and being trained by the king in Babylon?

2. *Resolve and Identity.* In the shaping of the identity of these Jewish youths what was the significance of Daniel's dietary resolution?

3. *Rule and Identity.* In the shaping of the identity of these men what was the significance of God's sovereign acts?

Daniel 2

Being in the Know

The Nature of the Distinctiveness of Daniel: God's Sovereignty Revealed in the Giving of Unique Wisdom

FLOW OF THOUGHT FROM DANIEL 1

Daniel 1 begins with the contrast between God's kingship and that of Nebuchadnezzar. Ostensibly, at least by ancient standards, the conquest of Jerusalem and placement of temple articles in the treasury of the temple of Nebuchadnezzar's own god signaled the capitulation of Israel's god and his subordination under the rule of Babylon's king and gods. But from the outset the book of Daniel opposes the received wisdom of the ancient world. Notwithstanding the demise of God's people, king, and city, this book insists that God continues to rule. Even more than this, the calamity which befell Israel was one orchestrated by God himself. It is God's will and purpose that his people be exiled in Babylon.

But the reality of God's continuing sovereignty is only perceived by the implied reader and is opaque to Nebuchadnezzar and the Babylonian world. Daniel 1 kicks off the book by showing that God continues to control what happens in Babylon. However, the exercise of God's kingship is behind the scenes, out of view, mysterious and veiled, only recognized by the sympathetic implied reader. But it is a real exercise of kingship which is demonstrated in the way the official treats Daniel so favorably and in the success of Daniel and his three friends relative to that of all the other magicians and astrologers in Babylon. There has been no dramatic, obvious shaking of historical terra firma. Nevertheless clear evidence is provided that God has sovereignly endowed his four faithful servants with an immense wisdom which greatly impresses Nebuchadnezzar.

Daniel 2 follows on from this. So far God's sovereignty has been especially revealed in the sphere of wisdom, yet only in a veiled fashion. Further all that has been revealed is that the God-given wisdom of Daniel and his friends differs from that of the Chaldeans only *in degree*. Now in Daniel 2 God will openly reveal to Nebuchadnezzar that God-given wisdom differs also *in kind*.[1] God is not merely the transcendent one who lives in heaven, but he is accessible to his people.

DATE AND GENRE

The chapter is set "in the second year of [Nebuchadnezzar's] reign," that is, around 604/603 BC. Reynolds argues that an original court tale with a dream report has been transformed into an apocalypse.[2]

STRUCTURE

Following Lenglet, Goldingay notes that chapters 2 and 7 form the outer frames of a chiasm:[3]

2 A vision of four kingdoms and their end (Nebuchadnezzar)

3 Faithfulness and a miraculous rescue (the three friends)

4 Judgment presaged and experienced (Nebuchadnezzar)

5 Judgment presaged and experienced (Belshazzar)

6 Faithfulness and a miraculous rescue (Daniel)

7 A vision of four kingdoms and their end (Daniel)

1. Lawson makes a major mistake in his analysis of this passage by not treating verses 10–11 with sufficient care (see below). As a result, having stated that "the Mesopotamian mantic tradition . . . has been subsumed within and subordinated to the Hebrew tradition, and translated within their framework of monotheism for their own theological purposes," he erroneously concludes: "The difference between the two traditions is not one of kind, but quality." Lawson, "The God Who Reveals Secrets," 75.

2. Reynolds, *Between Symbolism and Realism*, 90. Reynolds disagrees with Collins' assessment that Daniel 2 is merely the proto-type of an apocalyptic vision, *Between Symbolism and Realism*, 98.

3. Goldingay, *Daniel*, 158.

Daniel 2 breaks down into four major sections:

1–13	Chaldean inability to tell and interpret the dream and the ordering of their execution: the impotence and inaccessibility of Mesopotamian deities.
14–24	Daniel finds favor with Arioch, averts immediate disaster, and receives the revelation of the mystery in response to urgent prayer: Daniel, in contrast with the Chaldeans, experiences the power and accessibility of his God.
25–45	Daniel tells the dream and its interpretation to Nebuchadnezzar giving all the credit to God: Nebuchadnezzar experiences the sovereignty of God in the bestowal of otherwise inaccessible wisdom.
46–49	Nebuchadnezzar greatly honors Daniel (along with his three friends) and acknowledges Daniel's God as the revealer of mysteries: Daniel's God is acknowledged as absolute sovereign because of his bestowal of otherwise inaccessible wisdom.

Dorsey[4] proposes a chiastic structure:

A Introduction: Nebuchadnezzar has disturbing dream (1)

  B Magicians fail to recount and explain king's dream (2–13)

    C Daniel and Arioch: Daniel goes to king with proposal (14–16)

      D CLIMAX: God reveals and explains dream to Daniel (17–23)

    C' Daniel and Arioch: Daniel goes to king with answer (24–25)

  B' Daniel succeeds: he recounts and explains king's dream (26–45)

A' Conclusion: Nebuchadnezzar glorifies God and promotes Daniel (46–49)

Significantly, it is a poetic passage (vv. 20–23), with affinities to thanksgiving psalms and wisdom psalms, which centers the narrative. Following Prinsloo, we can identify four functions achieved by the insertion of this poem:[5]

1. Foregrounding. "It catches attention and prepares the reader for something out of the ordinary."

2. Heightening tension.

3. Delaying pace. This helps the reader to focus on the extraordinary.

---

4. Dorsey, *The Literary Structure*, 261. Similarly, see Prinsloo, "Two Poems," 98–99.

5. "Two Poems," 101.

4. Making the important theological statement concerning God's sovereignty with respect to wisdom, its impartation and the control of history this involves.

Towner studies this particular poem along with three other passages of a poetic character in chapters 1–6, namely 4:1–3; 4:34–35; and 6:25–27. He argues that there is close resemblance to the hymn-form of Israelite religious poetry.[6] He finds them to be expressive of a "universalist theodicy," noting that:

> . . . the prayers focus the point of the narratives roughly as follows: God's decision to allow evil its hour of ascendancy will be vindicated before the eyes of all nations when good ultimately triumphs; this vindication will come about because of God's transcendent power and endurance; to this fact the evil powers of the world will themselves be obliged at last to testify.[7]

THE JOSEPH–DANIEL PARALLEL

Think about this description:

> A handsome, impressive Jewish youth who comes from a great home is violently uprooted from his land and taken, against his will, to another country, the greatest world power of the day. He is forced into a life of service and lives in this foreign land with a foreign name which is given to him by the ruler. But God blesses this youth and endows him with such ability that he stands out as one worthy to assume high responsibilities which become more and more substantial as his life progresses. At one point he is treated favorably by the ruler's "captain of the guard." His moral integrity is challenged early in his life but he emerges from this with shining colours. He gets into great trouble which is not of his own making. But in that very context he displays his diplomatic skills and great wisdom. The ruler—the most powerful man on earth (politically speaking)—has nightmares which are caused by God and which terrify him. He senses that the future holds terrifying possibilities which are beyond his control. He is desperate for someone to interpret these frightening visions and, in this context, the youth, whose Hebrew identity is emphasized, emerges as the one who alone can interpret the great

---

6. "Poetic Passages," 321.

7. Towner, "Poetic Passages," 322–23.

ruler's dreams. This youth insists that he is not personally able to interpret the dreams but that he is mediating God's revelation to the ruler. The ruler recognizes the incomparable nature of this youth's wisdom who is described as one "in whom the spirit of the gods" is to be found. He is exalted by the ruler—at one point, second only to the ruler himself. Yet, notwithstanding the prosperity and high position this Hebrew man enjoys he always longs to return to the promised land.

Which biblical character have I just described? This fairly detailed portrait *precisely* fits two persons—Joseph and Daniel. Clearly the presentation of Daniel in this book is intended to invite the readers to compare, and perhaps even contrast, the lives of Joseph and Daniel respectively.

Rindge demonstrates that Daniel 2 involves a reconfiguration of Genesis 41.[8] In addition to the shared theme of a Jew serving in the court of a foreign king, he identifies 18 similarities in the plot structures of these chapters:

1. Each narrative begins with the ruler of a nation who has a dream (Gen 41:1; Dan 2:1).

2. The timing of each dream is associated with "two years."

3. Each dream results in the ruler's spirit being troubled (Gen 41:8; Dan 2:1).

4. The ruler responds to the dream and his troubled spirit by calling for magicians and others (Gen 41:8; Dan 2:2).

5. Those called before the king are incapable of providing what he desires (Gen 41:8c; Dan 2:10–11).

6. A new character is introduced who serves as an intermediary between the king and a potential dream interpreter. This potential dream interpreter functions in the narrative as a signal of hope that the ruler's dream may be interpreted (Gen 41:12–13; Dan 2:16).

7. The intermediary identifies the ethnicity of the potential dream interpreter.

8. The dream interpreter is brought before the ruler (Gen 41:14; Dan 2:25).

9. The ruler initiates dialogue by speaking to the interpreter regarding the interpreter's ability to interpret dreams (Gen 41:15; Dan 2:26).

---

8. Rindge, "Jewish Identity," 88–89. See too Hamilton, *Clouds of Heaven*, 230–31.

10. The interpreter responds with a twofold answer in which he downplays his own role in the interpretive process and highlights God's role as the one who is able to interpret dreams (Gen 41:16; Dan 2:27–30).

11. The content of the dream is described (Gen 41:17–24a; Dan 2:31–35).

12. In each case the dream is a "symbolic" dream.

13. The interpreter provides an interpretation of the dream (Gen 41:25–31; Dan 2:36–45a.).

14. The dream is interpreted to refer to future events (Gen 41:25, 28–31; Dan 2:39–45a).

15. The interpreter emphasizes the certainty or trustworthiness of the interpretation (Gen 41:32; Dan 2:45c).

16. The ruler is pleased with the interpreter's response (Gen 41:37; Dan 2:46).

17. The ruler affirms the ability of the interpreter and acknowledges God's role in the interpretive process (Gen 41:39; Dan 2:47).

18. The ruler rewards the interpreter by giving him gifts and a promotion to rule over an entire region (Gen 41:41; Dan 2:48).

As I will indicate below the life of Daniel is not merely presented as a recapitulation of the life of Joseph.[9] The portrayal of Daniel is much more complex than this. There are also significant differences.[10] In Daniel 2 we see Daniel not merely interpreting the king's dream, but also relating back to Nebuchadnezzar the very content of the dream itself. In Daniel 2 the lives of Nebuchadnezzar's magicians and company are at stake, whereas in Genesis 41 it is Joseph's freedom rather than the threat of death that is at

9. Those who reduce Daniel to the level of being but a new Joseph, typically exaggerate the affinity of the Danielic narrative with such works as the pseudepigraphical *Testament of Joseph* and the romance *Joseph and Asenath*, and also typically dismiss the narrative as a literary fabrication. The crucifixion of Christ is a unique historical event, but this does not prevent the Gospel writers from finding many significant Old Testament patterns fulfilled in that event. It is a curious logic which concludes that a literary emphasis on such correspondences presupposes a fictionalizing of the historical event concerned (e.g., Towner, *Daniel*, 29–31).

10. Some of the contrasts that Rindge proposes are dubious. For example, he thinks Joseph grows in humility and that his acknowledgement of God is progressive, whereas Daniel humbly acknowledges God from the outset. He also supposes that "God's role elevates the status of Joseph in Pharaoh's eyes, while Daniel elevates the status of God in the eyes of Nebuchadnezzar." "Jewish Identity," 94. It seems unlikely that the text of Daniel 2 insinuates that Joseph was less pious than Daniel. Rindge is making too much of differences between texts that are an inevitable consequence of the different functions they serve.

issue. In this context of high tension we see Daniel engaged in prayer, something conspicuous for its absence in the depiction of Joseph.[11] This aspect of Daniel's piety especially receives added focus at 6:10 and the extended prayer of chapter 9. Further, Daniel's dream interpretations, unlike those of Joseph, are typically eschatological in character. The future events foreseen by Joseph occur within his own lifetime.

In the man Daniel we see not only Joseph but also a summation of Israel's experience in Egypt and even relevant glimpses of Moses. At the same time Daniel also illustrates the intense relevance of these precedents to the lives of God's people in the new world order of which they are a part.

In the first instance the correspondence between Daniel and Joseph, and Israel and Moses is something effected by God through the particular historical events he brings about. Only those who repudiate the historicity of Daniel will see the correspondence as a purely literary creation and such scholars need to take much more seriously than is customary the fact that the parallels between Daniel and the lives of Joseph, God's people in Egypt, and Moses are as restrained as they are. For example, it would have been quite easy to have presented the miracles of Daniel in a way which much more closely approximated the signs and wonders performed in Egypt, but, arguably, the concern of the writer to remain true to the discrete historical facts constrains him from overdoing it. However, the above-mentioned parallels are certainly accentuated by the particular way in which the book of Daniel has been written. Arguably, they are explicable as means by which the writer seeks to prepare God's people to face suffering under blasphemous rule.

At the fundamental level history bears the same essential character. The parallelism involving Daniel goes beyond a mere correspondence between the personal careers of Daniel and Joseph. Daniel simultaneously represents the whole of Israel in Egypt and also, in some respects, the career of Moses as well. For Babylon is a new Egypt. The whole Egyptian experience is in some sense recapitulated, with Daniel (and his three friends) effectively representing God's people as an oppressed, captive people in the hands of the mightiest power on earth—a power which is capricious and often cruel. In Egypt God was committed to preserving his people and making a sharp distinction between them and the Egyptians. So too in Babylon, as epitomized by Daniel and his three friends, God sovereignly protects and miraculously delivers his people who are sharply distinguished by their moral integrity and wisdom from their Babylonian peers. The king of the day is humbled,

11. Rindge, "Jewish Identity," 92–93.

even humiliated, and forced to acknowledge the peerless nature of God's sovereignty and power.

Just as Moses was sent by God to confront Pharaoh so too Daniel performs something of this role in this book. There are very strong inter-connections between the book of Daniel and prophetic literature—much more so than with the inter-testamental apocalyptic writings—and Daniel functions not merely as a Joseph-like wise man but, to a limited degree, also as a Mosaic prophet who, as a traditional covenant mediator, confronts idolatrous human rule, and communicates God's irrevocable word of judg-ment upon it (see especially Daniel 5).[12] To this extent, Rindge is justified in drawing a contrast between Daniel and Joseph, in that Joseph is never portrayed as confronting Pharaoh.[13]

In many respects the book of Daniel, in encouraging readers to line up the Babylonian experience of God's people with that of Egypt, is presenting a grim picture of future history. In the short term, as Daniel 9 indicates, there is the prospect of God doing again what he once had done in Egypt—returning his people to the land and enabling the rebuilding of Jerusalem and the temple. However, the book of Daniel also teaches that the recur-rence of the Egypt experience in Babylon is an omen that there will never be untroubled security and freedom from attack for God's people in "the beautiful land" until blasphemous human rule (epitomized by Pharaoh and the rulers of *Daniel*) is once and for all conclusively destroyed. The destruc-tion of Jerusalem and the desecration of the temple will recur and the beasts of blasphemous human rule will seek to destroy God's people. Indeed, if anything, things will eventually get worse—as "the little horn" prophecies

12. Wooden remarks, "Daniel seems to act more as a prophet who has access to the council of God, than as someone who interprets what another receives. He does not interpret the dream using his own superior intellect, but merely passes on the interpre-tation given him in his vision." *Daniel and Manticism*, 214.

13. Rindge argues that "a pattern emerges in which Daniel is consistently portrayed, in contrast to the assimilation of Joseph, as one who resists the claims of empire" ("Jew-ish Identity," 95). This is excessive and unfair to the very different functional intent of the Joseph narrative. It is also an unbalanced treatment of Daniel's relationship to the state, given that there is immense and persistent stress on the fact that he and his friends are the most loyal servants a king could possibly have. It is wrong to see Daniel and his friends as in any sense intentionally subversive, as Rindge does, even though he recog-nizes that Daniel's model does not condone the rejection practised by the Maccabees ("Jewish Identity," 103). If forced to choose, Daniel and his friends will always put first their primary allegiance to Yahweh, but this is never an expression of defiance. Rindge incorrectly considers Daniel's refusal to eat the king's diet (1:8–17) as setting a pattern of resisting the empire (96). Rather, as I have endeavored to show, the concern is with preserving his essential identity as Yahweh's servant and, furthermore, Daniel refrained from the king's diet only for a limited period.

envisage. Yet God will preserve his kingdom and just as he dealt with Egypt and Babylon so he will deal with blasphemous human rule until that time when he once and for all destroys it and gives to his people an everlasting kingdom which encompasses the whole globe.

Thus the parallelism between Babylon and Egypt is intended to say to Daniel's readers that for God's people the pattern of suffering under blasphemous human authority and God's sovereign preservation of his people ("the wise") in that context is normative. However, it also implies that such history is inexorably moving towards the final showdown when blasphemous human authority, having assumed its most terrifying proportions, will be destroyed forever and replaced by the eternal kingdom of God.

The correspondences between Daniel and Joseph bring to the fore the importance of wisdom and its role in keeping perspective as to who really controls the course of history. In the kind of world anticipated in Daniel it would be easy to conclude that the throat of history is being clutched by the vice-like grip of awesome human power. If God's people are to endure and remain strong then it will be because they too have the Danielic wisdom which enables them to recognize the overarching sovereignty of God—even if, at times, as in Daniel's case, with a measure of perplexity. In this way the figure of Daniel takes on board the particular wisdom of Joseph and shows that in the new world order it is this kind of wisdom that all God's people now need. That is, as the wise man Daniel is not only a new Joseph but, more importantly, represents the *maskilim*, the wise, God's faithful people.

BROAD OVERVIEW OF 2:1–13

> *Narrative* (vv. 1–2). King troubled and issues an order accepting wise men as potential interpreters.
>
> *Direct Speech*
>
> First and second interchanges (vv. 3–4; 5–8). King tests the ability of wise men to act as potential interpreters.
>
> Third interchange (vv. 8–11). Wise men admit their inability to act as potential interpreters.
>
> *Narrative* (vv. 12–13). King furious and issues an order rejecting wise men as potential interpreters.

2:12–13 correspond with 2:1–2 and also constitute a contrast with those verses. The narrative provides a frame for this whole scene. This frame shows a primary interest in two matters[14]:

14. Milne's attempt (*Vladimir Propp*, 211) to describe verses 1–3 in terms of Propp's

1. The King's State of Mind. The scene begins with the king being troubled and ends with him shaking with fury.

2. The King's Disposition Towards the Chaldeans. The scene begins with the king issuing a command to bring in the Chaldeans to remove his distress through an explanation of the dream. The scene ends with the king issuing a command to destroy the wise men in order to satiate his rage.

With regard to narrative style note the use of the popular storytelling device of trebling. Three times the king makes his request to the sages and three times he is answered. Such trebling is used here to build tension.[15]

The above broad outline indicates how Daniel 2 follows on from Daniel 1. The first chapter has made a special point of comparing and contrasting Daniel and his friends with their Babylonian peers (the youths in training and the established class of Chaldeans). This was intended to demonstrate the surpassing wisdom of the Hebrew youths. Already in Daniel 1 it is indicated that the essential point of distinction between their wisdom and that of their Babylonian peers is that "God gave them knowledge and understanding." As twenty-first-century Christians who are used to this kind of lingo we are prone to be blasé when reading such words. But in the context of Daniel they are of extraordinary importance. For Daniel 2 goes on to highlight how, in the minds of the Babylonian wise men, it is unthinkable that humans can be privy to that which only the lehîn, the superhuman beings,[16] can know: "No one can reveal it to the king except the gods, and they do not live among men" (2:11). Only God can reveal such a thing: "there is a God in heaven who reveals mysteries" (2:28). This is in keeping with Keel's observation that the "gulf between god and man is generally greater in Mesopotamia than in Egypt, where it is bridged by the divine king."[17] In this context the estrangement from the gods of the wise men and even of Nebuchadnezzar himself is accentuated.

---

model, as performing the function of "a difficult task," evacuates these verses of their central thrust: the king's state of mind and disposition towards the Chaldeans. Anyway, by the end of verse 3 there is absolutely no indication that this will in fact be a difficult task. Indeed, the response of verse 4, suggests that the astrologers are keen to show how well trained and capable they are in meeting the king's need.

15. Fewell, Circle, 24.

16. In Daniel this plural form seems to encompass not merely pagan, but also all superhuman beings. Hartman and Di Lella note LXX versions which use it to refer to angels; Daniel, 138–39.

17. Keel, The Symbolism of the Biblical World, 78. Widder finds the Chaldeans' statement perplexing, given that the gods were believed to be present in the temples built for them ("Court Stories," 1120). But there need be no confusion. They clearly

Here is the point of contrast that is sorely missed by Lawson, in his otherwise helpful treatment of the Mesopotamian mantic tradition. Lawson maintains:

> Any attempt to characterize the Mesopotamian tradition as non-revelatory is patently wrong and can only rest upon a false distinction between biblical and non-biblical views of revelation. The only real distinction in Daniel is the *identity* and *competence* of the deity doing the revealing, not any doctrine of revelation itself; for in the final analysis, the effective ingredient in Daniel's dream interpretations was divinity, just as it was and always had been in the oneiromancy and other mantic acts of Mesopotamia.[18]

This is plain wrong. As verses 10–11 clearly teach there is a massive and fundamental difference between Mesopotamian revelation, no matter how divine such revelation was deemed to be, and the revelation that actually—and not merely in a literary manner—was imparted to Daniel.[19] It is not merely the case that "the God of heaven" has a different competency from Mesopotamian deities. The bottom line is that no Mesopotamian deity was able to reveal the dream itself. We are not merely talking about interpretation of dreams here! Only God is able to reveal such particularity and, as becomes apparent in the very relating of the dream and its interpretation, the further point is being made that only God is able to reveal the future in particular detail. When the theology implicit in verses 10–11 is set against the broader context of Scripture we can go further and say that there is no other supposed god, whatever "revelation" may be associated with it, that

---

understood that for all this there was in reality a gulf between the gods and themselves, as made manifest by the sheer absurdity of expecting their gods to supply the contents of the dream.

18. Lawson, "The God Who Reveals Secrets," 75.

19. This same failure to see the gulf between what people can know and what is only knowable through divine revelation is evident in Mol's attempt to read the dreams of Nebuchadnezzar in a purely naturalistic manner, in accord with a modern psychoanalytical understanding of dreams. So Mol speaks of dreams "'compensating for' and 'completing,' daily experiences and events that otherwise would be left dangling in emotional limbo." He adds, "The brain 'restores' and 'unifies' these experiences and events in order to integrate the memory bank." Furthermore, "this 'compensating' and 'completing' takes place wholly and entirely outside human reason and direction. Rather than understanding these latent forces to 'suffocate intelligence' as Calvin thought, they 'heal' and contribute to sanity and wholeness independent of the human will." Mol, *Calvin*, 20. This is all well and good, but to whatever extent Nebuchadnezzar's brain was processing experiences and events in an involuntary manner, this did not leave him more sane or whole. Quite the opposite. No modern psychoanalyst would have been any better placed than the ancient Chaldean to interpret Nebuchadnezzar's dream.

can actually reveal what God alone can and does reveal, precisely because he is the true and living God who has actual relations with his people.[20]

In chapter 3 it will become evident that this God does not merely dwell in a remote locality; he is present in a mysterious godlike figure who walks in the furnace with Daniel's three friends (see Daniel 6). In chapter 4 Nebuchadnezzar recognizes that "the spirit of the holy gods is in him" (4:8; see v. 9, 18; 5:11, 14). In the book of Daniel, God is a God who does "live among men." He is accessible to Daniel who, therefore, can reveal mysteries to the king. Incidentally, this emphasis in the book upon God's immanence, his presence with Daniel and his friends, assumes considerable importance in the debate as to whether the book of Daniel can be classified as an apocalypse. For in apocalypses the transcendence of God is greatly stressed. Thus 2:11 is an important indication that Daniel cannot be lumped together with other apocalypses in a simplistic manner.

The broad outline of verses 1–13 also indicates the continuance of another motif—the king's testing of the wise men. Daniel 1 closes with the king testing those who have undergone his training program. Daniel 2 has the king also testing the limits of the wisdom of the Chaldeans. Both chapters show that the wisdom of the Chaldeans falls far short of that attained by Daniel and his friends. But Daniel 1:20 suggests that the king has merely concluded that the Hebrew youths are more advanced than their Babylonian peers with respect to the Babylonian wisdom in which they have been inculcated. The king as yet has not realized that the wisdom of Daniel and his friends is radically different. One of the key purposes of Daniel 2, evidently, is to place beyond all doubt not merely that Daniel's wisdom is superior but that it *is* fundamentally different. The wisdom of the Chaldeans is humanistic because as they themselves confess they have no substantial contact with the gods.[21] By contrast the God of heaven reveals mysteries to Daniel and his presence with Daniel is discerned, even if not understood, by the various kings with whom he has to deal.

20. "Unlike the Babylonian sages, who argue that the gods dwell far from humans, the author shows that Daniel believes in a God who is intimately connected with the human community." Pace, *Daniel*, 66.

21. Hebbard comments, "Here in this short statement is their admission that they cannot possibly attain any status as theological hermeneuts. A hermeneut is precisely one who, while acknowledging the supernatural and being aware of the supernatural 'otherly' habitat, acts as a link to bridge the gap between a transcendent deity and immanent mortal. By the very nature of hermeneutics, we must conclude that a hermeneut is one who is the messenger—and hence interpreter—of the gods." *Reading Daniel*, 83.

CHARACTER CONTRAST IN DANIEL 2:1-13

These verses contrast the absolute power of the king with the complete impotence of the Chaldeans. It emphasizes that, following his nightmare, Nebuchadnezzar has a deeply troubled mind (vv. 1, 3). Whether the Chaldeans will perish or prosper depends not only on their ability to interpret the dream (vv. 2–3) but on being able to prove that they know what Nebuchadnezzar had actually dreamed (vv. 5–9). He orders their execution when they prove incapable of meeting his demand (vv. 12–13).

By contrast, the Chaldeans are shown to lack any truly God-given wisdom. They find themselves required to interpret the dream (v. 2a) but insist they can only do this if the king tells them what he dreamed (vv. 4, 7). When he refuses to do his, they declare that his request has placed them in an impossible position because what the king asks is beyond the reach of any human (v. 10). They argue that this is impossible because the gods are not present with humans (v. 11).

THE LINGUISTIC CHANGE

As the text itself indicates from 2:4b onwards Aramaic/Chaldean is used instead of Hebrew. Edlin reasons that since "the Aramaic section includes both stories and visions, it becomes a means of assuring that the reader will interpret the visions of chs 7 to 12 in reference to the stories of chs 1 to 6. The two sections of the book have been brought together by the use of Aramaic."[22]

The native language of Babylon was actually Akkadian, a Semitic language with strong similarities to Hebrew. However, the Chaldean ethnic group in power at the time spoke Aramaic. Anderson points out that this language became widely used throughout the ancient Near East from the seventh century BC.[23] Interestingly, it is incorporated into the book of Ezra in Ezra 4:8–23, 5:1–6:18 and 7:12–26. Anderson also notes the use of Aramaic in Jeremiah 10:11 and in two words used in Genesis 31:47.

The change at 2:4b from Hebrew to Aramaic has puzzled commentators. In terms of original composition there are only three possible explanations:

22. *Daniel*, 64.

23. Anderson, *Signs and Wonders*, 13. Harman observes that it had become the major commercial language of the Near East, "probably because of its comparatively simple alphabetic script." *Daniel*, 54.

1. The book was originally written entirely in one language—Hebrew or Aramaic—and later partially translated into the other language.[24]

2. The book was originally written in two languages, as per the present form of the book.

3. The book was originally written entirely in one language, then translated entirely into the second language. However, the original translation was partially lost and the gap was filled in with the second language.[25]

As Leatherman notes: "every proposal for explaining the bilingualism of the book requires the multiplication of hypotheses."[26] Other assumptions, combined with the above, have led to the making of various proposals:[27]

1. The Absent-Minded Writer

Least convincing, perhaps, is Driver's proposal "that the author began in Hebrew and switched to Aramaic when reporting direct speech in that language" but then "forgot to revert to Hebrew."[28] Driver also believed the author, not Daniel, was using Western Aramaic which was not used in Babylon, but this position has been criticized for its dependence on late evidence and for making a distinction between Eastern and Western Aramaic which did not exist in pre-Christian times.[29] Notwithstanding its use of Aramaic, Ezra was accepted as a document from the middle of the fifth century BC.[30] Why should Daniel be treated differently?

2. Sensitivity to Audience

Many have held the view that *Daniel* intended the Hebrew portions for Hebrew ears and the central Aramaic bloc for Gentile ears. So Wood maintains

---

24. For example, Charles conjectured that the book was first written in Aramaic with parts of it subsequently translated into Hebrew. Charles, *Daniel*, xii. Charles engages in a critique of various other arguments: (1) that Aramaic was the vernacular of Babylonia, and was accordingly used in the sections relating to that country; (2) the diversity of language is to be explained by a diversity of origin (e.g. Meinhold, Dalman); (3) the author introduced the Chaldeans as speaking the language he believed to be customary with them; (4) the book was originally written in Hebrew and later translated it into the Aramaic vernacular so as to be intelligible for ordinary people; (5) that chapters 2–7 of the version of the LXX were made directly from the Hebrew, and not from the Aramaic (xix–xxvi).

25. Leatherman, "Apparent Indicators," 155; Valeta, *Lions*, 29.

26. "Apparent Indicators," 156.

27. See Davies, *Daniel*, 35.

28. Davies, *Daniel*, 35.

29. Walvoord, *Daniel*, 15.

30. Walvoord, *Daniel*, 15.

that the Aramaic portion "deals with matters pertaining to the Gentile world, with little notice of God's people, the Jews."[31] Some have modified this position arguing the stories in chapters 2–7 were first written in Aramaic for Jewish ears with the visions of chapters 8–12 being added for a more sophisticated audience. After this, so the argument goes, Daniel added an introduction (1:1–2:4a) in Hebrew to replace the original Aramaic one.

3. A Patch-Up Job

Some would argue that the entire book was originally written in but one language. So Bevan guesses "that part of the Hebrew original had been lost and was replaced by an Aramaic version," while Charles maintains *Daniel* was composed in Aramaic.[32] Contrary to the view of those who hold that the complete *Daniel* was originally written in Aramaic with sections subsequently translated into Hebrew, manuscripts from both Cave One and Cave Four at Qumran validate the change from Hebrew to Aramaic at 2:4b and the change from Aramaic to Hebrew at 8:1. Hasel remarks: "The Hebrew/Aramaic Masoretic text of the book of Daniel now has stronger support than at any other time in the history of the interpretation of the book of Daniel."[33]

4. Angling for Canonical Recognition

Ginsberg argued that a partial translation was made from the Aramaic to the Hebrew with the book beginning and ending with Hebrew segments in order to receive canonical recognition. Against this Anderson comments,

> The least satisfactory answer to the . . . question [sc. Why was it thought necessary to translate the opening (1:1–2:4a) and closing sections into Hebrew?], but one popularly advanced, is that it was in order that the book should be received into the canon, i.e., an otherwise contraband article was smuggled into the canon by an innocent beginning and ending. A more likely reason is that a work which was to circulate among Hebrew people, particularly those under some duress from foreign authorities, should demonstrably be seen to be part of their own religious and national tradition. A reason advanced in reply to the . . . question [sc. why was the change to Hebrew made at 8:1?] is that the kinship of chs. 2 and 7 would require that they appear in the

---

31. Wood, *Daniel*, 15. More positively, Harman simply finds it "fitting that the *lingua franca* of the Persian period is used in the section of the book that has universal application." *Daniel*, 55.

32. Davies, *Daniel*, 36; see also Nelson, *Daniel*, 20.

33. Patterson, "The Key Role of Daniel 7," 248.

same tongue. This argument is less than convincing, for it could apply equally to ch. 8.[34]

Also speaking against this position is Lacocque: "as though the 'inspectors' or customs officials would content themselves with a cursory examination of the merchandise."[35]

5. Multiple Authors

Inevitably, others have proposed various theories about how multiple authors are responsible for composing different parts of the book, and those who argue this way also appeal to differences in genre and theology as buttressing their position.[36] So, for example, Casey reasons:

> . . . the two languages suggest two authors, and a reasonable hypothesis may begin from the unified literary structure of Dan. 2–7. This was written first. Its message is simple . . . and its function in time of persecution is clear and well known, that of fortifying the faithful. Aramaic was the natural language in which to write this material because it was intended to have popular appeal and Aramaic was the *lingua franca* of the time. The choice of Hebrew for the remaining material may be ascribed to deliberate nationalism. It is most natural to ascribe this change of policy to a change of author. In time of war and persecution, change of authorship in such an important and successful religious work may have a simple and unavoidable cause—the death of the first author.[37]

6. Different Thought Worlds

Alternatively, could it be that the change represents an invitation to enter the thought world of the Chaldeans? Daniel draws attention to the fact that "the astrologers answered the king in Aramaic." From 1:3–5 we can deduce the class of astrologers was made up not only of those born in Babylon, but of people who came from many different ethnic backgrounds. They had all been trained by the king who had insisted that each of them learn "*the language . . . of the Babylonians*" (1:4). Thus, irrespective of what their heart language might be, when they came into the presence of the king they were expected to speak to him in the language he had ordered them all to learn.

---

34. *Signs and Wonders*, 13.
35. Davies, *Daniel*, 36.
36. Davies, *Daniel*, 36–37.
37. Casey, *Son of Man*, 9–10.

It may even be the case that these graduates of Nebuchadnezzar's rigorous training program are called "Chaldeans" because they were united by their knowledge of the Chaldean language and literature (1:4). It also follows from the above that the fact all of them speak in Aramaic when they address the king underscores the fact that Nebuchadnezzar has successfully imposed his sovereign will on those he has personally trained.

The preceding context of 2:4b has strongly indicated Nebuchadnezzar's attempts to assert his own sovereign will. The opening three verses of chapter 2 continue this motif, especially when they are contrasted with Daniel's response to his somewhat corresponding dream in Daniel 7, which represents the other side of the chiasm bracketed by these two chapters (see above). When Daniel receives his disturbing dream and visions it is he who makes the approach to one of those standing in the assembly around the throne of the Ancient of Days (v. 16). It would, of course, be absurd for Daniel to summon someone to come to him and to insist that his dream be interpreted for him. It would be ridiculous for Daniel to threaten an angel with death if he failed to do so. The only proper response to understanding a God-given dream is for the recipient to approach God and urgently plead with him for revelation. This is precisely what Nebuchadnezzar does not do. As one who is yet ignorant of God, Nebuchadnezzar truly believes himself to be the supreme source of authority on earth and, accordingly, he seeks to command his own manufactured resources—the esoteric, elitist knowledge of his personally trained Chaldeans—to deal with perceived threat. Nor does he request an explanation of his dream, as Daniel does in Daniel 7. No! He demands it. In short, the preceding context has stressed Nebuchadnezzar's claim to absolute sovereignty. Thus, as soon as we hear the astrologers answering the king in Aramaic, we are encouraged to see again the immensity of Nebuchadnezzar's authority.

It follows from this that from 2:4b—7:28 the focus is upon this issue: the pathetic, futile attempts of pagan rulers to assert absolute sovereignty. Aramaic is presumably used because it belongs to a world which is supposedly under the control of the king, whoever he might be, who reigns in Babylon. Chapters 2:4b—7:28, beginning with the servile Chaldeans, play along with this idea and in chapter 7 a climax is reached in which it is shown conclusively that such claims to absolute authority by a Babylonian ruler are sheer pretentiousness. At the same time Daniel 7, following suit with Daniel 2, introduces a broader perspective of the future which, while it also serves to belittle Babylon as having a very limited tenure, also leads on, in chapters 8–12, to consider the broader issue of what history in general will mean for God's people.

Also in chapters 2–7 there is great stress on God's sovereignty over all nations. Dorsey argues that the use of the international language of Aramaic in these chapters serves to underscore this reality.[38] He sees the shift back to Hebrew as a simultaneous shift back to Israel's future, involving a particular concern with how two present world powers, Persia and Greece, will affect the Hebrew-speaking Jews, following the end of exile, in their restored homeland.[39]

The application by Valeta of Bakhtin's concept of heteroglossia buttresses the view being urged above that "the compositional history of the book . . . results from the actions of a single author or a significant, if not the final redactor of the book."[40] That is, the Aramaic serves a key literary purpose and functions to highlight conflicting ideological viewpoints—the pretensions of blasphemous and idolatrous human rule against divine rule.

ROYAL DREAMS

In many cultures still today dreams are taken seriously.[41] So it was in the ancient world.[42] It was believed that great events were often presaged by dreams. So, in *The Epic of Gilgamesh*, the appearance of Enkidu is foreseen in dreams. The third tablet of the so-called *Babylonian Theodicy* (*Ludlul Bēl Nēmeqi*) contains the turning point of the whole poem: three dreams that "are harbingers of divine pardon and return to grace."[43] In Mesopotamia

38. Dorsey, *Literary Structure*, 260.

39. Similarly Culver sees chapters 2–7 as dealing with "The Nations of the World—Their Character, Relation, Succession, and Destiny" and chapters 8–12 with "The Nation of Israel—Its Relation to Gentile Dominion and Its Future in the Plan of God." Culver, *Daniel and the Latter Days*, 109.

40. *Lions*, 31.

41. Tokunboh Adeyemo observes, "Across Africa, it is . . . believed that serious dreams are a means of communication between this world and the spirit world of the ancestors, divinities and the High God." He also recalls that in the late 19th century, "King Mswati I of Swaziland dreamed of a foreign guest arriving, holding a scroll and a round metal disc. The scroll was interpreted as the Bible and the disc as a coin. On waking, the king advised his subjects to welcome the guest and accept the book, which would bring peace and prosperity to the nation. But they should reject the coin, which would bring misery and greed. Soon after this, white missionaries from South Africa came to Swaziland to plant churches. Today, more than 83 per cent of Swaziland's population claim to be Christians." "Daniel," 1019.

42. See Mendelsohn, "Dream," 868–69; Ecklebarger, "Dreams," 641–43. To say that dreams were taken seriously does not mean that they assumed prominence in the day-to-day affairs of the court. See Lenzi, "Secrecy," 336.

43. Oppenheim, *Ancient Mesopotamia*, 272. Van der Toorn, noting that *Ludlul* and *Ahiqar* both involve "the tale of the slandered and vindicated courtier," claims that the

the interpretation of dreams was one of the major methods of divination (oneiromancy). It is notable that in verse 2 Nebuchadnezzar does not look to a class of dream interpreters for the interpretation of his dream but to "magicians, enchanters, sorcerers and astrologers."[44]

Nightmares experienced by ordinary people were often attributed to the activity of sorcerers and evil spirits. But dreams experienced by kings and priests were considered to be of a different kind, vehicles of divine revelation. Kings sometimes sought to induce dreams by passing the night in a temple, so-called *incubation dreams* (e.g., the dreams of Gudea and Tammuz in Babylonia, and the dream of King Keret in Ugarit). Unintentional incubation dreams occur when a person happened to sleep in a holy place and received a message dream without consciously seeking one, e.g., Jacob at Bethel (Gen 28:11–15) and at Beersheba (Gen 46:1–4), and Samuel at Shiloh (1 Sam 3). Nebuchadnezzar's dreams were neither intentional nor unintentional incubation dreams. These dreams came to him unbidden while he lay on his bed. They were unwelcome dreams that deeply troubled him.

Recorded dreams from antiquity typically focus on three areas: religion, politics, and personal destiny. Ecklebarger summarizes: "Religious dreams called for piety and devotion to the gods. Political dreams supposedly forecast the outcome of battles and the future destiny of nations. Personal dreams guided family decisions and presaged serious crises."[45] The repeated dream ("dreams") experienced by Nebuchadnezzar in Daniel 2 is primarily a political dream, though the personal destiny of Nebuchadnezzar is also implicit in the dream (vv. 36–37).

According to the Mesopotamian philosophy of divination, dreams offered nothing more than an "omen."[46] That is, a dream was only meaningful when it was correctly interpreted by an expert. Dream interpreters used collections of dream omens in this enterprise.[47] Ashurbanipal's library

---

book of Daniel has an artificial (or secondary, if emanating from the Eastern, Babylonian diaspora) Mesopotamian setting which is fictionally created under the influence of *Ludlul* and *Ahiqar*; Van der Toorn, "Scholars," 52.

44. Van der Toorn, "Scholars," 41, observes that some of the more important specialists at Assyrian and Babylonian courts, namely physicians and lamentation priests, go unmentioned. But, presumably, the king would not expect such courtiers to have any ability to interpret dreams. Van der Toorn's research into Assyrian court life fails to find any mention of oneiromancers among the court sages. But again verse 2 answers this: the king did not look to a specialized class to provide the interpretation!

45. Ecklebarger, "Dreams," 642.

46. See Oppenheim, *Ancient Mesopotamia*, 222.

47. Although Porteous rightly captures the Danielic perspective in calling the Mesopotamian manuals of dream interpretation "worthless," Lawson points out that the Babylonians themselves saw the manuals as being the product of divine revelation;

contains fragments of such a "dream book." This contained spells and rituals for warding off the consequences of bad dreams, namely those dreams that predicted disaster and other ills. There were also rituals that were to be used prophylactically, to protect sleeping persons against ominous dreams. If such rituals were in use during Nebuchadnezzar's reign then they had singularly failed. This might help explain why Nebuchadnezzar distrusted his wise men and had no confidence in any interpretation they might give of his dream.

These measures for dealing with dreams were associated with a detailed categorization of activities dreamed by a dreamer, e.g., eating and drinking in one's dreams (including dreams of cannibalism and eating excrement), traveling (including dreams of ascending to heaven and descending into the nether world and dreams of flying), incest, losing one's teeth, quarreling with members of the family, receiving gifts, and carrying objects.[48] The abstracted nature of the dreams described in Daniel 2 and 4 may in and of itself have posed particular problems for traditional Mesopotamian dream interpreters.[49]

NEBUCHADNEZZAR'S TROUBLED MIND

The first occurrence of direct speech in 2:3 involves a reiteration of what we have already been told in the narrative of 2:1–2. Direct speech is regarded as being a better vehicle by which to express the high drama of the events recalled in Daniel 2. In verse 3 the significance of that which has been expressed in verses 1–2 is underscored. We learn that the importance of this incident is not merely that Nebuchadnezzar has had a mysterious dream. The narrator has already told us that Nebuchadnezzar was troubled in his mind by this dream. The relevant phrase can be rendered: "his spirit was agitated."[50] Now in verse 3 Nebuchadnezzar himself draws attention to this. The troubled state of Nebuchadnezzar's mind is therefore of considerable importance in understanding this event. It is not just that Nebuchadnezzar is curious to solve the conundrum posed by his enigmatic dream, as though

---

"The God who Revels Secrets," 63.

48. Oppenheim, *Ancient Mesopotamia*, 222.

49. Possibly, as Longman proposes, God revealed himself to Nebuchadnezzar in dreams rather than say through a multiheaded ox, because this afforded the closest point of contact between Babylonian religion and Daniel's faith; *Daniel*, 77. Widder, "Court Stories," 1126.

50. Goldingay, *Daniel*, 32. Edlin has "his spirit was struck," as of a hammer striking an anvil or a bell, *Daniel*, 71.

he had a mania for solving cryptic crosswords. We are dealing with something much more serious than this. Nebuchadnezzar knows that the dream he has had is of immense importance and, therefore, he feels he *must* know what it means. This is all the more so because in "Nebuchadnezzar's world dreams were respected as communication from the world of the gods."[51]

Dumbrell comments, "Neither the empire over which he presides nor the decisions that he takes provide reality for Nebuchadnezzar. The element of reality is the contact which the dream permits him with the controller of history."[52] Nebuchadnezzar senses that hidden in the dream is ultimate reality—a reality which as yet escapes him, and in so doing frustrates him out of his mind. It is when the dream is interpreted that Nebuchadnezzar will be enabled to see reality as it really is, and not merely as he has hitherto perceived it to be. And as Dumbrell rightly notes, Nebuchadnezzar is placed in touch with reality when he comes to appreciate who it is who truly controls the course of history.

We have already noticed the presence of irony in chapter 1, and this note is continued in Daniel 2. Nebuchadnezzar is blind to the nature of real kingship. At 1:1–2 it was indicated that Nebuchadnezzar was unaware of the real cause of his victory over Jerusalem. His own perception—as expressed by the depositing of temple articles in the temple of Marduk—had been that he himself, in the power of his god, had shown himself to be the absolute sovereign. He was oblivious to the fact that it was actually Yahweh who had enabled him to conquer Jehoiakim and to take the temple articles. It is Yahweh who, unbeknown to Nebuchadnezzar, has been directing the historical process. Daniel 1 describes history so as to suggest that Nebuchadnezzar had supposed that he himself was the one who determined what took place in history.

Nebuchadnezzar's blindness to the hidden reality of Yahweh's control of history makes the dream motif highly suitable. His kingship is palpable—he issues a lot of dire and truly terrifying threats—yet it is really illusory. Real kingship is hidden, obscure, mysterious, and its nature is to be conveyed through the dream world of king Nebuchadnezzar.

Scholars often comment on the extremity of Nebuchadnezzar's violent reaction to the inability of his wise men to meet his demand.[53] Goldingay claims the "portrait is cartooned."[54] Perhaps there is an element of carica-

---

51. Reid, *Kingdoms*, 41.

52. *Faith of Israel*, 260.

53. He threatens to have them "cut into pieces," i.e. "made into limbs." He also threatens to turn their houses "into piles of rubble," i.e., "made a dung heap." Meadowcroft and Irwin, *Book of Daniel*, 42.

54. *Daniel*, 53.

ture in the text but modern examples of despots like Hitler, Idi Amin, and Saddam Hussein show how realistic this portrayal actually is. It is not that many years later that Darius the Great describes the way he dealt with rebels:

> Phraortes was taken and brought unto me. I cut off his nose, his ears, and his tongue, and I put out one eye, and he was kept in fetters at my palace entrance, and all the people beheld him. Then did I crucify him in Ecbatana; and the men who were his foremost followers, those at Ecbatana within the fortress, I flayed and hung out their hides, stuffed with straw (*Behistun Inscription* 32).

There is no reason, apart from the prejudices of the commentator, to dismiss this account as the stuff of fiction.

A great deal of light is thrown upon the virulence of Nebuchadnezzar's rage once we recognize that he knows he must understand *this* dream, in order to come to grips with ultimate reality. Presumably, and this is arguably confirmed by Daniel's later explanation, Nebuchadnezzar senses that this dream foresees future catastrophe, and he fears that it is he himself who will be the victim. It is even conceivable that his remarks in verse 9 betray a suspicion (whether warranted or unwarranted) that the wise men may be implicated in a conspiracy to overthrow him as ruler, though this reading of his words involves a measure of speculation.[55] Possibly also the reference to this event occurring in Nebuchadnezzar's "second year" is not so much to date the events as to indicate that this took place at an early point in his reign when he was still vulnerable and politically insecure.[56] Political anxiety might explain the king's paranoia. If this hypothesis were correct it would all the more explain why Nebuchadnezzar was reluctant to divulge the details of the dream, thus making himself vulnerable to political manipulation. It would also help explain his apparent over-reaction to the wise men's inability to tell him the dream, if he saw in this situation an opportunity to rid himself of a political threat. But whether these surmises be correct or not, Nebuchadnezzar is possessed by a determination to settle for nothing but the real explanation of his dream. It would not do simply to be given a persuasive explanation. So devastating have been the effects of this

55. In verse 9, the phrase "till the times change" may imply "till another takes my place as king," or "until my mood changes;" Goswell, *Daniel*, 15. However, in verse 8, when the king says, "I am certain that you are trying to gain time," the idea may not be that of "buying time," but rather of seeking to "control the moment;" so Breed following Newsom, "A Divided Tongue," 119.

56. So Fewell proposes, *Circle*, 23.

dream upon his mind that Nebuchadnezzar will continue to be troubled until he is certain that he truly understands the dream.

It has been suggested that Nebuchadnezzar requires the telling of the dream from the Chaldeans because he himself has forgotten what he has dreamed.[57] Instead of translating Nebuchadnezzar's words in verse 3 as: "The thing is certain with me"/"This is what I have firmly decided," it is has been argued by some the statement should read, "The thing is gone from me"/"I have forgotten the dream."[58] But this seems unlikely. When the Chaldeans ask the king to tell them the dream first, Nebuchadnezzar's response in verse 5 is most naturally read as meaning: "I could divulge details of the dream but I have decided not to do so."[59] Further since chapter 2 persists with the contrast between Chaldean wisdom and Daniel's wisdom, the preceding context strongly encourages us to see the king as continuing the testing of the wise men. Later Nebuchadnezzar speaks of having "seen" the dream, indicating that it was highly vividly imprinted on his consciousness.[60]

It is in the providence of God that Nebuchadnezzar has responded in this way and demanded first to know the contents of the dream before receiving its interpretation. Here recall how in 2 Samuel 12 Nathan first used a *mashal*, a parable, with David, to make him more amenable to the stinging interpretation that followed.[61] Given Nebuchadnezzar's propensity for uncontrollable rage, we might well imagine the disastrous consequence that may have happened if Daniel had given him the right interpretation straight up. The very fact that Daniel is able to begin by first providing the *mashal* immediately puts the king in a more amenable frame of mind.

---

57. See Goldingay, *Daniel*, 46. Jerome reasoned, "There remained in the king's heart only a shadow, so to speak, or a mere echo or trace of the dream, with the result that if others should retell it to him, he would be able to recall what he had seen, and they would certainly not be deceiving him with lies." Jerome, *Commentary on Daniel*, 25.

58. Walvoord, *Daniel*, 49; Farrar, *Book of Daniel*, 147. Nelson recalls a Babylonian omen text which stated that a person who couldn't remember his dream was subject to his god's wrath. On this somewhat flimsy basis, Nelson speculates that Nebuchadnezzar feared his god's anger because of his inability to remember the dream and especially because the articulation of the dream was considered to have a cleansing, healing effect. *Daniel*, 80–1.

59. At the very least, Walvoord's reasoning is sound: "Even if the king was hazy as to the details of the dream and could not recall it enough to provide a basis of interpretation, he probably would have been able to recognize complete fabrication on the part of the wise men," *Daniel*, 51.

60. See Harman, *Daniel*, 64.

61. Olojede, "More than a Prophet?" 955.

THE INSECURITY OF NEBUCHADNEZZAR'S KINGSHIP

Daniel 2 also exposes the deficiencies in Nebuchadnezzar's own sovereignty and his subordination to the God of heaven—"the Lord of kings" (2:47). The first chapter has repeatedly indicated Nebuchadnezzar's claims to absolute sovereignty. His siege of Jerusalem and his placement of temple articles in the temple of Marduk, his selection of the cream of Jewish youth, his ordering of a rite of passage through which they must pass in order to be made his servants, his changing of their names, his securing of their political allegiance by compelling them to eat from his table (as he supposes they have done), his testing of them—all of these stress Nebuchadnezzar's easy assumption of total power and authority, his belief in himself as the controller of history.

Daniel 2 begins by exposing the chinks in Nebuchadnezzar's armor. He is not at all the great king he thinks himself to be. There were already suggestions in Daniel 1 as to the hollowness of Nebuchadnezzar's claims to absolute sovereignty. While the verbs of 1:1–2 stress Nebuchadnezzar's decisive acts and his perception that Marduk has granted him victory (as expressed by the depositing of the temple articles in the temple of Marduk), they also state a reality which was hidden from Nebuchadnezzar—that it was the Lord who had delivered Jehoiakim into his hand. Further, while Nebuchadnezzar seeks to dictate terms as to the who and how of the servants he will train, it transpires in the providence of God, that action is undertaken by Daniel which countermands the direct orders of Nebuchadnezzar. Yet Daniel and his friends are divinely enabled to pursue their independent policy because Nebuchadnezzar remains completely incognizant of the way in which his sovereign will has been successfully challenged. That is, Nebuchadnezzar is not in complete control over what happens even under his nose, in the royal court.

It may also be the case, as we have indicated above, that Nebuchadnezzar's extreme reaction against his diviners partially stems from a deeply held suspicion that a conspiracy is brewing. If so this further consolidates the growing bank of evidence to the effect that Nebuchadnezzar does not possess the control he fancies himself to have—a conclusion he will continue to be very slow to reach for himself. But the irony of the situation is that it was Nebuchadnezzar himself who set the syllabus for the "manufacture" of a wise person, yet he has no confidence, when it comes to the crunch, in the end product. Deep down Nebuchadnezzar does not believe that he himself is able to produce what he really needs. His deficiency and insecurity as a king is revealed in this. Thus the proposed purge of all wise men speaks volumes. At the point at which he issues the decree of execution the wise men, in his mind, are all completely useless. For the narrator of Daniel 2 this implies that the whole Babylonian educational system is a sheer waste of resources when it comes to producing the kind of wisdom that really matters, that is, knowledge of the One who controls the course of history.

THE INTERCHANGE BETWEEN NEBUCHADNEZZAR AND THE CHALDEANS

The Chaldeans begin with a standard way of addressing the monarch, "O king, live forever!" This may be roughly equivalent to "your majesty."[62] However, it may have an added significance as that which marks the beginning of the elaboration of the Chaldean worldview. The privileges enjoyed by the Chaldeans are dependent on keeping the king happy and, therefore, there is a vested interest in securing the throne. The ensuing narrative will emphasize Nebuchadnezzar's personal commitment to ensuring the perpetuity of Babylonian rule. It is ironic that this sentiment of the king living forever should be expressed so soon after the narrator has indicated Babylonian rule will give way to Persian rule (1:21). The very dream Nebuchadnezzar has had is also at odds with the sentiment expressed by the Chaldeans, for it presages the end of the Babylonian empire.

In verse 4 the Chaldeans express their readiness to "unloose," that is, "explain" the dream. As Goldingay notes, the word they use—*pesher*—"does not denote interpretation generally, but interpretation by magical means or by supernatural revelation, with special reference to what something presages."[63] Thus the Chaldeans lay claim to being privy to supernatural knowledge. Daniel 2 will contrast the so-called supernatural knowledge of the Chaldeans with the incomparably supernatural knowledge of Daniel.[64]

It may be that Daniel 2 is composed with Isaiah 47:12–15 in mind, a portion from a prophetic oracle which presages the fall of Babylon:

> Keep on, then, with your magic spells and with your many sorceries, which you have labored at since childhood. Perhaps you will succeed, perhaps you will cause terror. All the counsel you have received has only worn you out! Let your astrologers

---

62. Péter-Contesse and Ellington, *Handbook*, 33.

63. *Daniel*, 33.

64. Wooden's study of Daniel 1–6 leads him to conclude that there is nothing in these chapters which "should lead us to find a positive assessment of the 'mantics' in the Daniel stories. They function in the stories as little more than pathetic, pagan charlatans who could not interpret a real revelation from God, no matter how simple it was." *Daniel and Manticism*, 346.

come forward, those stargazers who make predictions month by month, let them save you from what is coming upon you. Surely they are like stubble; the fire will burn them up. They cannot even save themselves from the power of the flame. Here are no coals to warm anyone; here is no fire to sit by. That is all they can do for you—these you have labored with and trafficked since childhood. Each of them goes on in his error; there is not one that can save you.

This passage is all the more interesting because it suggests that the spells, counsel, and predictions of Babylonian astrologers, sorcerers, and sages were regarded as capable of altering the course of history. Against such a worldview this oracle lampoons the Chaldeans as not even able to save themselves. In Daniel 2, therefore, the interpretation Nebuchadnezzar seeks from the Chaldeans is not merely an academic solution to some mental conundrum. Nebuchadnezzar is not disturbed by his inability to solve some intriguing puzzle, but by his sense that control of history eludes his grasp; that irresistible historical forces are threatening to unseat him and his kingdom. Had the Chaldeans been able to interpret the dream then such an interpretation—an interpretation inevitably favorable to the king (for who would dare to present an adverse interpretation?)—would have been viewed, given the Babylonian magical mindset, as a powerful word able to reverse any threat perceived by Nebuchadnezzar in his dream. Except that Nebuchadnezzar himself evidently entertains serious doubts as to the genuineness of the power of the words of his sages.

It follows from this that Daniel's subsequent interpretation does not provide merely a satisfying intellectual explanation of Nebuchadnezzar's dream, but like the prophetic word it is, actually has power to effect the very things of which Daniel speaks. Though Daniel is highly respectful in his demeanor before the king, and validly emphasizes the God-given glory of Nebuchadnezzar, nevertheless the content of his interpretation is essentially bad news for Nebuchadnezzar and the Babylonian kingdom. We must not underestimate the immense courage Daniel possessed in relaying such a disturbing message. Nebuchadnezzar had already expressed his impetuosity and caprice. Would not Nebuchadnezzar be enraged by Daniel's effrontery in daring to tell him that his days and the days of the Babylonian kingdom were numbered? Nebuchadnezzar's previous demand to be told the dream itself now works in Daniel's favor. The fact that Daniel can repeat things, which were only known to Nebuchadnezzar himself, proves beyond doubt, in Nebuchadnezzar's mind, that the interpretation, no matter how unsavory, is the correct one. There can be no question, then, of venting wrath upon Daniel, but only of acknowledging his remarkable and unique possession of divine spirit.

It is in verse 18 that we first meet with the important word *raz*, "mystery" or "secret." In this chapter it is always connected to the verb *galab*, "reveal," thus contrasting Chaldean "interpretations" from the revelation of "mysteries" which only the God of heaven can give.[65] Mesopotamian scholars were closely associated with secrecy so that a royal inscription from Nabonidus's reign calls them those "who guard the secret of the great gods."[66] The citation reads:

> I gathered the elders of the city, the citizens of Babylon, the architects, (and) the learned, who dwell in the temple academy, who guard the secret of the great gods, who maintain the rite of kingship . . . the assembly of the scholars . . .[67]

Consequently, God's enabling of Daniel to know divine secrets forges a highly powerful point of contrast with the Chaldeans, given that guarding divine secrets was apparently integral to their role. This was all the more so since, as Lenzi points out, "the entire textual corpora of exorcism (*āšipūtu*), medicine (*asûtu*), divination (*bārûtu*), ritual lamentation (*kalûtu*), and astrology (*tuppšarrūtu*)—were secret documents." Indeed, scribal scholars explicitly used such words as "secret" or "secret of the gods" in describing this textual corpora, even seeking to restrict access to it.[68] Of course, the previous chapter has already sharply contrasted Daniel and his three friends with the Chaldeans with respect to their mastery of this textual corpora (1:17, 20), so that indeed they have an access to divine secrets with which their peers cannot compete. Such a contrast implies the humiliation of the Chaldeans since they considered themselves to be *the* experts in secret matters.[69] Truly, God makes the wisdom of this world foolish.[70] Further,

65. Meadowcroft and Irwin, *Book of Daniel*, 47.

66. Lenzi, "Secrecy," 337.

67. Lenzi, "Secrecy," 337.

68. Lenzi, "Secrecy," 337. Lenzi provides illustrations from the medical and lamentation corpora: (1) "Ea fully endowed me with his wisdom from the Apsu. He gave me the tablet stylus from his hands. The physicians' corpus, the secret of the gods, he made my responsibility;" (2) "I wrote on tablets, collated, (and) checked the wisdom from Ea, the lamentation corpus, the secret of the sage, which is suitable for appeasing the heart of the great gods, according to the original tablet of the land of Ashur and the land of Akkade" (337–38). Ea, the god of wisdom, was strongly associated with secrecy, even called "lord of the secret," with his sanctuary in Marduk's temple in Babylon (Esagil) called "House of the Secrets of Heaven and Earth." An example of a "secrecy label" seeking to restrict access is the following text: "Secret of the great gods. The expert ["one who knows"] may show an(other) expert. A non-expert may not see [i.e., read] it. A restriction of the great gods." Lenzi, "Secrecy," 339.

69. Lenzi, "Secrecy," 339.

70. "It proves to me, in brief utterance, that all the religions, arts, sciences,

in revealing the secret to Daniel God causes Daniel to attain social power among his peers.[71]

AN ANALYSIS OF 2:13–19A

Note that verse 13 serves as a transition verse bridging the two initial scenes.

Narrative:	
Men sent to execute wise men	Arioch sent to execute wise men
Daniel targeted for execution	Daniel wisely deals with potential executioner
"to put the wise men to death;" "men were sent" (v. 13)	"to put the wise men to death;" "Arioch . . . had gone out" (v. 14)
Direct Speech:	
"He asked the king's officer, 'Why did the king issue such a harsh decree?'" (v. 15)	
Narrative:	
"Arioch . . . explained the matter" (v. 15b)	"Daniel . . . explained the matter" (v. 17)
Daniel asks for more time to interpret the dream (v. 16)	
"this mystery" (v. 18)	"the mystery" (v. 19a)

The NIV describes Arioch ("lion") as being "commander of the king's guard." Goldingay points out the word rendered "*guard*" is etymologically "slaughterman," but elsewhere it simply means "guard/police."[72]

The fact that the lives of Daniel and his friends are in grave danger because of someone else's failure to perform a difficult task constitutes a major departure from "fairy tales" and "court tales." Still, there are other ancient courtier narratives which involve a previously unknown or forgotten hero entering a crisis situation to save the day.[73]

---

philosophies, attainments, and powers of man, apart from God's inspired prophets, and an all-glorious Christ, are but emptiness and vanity as regards any true and adequate knowledge of the purposes and will of Jehovah or of the destinies of man." Joseph Seiss, cited by Gangel, *Daniel*, 42.

71. Lenzi, "Secrecy," 342.

72. *Daniel*, 33.

73. Holm, (*Courtiers*, 427) notes that in *Ahiqar*, the Assyrian king is trying to answer an Egyptian king's riddles, with Ahiqar, though presumed dead, dramatically reappearing alive and enabling the king to succeed. Another story (*Merire and Sisobek*) involves a previously hidden magician, Merire, suddenly being produced by his peers to deal with king Sisobek's mortal illness.

Our analysis above indicates that Daniel's question in verse 15 is of considerable importance: "Why did the king issue such a harsh decree?" Goldingay comments that the word rendered *harsh* "seems to mean "bare-faced/hardfaced," thus "peremptory, uncompromising, arrogant."[74] The wording of Daniel's question draws attention to a number of important things:

1. The distinction between Daniel and the Chaldeans

Daniel asks this question because he is ignorant of the events which have led to this crisis. Daniel had not been included among the wise men initially summoned by Nebuchadnezzar and, therefore, he is ignorant of the facts concerning this situation.

In verse 2 we learn that "the king summoned the magicians, enchanters, sorcerers, and astrologers." The fact that Daniel and his friends are not summoned indicates clearly that they were not considered to fall into any of these categories—indeed, they were still in training (1:5). Yet when the king issues the decree of execution it applies to "the wise men of Babylon" (verse 12). It is Nebuchadnezzar's conception at this time that only one who could be called a magician, enchanter, sorcerer, or astrologer could produce the kind of wisdom for which he was seeking. But the decree of execution applies to Daniel and his friends indicating that there were in fact "wise men" in Babylon whom Nebuchadnezzar had ignored in his search for an answer. It had not occurred to Nebuchadnezzar that there were those he had earlier identified as being especially wise whom he had not asked to interpret his dream. Daniel and his friends are unique. Their brand of wisdom is without precedent. When the king seeks wisdom he does so in the traditional manner. Because Daniel and his friends are representatives of a non-traditional wisdom, and fall outside of traditional wisdom categories, they are never given the chance to prove their superiority.

Daniel is further distinguished from the Chaldeans by being granted additional time, whereas the Chaldeans were denied this.[75] But the difference is that Daniel has already indicated his intent to provide the king with what he has asked for, whereas the Chaldeans have already ruled out such a possibility. In addition, the fact that Daniel is granted extra time precisely accords with the underlying reality to be revealed, namely, that God controls "times and seasons" (v. 21).[76]

---

74. *Daniel*, 33.

75. See Hebbard, *Reading Daniel*, 84.

76. See Goswell, *Daniel*, 17.

2. Nebuchadnezzar has lost control

Within the wider context Daniel's question carries another implication: the king has lost control. Why indeed did Nebuchadnezzar issue such a decree when, in fact, there was somebody able to meet his demand. Nebuchadnezzar begins with a troubled mind and is unable to control his own psychological state, now being propelled into hasty and premature action by his own rage.

AN ANALYSIS OF 2:19B–23: THE PRAYER OF DANIEL

> *Response to Revelation*
> Daniel praised "the God of heaven" (vv. 19b–20a)
> *Significance of Revelation: With Respect to God*
> God possesses wisdom and power: "wisdom and power are his" (v. 20b)
> *Content of Revelation*
> "He changes times and seasons; he sets up kings and deposes them" (v. 21a)
> *Significance of Revelation: With Respect to People*
> It imparts wisdom and knowledge; it is the revelation of that which is completely hidden: "he gives wisdom to the wise" (vv. 21b–22)
> *Response to Revelation*
> Daniel praises God as "God of my fathers" (v. 23a)
> *Significance of Revelation: With Respect to Daniel and Friends*
> Recipients of *wisdom* and power; answered prayer; knowledge of the dream itself: "You have given me wisdom and power" (v. 23b–c).

The above analysis shows that the theme of wisdom is central to Daniel's prayer. We learn the following things about wisdom:

1. God is the source of wisdom

Daniel 2 plainly deviates from the typical folk tale plot in which the wise succeed by their own ingenuity. Ultimately it is revelation from God that makes one truly wise.[77]

The solution to the mystery comes to Daniel at night, just as the mystery dream-text came to Nebuchadnezzar at night in the dark, "thus

---

77. Wooden, *Daniel and Manticism*, 204–205. God possesses "wisdom and power" and gives this to Daniel (v. 23) and it is arguable that "power" extends the idea of "wisdom," connoting "mental prowess." So Wooden, *Daniel and Manticism*, 208–209, 212.

attesting to the ability of God's light of illuminating revelation to pierce the darkness of ignorance."[78]

Daniel addresses his God as "the God of heaven." Anderson notes that this name does not appear in pre-exilic literature, save for Genesis 24:7, but becomes increasingly common in texts both biblical and extra-biblical from the postexilic period, e.g., Nehemiah 1:4; 2:5, 20; Ezra 1:2; 5:11, 12: Jonah 1:9; Judith 5:8; "Lord of heaven," Tobit 10:12; 1 Enoch 13:4. He also speculates that the "later abandonment of this epithet was due most likely to its closeness to the Hellenistic 'Zeus Ouranios.'"[79] The association of deity with the sky or with heaven comes as no surprise and in the ancient Near East many examples are found of this. Goldingay takes Daniel's use of this designation as implying his concurrence with the opinion expressed by the Chaldeans in verse 11: "Here he takes up the sages' confession that the gods' dwelling is not among mere humanity . . . yet denies that this makes God inaccessible; God is in heaven, but he reveals things on earth . . . ."[80] But this misses the essential point of contrast introduced in Daniel 2 and developed in the book, namely that despite his awesome transcendence God does in fact live with man. The revealing of the mystery of the dream begins the process of overturning the opinion of the Chaldeans. The next chapter will strengthen emphasis on God's immanence by stressing the presence of the angelic figure with Daniel's three friends in the fiery furnace. Nebuchadnezzar and Belshazzar will in fact acknowledge Daniel to be unique as one in whom the spirit of the holy gods reside.

Though the association of God with heaven does suggest God's transcendence it also accords with another major stress in Daniel, namely upon the absolute sovereignty of God. For "heaven" is the place of ultimate rule. In Daniel what happens on earth occurs because of what has happened in heaven. For example, in Daniel 7 heaven is conspicuously associated with "*thrones*," and especially with the throne of "the Ancient of Days." The coming of the "son of man" into the presence of the Ancient of Days upon "the clouds of heaven" to receive supreme authority describes the delegation of divine rule, and this portrait is matched by 7:26–27 which spells out how, following the "sitting of the court," the outworking of this supreme authority will result in the handing over of all kingdoms "under the whole heaven" to "the saints, the people of the Most High." Thus when Daniel reverently addresses God as "the God of heaven" it is in acknowledgment of his awesome, matchless sovereignty.

78. Hebbard, *Reading Daniel*, 87.

79. *Signs and Wonders*, 15.

80. *Daniel*, 47.

Further Daniel's recognition of his God as "the God of heaven" probably involves a contrast with "the religious superstitions of the Babylonians who worshiped the starry heaven." God controlled those heavens too.[81] As Fyall comments, "Not by horoscopes, séances and divination would enlightenment come, but from the *God of heaven* . . . the God who rules the heavenly bodies, the study of and attempt to manipulate which lay at the heart of Babylonian religion."[82]

There may be even more implicit in Daniel's use of this name. For, as Daniel is painfully aware, the sanctuary is desolate (9:18). Consequently while Daniel prays facing Jerusalem he is not able to address God as the one who dwells in the earthly temple. Thus the name "God of heaven" is a highly appropriate name for Daniel to use in prayer given all that has happened to the land and the temple, especially since his mode of praying indicates his acute awareness of Solomon's prayer in 1 Kings 8 in which Solomon prays, "But will God really dwell on earth? The heavens, even the highest heaven, cannot contain you. How much less this temple I have built!" The destruction of the temple does not shake Daniel's confidence in the greatness and sovereignty of his God for his God is "the God of heaven."

In addition to the above, Daniel evidently understands heaven to be not only the sphere of ultimate sovereignty but also of ultimate wisdom. The God who rules in and from heaven is not only supremely majestic and mighty, but is also superlatively wise. Thus in Daniel 7 Daniel's vision of this God is of one he calls "the Ancient of Days," that is, the God who takes his seat on the throne of ultimate and absolute rule is like an exceedingly old man. Clearly the point of this image is not to suggest any frailty in God. The context plainly shows the reverse is intended. No! What this portrayal achieves is to underscore that God is uniquely qualified to exercise absolute and ultimate rule because he is the "oldest," and therefore the wisest person in the entire universe (see 7:9).

As if this is not enough, it will be recalled that the Babel builders sought to build a tower with its top reaching "the heavens" (Gen 11:4), with Yahweh "coming down," implicitly from heaven, "to see the city and the tower," since it was so utterly inconsequential from a divine perspective. Given the extensive Babel allusions in Daniel it is conceivable that "God of heaven" evokes similar connotations, especially as the dream interpretation does indeed involve a tower-of-Babel-like statue, so seemingly impressive but so easily destroyed.[83]

81. Walvoord, *Daniel,* 55.

82. *Daniel,* 34.

83. See Kim, *Biblical Interpretation,* 77.

2. Wisdom is inseparable from power

In the book of Daniel God's sovereignty is not displayed by superior show of might on the battlefield, but through wisdom. The wisdom of Daniel has already worked to stay the execution order issued by the king. The fact that the king issues a decree of execution and then later reverses his decision is itself an indication that the sovereignty of Nebuchadnezzar, despite his personal pretensions, is not absolute, but subject to forces of wisdom and power which transcend him. God's sovereignty in the book of Daniel is made manifest especially in the sphere of wisdom.

Gnuse observes:

> Israel differs somewhat from other cultures in the understand-
> ing of dreams. Dreams are not seen to come from the realm of
> the dead, magical practices for incubation are lacking, and the
> art of interpretation is connected only with Joseph and Daniel
> where special effort goes into attributing the power of interpre-
> tation to God, so that Joseph and Daniel appear as prophets not
> oneirocritics. Dreams are clear messages freely given by God.[84]

Smith-Christopher recognizes that in the context of the Daniel stories,

> . . . dreams represent a politically significant power that is greater
> than the worldly power of the conquerors. To assert the power
> of God over Nebuchadnezzar is an inherently political act and
> it is furthermore to identify the Jews with the power that even
> Nebuchadnezzar cannot resist.[85]

Accordingly, Smith-Christopher sees the interpretation of dreams as "an act of spiritual warfare." However, this is not to be viewed as a political stance initiated by Daniel. It is God who is in conflict with human rule. But the phrase "wisdom and power" forms an inclusio (vv. 20, 23) that does suggest, as Smith-Christopher puts it, "that God, the greatest power, 'deputizes' Daniel and his companions."[86] Indeed, the conviction Daniel expresses in his prayer that God "sets up kings and deposes them" is realized in the life of Nebuchadnezzar, temporarily (Dan 4), and in the life of Belshazzar, permanently (Dan 5). Ironically, as we will discover, the interpretation of the dream carries the probable implication that Daniel and his three friends, the wise ones, are the very ones through whom God undermines the Babylonian empire.

---

84. Smith-Christopher, "Prayers," 281.

85. "Prayers," 282.

86. "Prayers," 286.

3. God only gives his wisdom to those who fear him

This is what is meant by the statement that God gives his wisdom to the wise. Daniel is *"discerning"* not so much because he has a knack of perceiving the significance of what God reveals but because in his wisdom he perceives that God is the source of wisdom. Further, Daniel reveals by his response to this revelation that he does indeed fear God more than he fears Nebuchadnezzar. For, as Thompson points out, when the meaning of the dream is made known there is a sense in which the situation is worse for Daniel than before, now that he realizes he must tell the king that his rule will not last forever.[87]

4. God is able to reveal what is otherwise totally inaccessible to the human mind

Note here the parallelism between verse 22 and verse 23c. As far as the Chaldeans were concerned Nebuchadnezzar's dream was a "deep and hidden thing," something which "lay in darkness" and was only penetrable to "the gods." The word "mystery" (*raz*) is only used nine times in the Old Testament, with all occurrences being in Daniel (2:18, 19, 27, 28, 29, 30, 47 [2x]; 4:6). It may also be rendered "secret," for its usage indicates the meaning is that of a secret which only God can divulge. Lenzi observes that the term is often accompanied by the verb "to reveal" (2:19, 28, 29, 30, 47 [2x]).[88] Lenzi suggests that the use of *raz* suggests that Daniel enjoys prophetic privilege; though, given the apocalyptic character of the book of Daniel, it has a particularly eschatological significance.[89] Goldingay notes that this term becomes almost a technical term for this idea at Qumran.[90]

We should also observe that, when analyzed, Nebuchadnezzar's dream involves a series of metaphors.[91] At least some of these, for example, the

87. "Wisdom in Babylon."

88. "Secrecy," 332.

89. "Secrecy," 332. To the extent that Daniel adopts a stance with respect to the king comparable to that of a prophet Olojede, "More than a Prophet?" 953, finds this difference: "Nebuchadnezzar had the *mashal* but Daniel provided the *peshar*." But on further reflection this difference fades away, precisely because Daniel himself has to provide the *mashal* before giving his interpretation.

90. *Daniel,* 47. Pace understands that this technical use of *raz* involves "crucially important information concerning God's plan for human history or for the end of days, determined from the foundations of creation and given by God (often by means of an angel) to an elected individual." *Daniel,* 58.

91. Meadowcroft observes that "a central component of the dream is often a metaphor, and a key to the interpretation of such dreams is an appreciation of the metaphors therein and the impact of those metaphors on their interpreters." Cited by Olojede, "More than a Prophet?" 951.

"stone" and "the mountain," together with in-built allusions to the Tower of Babel episode, necessarily presupposed that only a Jew privy to the significance of such metaphors and allusions would be able to make sense of the dream. Even if the Chaldeans had known the details of the dream they would have been incapable of understanding its true import.

The equation of wisdom with "light" (v. 22) is taken by Smith-Christopher as accentuating the expression of God's power over earthly powers.[92] However, there is no hiatus in verse 22 that corresponds to that of the Qumran War Scroll's "children of light" and "children of darkness." In verse 22 "darkness" is not descriptive of human rule but of that which is "deep and hidden." However, the wisdom–light association does connect well with the image of the wise shining like the brightness of the heavens (12:3).[93]

Before moving on, there are two further points to note about this prayer. First, that it provides a model of hope for all God's people in that God hears the cry of his people even when not accompanied by a sacrifice.[94] Secondly, it is a notable feature of Daniel 2 that the chapter centers very much on Daniel's role in proceedings, and yet in this section attention is drawn to the friendship between Daniel and his three friends.[95] This indicates that whenever the book focuses on Daniel it is understood that he functions not as an individual but as the representative of his people.

THE MEANING OF THE DREAM ANTICIPATED

There is one statement in Daniel's prayer which stands out as not directly bearing on the theme of wisdom: "He changes times and seasons; he sets up kings and deposes them" (v. 21a).[96] The mystery of the dream has already been revealed to Daniel (v. 19). The other words of praise uttered by Daniel all have to do with the act of revelation itself. The statement of verse 21a stands out because it is not concerned with the act of revelation but with the content of that revelation. In particular, this truth sweeps aside the fatalism of Babylonian astral religion. Day passes into night, winter to spring, etc., because God controls the natural phenomena, not because of a

---

92. "Prayers and Dreams," 286–88.

93. Smith-Christopher, "Prayers and Dreams," 288.

94. Pace, *Daniel*, 61.

95. Note the use of the pronouns "we" and "us" in verses 23 and 36. Daniel's prophet-like distinctiveness is nevertheless brought out. He is uniquely the one who "could understand visions and dreams of all kinds" (1:17).

96. There may be an intended contrast in 7:24–25 (Walvoord, *Daniel,* 57).

deterministically ordered universe.[97] Further, this statement may anticipate 7:25, the threat posed by Antiochus IV Epiphanes, who, it is predicted, will "try to change the set times and laws."[98] The attached "he sets up kings and deposes them" also forms a suitable counter to 7:24, which predicts that Antiochus "will subdue three kings." Consequently, verse 21 parallels 7:26 which predicts that Antiochus's "power will be taken away."[99]

The statement of verse 21 crystallizes the fundamental conclusion reached by Daniel as to the significance of Nebuchadnezzar's dream. Throughout the whole experience God has shown that he is in control of history. It is he who set the present events in motion by causing Nebuchadnezzar to have such a disturbing situation; it is he who has orchestrated events so as to demonstrate the gulf which stands between the humanistic wisdom of the Chaldeans and the divinely revealed wisdom of Daniel; it is he alone who has revealed what no mortal could possibly reveal, the inner workings of Nebuchadnezzar's private thoughts; it is he who in the telling of the dream and the interpreting of its significance declares himself to be the absolute sovereign who determines who will reign and when their reigns will end. God is the Lord of history. This is the central meaning of the entire dream event and dream interpretation.

AN ANALYSIS OF 2:24–28A

	Present Passage	Corresponding Precedent
Daniel Blocks Royal Purpose	Daniel asks Arioch, the appointed executioner, not to execute the wise man and to take him to the king (v. 24)	Daniel wisely speaks with Arioch, the appointed executioner of the wise men (v. 14)
Daniel in King's Presence	Daniel introduced to the king as a Jewish exile who can interpret his dream (v. 25)	Daniel asks the king for time to interpret his dream (v. 16)
King Tests Daniel's Ability	Daniel asked if he can replicate the king's dream and interpret it (v. 26)	Chaldeans ordered to replicate the king's dream as proof of their ability to interpret it (v. 9c)

97. Sims, "Daniel," 329. The Babylonian view of history, locked into an inevitable cycle of "times and seasons," implied the gods did not control history. Péter-Contesse and Ellington, *Handbook*, 46.

98. Segal, "From Joseph to Daniel," 147.

99. Segal, "From Joseph to Daniel," 148.

Admission of Impossibility for Humans	Daniel declares that it is impossible for anyone, no matter what their abilities, to replicate the dream (v. 27)	Chaldeans declare that it is impossible for anyone, no matter what their abilities, to replicate the dream (v. 10a)
Gods and the Revelation of Mysteries	Daniel is able to explain the mystery, not because he possesses innately superior wisdom, but because the God of heaven has revealed it to the king through him (vv. 28–30)	The Chaldeans are not able to explain the mystery because the gods do not live among people and do not reveal such a mystery through them (v. 11)

THE SIGNIFICANCE OF DANIEL'S ROLE AS THE INTERPRETER OF HISTORY

In verse 24 we read how Daniel goes to Arioch and asks to be taken to the king so that he might interpret his dream for him. Segal follows various others as seeing this as a contradiction of verse 16, which has already informed us that Daniel went to the king and secured permission to have more time to seek an interpretation of the dream.[100] However, it is not necessary to see a contradiction here. First, Lucas,[101] following Whybray, notes the implausibility of the assumption that an ancient author should be "credited with a consistency in the avoidance of repetitions and contradictions which is unparalleled in ancient literature (and even in modern fiction)." Secondly, it ignores the possibility that the writer employs such a contrast for aesthetic and literary purposes.[102] Thirdly, verse 16 is extremely terse and the language of going "to the king" allows for an ancient Near Eastern reader to assume Daniel had to follow all the normal court protocol to make his request, it being quite possible he never actually saw the king himself but received his permission through a senior court official. Indeed, Collins takes yet another view that also accounts for any apparent discrepancy, namely that in verse 16 Daniel approached the king directly, whereas in verse 24 he followed correct protocol.[103]

100. "From Joseph to Daniel," 126.

101. *Daniel*, 71.

102. Segal, failing to appreciate the literary artistry of the chapter, is intent on finding evidence to support his thesis that the narrative of Daniel 2 is a composite of various spliced together sources.

103. Collins, *Daniel*, 160.

Segal makes a further attempt to find a contradiction in the way Daniel was permitted more time to find an interpretation, while the other wise men's attempt to buy time was rejected.[104] Here Segal is simply not reading the text as it stands. For the wise men do not in fact ask for more time to interpret the dream but simply state their inability to do what the king asks of them without knowing the dream itself.

The NIV informs us that Arioch took Daniel to the king "at once" (v. 25a). Goldingay proposes "with excitement." The NEB prefers "in trepidation," but this is perhaps unlikely given the confidence which seems implicit in Arioch's declaration to the king (v. 25b). At any rate, as Goldingay notes, the word "suggests strong feelings, not just speed of motion," hence Goldingay's own translation "with urgency."[105]

It has been suggested that Daniel represents Israel since, in prior biblical revelation, "only Israel, only the community of faith, has the answer as to the direction history will take."[106] When Arioch presents Daniel to Nebuchadnezzar as the one who can tell him what his dream means he does so in a way that attaches no importance to Daniel's individuality and personal talent. He is introduced simply as "a man among the exiles from Judah." He comes to the king to interpret his dream as a representative of the Jewish exiles. This ability to take what God has revealed and to interpret its implications for the times in which we live is one which has continuing pertinence for God's people today.

The wisdom of Daniel is manifested in the way he defends the sages as being right when they said none but God can reveal mystery (cf. 2:10–11), though at the same time, fulfilling a polemical objective in the narrative, he rejects any notion that they have any ability to know such a divine secret (v. 27).[107] Their fate is in Daniel's hands, or more specifically depends on what Daniel says. The very words which deliver the Babylonian wisdom representatives from death are, ironically, the very words which indicate the impotency of their wisdom! Fewell[108] misses the point of the chapter

104. "From Joseph to Daniel," 128.

105. *Daniel*, 34.

106. Dumbrell, *Faith of Israel*, 260.

107. Lenzi, "Secrecy," 346–47.

108.. "But what Daniel's speech *does* is to point out to Nebuchadnezzar that he has merely relied on the wrong sages. If he had, from the beginning, depended upon someone like Daniel, his problem would have been solved long ago without the distasteful threats," *Circle*, 31. She believes that Daniel also minimizes the judgmental nature of the dream and provides a "one-sided view of the dream's content," *Circle*, 33. "Daniel minimizes Nebuchadnezzar's culpability," *Circle*, 35 and presents a version of the dream which is but "the version of diplomacy," *Circle*, 35. "Daniel's private political hopes are more complex than those he is willing to express in public," *Circle*, 36. Cynically, Fewell

and blunts its force by suggesting that Daniel's comments carry with them a hidden agenda of self-interested political machination, leading him to insinuate that the king should depend on himself rather than the other sages.

As observed by Nelson, the structure of verses 27–30 also stresses Daniel's humility and the way he gives glory to God[109]:

2:27–28	2:29–30
as you lay on your bed	as you were lying there
what will happen in days to come	things to come . . . what is going to happen
he has shown King Nebuchadnezzar	showed you
there is a God in heaven who reveals mysteries	this mystery has been revealed to me
no wise man, enchanter, magician	not because I have greater wisdom
or diviner can explain to the king the mystery he has asked about	than other living men
your dream and the visions	that you may understand
that passed through your mind	what went through your mind

Verses 27–30 serve to distinguish the narrative of Daniel 2 from typical court tales in which the hero of the story is exalted.[110] By contrast, in chapter 2 Daniel stresses his subordination as a wise man to his God, "the revealer of secrets."[111] This makes Daniel 2 unique, though, ironically, in stressing that God is "the revealer of secrets," as Nebuchadnezzar himself acknowledges (v. 47), Daniel nevertheless assumes great significance as the human agent through whom such secrets are revealed (see 4:6—hence the authoritative nature of the entire book.[112]

---

asks, "Is it *because* Daniel's god is god of gods that Daniel is able to reveal the mystery? Or is his god now god of gods *because* Daniel is able to reveal the mystery?" *Circle*, 37.

109. *Daniel*, 86.

110. For example, contrast this account with that in Setne II, where an ancient magician (Hor-son-of-Paneshy) who had saved Egypt centuries earlier, appears in the guise of a young boy, Si-Osire, and, coming before Ramses II, reads a bound scroll without opening it. The tale ends with the revelation of his true identity. Holm, *Courtiers*, 427.

111. Daniel's humility is impressive. Goswell, *Daniel*, 18, comments, "In prayer we are quite willing to give all the glory to God and we tell him we are nothing and can do nothing without him, but in the public arena we find it very hard not to steal just a little bit of the credit for ourselves. We want people to think well of God, but we also want them to think how clever and faithful we are! Let us repent of this inconsistency."

112. Lenzi, "Secrecy," 344–46.

THE INSEPARABILITY OF
HISTORICITY AND THEOLOGY

Collins effectively emasculates the very theology of this chapter when he states categorically, "No claim can be made that this story is historical."[113] On this basis the teaching of Daniel 2—that God's supreme sovereignty is proved by the fact that he alone can reveal specific information which is otherwise totally and absolutely inaccessible to man—is treated as being a mere literary fabrication which has no substance or relationship to the real world in which we live. The staggering irony of Collins' position is that he himself claims (apparently) certain knowledge of a situation of which he had no personal experience. It is impossible that he should know the true facts of what or what did not happen. Yet this does not prevent him from declaring, for example, that Nebuchadnezzar's threat to execute the wise men was not rooted in history, but was just a literary "device to heighten the drama of the story." When scholars speak like this are we to conclude "the spirit of the holy gods" must be in them, enabling them to pontificate with such confidence?

AN ANALYSIS OF 2:31-45

Nebuchadnezzar's Dream is Miraculously Revealed and Interpreted (2:31–45)

> Introduction to the Dream Proper (2:28–30)
> The Dream and its Interpretation (2:31–45)
> Conclusion (2:45b)

Nebuchadnezzar's Response (2:46–49)

> Introduction to the Dream Proper (2:28–30)

> " . . . but there is a God in heaven who reveals mysteries. He has shown King Nebuchadnezzar what will happen in days to come . . ."

---

113. *Apocalyptic Vision*, 34–35. The same applies to the handling of this passage by Kruschwitz and Redditt. These authors hold the view that the "book of Daniel is much more a study in reading Israel's past than in predicting the world's future"; "Nebuchadnezzar," 416. Assuming a second century composition of the book, they maintain that the "prophecy" of Daniel 2, as per all other like material in the book, is written after the events to which they refer. They also contend that all verses which look to the future—2:44–45; 7:27; 8:25b; 9:26b–2—"say nothing about the time after 163 BCE;" "Nebuchadnezzar," 400.

The words "in days to come" are etymologically "at the end of the era," or word-for-word "at the end of the days." Comparing "end" ('acharîth) with its use in 8:19, 23; 10:14; 11:4; 12:8, Goldingay maintains it "denotes not a single moment . . . but the last part or the aftermath of something," and that more precisely "the days" represent "a possibly long, but not interminable period that will or must elapse before certain predictions, promises or warnings are fulfilled."[114] He concludes, "The phrase thus refers to 'the time of fulfilment.' This may come at the End of the Age, though the phrase itself is not of eschatological meaning; it only acquires this association through being used in such contexts." Thus "the days" denotes the whole period of history from Nebuchadnezzar onward, while "end of the days" refers more specifically to the events that bring that whole period to a close.

Building on the above, it is arguable that in Daniel "end" is in fact often (if not always) used in an eschatological fashion.[115] The interpretation of the dream associates the setting up of the final, everlasting kingdom, which apparently replaces and succeeds all human kingdoms (2:44). Also arguable is that "the stern-faced king . . . master of intrigue" of 8:23 is not merely to be associated with Antiochus IV Epiphanes but with final anti-God human rule. Certainly 12:8 would seem to require an eschatological interpretation since the "end" marks the time of general resurrection when Daniel "will rise to receive his allotted inheritance" (12:13).

THE TELLING OF THE DREAM	THE INTERPRETATION OF THE DREAM
	2:36 This was the dream, and now we will interpret it to the king.
2:31 You looked, O king, and there before you stood a large statue—an enormous, dazzling statue, awesome in appearance.	
2:32a The head of the statue was made of pure gold,	2:37 You, O king, are the king of kings. The God of heaven has given you dominion and power and might and glory; 38in your hands he has placed mankind and the beasts of the field and the birds of the air. Wherever they live, he has made you ruler over them all. You are that head of gold.
2:32b its chest and arms of silver,	2:39a After you, another kingdom will arise, inferior to yours.

---

114. *Daniel*, 48–49.

115. See Walvoord, *Daniel,* 59–61.

2:32c its belly and thighs of bronze,[116]	2:39b Next, a third kingdom, one of bronze, will rule over the whole earth.
2:33 its legs of iron, its feet partly of iron and partly of baked clay.[117]	2:40 Finally, there will be a fourth kingdom, strong as iron—for iron breaks and smashes everything—and as iron breaks things to pieces, so it will crush and break all the others. 41 Just as you saw that the feet and toes were partly of baked clay and partly of iron, so this will be a divided kingdom; yet it will have some of the strength of iron in it, even as you saw iron mixed with clay. 42 As the toes were partly iron and partly clay, so this kingdom will be partly strong and partly brittle. 43 And just as you saw the iron mixed with baked clay, so the people will be a mixture and will not remain united, any more than iron mixes with clay.
2:34 While you were watching, a rock was cut out, but not by human hands.	2:44a In the time of those kings, the God of heaven will set up a kingdom that will never be destroyed, nor will it be left to another people.
2:35 It struck the statue on its feet of iron and clay and smashed them. 36 Then the iron, the clay, the bronze, the silver and the gold were broken to pieces at the same time and became like chaff on a threshing floor in the summer. The wind swept them away without leaving a trace. 37 But the rock that struck the statue became a huge mountain and filled the whole earth.	2:44b It will crush all those kingdoms and bring them to an end, but it will itself endure forever. 45a This is the meaning of the vision of the rock cut out of a mountain, but not by hands—a rock that broke the iron, the bronze, the clay, the silver and the gold to pieces.

116. This word can also be translated "copper," but bronze, being stronger, was more commonly used; Goldingay, *Daniel*, 35.

117. Goldingay comments, "The word suggests decorative tiling or potsherds, . . . tatty decoration when strength of structure is really needed." *Daniel*, 35.

THE DREAM AND ITS INTERPRETATION (2:31-45)

The Statue Described

"You looked, O king, and there before you stood a large statue—an enormous, dazzling statue, awesome in appearance."

The very description of the statue indicates why Nebuchadnezzar was so terrified. It was "before him," that is, it was in his space, intimidating. It was "enormous," something which towered above him, evoking memories of the tower of Babel.[118] It conveyed to him an overwhelming sense of kingly power and splendour—"dazzling," evidently with a majestic splendor even he did not possess; and "awesome in appearance," instilling in him a deep sense of dread.[119]

The Statue: Four Human Reigns, One Empire

Regarding the interpretation of the statue in Daniel 2, Collins[120] finds a combination of two complexes of traditional ideas:

1. A sequence of four kingdoms, followed by a lasting kingdom

Collins finds this to be a widely used sequence in political propaganda in the Hellenistic Near East; e.g., a fragment of the Roman chronicler Aemilius Sura (who wrote shortly before 171 BC); the fourth Sibylline Oracle (a Jewish work from Egypt which argues that the eruption of Vesuvius constitutes divine punishment for the destruction of Jerusalem); Persian Bahman Yasht (Zand-i Vohuman Yasn 1). Following Swain, many believe that both the four empires scheme of Daniel 2 and Daniel 7, plus the ten kings series of Daniel 7, are attributable to Persian influence.[121]

Daniel is in fact by far the earliest known example of a four empires scheme. In perhaps the early part of the second century BC, Roman writer Aemilius Sura presents a list of four empires: Assyrian, Median, Persian, and Macedonian. To these he adds a fifth: Rome.[122] Next to this comes Sibylline Oracle 4. In the 4th Sibylline Oracle the same sequence of five kingdoms is

---

118. So many, e.g., Kim, *Biblical Interpretation*, 77.

119. Cf. Walvoord, *Daniel*, 63.

120. *Apocalyptic Vision*, 37–43.

121. Lucas, "Origin," 185. So Russell thought this four world empire schema (which he also saw as influenced by Greek thought) as characteristic of the teaching of Zoroastrianism. Hasel, "Four World Empires," 17.

122. Lucas, "Origin," 190; Hasel, "Four World Empires," 18–19.

observed as in Sura: the first kingdom is that of the Assyrians (lines 49–53); the second that of the Medes (lines 54–64); the third that of the Persians (lines 65–87); and the fourth that of the Macedonians (Alexander the Great's empire; lines 88–101). This is followed by the Roman Empire (lines 102 onwards), which will involve the destruction of Jerusalem and the Temple (lines 115–129), the catastrophic eruption of Vesuvius in 79 AD (lines 130 onwards). This is the final kingdom before God destroys the whole world by fire (lines 171 onwards), and there is never a suggestion that the Roman Empire will last forever. The Sibylline Oracles are much later than Daniel with Davies suggesting that the passage in question is based on a Hellenistic oracle dated to 80 AD, that is, soon after the latest event it recorded, the eruption of Vesuvius.[123]

Around 400 AD Servius reports that the Cumean Sibyl divided the generations by metals and said who would rule each generation, saying that the Sun would be the tenth and last ruler. However, it is not clear whether each generation was associated with a different metal.[124] A Persian text from the Middle Ages, the Bahman Yasht (cf. also the Zoroastrian text Denkard IX.8),[125] "tells of a dream of Zoroaster consisting of a tree with branches of gold, silver, steel, and mixed iron, representing four periods of time yet to come."[126]

Even more tenuous is Hasel's proposal that the "Dynastic Prophecy" from Babylon is a possible source of influence.[127] As Davies notes, while four kingdoms may be described in the course of the prophecy (though the text is very fragmentary), "there is no evidence of a four-empires scheme as such."[128] Regarding a four kingdom schema it is of interest only that one Jewish tradition (Lev. Rab. 13:5) likens the four rivers of Eden to four empires: Babylon, Media, Greece, and Edom.

Clearly there is no substantial reason to link any of the above sources in any way with Daniel's presentation of four kingdoms and they should not be allowed to influence our interpretation of Daniel 2. Lucas maintains: "rather than being the result of a combination of adherence to a traditional

123. *Daniel*, 44; see too Lucas, "Origin," 185; Hasel, "Four World Empires," 19.

124. Lucas, "Origin," 191.

125. Lucas, "Origin," 191.

126. Davies, 44; cf. Hasel, "Four World Empires," 20. Hasel stresses the significant differences between both dreams: (1) tree not statue; (2) steel not bronze; (3) "mixed iron" not iron; (4) nothing after "mixed iron" against "mixed with clay" after iron; (5) metals symbolizing kings not empires. As our own exegesis indicates, this last point of supposed difference is debatable.

127. For the argument see Hasel, "Four World Empires," 17–30, esp. from 22.

128. *Daniel*, 45.

scheme and an inaccurate knowledge of history, the sequence of world powers in Daniel 2 and 7 expresses a Jewish perception of history from the fall
of Jerusalem to the expected intervention of God to restore his kingdom."
Lucas then goes on to seek to identify the four kingdoms: "During this
period those Judeans and Israelites who are experiencing God's chastise-
ment and who will, if they are faithful, share in the kingdom, experience the
power of Babylon, Media, Persia, and Macedonia."[129] Later we will consider
whether it is legitimate to identify the four kingdoms with these particular
four world powers.

2. A distinction of four world ages identified by metals.

The original purpose of this schema was to signify a gradual deterioration of the world.

In the eighth century BC, Hesiod (*Works and Days*; cf. Ovid, *Meta-
morphoses*[130]) spoke of a sequence of Five Ages in which man has moved
from the race of gold to the iron generation of Hesiod's contemporaries.[131]
Actually, the sequence is gold, silver, bronze, iron, followed by Hesiod's own
age.[132] Davies observes, "Many scholars believe that here is the source of
Daniel 2 mediated either directly or, more plausibly, through a widespread
diffusion of the idea in the Eastern Mediterranean." However, long before
Hesiod a sequence of four ever-deteriorating world ages—gold, silver,
bronze, and iron—was an integral part of Vedic philosophy.[133]

But while interesting the similarity is purely superficial. To begin
with, it is not at all apparent that the movement from head to feet involves
a process of sustained deterioration. True, the reign that follows upon that
of Nebuchadnezzar's is said to be *"inferior"* (v. 39), presumably as silver is
inferior to gold. But the third reign is evidently commensurate in power
with that of Nebuchadnezzar. The fourth kingdom, while vulnerable, is also
of great might and indeed so much so "it will crush and break all the others"
(v. 40). In general usage gold and silver stand for that which is precious and
bronze and iron for that which is strong and hard.[134] Thus, there is no appar-

129. "Origin," 194. This schema is also observed by Gurney, *God in Control*, 30–34.

130. Lucas, "Origin," 191.

131. Anderson, *Signs and Wonders*, 21.

132. Hasel, "Four World Empires," 20.

133. Ancient Vedic philosophy, as taught in the Vedic Puranas, now assimilated
into Buddhism and Hinduism, conceives of the universe as going through a series of
cycles of immense time-length before coming to a cataclysmic end, then being reborn
and repeating the same four cycles, ad infinitum. Essential to the structure of these
ever-recurring cycles is a series of four sub-ages or *yugas*, called Satya, Treta, Dvapara,
and Kali. They are also referred to in sequence as the Gold, Silver, Bronze, and Iron ages.

134. Goldingay, *Daniel*, 49.

ent diminution of power as we move from head to feet, though it is probably valid to speak of a decrease in splendor from reign to reign. Perhaps the underlying notion is that given time, as the gloss wears off, anti-God human rule always becomes more and more a matter of the exercise of brute, raw power.

Actually, Gooding helpfully points out that with respect to pagan rule there is a discernible pattern of decline:[135]

Chapter 1 Nebuchadnezzar idolatrously, but reverently, places God's vessels in the house of his idol: but he does not ban the Jews' worship of God.

Chapter 3 Nebuchadnezzar tries to force Jews to worship his god, but does not ban their worship of God, and in the end worships their God himself.

Chapter 5 Belshazzar sacrilegiously drinks from God's vessels, but even so does not ban the worship of God nor deify himself.

Chapter 6 Darius temporarily bans prayer to God, and is sorry.

Chapter 7 The little horn speaks words against the Most High.

Chapter 8 Antiochus stops the regular sacrifice, casts down the sanctuary of God, magnifies himself *even* to the Prince of the host.

Chapter 11:31 Antiochus sets up the abomination of desolation in the sanctuary.

Chapter 11:36 "The king" magnifies himself *above* every god and speaks unheard-of things against the God of gods.

While admitting there is no precise parallel with Hesiod's schema, Davies comes to the extravagant conclusion:

> ... it can be safely said. . . that the idea did not arise independently in Daniel, and that it was used elsewhere in the Hellenistic period as a device of political propaganda against Hellenistic monarchies. Its function in Daniel is not necessarily the same, but the idea of a sequence of kingdoms does play an important part in the construction of the whole book.[136]

Davies has no substantial evidence for making such an assertion. In Daniel 2 we are told that God gave Nebuchadnezzar the dream and thus presented this schema; it was God who brought out the significance of this

135. Gooding, "Literary Structure," 55–57.
136. *Daniel*, 45.

four-reign schema via Daniel's interpretation. There is at least as much evidence to say the schema was brand new. It is possible that in presenting this sequence of kingdoms God was employing a pattern familiar to Nebuchadnezzar because of similar presentations in the ancient world. But this is speculation. What we do know is that insofar as our scant collection of ancient texts permits, the schema, as presented in Daniel 2, is quite unique, especially for its time.

The problem with Collins' approach to Daniel 2 is that he reads the above kinds of background into the passage, thus concluding that Daniel 2 also involves a sequence of four kingdoms. But, as we will observe below, it is more probable that what is envisaged is a sequence of four kings ruling over a single empire.

The Statue as a Unit

Fewell contends,[137]

> Daniel is one who tells the truth but not the whole truth. Daniel's reading of the dream is an underreading. There are elements of the dream for which he has not given account to the king. The image, though built of multiple components, is still a singular entity, a unified structure that stands as one and falls as one. As a singular construct, its temporality is marked, not by succession, but by synchrony.[138]

Fewell caricatures Daniel as a political machinator who unfaithfully relays to the king what God has told him, by imposing his own self-promoting emphases upon the interpretation given, and by cunningly omitting to explain certain features of the dream. But this conclusion presupposes a knowledge that is out of Fewell's reach: the knowledge of what God actually revealed to Daniel and required him to relay. Fewell's conclusions therefore presuppose she has more ability to uncover secret things than did Daniel himself!

Notwithstanding these critical remarks, Fewell is correct to stress the statue's nature as a "singular construct." Young approves Darby's comment:

> We may first observe that the Gentile kingdoms are seen as a whole. It is neither historical succession nor moral features with respect to God and man, but the kingdoms all together forming,

---

137. *Circle*, 34.

138. Indeed, the destruction moves from bottom to top, after the stone strikes the statue at its base. Goswell, *Daniel*, 19.

as it were, a personage before God, the man of the earth in the
eye of God—glorious and terrible in his public splendour in the
eyes of men.[139]

Fewell sees the image as not so much an idol of a divine being, but of
humanity.[140] She notes that the elements of which the image is composed are
those "usually worked by human hands and valued by human society." That
is, gold and silver are used for adornment and to furnish economic power;
bronze and iron to make tools and weapons; and pottery for literary and
domestic purposes. Given this, she sees the top-heavy imagery as indicating
"a humanity that has over-reached itself." The antithesis to this image, the
stone, is by contrast "a power completely devoid of human characteristics, a
force that is completely 'other.'" The stone, in contrast to the elements used
in the image, is a natural element which does unnatural things:

> It divorces itself from its surroundings, it propels itself against
> the image, it grows as if an organic entity, into a mountain that
> fills the entire earth. The mountain, in contrast to the image, is
> raw and undomesticated. It represents something that cannot be
> tamed by human power

Fewell suggests the dream is loaded and that it has not only diachronic
significance, as openly explained by Daniel, but also a synchronic significance, which Daniel, for diplomatic reasons, leaves unsaid. The synchronic
significance is that those under Nebuchadnezzar right now pose a threat
to the security of his rule. Fewell seeks nuances in the text to support this
view.[141] She draws attention to Nebuchadnezzar's accusation that the wise
men are "buying time" and also the phrase in verse 8 "until the time is
changed." Is it Nebuchadnezzar's idea that should he give them time these
wise men will be his undoing? This interpretation stretches the text a good
deal, relying heavily on eisegeted innuendoes rather than upon exegetically
derived conclusions. Notwithstanding this, it is likely that the threat does lie
under Nebuchadnezzar's nose, but not in the persons of the Chaldeans, but,
ironically, in the persons of the Jewish exiles (v. 25), through whom God's
rule is being established "in the time of those kings."

139. *Daniel*, 76. Similarly, Goswell (*Daniel*, 19): "The picture. . .cannot be reduced
to a simplistic schema of four chronologically successive kingdoms. In the dream the
last kingdom is destroyed first!"

140. *Circle*, 34.

141. *Circle*, 35.

The NIV speaks of "kingdoms" in verses 37, 39, 40, 42, 44. The Aramaic word used is *malkû*. Goldingay points out[142] that "empire" ("kingdom") is only one option for translation, and that the Aramaic word can also mean "royal authority," "realm," or "individual reign." Gammie likewise insists that this is the right understanding of the word.[143] Goldingay reasons that since Nebuchadnezzar as an individual is represented as being the head of a unified structure (statue) it cannot be said that Nebuchadnezzar is the first "empire," but rather that he constitutes the first "reign." It is especially to be noted in this regard that before conveying the meaning of the dream to Nebuchadnezzar Daniel praises God as the one who "sets up kings and deposes them" (v. 21). Further in 2:44 Daniel explicitly speaks of "the time of those kings."[144] It thus makes more sense to see the dream as involving the reigns of four kings over a single empire that is finally destroyed at one blow by the "rock."

Nebuchadnezzar as the Head of Gold

Daniel, in his interpretation, identifies Nebuchadnezzar as the "head of gold" and thus implies that his reign is the golden age. This is yet further evidence telling against any idea of Daniel being a model for *Hasidim*. Rather, as exemplified in the book of Judith, Jews consistently remembered Nebuchadnezzar as an evil king, indeed the monster who conquered Jerusalem and destroyed the temple.

However, there is evidence that during the Hellenistic period the Babylonians recalled the reign of Nebuchadnezzar as a golden age. Berossus, writing about 275 BC, exalted Nebuchadnezzar above all previous kings of Babylon. According to Megasthenes, he surpassed even Heracles. His exploits were developed to surpass those of Alexander the Great and Seleucus. Collins cynically regards the identification of Nebuchadnezzar with the head of gold as being far more appropriate in the mouth of a hellenistic Babylonian than in that of a contemporary Jew. But Daniel 2 presents a definite divine revelation of God to Daniel in space-time history, which Daniel was duty-bound to relay to Nebuchadnezzar, regardless of what he may personally have felt. It may well have been a repugnant idea to Daniel for Nebuchadnezzar to be compared with the "head of gold," but this is the meaning of the dream as God revealed it, and Daniel is not free to interpret

142. *Daniel*, 49.

143. "Classification," 199–200.

144. Fyall takes the view that this phrase refers to rulers of the fourth kingdom, *Daniel*, 41.

the dream as he pleases. The total preceding context has labored to stress that Daniel did not work this all out for himself, but that God revealed to him the content and meaning of the dream.

Daniel begins his interpretation of the dream by telling Nebuchadnezzar that though he is "the king of kings" he must recognize that his "dominion and power and might and glory" have been given to him by "the God of heaven" (v. 37).[145] This rubs right against Nebuchadnezzar's own belief that Nabu, his guardian deity, is "the bestower of thrones in heaven and on earth" (*Borsippa Inscription* 1.43).

Further to this, the ensuing chapters reveal that Daniel was so personally convinced as to the sovereignty of God that he was able to accept his situation as the king's servant in a wholehearted manner, and indeed to accord genuine, heartfelt respect for the pagan ruler whom God had placed in control (e.g., 4:19). In the light of the clear teaching of passages such as Romans 13:1–7, 1 Peter 2:13–14, 18–21, submission to and respect for ruling powers is a characteristic of godliness. Since Daniel is presented as a model of godliness there can be no problem with Daniel's positive regard for Nebuchadnezzar. To treat this as humbug is to repudiate central claims made in the book, and also represents a failure to come to terms with biblical godliness.

From Head to Foot

In Daniel's relation of the dream he speaks of the statue having legs of iron and feet "partly of iron and partly of baked clay" (v. 33); of a rock striking the statue on its feet of iron and clay and smashing them (v. 34); of "the iron, the clay, the bronze, the silver, and the gold" being "broken to pieces at the same time" and becoming "like chaff on a threshing floor in the summer" (v. 35). In his interpretation Daniel speaks of a fourth kingdom, "strong as iron—for iron breaks and smashes everything—and as iron breaks things to pieces, so it will crush and break all the others" (v. 40). However, the fact that the feet and toes are an admixture of baked clay and iron indicates that this fourth kingdom will become "a divided kingdom," "partly strong

145. Kim finds here an indication that Nebuchadnezzar should see himself as "a vassal of the celestial sovereign." *Biblical Interpretation*, 77. It is true that the suzerain-vassal model would have been very familiar to ancients. But Kim's reading goes beyond the text and ignores the fact that communication between the parties is presupposed in such a model. Nebuchadnezzar has been given no prior reason to see Daniel's God as his suzerain. At best we can say that Nebuchadnezzar is as accountable to the ultimate superpower, God, as a relatively weak vassal would be to an immensely powerful suzerain.

and partly brittle" (vv. 41–2). Given prior references to Babel it may well be that the mixture involved here echoes the way in which God "mixed" the language of the Babel-builders so as to scatter them all over the earth (cf. the wind sweeping away all the broken pieces of the statue after it is toppled, v.35). This possibility is enhanced by the fact that "clay" was rejected by the Babel builders as a building material (Gen 11:3). It may be implied, therefore, that the statue was actually weaker than the tower of Babel. On top of all this, recall that it is "stone," the other building material rejected by the Babel-builders, which brings down the statue. The tower of Babel was built by human hands but the whole enterprise was "brought down" by that which was not produced by human hands, just as in the case of the statue.[146]

The political manifestation of the mixing of iron and clay is made clearer in verse 43. Here it is especially important to note the translation of the Aramaic as provided in the NASB: "And in that you saw the iron mixed with common clay, they will combine with one another in the seed of men; but they will not adhere to one another, even as iron does not combine with pottery."[147] The notion of "combining" or "mingling" (KJV) "in the seed of men" is commonly understood to denote a unity formed through marriage.[148] But one which proves to be unsustainable: "but they will not adhere to one another." To use a pun, this supposed marriage-based unity proves to be "the Achilles heel" of the statue.

Those who see a marriage-based unity take either of two broad positions:

1. It refers to a particular marriage alliance in history that brought together two peoples.

2. It refers to general intermarriage between different peoples within the kingdom.

A Particular Marriage Alliance?

Ginsberg and Rowley are illustrative of a number of scholars who find in verse 43 an allusion to a particular marriage alliance.[149] Rowley's concern is to show that Daniel 1–6 was written by the same author who wrote Daniel

146. See especially Kim, *Biblical Interpretation*, 78–80.

147. Cf. Harman's literal translation: "As you saw iron mixed with ceramic clay, they are mixing with the seed of mankind; and they are not cleaving this to this as iron does not mix with the clay." *Daniel*, 68.

148. For example, Meadowcroft and Irwin, *Book of Daniel*, 56.

149. See Ginsberg, "Composition."

7-12. Since he believes the entire book is a united work written during the time of Antiochus IV Epiphanes, it seems to him that the best way of understanding 2:43 is as an allusion is to an important marriage close to this time. Hence his proposal that 2:43 has in mind the marriage of Antiochus III's daughter Cleopatra to Ptolemy V in 194/193 BC.[150] Providing some support for this view would be the apparent allusion to this very marriage at 11:17:

> He will determine to come with the might of his entire kingdom
> and will make an alliance with the king of the South. And he
> will give him a daughter in marriage in order to overthrow the
> kingdom, but his plan will not succeed or help him.

Ginsberg is scathing in his rejection of Rowley's hypothesis because it is unthinkable to him that Daniel 2, or indeed Daniel 1-6 as a whole, could have an Antiochean provenance. Ginsberg believes that 2:43-44 has in mind the consequences of a marriage alliance that have "world-shattering events."[151] He insists that the marriage of Cleopatra and Ptolemy V was nothing of the sort.

To Ginsberg it is virtually beyond question that 2:41-3 must be an interpolation since the interpretation interprets the phrase "and the toes"— something the dream, as related, knows nothing about.[152] Further, Ginsberg believes he finds in this interpolation one of the keys to dating the entirety of Daniel 1-6. Ginsberg dates this portion in the period 307-301 BC, rightly pointing out the foolishness of Rowley's attempts to treat the representations of kings in Daniel 1-6 as veiled caricatures of Antiochus IV. Alongside of this dating, Ginsberg finds in 2:43 an allusion to the marriage of Antiochus II and Berenice in 252 BC and believes that it was the War of Laodice in 246 BC which gave (false) hope to the writer that now at last God's great (fifth) kingdom would be ushered in.[153]

---

150. Similarly Kim, following Collins, thinks of intermarriage between the Seleucids and the Ptolemies, *Biblical Interpretation*, 78.

151. "Composition," 250-51.

152. "Composition," 253.

153. "Composition," 250. Gammie ("Classification," 200) similarly looks of a particular marriage alliance and favors the marriage of Ptolemy IV to his sister Arsinoe. This is in keeping with his highly speculative and, in our opinion, forced view that the four reigns of Daniel 2 are to be identified with the reigns of the first four Ptolemaic kings of Egypt.

General Intermarriage?

There is no mention in either the dream or its interpretation of two *kingdoms* being united by marriage. Rather, the reference, as it stands, is to the mixing of iron and clay *within* the kingdom. This does not mean that marriage alliances with other states are ruled out. Only that any such alliances are by way of uniting the peoples of the kingdom itself and not as a means of uniting different kingdoms.

Rather than marital unities being presupposed, the idea seems to be that of a cosmopolitan kingdom made up of different people groups. Some of these peoples bring strength to the kingdom (iron) while others weaken it (clay). Keil and Delitzsch explain,

> If, then, the "mixing themselves with the seed of men" points to marriages, it is only of the mixing of different tribes brought together by external force in the kingdom by marriages as a means of amalgamating the diversified nationalities.[154]

They further point out that the image of mixing by seed is fundamentally an agricultural one, "derived from the sowing of the field with mingled seed." Given this, we need to go beyond intermarriage in understanding what is meant by "they will combine with one another in the seed of men." This "denotes *all the means* employed by the rulers to combine the different nationalities" (my stress), though intermarriage would doubtless be one of the main methods.[155]

Keil and Delitzsch also observe that the expression "the seed of men" serves to contrast "the vain human endeavor of the heathen rulers" with "the doings of the God of heaven."

Is it Possible to Identify the Four Reigns?

Harman observes that while the "kingdoms" are described in sequential order their destruction occurs simultaneously and he rightly identifies this as "an interpretive key to the dream." Simultaneity rules out the identification

---

154. Keil and Delitzsch, "Daniel," 109.

155. "The text does not define the subject of the verb 'to mix.' Though some suggest that it means the kings referred to in the next verse, it is best to assume that it refers to the people of the kingdom that is being described. In some way, possibly by racial or ethnic division, the population of the kingdom does not adhere, so that the lack of coherence will contribute to its downfall." Harman, *Daniel*, 68–69. My proposal is that is especially the presence of God's people in the kingdom that makes impossible the godless unity that might otherwise stabilize it.

of these "kingdoms" with such empires as the Babylonian, Persian, Greek, and Roman.[156] It is said of the fourth reign that "it will crush and break all the others" (v. 40). In similar vein in verse 44 the God-established reign "will crush all those reigns and bring them to an end." Clearly in neither case can this mean that the reign concerned will destroy all of the preceding reigns in one blow since it is not possible for them to coexist together at one time: the time of the new destructive reign. But once we think of the four reigns as being over one continuous empire, rather than of four distinct kingdoms, it is possible to think in terms of a new reign which will bring to an end all that preceding reigns have accomplished in the one empire.[157]

Many scholars take verses 40–43 (what we call "the Fourth Reign") to be referring to the kingdom of Antiochus IV Epiphanes (175–163 BC). But as Goldingay points out the vagueness of the depiction used in these verses makes it equally valid to apply it to the Babylonians or Persians.[158]

One of the reasons why many feel confident to identify each of the four reigns with particular kingdoms is because they see the four reigns of Daniel 7 as standing in precise or at least close parallelism.[159] But even if this is so, and this is debatable, it is still arguable that in Daniel 7 as in Daniel 2 the number four is used to suggest the comprehensiveness of human rule in its various manifestations rather than to identify particular reigns. Against this it can be urged that Daniel 8 explicitly identifies the kings of Media and Persia and of Greece (8:20–21) and that their symbolic equivalents in the vision, the ram and the goat, are to be identified with the second and third beasts of Daniel 7 respectively. But even if this latter point be true it does not logically follow that, as used in Daniel 7, the second and third beasts represent the Medo-Persian empire and the Greek empire respectively. It is equally arguable that the Medo-Persian and Greek empires represent particular historical manifestations of the general types of rule spoken of in Daniel 7. It is therefore precarious to use Daniel 8 to fix the reference point of each of the beasts in Daniel 7 and parts of the statue in Daniel 2.[160]

In the twenty-three years which followed Nebuchadnezzar's reign, there were five Babylonian rulers, including the regency of Belshazzar, and

---

156. *Daniel*, 69.

157. It is not necessary to see the second, third, and fourth kingdom as contemporaneous, contra Harman, *Daniel*, 69.

158. *Daniel*, 50.

159. E.g., Walvoord, *Daniel*, 67.

160. Barker, apparently blind to this other progressive reading of the four kingdoms schema, over-confidently declares, "These identifications become virtually certain in light of a correlation of the data of chapter 2 with those of chapters 7 and 8, notwithstanding Goldingay and others to the contrary." Barker, "Premillenialism," 28.

the four reigns of Daniel 2, as Goldingay suggests, may well refer to four of these kings. Other scholars have tried to identify them with Assyrian kings, Persian kings, and Ptolemaic kings. Goldingay himself thinks that that the three reigns which follow Nebuchadnezzar's are those of Babylonian rulers, with the "rock" being Cyrus, in line with the role assigned to him in Isaiah 41:25; 44:28; 45:13. Goldingay notes that in the book of Daniel, Belshazzar, Nebuchadnezzar's successor, is presented as an inferior king, and argues that Darius the Mede represents the third, and Cyrus the fourth of the rulers symbolized by the four respective parts of the statue.[161] But this too seems highly unlikely. There is no attempt in Daniel to portray a history which corresponds to such a schema. In fact the demise of the Medo-Persian ram in Daniel 8, before the all-conquering might of the Greek goat, is at odds with Goldingay's proposal. It stretches credulity to argue Greek rule represents the rock and illustrates the endless speculation that results from trying to precisely identify the four reigns of Daniel 2.

It is probably a mistake even to try to identify the four kings with four specific historical figures. In Daniel numbers are often used in a symbolic fashion and certainly the number four was often used in the ancient world to convey the idea of completeness, corresponding especially to the four corners of the earth, and the four seasons. Thus the four reigns of Daniel 2 may represent the comprehensiveness of human rule; a rule which expresses itself in different ways, corresponding to the different parts of the body of the statue. As history progresses the glory of human rule will increasingly tarnish, though its might will remain. But ultimately it is vulnerable and incapable of holding its subjects under its power. In the end it will be destroyed and succeeded by God's eternal kingdom.

To many the wording of verse 44—"the God of heaven will set up a kingdom that will never be destroyed"—indicates that the historical fulfillment of Daniel's prophecy (the details of which were probably not even known to Daniel; cf. 1 Peter 2:10–12) coincides with the coming of Christ. Thus it is argued that the fourth part of the statue—the legs and feet—surely represent the eschatological human kingdom. The reasoning then goes that within the whole corpus of biblical literature there is not the slightest suggestion that the time of Antiochus IV Epiphanes was of any significance in the establishment of God's eternal kingdom. Certainly the New Testament shows complete disinterest in this historical period, and following the immediate post-exilic period there were some 400-odd years known as the time of the "quenching of the Spirit" when the voice of biblical prophecy was silent.

161. *Daniel*, 51.

However, a closer look at the language of verse 44 shows that it does not demand an interpretation which dates the emergence of this God-established kingdom at the time of Christ's coming. Verse 44 begins "in the time of those kings, the God of heaven will set up a reign that will never be destroyed, nor will it be left to another people" (NIV modified by "reign" for "kingdom"). In interpreting this it is important to note that verses 37–38 reflect Daniel's meditation on Jeremiah 27:5–7. Later the importance of Jeremiah for Daniel will be made explicit (9:2). Our immediate interest is in Jeremiah 27:7—"All nations will serve him and his son and his grandson until the time for his land comes; then many nations and great kings will subjugate him." This verse is important because it recognizes that a number of kings will succeed Nebuchadnezzar. When the demise of Babylon eventually comes, that is, after the prescribed "seventy years," God will punish "the king of Babylon" (Jer 25:12). Clearly the point of this is not that God will punish the particular king who happens to be reigning at the time of God's judgment on Babylon, but that "the king of Babylon" is a collective figure who comprehends the entirety of Babylonian rule.

This background lends support to the view that in Daniel 2 the dream and its interpretation, at least in the first instance, refer to the Babylonian empire and that the toppling of the statue of Babylonian rule corresponds with the end of the seventy-year period.[162] Goldingay maintains, "The statue represents the empire led by Nebuchadnezzar.[163] It is a single statue, a single empire, passed on from one king to another."[164] Hebbard, following Steinmann, likewise observes that here "all human empires are brought together in a single symbolic empire, and in order to add emphasis to this notion, the symbol of this unity is the form of a man."[165]

My own understanding of the dream is that it presents four typical, not actually identifiable kings as those who reign over a single world empire epitomized by Babylon of which Nebuchadnezzar is the head. That is, Daniel 2 is written to encourage God's people in all ages. Especially in these "latter days" it is appropriate for God's people to anticipate the termination of the fourth and final reign through the decisive intervention of God's eternal kingdom. If this is correct then the setting up of the God-established reign

162. This view is also proposed by Davies: *Daniel,* 48.

163. *Daniel,* 57.

164. Similarly, Olojede, "More than a Prophet?" 949. Redditt, *Daniel,* 49. Redditt believes the statue *originally* represented Babylonian kings but was then modified. He maintains that in its present form the kingdoms are the Babylonian, Median, Persian, and Greek: *Daniel,* 59. However, this latter conclusion is only formed by reading back into Daniel 2 the later identifications of Daniel 8—a mistake in my opinion.

165. *Reading Daniel,* 90.

"in the time of those kings," means Daniel is describing what God is doing in the entire course of history which extends from the rule of Nebuchadnezzar to the very end of that point *in* history when blasphemous anti-God rule will be destroyed for evermore and replaced by indestructible divine rule.

Martin Noth sees this. He once presented an oft-quoted lecture entitled "*The Understanding of History in Old Testament Apocalyptic*" in which his consideration of the four-empire scheme leads him to draw a major conclusion concerning the apocalyptic understanding of history: that

> . . . the four world empires are not mentioned and described because they follow one another in time; the round number four is intended to bring out "that the coming of the Kingdom of God is always a matter for the whole of world history."[166]

Empires give way in a sequence of decreasing splendor though increasing strength (gold–silver–brass–iron). But the image is destroyed as a whole. Dumbrell's suggestion is likely:

> Perhaps the four kingdoms are a picture of the totality of human government, representative of the human power structure, of the human image. Clearly the historical sequence of kingdoms which is presented is simply various fine-tunings of the anti-God power structure. Progressive human government will inevitably exhibit the same innate tendencies to search for its centre within itself.[167]

It is interesting to observe that John's use of Babylon in the book of Revelation is consistent with the above (Rev 14:8; 16:19; 17–18). Though it could be argued that John has developed his own way of referring to Babylon (for example, as a cryptic reference to Rome), it is also arguable that in using Babylon as a cipher for the totality of anti-God human rule John is simply picking up what had already been intended by Daniel's own use of this imagery.

The Identification of the Fifth Kingdom

In seeking to find historical placement for the fifth kingdom, Ginsberg makes much of the phrase "in the time of those kings" (v. 44) which he

---

166. Koch, *Rediscovery*, 39. See too Goswell, *Daniel*, 20: "It is best to view the four sections of the statue as symbolizing all the kingdoms of history (however many there will be), with the number four expressing the ideal of universality."

167. *Faith*, 260.

insists should be rendered "in the days of those kingdoms."[168] He maintains that this implies the first three kingdoms still have a continuing existence at the time the fourth kingdom comes to its end.

We have argued above that Ginsberg erroneously reads 2:43 as an allusion to the particular marriage alliance between Antiochus II and Berenice in 252 BC. Ginsberg, believing 2:41–43 to be an interpolation, now takes this out of the equation in seeking to fix a date for the rest of Daniel 2. He presupposes, with Rowley, that the four kingdoms are respectively Babylonia, Media, Persia, and Macedonia.[169] He then argues that, in some sense, it can be said that Babylonia, Media, and Persia all continued to exist down to the period 307–301 BC.[170] Therefore, he believes that at this time the author of Daniel 2, and indeed of Daniel 1–6, made the prediction that the Macedonian kingdom would be brought to an end by a fifth kingdom. He goes on to claim that it was this very prediction that inspired another writer in the period 176–167 BC to write an up-to-date version of that prediction in the shape of what he refers to as "the primary text" of Daniel 7. He believes that chapters 8–12 were then tacked on successively.

But against this the expression "in the time of those kings" does not require that we understand the first three kingdoms as having a continuing existence at the time the statue falls, though, as we noted above, the statue must be treated as a unit. The following translations capture the force of what is being said:

> "But throughout the history of these kingdoms, the God of heaven will be building a kingdom that will never be destroyed" (The Message).
> "During the reigns of those kings, the God of heaven will set up a kingdom that will never be destroyed" (NLT).

Although God's eschatological kingdom replaces the fourth kingdom, and indeed the entire statue of human rule, it does not *begin* at the time when the statue is toppled. Rather, it is a kingdom that God progressively establishes throughout the entire course of human history whatever its contemporary expressions of human rule might be. In Daniel itself we discover that this eschatological kingdom does have a particularly Jewish character.

This is denied by Collins who, speaking of the fifth kingdom, contends:

> The statement that the kingdom will never pass to another people would most naturally be understood by Nebuchadnezzar to

---

168. "Composition," 248.

169. Siegman declared this to be "practically certain." Siegman, "Stone," 367.

170. "Composition," 249–50.

mean that this kingdom will belong to the Babylonian people. The fact that a kingdom is set up by the god of heaven does not necessarily mean that it is a Jewish kingdom. All the peoples of the ancient Near East believed that their kingdoms were set up by a god. The text nowhere suggests that this final kingdom is Jewish. If Nebuchadnezzar understood the final kingdom to be a reconstitution of the Babylonian kingdom, his enthusiastic reaction to Daniel becomes much more readily explicable.[171]

Unfortunately Collins chooses to read only that part of the text that suits his purpose and to simply ignore the rest. He goes further than this, reconstructing the whole text, in order to bolster his thesis.

The kingdoms have been described clearly in the dream and its interpretation. And in 2:44 it is plainly indicated that the fifth reign cannot be confused with any human kingdom (indeed it is explicitly represented (2:45) by a "rock cut out of a mountain, but not by human hands"), and that it will crush all of the four kingdoms described by Daniel. Indeed, not a trace will be left of that human rule—it will be as though it never existed (v. 35).[172]

Seow notes that the language of "a rock cut out" (v. 34) is quarry language which invites comparison with Isaiah 51:1–2:[173]

> Listen to me, you who pursue righteousness and who seek the Lord: Look to the rock from which you were cut and to the quarry from which you were hewn; 2 look to Abraham, your father, and to Sarah, who gave you birth. When I called him he was only one man, and I blessed him and made him many.

It is significant that here the "stone" cut from the Abrahamic rock is identified with God's people. The image of verse 45 may involve divine comedy. For the language of a rock or stone "cut out of a mountain" is precisely the language used to describe the bricks of stone "cut out of mountains" and used by Nebuchadnezzar in his massive building projects (e.g., *Borsippa Inscription* 5.44). In recent times Saddam Hussein constructed brickwork over the ruins of Babylon. The original bricks were inscribed with the name of Nebuchadnezzar. It gives some idea of the immensity of the number of bricks used by Nebuchadnezzar to build his kingdom that Saddam Hussein

---

171. *Apocalyptic Vision*, 42.

172. Olyott expresses it well: "At once the whole image collapsed, and was reduced to powder. The wind blew over it, and very soon there was no sign that it had ever been there. What had been so terrifying, and what had appeared so permanent and formidable, was gone." *Dare to Stand*, 30.

173. Cited by Olojede, "More than a Prophet?" 950.

had over 60 million bricks inscribed with his own name, seeing himself as successor to Nebuchadnezzar. Seen in this context how humorous it is to see all of this massive empire, symbolized by the giant statue, being brought down by one solitary "stone" or, we might say, brick!

Olojede comments, "The invisibility of the hand that cut the stone underscores the ephemeral nature of the image and the kingdoms it represents. The abstract hand destroys the concrete image!"[174]

Since the formation of this kingdom is not achieved by human hands it stretches the imagination too far to identify the rock with Cyrus, as suggested by Goldingay.[175] Further, Daniel does not refer to just any god, but specifically to the God of heaven who in this entire experience is revealed to be utterly unique and to be distinguished from all other gods—as Nebuchadnezzar himself acknowledges (v. 47).[176] In the ancient world all gods were associated with particular peoples. Daniel stands before Nebuchadnezzar as "one of the exiles from Judah" (v. 25) and thus the unique, incomparable "God of heaven" who alone reveals such mysteries—for one cannot expect this of other gods because they do not live among men (v. 11)—is identified with the people whom Daniel represents in his own person, the people of Judah. Daniel 7 involves the same eschatology: the replacement and succession of all expressions of human rule by the eternal reign of God. Most significantly, this reign of God is a "kingdom" received by "the saints of the Most High" (7:18), for "the sovereignty, power, and greatness of the kingdoms under the whole heaven will be handed over to the saints, the people of the Most High" (7:27).

Kim rightly notes the strong affinity of the dream's imagery with Isaiah 41:14–16:[177]

> Do not be afraid, you worm Jacob, little Israel, do not fear, for I myself will help you, declares the Lord, your Redeemer, the Holy One of Israel. 15 See, I will make you into a threshing sledge, new and sharp, with many teeth. You will thresh the mountains and crush them, and reduce the hills to chaff.

174. "More than a Prophet?" 950–51.

175. *Daniel*, 51.

176. Lawson, God Who Reveals," 72, sees this statement as "perfectly in keeping with the Mesopotamian tradition of divine revelation." Divorced from its context, this statement does accord with this tradition. However, it is precisely the context that enables us to interpret this statement correctly. Nebuchadnezzar is clearly recognizing that an unprecedented revelation has taken place, the impartation of secrets, of mysteries, unobtainable through Mesopotamian arts: the very particular retelling of the dream itself and the revelation of the future in a particular manner.

177. See Kim, *Biblical Interpretation*, 80.

16 You will winnow them, the wind will pick them up, and a gale will blow them away. But you will rejoice in the Lord and glory in the Holy One of Israel.[178]

Observe the following points of contact:

1. The simile of chaff and wind.

2. The image of threshing: "became like chaff on a threshing floor."

3. The image of crushing: "and smashed/crushed them."

As Kim points out, Isaiah has in mind God using his people, exiled Israelites, to judge the foreign nations which persecute them. Significantly, the parallel dream-vision of Daniel 7 similarly culminates with "the Son of man" and "the saints of the Most High" as triumphant. Porphyry understood the "stone," together with the "Son of Man" figure of Daniel 7, to be representations of the victorious Jewish people.[179] This view is also represented in later rabbinic exegesis.[180] This is consistent with a point I have been pressing in our overview of these early chapters in Daniel: God uses Daniel, with his friends, to render impossible the achievement of the unity deemed essential for the ongoing stability of Babylon, and to effect its ultimate downfall (especially through the irresistible, history-changing divine word relayed via Daniel).

Many commentators note the similarity between the way this stone brings the giant statue tumbling down and the way David with a stone felled Goliath (1 Sam 17).[181] But in this case Nebuchadnezzar is described as the head of gold and the weakness is not represented as located in the head but in the feet. Perhaps irony is intended here and it is not impossible that the allusion also hints at the stone having Davidic associations. Perhaps messianic associations are not as absent as is often thought.[182]

178. Hamilton, *Clouds of Heaven*, 89, sees Daniel 2:35 as alluding to Psalm 1:4: "Not so the wicked! They are like chaff that the wind blows away."

179. Davies, *Daniel*, 16. The Son of Man is linked with the stone in *4 Ezra*. Evans, "Daniel in the New Testament," 507.

180. In Esth.Rab 7.10 (on Esther 3:6), the midrash compares Israelites to stones, linking together Genesis 49:24; Psalm 118:22; Isaiah 30:14; and Daniel 2:45. Evans, "Daniel in the New Testament," 508.

181. For example, see Anderson, *Signs and Wonders*, 19.

182. So Lacocque, cited by Anderson, *Signs and Wonders*, 25. In later rabbinic exegesis we find a midrash in *Tanhuma* (*Terumah* #7) that explicitly identifies the stone of Daniel 2:34 with the Messiah, linking also Genesis 49:24, Isaiah 11:4, and Ezekiel 28:26 (Evans, "Daniel in the New Testament," 507–8). Hippolytus and Tertullian make the same connection (Evans, "Daniel in the New Testament," 508–9).

Indeed the symbol of the stone/mountain, to represent the fifth reign, would cause Jews to anticipate the eschatological exaltation of Zion (see Isa 2:1–4; Mic 4:1–5): "In the last days the mountain of the Lord's temple will be established as chief among the mountains; it will be raised above the hills . . . "[183] Davies comments: " . . . the mountain probably stands for Zion, and the dream depicts the imminent restoration of the Jewish people to their home which will soon become the centre of the earth."[184]

Certainly the language of verse 35—"the rock . . . became a huge mountain and filled the whole earth"—is conducive to the notion of Jerusalem as the world center. The symbol of the rock being cut from a mountain may not have meant much to Nebuchadnezzar, but the Jewish people, for whom the book is written, would naturally associate the imagery of the huge mountain which fills the earth with Mount Zion, and all the more given the central significance accorded to the Jerusalem Temple in the book of Daniel. Both here and at 9:16–17 (where "holy mountain" and "sanctuary" are juxtaposed), the kingdom of God is associated with the sanctuary but not identified with it. That is, "God's kingdom will be established because of what takes place in His sanctuary."[185] Further, the fact that God's own kingdom will eventually fill the earth reverses the outcome of the tower of Babel episode which saw rebels filling "the whole earth" (Gen 11:9).[186]

Isaiah 28:16 corresponds closely to Daniel's choice of imagery: "See, I lay a stone in Zion, a tested stone . . ." This associating of the Danielic stone with Zion is consistent with prophetic eschatology regarding the establishment of Jerusalem as the ideal world center.[187] It thus is antithetical to "the land of Shinar" of 1:2, a phrasing that seems intended to identify Babylon, as per Genesis 11, as the world-center proposed by man.

It is highly significant that in Mark 14:58 an evident allusion is made to Daniel 2:34 with the following words: "We heard him say, I will destroy this temple that is made with hands, and within three days I will build another made without hands." Mark's irony is sublime. Jesus' enemies are convicted by their slander of Jesus. The present temple is idolatrous, "made with hands." But it will be replaced by the temple "made without hands," the representation of the unadulterated reign of God. The temple is the locus of divine rule—the implication of the opening verses of the book. This raises questions as to what future shape the rule of God will assume in the time of the kings

183. See Siegman, "Stone," 370–71; Nelson, *Daniel,* 88.

184. *Daniel,* 48.

185. Vogel, "Cultic Motifs," 26.

186. See Kim, *Biblical Interpretation,* 88.

187. Dumbrell, *Faith of Israel,* 260.

of this world; the time when history will be characterized by the sustained domination of a humanistic empire which parodies the image of God in the form of the blasphemous statue. Daniel and his friends are inseparably linked to Zion. It is even true that God's rule works through the prophecies of Daniel to effect the end of human reigns. For Daniel's word is not merely predictive. It is the word of God, which effects that which it declares.

Returning to Collins' view above, it is baffling to understand why Collins finds Nebuchadnezzar's response to be inexplicable apart from the interpretation he offers. How would he have responded if he had had a nightmare of a dream, as Nebuchadnezzar had done, and had had someone tell him what is impossible for another to know—the precise details of what he had seen only in his own head and never divulged to any other person? This is nothing short of a most astounding miracle which displays the truly magnificent nature of God's sovereignty. Thus Collins's whole approach to this matter is distorted by his failure to accept the essential historicity of the event.

The fifth kingdom, as noted above, is set up "in the time of those kings." Thus the dream and its interpretation are immensely relevant to the historical situation depicted in Daniel. "The rock" describes a rule that is set up during the reign of Nebuchadnezzar and extends down to the end of that phase of history characterized by blasphemous anti-God rule. Certainly this rock ultimately becomes the rule of Christ,[188] but this is not its initial form. Daniel and his three friends are expressions of this rule epitomized by the rock. Daniel and his friends are themselves primary evidence of the fact that "the kingdom of God," that is, God's dynamic rule, is being set up even in the time of the reign of the first king, symbolized by the head of gold, that is, Nebuchadnezzar. Daniel and his friends evidence the fact that this kingdom will never be destroyed, and the very next chapter which tells of how God delivers Shadrach, Meshach, and Abednego from the fiery furnace is designed to drive home this truth. Similarly the deliverance narrative of Daniel 6 achieves the same purpose.

The Association of Humanistic Rule with Idolatry

It is of immense importance to recognize that the word translated "statue" is the Aramaic word *tselem*, "image," which precisely corresponds to the

188. Irenaeus (130–200 AD) taught that the stone which smashes the statue is Jesus, that is, not conceived through any human agent (sc. virgin birth). Jesus will destroy temporal kingdoms and fill the earth and establish an eternal kingdom. In *Against Marcion* Tertullian identifies the stone with the church. Cyprian maintained the stone was Christ but that he would fill the earth through spiritual children born to him and his bride the church. Gammie, "A Journey," 144, 146, 149.

Hebrew word *tselem*, "image." We have here a clear allusion to the creation of human beings in the "image" (*tselem*) of God (Gen 1:26,27; 5:3; 9:6). That it is a "clear" allusion is made apparent at Daniel 2:38. Nebuchadnezzar is described with language taken from Genesis 1:28 (via Jer 27:5–8 and Ps 8: 6–8) in describing the role assigned by God to Nebuchadnezzar.[189] This is not by way of endorsing Nebuchadnezzar's right to act as a New Adam, but by way of bringing out into the open the essential nature of such rule as exercised by Nebuchadnezzar.[190]

The word *tselem* is used eleven times in the very next chapter to describe the man-made idol set up by Nebuchadnezzar and, significantly, is sometimes used to denote idols in the Hebrew Bible (e.g. 2 Kgs 11:18; 2 Chron 23:17; Ezek 7:20; Amos 5:26). It may not have been obvious to Nebuchadnezzar, but to the Hebrew reader the dream interpretation plainly insinuates that the entire "statue" is a radical perversion of what it truly means for human beings to live and act as those created in God's image.

Given this, Collins is quite correct to read the "image of gold" (3:1) alongside "the gods of silver and gold, of bronze, iron, wood, and stone" (5:23), and to conclude that the metals in the dream of Daniel 2 correspond to idols.

Therefore, insofar as the redactor of Daniel 2 is interested in the content of the dream, he is concerned less with the future rule of the world than with the transcendent power of God to destroy all idols and the human kingdoms which worship them . . . The main emphasis of the dream and interpretation falls on the destruction of idolatry.[191]

Indeed, the image presented in verse 45 of a stone cut without hands is by way of contrasting it with idols which, as Old Testament writers often remind God's people, are made by the hands of people. Thus in this context the stone cut without hands contrasts with the idolatrous statue of Nebuchadnezzar's dream. Indeed, Siegman is confident that the "stoning" of the idolatrous statue recalls stoning as the punishment for seduction to idolatry (Deut 13:6, 10).[192]

189. Nelson also considers a possible allusion here to the hunting practices of Mesopotamian kings. He notes reliefs in which they are portrayed as hunting lions and sometimes putting wild animals in captivity, as expressions of their power. *Daniel*, 90.

190. The 4th century Syrian saint, Ephrem, in his *Hymns on Paradise*, comments: "The king of Babylon [sc. Nebuchadnezzar] resembled Adam king of the universe: both rose up against the one Lord and were brought low; He made them outlaws, casting them afar [sc. allusion to Dan 4]. Who can fail to weep, seeing that these free-born kings preferred slavery and servitude. Blessed is He who releases us so that His image might no longer be in bondage." Henze, "Nebuchadnezzar's Madness," 559.

191. *Apocalyptic Vision*, 44.

192. "The Stone Hewn," 370.

This implicit critique of the arrogant self-sufficiency of Nebuchadnez-zar's reign was already suggested by the loaded use of "Shinar" in Daniel 1:2, and this same issue is developed in Daniel 3 with Nebuchadnezzar's self-glorifying construction of the idolatrous statue, and is explicitly brought to a head in Daniel 4 which focuses on God's judgment upon Nebuchadnez-zar's conceit. Thus, the application of Adamic language to Nebuchadnez-zar in 2:38 indicates that his kingship is fundamentally a perversion of the image; it is idolatrous in a rudimentary manner. By way of cementing this point nothing could be more natural than to move from the dream statue of Daniel 2, with its implications of Nebuchadnezzar's reign involving image-perversion, to the blatantly idolatrous statue of Daniel 3.

NEBUCHADNEZZAR'S RESPONSE (2:46–49)

> Then King Nebuchadnezzar fell prostrate before Daniel and paid him honor and ordered that an offering and incense be presented to him.
>
> The king said to Daniel, "Surely your God is the God of gods and the Lord of kings and a revealer of mysteries, for you were able to reveal this mystery."
>
> Then the king placed Daniel in a high position and lavished many gifts on him. He made him ruler over the entire province of Babylon and placed him in charge of all its wise men.
>
> Moreover, at Daniel's request the king appointed Shadrach, Meshach, and Abednego administrators over the province of Babylon, while Daniel himself remained at the royal court.[193]

This is an ironic passage because, if our interpretation has been cor-rect, it indicates the beginnings of the fulfillment of that which Daniel has already foreseen in the dream and his interpretation: the setting up of the fifth reign. The irony is that Nebuchadnezzar himself, in exalting Daniel and his three friends, becomes the instrument of God's rule, in setting up that to which his own rule is inextricably opposed in its essence. Perhaps it is even the case, though we cannot be sure, that here "Daniel epitomizes the Jewish people who, on behalf of their God, will receive the submission of the nations."[194]

---

193. "Court" is literally "gate." Harman notes that this is not a surprising usage since the gate of the city was the place where justice was often administered and where prop-erty transactions were carried out, *Daniel,* 74.

194. Anderson, *Signs and Wonders,* 26, summarizing Lacocque's proposal.

Nebuchadnezzar falls prostrate before Daniel and accords him honor. Goldingay summarizes three contexts in the Hellenistic world which would occasion such behavior on the part of a king: (1) the honoring of a benefactor; (2) the "demythologizing" of deified kings; (3) honoring the God Daniel represents.[195] According to Josephus, on one occasion Alexander the Great behaved similarly in paying homage to the high priest of Jerusalem and explained he was not worshiping the man but the God whom he represented.[196]

In this case Nebuchadnezzar is overwhelmed by the magnitude of the miracle performed by Daniel. His words honor God.[197] Yet the stress of the text is on the way in which Nebuchadnezzar behaves before Daniel and treats him. For Nebuchadnezzar "god" is subordinated to Daniel.

Nor must we miss the satire, the biting yet humorous tone of which has pervaded the entire chapter. It is ludicrous for Nebuchadnezzar to prostrate himself before an exile and the image painted here belittles and makes fun of him. As Valeta expresses it so well: "He has been turned from a vicious, violent victor to a snivelling, submissive supplicant."[198]

Farrar,[199] Fewell,[200] and some Talmudic texts[201] criticize Daniel for accepting this homage. But this is to misread the text. What is indicated here is that Nebuchadnezzar still has not got the essential point and that something else is needed to drive the point home; hence the next chapter and what follows.

There is a marked and apparently deliberate similarity between Daniel and Joseph.

> Both were captives at the royal court, both succeeded where the
> professionals failed, both were promoted as a result, and most
> important, both operated in an Israel that stood before an exo-
> dus, a major impending change."[202]

195. *Daniel*, 52.

196. Hartman, adopting this reading of the passage, follows Montgomery: Anderson, *Signs and Wonders*, 25.

197. Widder observes the contrast between Nebuchadnezzar and the Pharaoh of Genesis 41 who gives no indication that he acknowledges the sovereign superiority of Joseph's God. "Court Stories," 1116.

198. Valeta, *Lions*, 77.

199. *Daniel*, 50.

200. *Circle*, 36–37.

201. Anderson, *Signs and Wonders*, 26.

202. Dumbrell, *Faith of Israel*, 260. Similarly, Hamilton proposes that Daniel saw himself as a new Joseph preparing the way for a new exodus; *Clouds*, 227, 231.

A leading characteristic of the wise is their ability to understand and use riddles and parables.[203] Daniel, like Joseph, rightly is placed in charge of all the wise men of the court because he alone will be able to decipher and decode the ultimate messages received by the king, messages from the Most High, since they involve images, metaphors, and language, the significance of which only a Jew like Daniel could understand.

In closing it is essential to pay particular attention to the direct speech climax of verse 47: "The king said to Daniel, 'Surely your God is the God of gods and the Lord of kings and a revealer of mysteries, for you were able to reveal this mystery.'" In the exilic context God's kingship is not revealed in military conquest but in the transcendent wisdom he imparts, a wisdom inaccessible to man. It has also been revealed in the way that the "one language" of Babylon could not reach into heaven to grasp this wisdom. The very media of dreams are used by God to highlight the transcendence of divine language, inaccessible to humans unless revealed.[204]

A POPULAR APPROACH TO IDENTIFYING THE FOUR KINGDOMS

The interpretation which follows, as noted by Anderson,

> . . . is to be found consistently in the Talmud . . . and among medieval Jewish commentators . . . This lead has been followed, in the main, within traditional Judaism . . . Early Christian exegesis tended to be influenced by the earlier Jewish identification of the fourth kingdom with the secular Roman empire.[205]

Walton observes that this is not just a recent consensus, for Luther commented, " . . . in this interpretation and opinion all the world are agreed, and history and fact abundantly establish it."[206]

203. See Olojede, "More than a Prophet?" 954.

204. See Kim, *Biblical Interpretation*, 74–76: "Here we find the analogy in function between the common language in Genesis 11 and the dream vision in Daniel 2. In both biblical chapters God is shown as manipulating language to subdue rebels in Babel. Fascinatingly, the author of Daniel 2 modifies the character of God, the Master of language in control of Babel. In Genesis God thwarts Nimrod's building project in Babel, precluding the tower-builders from understanding *their* own language (Gen 11:7). In Daniel, by contrast, God frustrates Nebuchadnezzar's political project for Babel, preventing imperial intelligentsia from understanding *God's* language."

205. *Daniel*, 21–22.

206. Walton, " Four Kingdoms," 25. Holm, *Courtiers*, 428, compares the interpretation of Nebuchadnezzar's dream with that provided in the *Oracle of Hystaspes* which divides history into seven periods and predicts the end of Rome.

With sweeping and dubious assumptions as to the origins and identification of the four kingdoms, Breed illustrates how the popular view
has been re-applied by some so-called "Christian fundamentalists" and
dispensationalists.[207]

Here is a popular way of identifying the four kingdoms:[208]

Daniel 2	Daniel 7	Daniel 8	Empire
Head of gold	Beast like lion with eagle's wings		Babylon
Chest and arms of silver	Bearlike beast	Ram with two horns	Medo-Persia
Belly and thighs of bronze	Beast like "leopard/panther" with bird's wings	Goat with prominent horn	Greece
Legs and feet of iron and clay	Terrifying beast with large iron teeth		Rome

Inevitably there is considerable controversy as to which kingdoms are
referred to by which metal. Some[209] would prefer the following structure:

Head	Gold	Babylon
Chest and arms	Silver	Media
Belly and hips	Bronze	Persia
Legs	Iron	Alexander's kingdom
Feet	Iron and clay pottery, mixed	Alexander's divided kingdom

Anderson provides a number of inconclusive arguments for this position:[210]

1. It is compatible with Daniel 11.

207. See Breed, "Daniel's four Kingdom Schema," 182. Breed simply declares that
the four kingdoms are the Babylonians, Medes, Persians, and Greeks, and that the
multiple-kingdoms schema originated in Persia. He notes how the schema was typically
used as propaganda for the kingdom which was last in the sequence and sees Daniel 2
as converting propaganda into oppositional literature.

208. So many scholars, e.g., Wood, *Daniel*, 38–39. See Anderson, *Signs and Wonders*, 21.

209. For example, Hartman and Di Lella, *Book of Daniel*, 69. See too Davies, *Daniel*,
28–29; Towner, *Daniel*, 36; Nelson, *Daniel*, 90.

210. *Daniel*, 22–23.

2. It accords with the schema of Herodotus (fifth century BC) and Ctesias (fourth century BC) who both adopted the order Assyria, Media, and Persian.

3. Certain prophetic passages isolate the role of Media in the destruction of Babylon: Isaiah 13:17; Jer 51:11, 28–29.

4. This schema makes the entire book relevant to the first addressees of this book whereas the Roman empire lay beyond their experience. This presupposes that Daniel is preoccupied with the atrocities committed by Antiochus and is to be dated in this period.

The distinguishing of the Median empire from the Persian empire is problematic because Media ceased to exist as an independent kingdom some eleven years prior to the fall of Babylon. Further Daniel 8:3–4 provides evidence that the book of Daniel presupposes a unified Medo-Persian empire.

In weighing these competing views, a major bone of contention is the identification of the fourth kingdom. Above we see there is a tradition of understanding the fourth kingdom to be identifiable with Greece.[211] Young[212] explains why the Roman view came to the ascendancy in New Testament times:

1. Our Lord identified himself as the Son of Man, the heavenly figure of Daniel 7, and connected the "abomination of desolation" with the future destruction of the Temple (e.g., Matt 24).

2. Paul used the language of Daniel 7 to describe the Antichrist, and the book of Revelation employed the symbolism of Daniel 7 to refer to powers that were then existent and future.

Wood finds a stress on the toes in Daniel 2:42 and from this concludes there is an implicit correspondence with the ten horns of the fourth beast of Daniel's vision in 7:7. He proposes that since in ancient history Rome never had ten contemporaneous kings that Daniel's vision of ten toes must presage a restored form of the Roman empire.[213] Needless to say this is all highly speculative and all the more so since there is in fact no explicit reference to ten toes at all in Daniel 2. Assuming this speculative position, Wood goes on to argue that the complete destruction of the image from one blow of the stone must be an implicit reference to the second coming of Christ which will result in the establishment of his millenial kingdom.

---

211. See Gurney, "The Four Kingdoms;" Mendez, *Hellenistic World*.

212. Summarized by Walton, "Four Kingdoms," 26.

213. *Daniel*, 39–40.

The identification of the fourth beast with Rome was quite understand-ably adopted in Jewish traditions[214] reflecting a time when the Roman empire was firmly in place. In the first century AD the Apocalypse of Baruch (39:1–8) may identify the fourth beast with Rome. 4 Ezra (12:10–12) is clearer: an eagle with twelve wings is likened to the fourth beast of Daniel and identified by cryptic description as Rome. Further, Josephus openly states "Daniel also wrote concerning the Roman government, and that our country should be made desolate by them" and the Talmud consistently adopts this view, quot-ing Rabbi Johanan's view that the fourth kingdom is Rome.

Since the Church Fathers also lived during the time of the Roman em-pire it is not surprising that they too typically identified the fourth kingdom with Rome; e.g., Irenaeus, Hippolytus, and Origen.

Walton identifies three common evangelical positions that identify Rome with the fourth kingdom:

> (1) The fourth empire and the ten horns are all in the past, and the kingdom of God is represented and fulfilled in the Church. Fulfillment is viewed as complete. This view is at least as old as Augustine. (2) The fourth kingdom is still in power through the continued influence (political, religious, cultural, etc.) of the Roman empire, but the ten-horns stage is still future. An early proponent of this view is Jerome, and it seems to be the most popular view, historically speaking. But it is held by very few today because of the historical difficulties. (3) The fourth kingdom is over, and we are now in a prophetic gap that will end when a ten-nation confederacy reconstitutes the Roman empire. This view is scarce, if not nonexistent, prior to the nineteenth century.[215]

Despite such traditions, although the New Testament does take up Daniel 7, there are no clear grounds within the New Testament for identify-ing the fourth kingdom with Rome. Indeed in Revelation 13 John speaks of one beast, not four (see above exegesis for further reasons for disassociating the identification of the fourth kingdom from Rome).

It is common for commentators to understand the mix of iron and clay as an allusion to the division of Alexander's empire into smaller kingdoms. The NIV speaks of a "divided kingdom" (v. 41) but there is no reference to a process of division, only a description of the existing state of the fourth "kingdom." Goldingay points out the word rendered "clay" actually "sug-gests decorative tiling or potsherds . . . , tatty decoration when strength of

214. See Walton, "Four Kingdoms," 36.
215. "Four Kingdoms," 28.

structure is really needed."[216] Indeed it is arguable, as Goldingay suggests, that the notion is either of an internally divided "kingdom" or of a "composite kingdom." Since, as we have noted, the first "kingdom" is actually the first "reign," namely of Nebuchadnezzar, it is perhaps better with respect to the so-called fourth "kingdom" to think rather of a fourth "reign" which is weakened by the fact that the king concerned is too much concerned about his own image before his subjects and not sufficiently about the strength of his position. If, as I have suggested, the four reigns are representative of all rules in all ages from Nebuchadnezzar's own rule to the end of that period of history characterized by blasphemous anti-God rule, then it is dubious that the fourth reign can be identified with Alexander's divided empire.

SUMMARY

Daniel 2 continues to develop two fundamental aspects introduced in Daniel 1: the distinctiveness of the *maskilim*, as epitomized by Daniel, and the continuing and overarching sovereignty of God, notwithstanding Babylonian power. The following represent key features of Daniel 2:

1. To prepare God's people for suffering under blasphemous rule, Daniel is portrayed in terms which especially recall the experience of Joseph, but also that of Israel in Egypt and Moses as well.

2. The reader is invited to enter the thought world of the Chaldeans.

3. Nebuchadnezzar's claim to absolute sovereignty is belied by the impotence of his own resources, as represented by his personally trained Chaldeans, to meet the threat to his rule posed by his nightmare.

4. God-given wisdom differs from Babylonian wisdom not only in degree but also in kind.

5. God now reveals his sovereignty by the granting of unique, otherwise inaccessible knowledge. This demonstrates that:
   - There is no other god comparable to God.
   - God controls history.
   - God "lives among men," that is, with the *maskilim*, as epitomized by Daniel.

6. All expressions of human rule, as epitomized by the Babylonian empire with Nebuchadnezzar as its head, are one of a kind. For all its

216. *Daniel*, 35; cf. Walvoord, *Daniel*, 69–70.

glory and power, human rule is always vulnerable and ultimately will be destroyed by God's eternal kingdom, vested in his saints.

7. The arrogant self-sufficiency of human rule, as epitomized by Nebuchadnezzar, is an idolatrous perversion of the *Imago Dei* (Gen 1:28).

POINTS OF CONTACT WITH THE NEW TESTAMENT AND WITH LIFE

1. The distinction between Daniel's wisdom and that of the Chaldeans is mirrored in the difference between the wisdom of God and the wisdom of the world in 1 Corinthians 1:20–21, 30; 2:6–16; 3:18–23. Here again God's wisdom is concerned with revelation and displays God's awesome control of history. The "rulers of this age" do not control history and act in an ignorant and blasphemous, God-defying manner (1 Cor 2:8).

2. 1 Corinthians 15:24 anticipates the eschatological triumph of the kingdom of God, consequent upon the destruction of all anti-God rule by Christ. Here, as in Daniel 2, all anti-God rule (human and demonic) is monolithic in nature.

3. John's depiction of Babylon in Rev 14:8; 16:19 and 17–18 bears close correspondence with the presentation of human rule in Daniel 2. In the first instance, the four reigns represented by the statue in Daniel 2 concern a single, "Babylonian" empire which, as in Revelation, epitomizes arrogant, idolatrous human rule in all its manifestations.

POSSIBLE SERMON OUTLINE

Title: "Wise Guys" (the chapter hinges on the distinction between the impotence of Chaldean wisdom and the awesome nature of divinely revealed wisdom, through Daniel)

1. *Control freak.* Nebuchadnezzar's rage expresses his sense that he does not have the absolute control he covets. But Nebuchadnezzar loses far more than his temper. He comes to realize that he cannot control knowledge of the future and, even more importantly, cannot control the future itself.

2. *Clueless.* When it comes to being able to relate the details of Nebuchadnezzar's dream the Chaldeans are completely helpless. Nebuchadnezzar refuses to give them any clues because he doesn't want to hear
a cleverly constructed case built on circumstantial evidence but wants
to get to the bottom of the mystery which so troubles him.

3. *Clay feet.* Human rule, in all its manifestations, is like an impressive
statue which is ready to topple. Once shattered, it will be replaced by
God's everlasting kingdom.

Daniel 3

The Unbowed

Ultimate Commitment to Distinctiveness: God's Sovereignty Revealed in Rescuing his Servants from the Place of Certain Destruction

INTRODUCTION

Most scholars recognize there is considerable similarity between the stories of Daniel 3 and Daniel 6. However, there is no consensus as to what genre they represent. Nickelsburg designates them "wisdom tales." Hartman and Di Lella disagreed as to whether this story is primarily a martyr story or a court tale. Porteous argued that there are two kinds of martyr stories. In one type the martyr is faithful to death and in the other a miracle occurs and the hero is saved.[1] However, it is much more satisfactory to read this chapter as a Menippean-like satire. As Valeta observes, "The overall effect of Daniel 3

---

1. See Milne, *Vladimir Propp*, 239–42. Milne is able to demonstrate that Propp's model is much more applicable to Daniel 3 and 6 than to Daniel 1, 2, 4 or 5 (239–56). She concludes, however, that though both of these stories share many of the structural elements belonging to the fairy tale, nevertheless neither Daniel 3 nor Daniel 6 can be described as an heroic fairy tale on the basis of structure (254).

is a portrayal of a king who blusters and splutters, issuing royal commands that are in the end thwarted and frustrated."[2]

Gooding's recognition that in addition to the offsetting of chapters 3 and 6 there is a pairing of chapters 2 and 3 leads to an interesting observation. In both chapters Nebuchadnezzar is taught about the limits of Gentile imperial power. In chapter 2 the interpretation of the dream teaches that a predetermined limit is set to the *tenure* of imperial power, whatever form it might assume in history. Chapter 3 adds to this by teaching that "a limit must be set to the scope and exercise of political power." As Gooding puts it: "the imperial political power must not lay claim to that loyalty and devotion on the part of its subjects generally, and of Jews in particular, that is properly reserved for God alone."[3]

STRUCTURE

Breakdown

The King Implicates All People in Idolatry (1–7)

> Exaltation of the Image in the Province of Babylon (1)
> The King, in Control, Commands: Implication of all Leaders in Idolatry (2)
> Obedience is Complete and Voluntary (3)
> The King, in Control, Commands: Implication of all People in Idolatry (4–5)
> The Fire: The King's Extreme Penalty for Failure to Commit Idolatry (6)
> Obedience is Complete, Voluntary, and Instantaneous: all Commit Idolatry (7)

The Disobedient Jews: Identified and Confronted (8–18)

> The King is Reminded of his Command: Idolatry Reinforced (8–10)
> The King is Reminded of his Extreme Penalty for Disobedience (11)
> The King is Disobeyed! Idolatry Undermined (12)

2. *Lions*, 87.
3. "Literary Structure," 62.

The King Out of Control Commands (Summons) (13a)
Obedience is Forced (13b)
The King Confronts the Reported Disobedience: Idolatry De-
manded (14)
The King Commands ["Back to square two"]: Idolatry Demand-
ed (15a)
The King's Extreme Penalty for Disobedience (Failure to Com-
mit Idolatry) (15b)
Fire is Place of Certain Destruction: King Denies any God can
Rescue them (15c)
The Jews Claim God can Rescue them from the Place of Certain
Destruction (16–17)
The Three Jews Refuse to Commit Idolatry (18)

Into the Place of Certain Destruction (19–23)

Execution of the Extreme Penalty: The King Out of Control
Commands (19–20)
Execution of the Extreme Penalty: Obedience is Complete (21)
The Fire as the Place of Certain Destruction: Extreme Penalty is
Inescapable (22)
The Jews in the Place of Certain Destruction: Extreme Penalty
Experienced (23)
[C[The Rescue (24–27)
Rescue from the Place of Certain Destruction: God the Savior
(24–25)
Rescue (cont'd): The King Summons the Three Men from the
Fire (26a)
Rescue (cont'd): Obedience is Complete (26b)
Examination: Rescue from the Fire Complete (27)

The King Exalts God and Jews who Undermined his Plan (28–30)

The King Acknowledges God Rescued them (28a)
The Uncompromising Refusal of the Three Jews to Commit
Idolatry is Commended (28b)
The King Orders Extreme Penalty for all who Blaspheme God
(29a)
The King Acknowledges God is a Unique Saviour (29b)
Exaltation of the Three Jews in the Province of Babylon (30)

Broad Outline

- The King implicates all in idolatry to secure a united kingdom (1–7)
- Disunity is injected by non-idolatrous Jews who are identified and confronted (8–18)
- The non-compliant Jews are consigned to a place of certain destruction (19–23)
- The Jews are miraculously rescued from the place of certain destruction (24–27)
- The King exalts God, the Rescuer, and the Jews who made a united kingdom impossible (28–30)

For those who like chiastic structures the one proposed by Lucas is appealing[4]:

A Nebuchadnezzar's decree to worship the golden image (1–7)
   B The Jews accused (8–12)
      C The Jews threatened (13–15)
         D The Jews confess their faith (16–18)
      C' The Jews punished (19–23)
   B' The Jews vindicated (24–27)
A' Nebuchadnezzar's decree honouring the Jews and their God

THE MAJOR MOTIFS OF DANIEL 3

A. Exaltation in the province of Babylon (1, 30)

B. The King demands idolatry: implication of leaders and people in idolatry (2–5, 7–10, 13a–15a)

C. The King's extreme penalty and place of certain destruction: Fire/Cutting to pieces and reducing houses to rubble (6, 11, 15bc, 19–23, 29a)

D. Refusal of the three Jews to commit idolatry (12, 18, 28b)

E. Rescue from the place of certain destruction: God as savior (16–17, 24a–28a)

F. The King acknowledges God to be unique as Savior (29b)

---

4. *Daniel*, 86.

The chapter begins with heavy emphasis on King Nebuchadnezzar's attempt to implicate all in his idolatry (note the heavy concentration of verses under "B"), and ends with great stress on God's ability to save his people from the place of certain destruction (note a heavy concentration of verses under "E"). The middle of the chapter emphasizes that the fire is the place of certain destruction ("C"). This prepares the reader to share Nebuchadnezzar's amazement that anyone should survive, and to confess with him: "for no other god can save in this way."

THE IMPORTANCE OF REPETITION

The repetition that marks the narrative probably presupposes the account will be read out loud to Jewish listeners. If so, it would no doubt have induced laughter and succeeded in mocking idolatry:

> You can almost imagine Jews sitting in a synagogue hearing the passage read out and laughing among themselves as they conjured up in their minds a picture of the great ones of the Babylonian world bowing and scraping in unison to the sound of music.[5]

Further, as Avalos remarks, "In effect, the iteration of enumerations helps to portray those pagans as a version of Pavlov's dog."[6]

It should also be observed how the device of repetition is skillfully used to build up tension, especially to underscore the immense peril into which the three courageous, unflinching Jews place themselves: they are defying the greatest king on earth whose will is law, whose every command is unquestioningly and unhesitatingly obeyed. Further Nebuchadnezzar is an exceedingly dangerous king known for his explosive temper and possessing terrifying power to secure the utter destruction of all who meet with his displeasure. Can there be any other future in resisting such a king than a horrible and certain death?

To develop this drama we are reminded over and over again how what the king commands and says goes. It is unthinkable to stand in the path of this steamroller of a monarch! Over and over again it is stressed how all people accept the idolatrous worship enjoined by Nebuchadnezzar. How completely isolated are these puny three Jews! Is not their defiance of pathetic proportions?

---

5. Reid, *Kingdoms*, 77; cf. Gooding, "Literary Structure," 52.
6. Avalos, "Comedic Function," 585.

The certain death that awaits them is emphasized by a number of points of repetition. Three times we are reminded that they were tied up by Nebuchadnezzar's strongest soldiers. The wrath of Nebuchadnezzar is emphasized by repetition and, significantly, is immediately linked to the death-dealing heat of the inferno. Twice we are told how the furnace is heated to an extraordinarily high temperature.[7] Of course, death for the defiant was already certain, so the increasing of the temperature signifies the immense fury of the king against these little upstarts. It is a terrifying thing to resist this awesomely powerful king who holds the power of life and death in his hand. How hopeless and pointless their stubbornness now appears!

NEBUCHADNEZZAR'S ATTEMPT TO REMOVE ALL WEAKNESS FROM HIS KINGDOM

The statue clearly connects with the dream-statue of the previous chapter.[8] In Daniel 2, Daniel had explained to Nebuchadnezzar that the Chaldean empire would one day topple because of an inherent weakness within it, for a king will eventually rule over a seriously disunited people. Daniel 3 begins with Nebuchadnezzar's apparent attempt to root out of his kingdom any possibility of such disunity occurring. To do this he sets up an enormous image of gold (90 feet high by 9 feet wide/27.5 by 2.75 meters)[9] in the province of Babylon and requires all his leaders and the peoples of all nations and languages to unite in falling down before, and worshiping the image of gold. Furthermore, the chapter commences by stressing how the king's imperious will is in fact obeyed. At first sight it does appear the king has succeeded in his strategy.

There appears to be a consensus among scholars that the plain of Dura (Dura means "a walled place") was located in the region south of Babylon near Hilla.[10] However, if Edward Cook is right[11] then the relevant phrase should be translated "in the plain of the wall in the city of Babylon" and, on this basis, presumably portrays the image as being set up in the plain

7. That is, "seven times hotter than usual" = as hot as possible.

8. Hebbard favours Longman's assessment as to the implication of this correlation: "behind every idol is the self." *Reading Daniel*, 93.

9. Walvoord notes Leupold's comparisons of the image with that of Zeus in a Babylonian temple; the golden images on top of the Belus temple with one reaching 40 cubits high; and the famous Colossus of Rhodes which stood 70 cubits high (*Daniel*, 80).

10. Anderson, *Signs and Wonders*, 30. For further discussion see Walvoord, *Daniel*, 81–82.

11. Cook, "In the Plain of the Wall," 115–16. Cook takes the "area" also to be referring not to a province but to the city of Babylon.

between Nimit-Enlil, the great outer wall built by Nebuchadnezzar and described in detail by Herodotus, and the city proper. More significantly, the reference to the "building" of this image on any plain in Babylon necessarily evokes memory of the building of the tower of Babel on a plain in the land of Shinar (Gen 11:2, 9).[12]

A lot of ink has been spilled in trying to determine the nature of the statue. Was it a stele? Was it a statue of Nebuchadnezzar himself?[13] Was it a statue of Nebuchadnezzar's god? If so, which one? Whatever the physical appearance of the statue it is plain from verses 12 and 18 that worship of the image was intimately associated with worship of Nebuchadnezzar's gods.

There is an obvious correspondence in all this with the Tower of Babel episode (Gen 11). It is as though Nebuchadnezzar is recapitulating the way in which (in terms of biblical polemic) Babylon began. On that occasion God judged the Babel builders, recognizing that the extraordinary unity they had achieved would enable them all the more to endeavor to control the course of history and, unitedly, defy him. God therefore injected disunity into the situation. Now in Daniel 3, Nebuchadnezzar is fighting to assert his right to hold the reins of history[14] and he too relies on an extraordinary unity to effect this. Recalling Genesis 11, Nebuchadnezzar may even be trying to overcome the potentially divisive nature of human language by replacing it with the sound of music.[15] But in actuality the traces of disunity, which will ultimately lead to the fall of the Chaldean empire, are already present, in an embryonic form, within Nebuchadnezzar's very own empire.

Significantly, it is God's people, as represented by the three Jews, who undermine Nebuchadnezzar's policy. As our analysis of the structure of the chapter would seem to indicate, there is an inclusio of sorts formed by the contrast between the way the chapter begins: with the exaltation of the image of gold "in the province of Babylon," and the way the chapter ends: with the exaltation of the three Jews "in the province of Babylon."

Also, in the early portion of Daniel 3, Nebuchadnezzar imposes an extreme penalty on all who would dishonor his image of gold, while the chapter closes with a similar extreme penalty being leveled against all who would dishonor God. Ironically, at the end of proceedings, Nebuchadnezzar is forced to accept that it is impossible for him to control the situation and

12. Kim, *Biblical Interpretation*, 95–96.

13. A view advanced by the priest Hippolytus in the early 3rd century AD. Anderson, *Signs and Wonders*, 30.

14. Others have also seen this implication, e.g., Anderson, *Signs and Wonders*, 30.

15. So Kim, *Biblical Interpretation*, 99–100.

enforce perfect unity in his kingdom. A measure of disunity is unavoidable simply because it is God, not Nebuchadnezzar, who really controls history.

This situation can only be so because God's supreme rule over the affairs of men is not reducible to a matter of doctrine, but is a reality. He *really does* control what happens in Nebuchadnezzar's kingdom, showing this through his miraculous rescue of the three Jews. Without God intervening in such a manner to protect and deliver his people, there would be nothing to stop despots like Nebuchadnezzar actually achieving their goal of complete unity along with a real and actual control of the course history will take. Thus Daniel 3 must not be regarded as legend for to do so is to undermine the whole theology of Daniel. God actually did what he is described as doing, no matter how unusual and extraordinary it now seems for many moderns. He *is* the God of the nations and the Lord of history.

But the implications of all this are even more profound. Not only does Daniel 3 reinforce the dream interpretation of Daniel 2 by drawing attention to the inevitability of disunity in the Babylonian empire as a manifestation of God's ultimate sovereignty, but it also draws attention to the means God will use to undermine such human rule.

Daniel 2 had revealed that it would be a stone or rock "cut out of a mountain, not by human hands" that would exploit the Achilles-like weakness of the world empire represented by the statue. In Daniel 3:12 Shadrach, Meshach, and Abednego are portrayed by Chaldeans, in an evidently derogatory fashion, as "some Jews" who, because they are Jews should not be doing what they are in fact doing (an implicit criticism of the king—a yet further indication of disunity?), that is, exercising positions of responsibility with respect to the affairs of the province of Babylon. Yet just prior to this we have read: "as soon as they heard the sound of [the musical instruments], all the peoples, nations and men of every language fell down and worshiped the image of gold that King Nebuchadnezzar had set up." Thus the "Jews" are set in contrast with all other peoples in the world. It is Jews alone who refuse to comply with Nebuchadnezzar's demands.

In Daniel 3 it is stressed that Shadrach, Meshach, and Abednego are Jews (vv. 8, 12) and it is they who succeed in thwarting Nebuchadnezzar's universalistic ploy. Not that they do so actively or with any intention of undermining Nebuchadnezzar's right to rule. Nor, even in a passive way, do they deliberately seek to issue a telling protest against Nebuchadnezzar's policy. Rather, in this chapter they are portrayed as completely passive. And this complete passivity extends to their rescue, and indeed, from a literary standpoint, prepares for the decisive role God himself will assume as their savior.

Notwithstanding this passivity, it is these Jews whom God uses to entrench disunity in the Chaldean empire, the very kind of disunity which will ultimately make such a world empire fatally vulnerable. These three men represent a rule which is not constructed by human hands; a rule which, within the terms of reference set down by the book of Daniel, is associated with the Jewish people, a people whose identity is inseparably tied up with Jerusalem and the temple, that is, with "the mountain."

Therefore, Daniel 3 begins to explain how the people of God are "the rock" God uses to topple the world empire. In this connection Daniel's own prophetic role in Daniel 2 must not be ignored. When Daniel relayed God's word to Nebuchadnezzar, it was not merely as a messenger boy, but as one who's very identity, in the mind of Nebuchadnezzar, was inextricably tied up with the God he represented. Consequently, Daniel, like all other Old Testament prophets, uttered a word which itself was dynamic, and effective, and achieved the very purposes it pronounced. When Daniel told Nebuchadnezzar what God had shown to the king concerning future events, he was simultaneously God's effective instrument in bringing that future to pass. Therefore, the fall of the world empire is in a very real way achieved by Daniel and his fellow Jews. Ultimately it is his own people whom God uses to bring about the demise of blasphemous, defiant human rule.

There are scholars who reject the historicity of Daniel 3 on the grounds that there is no historical evidence that the Babylonian empire practiced religious intolerance. Davies, commenting on such accounts of persecution in Daniel, maintains,

> These are not mere arguments from silence, for in the case of persecution the historically attested reluctance of Jews to leave Babylon (while remaining religiously as well as ethnically Jewish) suggests tolerance of their religion.[16]

But notwithstanding such a disclaimer Davies is presenting an argument from silence. His reasoning is illogical. Why should it be assumed, as he does, that the conditions of "tolerance" which existed at the time of return from exile were consistently observed all throughout the exilic period? Besides, Daniel 3 is not describing a general anti-Semitic policy but the king's specific response to a particular incident that happened to concern Jews. Further, and this is most important, Davies's conclusion is only possible because he rejects from the outset the relevant Danielic accounts as authentic historical sources themselves. Davies does not merely interpret Daniel. He sits in judgment on it and adopts the stance "Guilty till proved innocent!"

16. *Daniel,* 31.

THE IMAGE OF GOLD

What is the relationship, if any, of this image to the statue that Nebuchadnezzar dreamed about in Chapter 2?

Some scholars ignore the fact that chapter 2 has also spoken of a similar statue. Some contend that the statue represents the god Nabu, being Nebuchadnezzar's own god as the first part of his name indicates.[17]

It does seem very probable that there is a direct relationship with the prior dream[18]:

1. In both cases the identical word *slm* is used. Nebuchadnezzar is actually exaggerating his importance and trying to exceed the role God had accorded him in history. He was not content to be the head but wanted to be the whole body.

2. In the dream interpretation Nebuchadnezzar was informed that "the God of heaven will set up a kingdom that will never be destroyed" (2:44). Significantly, no less than five times in the opening verses of chapter 3 we are told that this image was "set up," symbolizing Nebuchadnezzar's own intent to "set up a kingdom that will never be destroyed."[19]

3. In 2:31 the point is made that it was a "large statue—an enormous, dazzling statue, awesome in appearance." Correspondingly in 3:1 we learn that the image set up by Nebuchadnezzar was 60 cubits (90 feet) high and 6 cubits (9 feet) wide and, therefore, so "disproportionately heavy at the top so as to be in danger of toppling."[20]

4. In his dream the statue had a head of gold (2:32), and Daniel explained to Nebuchadnezzar that this was a representation of Nebuchadnezzar himself. The statue became increasingly weak from the head down and this augured the collapse of the statue.

17. For example, Harman, *Daniel*, 75.

18. Beaulieu, "Babylonian Background," 276, cites Hippolytus of Rome's understanding of the statue as made by Nebuchadnezzar in memory of his dream: "For as the blessed Daniel, in interpreting the vision, had answered the king, saying, 'Thou art this head of gold in the image,' the king, being puffed up with this address, and elated in his heart, made a copy of this image, in order that it might be worshiped by all as God." Some scholars, who focus more on an attempt to reconstruct sources than the final literary form of the book, have supposed that the absence of Daniel from Daniel 3 "suggests the tale of the worship of the gold statue originated separately and was joined to the other tales of the cycle—including the story of the dream vision of the fourfold statue in ch. 2—at a later date." Beaulieu, "Babylonian Background," 277.

19. Similarly, Thompson, "Faith in Babylon."

20. Kim, *Biblical Interpretation*, 98.

The dream of chapter 2 had communicated to Nebuchadnezzar that there is a weakness in his kingdom. He may be the head of gold but he stands on feet that are too weak to support the weight of the kingdom and enable it to stand firm when God's time comes for it to be toppled. Consequently, he makes the image completely of gold as though to forestall the possibility of such weakness occurring.

In our study of Daniel 2 we suggested the statue as a unit represented human government as a whole and was therefore applicable to the entire course of human history. Notably, the recurrence of the number six, the number of man (see Rev 13:18),[21] in denoting the dimensions of the statue, underscore this stress on human rule. It may also involve a parody of the true worship associated with the Jerusalem temple, given that the statue's height equals the first temple's width and is twice its height (1 Kgs 6:2).[22] As noted above, Nebuchadnezzar's making of this image is probably a response to the dream of Daniel 2.[23] In the first instance the different segments of the dream-statue would seem to pertain to successive reigns in the Babylonian kingdom, so that the ultimate destruction of the statue is effectively a destruction of the Babylonian kingdom that in turn symbolizes all human government.

If Nebuchadnezzar took Daniel's interpretation in this way, as foretelling the disintegration and destruction of the kingdom of Babylon, then there is an obvious significance in Nebuchadnezzar's making of a statue that is composed entirely of gold,[24] whether it was made of solid gold or, as many scholars conclude, was deemed a gold statue simply because it was completely overlaid with gold (cf. Ex 30:3; Is 40:19; Jer 10:3–4). It represents Nebuchadnezzar's rejection of the meaning of the dream, an attempt on his part to change the course of history. As Valeta observes, "It is as if

21. So Walvoord, *Daniel*, 81 and Irenaeus, *Against Heresies*, Book 5, Chapter 29.2; 30.1.

22. See Pace, *Daniel*, 90. She also notes that the width of the statue corresponds to the width of the support beams of both the first and second temples. Observing the importance of gold in Solomon's temple she concludes: "These connotations suggest that the traditional association of gold with the holiness of God's temple is to be contrasted with the self-aggrandizing policies of Nebuchadnezzar." 91.

23. At another level Beaulieu, assuming "that behind the Danielic Nebuchadnezzar lurks a memory of the historical Nabonidus," further speculates that the image of Daniel 3 presupposes the "horrifying cult image of the god Sin" made by Nabonidus, as referred to in the Verse Account of Nabonidus. "Babylonian Background," 275–76. In my judgment it is reckless to draw such conclusions on the basis of such flimsy evidence.

24. It is irrelevant to this exegesis that such statues may not have been made of solid gold but were rather gold plated. In the first place, we simply do not know how this particular statue was made. Secondly, even if it were gold plated, the point still remains that to all intents and purposes it is a statue of gold.

Nebuchadnezzar tries to topple the dream by building a statue that is entirely gold."[25] Hence appropriately in this chapter we see Nebuchadnezzar's kingship not merely tested in the dream world but in the world of events, the realm of history.

In order for him to succeed in this venture Nebuchadnezzar must undo the weakness inherent in the structure of Babylonian rule. He thus seeks to make his rule over the people perfectly strong; a rule which all will obey without question. The first seven verses stress the compliance of all important personages, and of all peoples, nations, and men of every language. Nebuchadnezzar appears now to exercise total and absolute control. How can such complete rule ever be weakened?

Fewell proposes that Nebuchadnezzar is trying to establish political security to counter a currently perceived threat.[26] Her thinking is based on a dubious reading of Daniel 2 that sees Nebuchadnezzar's extreme response to the Chaldeans as being rooted in his well-founded suspicion that they are cooking up political intrigue against him. This is not theoretically impossible but it is hard to find any textual warrant for this conclusion. Besides, in chapter 3 Nebuchadnezzar is doing much more than using the statue as an instrument for imposing his absolute will upon his subjects. The statue is not just one of many such instruments that he might have used. The statue has inherent significance, as is indicated by the clear link with the statue of Nebuchadnezzar's dream in the preceding chapter.

It is plausible that Nebuchadnezzar is engaging in sympathetic magic, and that seeing the image as a representation of the Babylonian kingdom: he believes the image is virtually one and the same as the reality it represents. What happens to the image is what will happen to the kingdom. This principle of identification was a familiar one in the ancient world. It meant that a temple could be identified with the creation mount itself, and was not viewed as being merely a symbol of the creation mount. It meant that inscribing the names of ones enemies on a pottery vessel and then shattering it would cause the destruction of those enemies. It meant that food placed in a tomb with a corpse would feed the spirit of the deceased in the afterlife. My proposal is that the statue of gold is Nebuchadnezzar's way of trying to ensure that the Babylonian kingdom remain forever strong and resplendent—a kingdom of pure gold.

25. *Lions*, 80.
26. *Circle*, 67.

THE IMAGE OF GOLD AND THE IMAGE OF GOD

There are strong indications from the context that the reader is invited to compare the image of gold which Nebuchadnezzar erects with the portrayal of man in Genesis 1 as one created in the image of God.

1. In Daniel 2:37–38 the language of Genesis 1 is applied to Nebuchadnezzar. Clearly this does not mean that Nebuchadnezzar is a perfect representation of what God intended when he created man to function as his image. But the dominion which Nebuchadnezzar presently exercises over the world is akin to the rule Adam exercised. When we compare Nebuchadnezzar's rule with that intended for Adam it becomes apparent that Nebuchadnezzar's absolute rule is a parody of God-intended rule, a perversion of the image of God.[27] It is chapter 3 which brings this out more clearly.

   Adam was created to serve as God's vice-regent. Human rule which is consistent with the God-intended meaning of the *Imago Dei*, is an expression of God's own rule through human instrumentality, so that ultimately the glory, and attendant worship and praise, belongs to God and not to the human agent. By contrast Nebuchadnezzar's parody of the absolute rule, which God intended for man to exercise on his behalf, involves compelling people to worship, not God, but the image which Nebuchadnezzar has set up.

   Nebuchadnezzar's kingship is a perversion of the image of God and as such inevitably leads people into idolatry. It is the idolatrous nature of Nebuchadnezzar's kingship that ultimately explains the inherent weakness of his kingdom. While in the first instance the weakness in the feet of the statue is explained as disunity in a kingdom, now it is made clear that the fundamental cause of damaging disunity is idolatry. Thus Daniel 3 is seeped in irony: the very method Nebuchadnezzar employs to extirpate weakness from his kingdom is the very thing that breeds it.

2. The linkage of Babylon with Genesis traditions was forged at the outset of the book with the identification of Babylon as "the land of Shinar," a phrase that is calculated to recall Genesis 11.

3. The structure of 3:1–7 is evocative of the royal fiat–unquestioned obedience sequences of Genesis. The king commands and it is done.[28]

---

27. Dumbrell, *Faith of Israel*, 260–62. Dumbrell sees a counter-image of man and a counter-tree of life, and an underlying presupposition that Babylon is the New Eden.

28. Milne, *Vladimir Propp*, 242–43, seeking to apply Propp's model, argues that the proclamation of verses 4–6 does not constitute the Proppian function of villainy (she

Nebuchadnezzar is not content to be the agent of God's rule (2:37–38). In true Genesis 3 style he reaches out in blasphemous fashion to be "like God," to exercise absolute rule.

All people involved in verses 2–3 are identified by political status, and this serves to draw attention to the absolute control the king claims to have. The long list of verse 2, its repetition in verse 3, and the analogous listing of musical instruments in verse 5 all function as skillful literary devices that accentuate the solemnity of the ritual of obeisance which Nebuchadnezzar has introduced. The narrative stresses pomp more than it does the meaning of the ceremony associated with the image, and thereby it draws attention to the bombast of the king. The precise people he summons (v. 2) are the precise people who come—indicating again his seemingly absolute power. All the people bowing down underscores the absolute power of this king. The image of all peoples, nations, every language bowing down before the statue is one which rightfully should pertain to the worship of the Creator-King.

This opening section anticipates the latter developments of the chapter. Verse 4 has a purpose that goes beyond merely recording the absolute rule which Nebuchadnezzar imposes on all peoples, nations, and languages. The point is that if the Jews as a people were included in this description then they, by their worship of the image, would have lost their identity as Jews. Similarly "if the Jews of the Babylonian exile (or any kind of exile for that matter) had conformed completely to the culture in which they found themselves, there would be no Jewish nation; there would be no story to tell."[29]

BABYLONIAN IDOLATRY

It is difficult to overestimate the central and gargantuan importance of the Babylonian ruler. Oppenheim rightly observes, "From the point of view of Mesopotamian civilization, there was only one institution in the modern sense of the word: kingship."[30] The divinity of the Babylonian ruler differed from that of the Egyptian Pharaoh since it was not metaphysical but functional deity. That is, the king was adopted to be the servant of the gods and to maintain their rule. Though he remained a man—an exalted human being— his divine election resulted in him being endowed with "divine," supernatural qualities.

---

dubs this "the problematic situation") but rather corresponds to a function from "the prepatory section," namely "interdiction/command." As yet this has not emerged as a problem since initially all seem to comply with this command (v. 7).

29. Fewell, *Circle*, 60.

30. *Ancient Mesopotamia*, 98.

Daniel 3 presents an anomalous situation. The Babylonian king was never worshiped. However, evidently there was a time when Nebuchadnezzar effectively, even if not formally, sought to elevate himself to the level of the gods. That time is recorded for us in this chapter. It is crucial to note the recurrence of similar phrases in connection with the idolatry here described:

- King Nebuchadnezzar made an image of gold . . . and set it up on the plain of Dura . . . (v. 1).

- He then summoned the satraps et al. to come to the dedication of the image he had set up (v. 2).

- So the satraps et al. assembled for the dedication of the image that King Nebuchadnezzar had set up (v. 3).

- Then the herald loudly proclaimed, "This is what you are commanded to do, O peoples, nations and men of every language: As soon as you hear the sound of the horn, etc. you must fall down and worship the image of gold that King Nebuchadnezzar has set up" (vv. 4–5).

- Therefore, as soon as they heard the sound of the horn, etc. all the peoples, etc. fell down and worshiped the image of gold that King Nebuchadnezzar had set up (v. 7).

- At this time some astrologers came forward and denounced the Jews. They said to King Nebuchadnezzar, "O king, live forever! You have issued a decree, O king, that everyone who hears the sound of the horn, etc. must fall down and worship the image of gold . . . But there are some Jews . . . who pay no attention to you, O king. They serve neither your gods nor worship the image of gold you have set up" (vv. 8–12).

- Furious with rage, Nebuchadnezzar summoned Shadrach et al. . . . Nebuchadnezzar said to them, "Is it true, Shadrach, [et al.] that you do not serve my gods or worship the image of gold I have set up? Now when you hear the sound of the horn, . . . if you are ready to fall down and worship the image I made, very good. But if you do not worship it, you will be thrown immediately into a blazing furnace. Then what god will be able to rescue you from my hand?" (vv. 13–15).

- Shadrach et al. replied. . . . "O Nebuchadnezzar, we do not need to defend ourselves before you in this matter. If we are thrown into the blazing furnace, the God we serve is able to save us from it, and he will rescue us from your hand, O king. But even if he does not, we want you to know, O king, that we will not serve your gods or worship the image of gold you have set up" (vv. 16–18).

The following features are noteworthy:

1. The enormous stress laid upon the fact that Nebuchadnezzar, as king, made and set up the image. The use of personal pronouns is of considerable importance in understanding the idolatry described in Daniel 3. The Chaldeans tell the king that the three accused Jews do not serve "your gods" (v. 12).[31] Nebuchadnezzar says he is furious because these men "do not serve my gods" (v. 14). The three Jews enrage Nebuchadnezzar all the more when they tell him that they refuse to worship "your gods" (v. 18). The idolatry described in Daniel 3 is not so much a description of general Babylonian religion but an exposé of Nebuchadnezzar's own overreaching pretensions. Clearly the image was an expression of Nebuchadnezzar's claim to absolute and total rule.

2. The considerable accent placed upon the coercive nature of this idolatry. All people were forced to worship all that was represented by the image—Nebuchadnezzar's greatness as king and the gods who stood with him in his reign.

3. The image was not merely associated with the worship of Nebuchadnezzar's gods but was itself an object of worship as the expression of the greatness of Nebuchadnezzar's own rule.

4. Following on from the above points, Nebuchadnezzar, in what is tantamount to self-deification, pits himself against any god. He is so full of confidence in his own divine power that he pontificates that no god is capable of rescuing the three Jews from his hand. This brings us full circle back to how the book begins—with God delivering Jehoiakim and the temple articles into Nebuchadnezzar's hand (1:1). In the interpretation of his dream, Nebuchadnezzar was told that God had placed "mankind and the beasts of the field and the birds of the air" in his hands. Nebuchadnezzar effectively denies this reality. He believes that he himself has the absolute power of life and death in his hands—the prerogatives of deity alone.

The representation of Nebuchadnezzar's implicit self-deification is skillfully indicated by another literary emphasis. Nebuchadnezzar burns with rage at the refusal of the three Jews to worship his gods and the image he has set up (vv. 13, 18) and the heating of the furnace seven times[32] hotter than usual is an outward expression of the self-

---

31. They scurrilously insinuate that these Hebrew youths rebel against Nebuchadnezzar in a widespread manner, though in reality it is only with respect to this one issue. Goswell, *Daniel*, 23–24.

32. Incidentally, this furnishes another illustration of the symbolic use of numbers.

made god-king. The wrath of this "god" is a fire which it is impossible to escape.[33]

Incidentally, the above is also consistent with an observation made by Oppenheim:

> A large part of what we assume to be Mesopotamian religion has meaning only in relation to royal personages—and for this reason distorts our concepts. The religion of the priest was centered primarily on the image and temple; it was concerned with the service the image required—not only in sacrifices but also in hymns of praise—and with the apotropaic functions of these images for the community.

But the . . .

> . . . common man. . . remains an unknown, the most important unknown element in Mesopotamian religion. . . religion's claims on the private individual were extremely limited in Mesopotamia; prayers, fasts, mortification, and taboos were apparently imposed only on the king.
> A similar situation prevails with respect to divine communications. The king could receive divine messages of certain types, but it was not considered acceptable for a private person to approach the deity through dreams and visions. Such practices on the part of private persons are recorded in our sources, but only quite rarely, mostly outside the Babylonian area (from Mari) and, later, from Assyria—possibly under Western influence.[34]

Consequently, insofar as we know anything about Babylonian religion it is first and foremost a royal cult. Further, Daniel 3 again represents an anomalous situation for Mesopotamia in that Nebuchadnezzar takes the extraordinary step of trying to force a particular religious ritual on the entire populace. Even so, the extent of religious involvement required of individuals remains limited. Evidently Nebuchadnezzar does not require of ordinary individuals such things as sacrifices, mortification, and fasts. What he imposes is a communal ritual. Indeed, all subjects are evidently free to

---

There were no thermometers (till c.1650 CE), so "seven times" hotter simply means to make the furnace as hot as possible. Redditt, *Daniel*, 70.

33. Less likely is Goswell's suggestion that Nebuchadnezzar had the furnace made hotter because he "fears the rescue that he boasts can never happen!" *Daniel*, 25.

34. *Ancient Mesopotamia*, 181–82.

hold to their own private beliefs and practices, provided that they will bow down to Nebuchadnezzar's image.[35]

THE NATIONS

It is significant that repeated reference is made to nations, clans, and languages (vv. 4, 7, 29, 31). For this recalls the "nations," "clans," and "languages" of Genesis 10 (vv. 5, 20, 31, 32), with the "earth" being the overall residence in both instances (cf. Gen 10:32 and Daniel 4:1).[36] Given the imposed unification of Daniel 3 we also have an allusion to Genesis 11:6: "one people speaking the same language."

THE DISTINCTIVENESS OF THE JEWS

Certain Chaldeans and Certain Jews

In verses 8–18 we are invited to compare and contrast the Chaldeans with Shadrach, Meshach, and Abednego, for we are told how "certain Chaldeans" (v. 8) denounce "certain Jews" (v. 12; cf. v. 8). Significantly, in so doing they begin by hailing the king with familiar words, "O King, live forever!" When this same phrase was used by them in the previous chapter it signaled their utter failure to give the king what he demanded of them.[37]

Prior Elaboration of Jewish Distinctiveness

In chapter 1 we first saw the development of the motif concerning the distinctiveness of Daniel and his three friends from their Chaldean counterparts. Daniel's decision not to defile himself with the king's food was a decision to maintain his distinctiveness and not to become a spineless

---

35. "You could be a private believer in the God of Israel . . . as long as you bow and worship the image that the king has set up. As long as you keep your own religious preferences to yourself, keep your faith as a private thing and do not challenge the values and structures and allegiances of the society in which you live you can escape the fire. In public you must be just like us. You must bow like the rest of us." Thompson, *Faith in Babylon*.

36. See Kim, *Biblical Interpretation*, 90. For example, the NIV of Daniel 3:4 has "peoples" (עַמְמַיָּא), "nations" (אֻמַיָּא) and "men of every language" (לִשָּׁנַיָּא). The corresponding terms in Genesis 10 (vv. 20, 31) are "nations" (גּוֹיֵהֶם), "clans" (מִשְׁפְּחֹתָם) and "languages" (לִשֹׁנֹתָם).

37. Hebbard, *Reading Daniel*, 95.

lackey of the king and just another Chaldean-like magician-sage. The result of their distinctive diet is a distinctively healthy appearance. Because God gave wisdom to Daniel and his friends—a wisdom he had not imparted to their Chaldean peers—the king was able to distinguish them from their counterparts. At this stage Nebuchadnezzar recognized that with respect to wisdom there was a considerable difference *in degree*. In chapter 2 God brings Nebuchadnezzar a step further—to the recognition that the point of distinction is much more radical than he first perceived. Their wisdom is different *in kind*.[38]

But chapter 2 uncovered for Nebuchadnezzar something of the fundamental nature of reality, a reality which, apart from God's deliberate act of revelation, was totally inaccessible to any man. The reality disclosed was that God is the ultimate sovereign who had even given Nebuchadnezzar the Adam-like dominion he presently exercised over the world, and that the entire course of history was in God's hands so that the inevitable demise of humanistic kingship, specifically the Babylonian kingdom, was assured. The distinctiveness of Daniel and his friends is that they alone have direct access to this God and thus to an understanding of ultimate reality and an understanding of the meaning of the historical process. The Chaldeans, by their own admission, are incapable of accessing that which only the gods can possibly know, and add that the gods do not live among men. Daniel and his friends are distinctive because, as Daniel's revelation of the dream and interpretation of it clearly indicated, God does live among these men.

In chapter 1 Daniel and his friends are described as exiles from Judah (1:6). In chapter 2 Daniel is introduced to Nebuchadnezzar by Arioch as one of "the exiles from Judah" (2:25). In both of these instances links with the southern kingdom, the realm of David, are suggested, and even more pointedly their status as exiles is underscored. We understand from this that Daniel and his friends are to be identified with their homeland; this identity is not erased. It is also to be noted that Shadrach, Meshach, and Abednego are always presented in this chapter, and indeed in the book, as a group, like the satraps, prefects, et al. (vv. 2–3, 27). They never appear as individuals. This leads Fewell to contend that the primary stress falls on the individual Nebuchadnezzar.[39] It is perhaps more accurate to see that the emphasis falls upon the clash between Nebuchadnezzar as the representative of absolute human rule, and the Jews as representatives of divine rule.

---

38. I find Wooden has reached a similar conclusion: "The authors/redactors of *Dan* did not want to portray Daniel as merely better than the other diviners in the court. They consistently portray him as doing something qualitatively different." *Daniel and Manticism*, 349.

39. *Circle*, 55–56.

Distinctiveness as Jews

Certainly there is also great attention given to the three men in chapter 3, and specifically to their identity as *Jews* (verse 8). It is as such that Shadrach, Meshach, and Abednego are denounced, a designation which is stressed again in the words of denouncement (v. 12). Doubtless the prior exaltation of these individuals by Nebuchadnezzar (2:49) has aroused the jealousy of the Chaldeans. But the significant thing is that their enemies treat them as being radically different, and that in these narratives Daniel and his friends are not simply heroes to be admired, but stand as representatives of the Jews.[40] Indeed, the absence of Daniel from chapter 3 serves to emphasize that there were others beside him who were also faithful to God in the midst of adversity, so as to disabuse us of any idea that the book is merely about Daniel.[41] The closing verse of chapter 2 also serves to pave the way for a focus on Shadrach, Meshach, and Abednego, with perhaps even an added implication that Daniel is not present in chapter 3 because he was occupied with special court responsibilities.

THE ROCK AND DISTINCTIVE RULE

If my interpretation of Daniel 2 has been correct then "the rock" which will bring about the destruction of the kingdom of Babylon, being the reign which God will set up "in the time of those kings" (2:44), is, in the first instance (though only embryonically), identifiable with Daniel and his friends. It is in and through them that God begins the process that will achieve the weakening of Nebuchadnezzar's kingdom.

This reign that God sets up "will never be destroyed" we are told in 2:44. This would seem to imply that the "rock" is not simply the active aggressive element that will topple the statue, but that attempts will be made to destroy this rock. The throwing of Shadrach, Meshach, and Abednego into the fire is thus to be viewed as an attempt to destroy the rock, God's rule, and this indeed, as we have argued above, fits the evident meaning which is conveyed by the very setting up of the statue in the first place. Namely, Nebuchadnezzar refuses to accept the message of the dream that God rules history. So he delegates authority to all human rulers (himself included), and, via the

40. Fewell comments, "The Chaldeans are not interested in simply turning in some disobedient Jews; they are interested in turning in *particular* Jews — Jews whom the king himself has appointed to administer the province of Babylon" (*Circle*, 46). While this is true, we must not ignore the fact that in the first instance they are simply "the Jews" (v. 8).

41. Schwab, *Hope*, 12.

statue, he seeks to actualize his own control of history and to guarantee the impregnability of the Babylonian empire. But Nebuchadnezzar's throwing of the three Jews into the fire does not destroy them, precisely because they are to be identified with the rock that God is setting up—a rule that by nature is indestructible. To this can be added that the building of the original Babylon involved the use of fire (Gen 11:3) and now Nebuchadnezzar is effectively using fire yet again to achieve the same result.[42]

Prior events have now established a clear distinction between the Jews, as epitomized by Daniel and his friends, and the Babylonians, and this distinction now leads to Chaldean hostility towards them,[43] a theme that will receive further treatment.

THE SERVILITY OF THE CHALDEANS

A clever literary technique is used to accentuate the servility of the Chaldeans. In verse 2 we read that Nebuchadnezzar summoned a wide range of officials, and these important personages are listed. In order to stress the completeness of obedience to the king's command the list is repeated in verse 3. Similarly in verse 5 the king requires compliance to his command whenever a wide range of instruments are sounded, and these too are listed. Given what has preceded, we might expect that complete obedience to the king's command will be expressed by an instant repetition of the list of musical instruments as in verse 3.[44] And this indeed is what happens, as

42. See Kim, *Biblical Interpretation,* 100–101.

43. Fewell sees strong parallels between Chaldean's approach to Nebuchadnezzar and Bathsheba's approach to David in 1 Kings 1 (*Circle*, 46).

44. It is not easy to identify these instruments given that the context provides no help and that these words only occur in the Bible at this point. Mitchell and Joyce identify *qeren* with "horn," very tentatively propose "flute" for *mashroqi*, suggest a kind of lyre for *qayteros*, speculate a kind of horizontal harp for *shabk*, and a triangular-shaped stringed instrument for *psalterion = pesanterin*. Identification of what is meant by *sumponeya* is particularly difficult and Mitchell and Joyce believe it is not impossible that this word does not in fact refer to an instrument at all but is used by Daniel to qualify the whole clause, signifying "in unison." Mitchell and Joyce, "Musical Instruments," 23–26. Dyer reasons that while *qeren* may have referred to an animal horn, there is evidence from Assyrian sources that suggests this had been replaced by wooden or metal horns for official functions and he proposes Daniel has in mind a wood or metal trumpet. Dyer, "Musical Instruments in Daniel 3," 428–429. With respect to the *mashroqi*, Dyer proposes that a double-reed pipe rather than a flute is more probable. A bas-relief from the reign of Ashurbanipal (seventh century BC) pictures Elamite musicians greeting the royal conquerors returning from battle, accompanied by two who play double-reed pipes. Having identified the first two instruments as wind instruments, Dyer believes the next three are stringed instruments. He takes *qayteros* to be a

recorded in verse 7. All of this is part and parcel of a satirical attack on the pretensions of blasphemous and idolatrous human rule which effectively casts the monarch as a string-pulling puppet-master and his subjects as marionettes. This is augmented by the strong possibility that "many of these instruments may have been associated with bawdy or lewd celebrations."[45]

The Chaldeans next "accused" or, more precisely, "ate the pieces of the Jews"[46]—indicating their "fierce devouring malice."[47] In bringing their accusation against "the Jews," they now repeat this list to indicate their own complete loyalty to the king. Their obsequiousness is further accentuated by their repeated addressing of Nebuchadnezzar with the phrase "O king" (v. 9, 10, 12) and by their reference to the decree and its precise contents, including the requirement that refractors be thrown into the blazing furnace.

transliteration of the Greek *kitharis*, a type of lyre attested by Homer and Herodotus, reasoning that the presence of a Greek instrument in the royal court of Babylon is not surprising given much evidence of contact and trade between the people of the Aegean and Mesopotamian region, with additional evidence of musical instruments being carried between countries; "Musical Instruments in Daniel 3," 430–431. While recognizing that *shabk* might refer to a seven-stringed lyre, Dyer favors correspondence with the Greek *sambuke* and therefore believes it was a kind of harp, though, noting Assyrian reliefs, suggests it had more strings than the four that would otherwise be implied by *sambuke*. He argues that the *psalterion* "was likely a trapezoid-shaped dulcimer either plucked or played with plectra;" "Musical Instruments in Daniel 3," 433. Dyer dismisses the translation of *sumponeya* as "bagpipe" and considers various speculations—the rendering "harmony" or "concord" or "sounding together," "concord harp" (Wellesz) and "drum" (identifying with Greek *tumpanon*). The latter, favored by Dyer, would provide a sequence of two wind instruments, three stringed instruments, and one percussion instrument. This has particular merit given that "it would have been unnatural for an orchestra not to have some percussion instrument" as confirmed by the evidence of ancient Near Eastern bas-reliefs; "Musical Instruments in Daniel 3," 435–36.

45. Avalos, "Comedic Function," 587.

46. Russell suggests: "they made mincemeat out of them!" Russell, *Daniel*, 65.

47. Farrar, 173–74. Wills observes that the "court narratives probably reflect not a situation of governmental persecution but, rather, one of relative religious freedom, in which the tension derives from the social and economic competition with other ethnic groups." Wills, *The Jewish Novel*, 49. Wills points out that "in the court conflicts of *Daniel* 3 and 6, it is the other courtiers, not the king, who instigate the antagonism, even if the king is enlisted in their efforts." This all needs some qualification insofar as in Daniel 3 Nebuchadnezzar is allowing for no religious freedom whatsoever with respect to his own demands. But Wills's point retains validity and he speculates that the social reality behind such a framing of the account might "simply be the day-to-day ethnic competition in the larger marketplace of the Hellenistic world, a situation reflected in the business records preserved in the Murashu tablets and Zenon papyri.

WHO ARE THE REAL IDOLATERS?

The Chaldeans charge the three Jews with failing to obey the king, serve his gods, and worship the image Nebuchadnezzar has set up.[48] Presumably by dobbing them in, the Chaldeans are lodging their claim to occupy the high positions which they trust will soon be vacated by the rebellious Jews. The irony is that the narrative has already suggested the idolatrous nature of Nebuchadnezzar's blasphemous actions, and yet it is those who refuse to be party to this idolatry who themselves are denounced as idolaters. The language of verse 12 is evocative, perhaps deliberately so, of Exodus 20:3–5. They are culpable in the eyes of the Chaldeans for obeying God's demand, as expressed in the Decalogue, that they not serve and worship the gods of Nebuchadnezzar. It is notable that the Chaldeans do not speak of "our gods" but of "your gods" (v. 12). Fundamentally the hiatus is not between the Jews and the gods of Babylon but between the Jews and Nebuchadnezzar.

THE REJECTION OF NEBUCHADNEZZAR'S ABSOLUTISM

Indeed the Chaldean accusers close by stressing that the non-compliance of these Jews amounts to being a personal repudiation of Nebuchadnezzar himself, for they are refusing to worship the image of gold which Nebuchadnezzar himself had set up (v. 12). Nebuchadnezzar interprets their action in the same light, hence it as one "furious with rage" that he summons Shadrach, Meshach, and Abednego. As Valeta observes, in Daniel 1–6 "Kings are portrayed as violent buffoons when measured against the calm, measured, steadfast, and effective acts of the Jewish protagonists of the stories."[49]

The Chaldean accusers are in fact quite correct. Ultimately it is the absolute rule which Nebuchadnezzar would claim for himself which is repudiated by the Jews. Nebuchadnezzar believes that his absolute power is demonstrated by his ability to destroy any who refuse to obey him, for telling the Jews that continued disobedience will result in them being immediately cast into the furnace, he challenges, "Then what god will be able to rescue you from my hand?" With such words Nebuchadnezzar presumes to hold absolute power in his hand. In Deuteronomy 32:39 it is Yahweh who

48. In referring to these Jews as those Nebuchadnezzar had appointed over the affairs of the province the insinuation is this: "You went out of your way to help these people and gave them jobs they didn't really deserve. Now see how ungrateful and defiant they are!" Fernando, *Spiritual Living*, 73.

49. *Lions*, 84.

declares that no god "can deliver out of my hand." It would seem that in verse 15 the narrative finds in Nebuchadnezzar's disdainful words—"Who is the god who will deliver you from my hands?"—a reversal of this truth, together with the implication that Nebuchadnezzar puts himself into the place of God. The language is also reminiscent of Sennacherib's attempt to take Jerusalem, especially as in that case too God's people are miraculously delivered (2 Kgs 18:13–19:37). This augments the total contextual idea of Nebuchadnezzar blasphemously acting like God, and usurping the place that is his alone.

The response of the three Jews is notable, not just as an expression of awe-inspiring heroism.[50] More than that, their confession concerning God in this particular context is of immense significance: "If we are thrown into the blazing furnace, the God we serve is able to save us from it, and he will rescue us from your hand, O king" (v. 17).[51] Again the words *"from your hand"* must be stressed, together with the words *"O king"* which only shortly before this were mouthed by the Chaldeans. The point is that Nebuchadnezzar is not able to absolutely control the lives of these men in his hand. These three men anticipate the probability that God will intervene and rescue them. When this deliverance takes place it will not primarily express the worthiness of these faithful men to be saved, but rather it will demonstrate that Nebuchadnezzar does not possess the absolute power he thinks he has.

Chapter 3 follows on from chapter 2. The dream has revealed that God is the controller of history, and at that time even Nebuchadnezzar recognizing the significance of this, declared, "Surely your God is the God of gods and the Lord of kings." But Nebuchadnezzar has not come to terms with

50. Hebbard, *Reading Daniel*, 105, notes that in the prior narrative Daniel has been presented as the leader of the group. He comments, "Now, with Daniel out of the scene, the three understudies of Daniel are put to the test. They prove themselves to be good disciples of Daniel . . . "

51. According to an alternative rendering of verse 18 by Montgomery and Lacocque, the three men question the ability and power of God to deliver them: "If our God whom we worship is able to rescue us from the fiery burning furnace (Lacocque: *the crematory oven*) and from your hand, O King, he will rescue. But if not, be it known to you O King. . ." (my emphasis). The reasoning here is that: "They cannot answer for God in this situation, but they can answer for themselves." Wharton, "Daniel 3:16–18," 173–74. Lucas, *Daniel*, 90–91, regards this as "the most obvious meaning of the text." Lucas doubts the validity of interpretations that involve either questioning God's "ethical ability" or see the youths as using *if* "for the sake of argument." If the youths were expressing doubt in God's ability to save then presumably this is mentioned to add a note of realism to the account. Their devotion to God whatever might happen is unquestionable. However, member of the NIV translation committee, Longman (*Daniel*, 101), defends the standard NIV on philological grounds and rightly regards the Montgomery-Lacoque-Wharton interpretation as theologically improbable.

the fact that this actually means that he himself does not possess absolute power. There is a big difference between what Nebuchadnezzar experiences in his dream state and what he must now experience in his waking state. Now the message of the dream will be rooted in concrete human experience by way of driving the point home.

PASSIVE OBEDIENCE

Even the way the three Jews come to Nebuchadnezzar distinguishes them from all others. Avalos comments, "In effect, the mechanical repetition of the lengthy enumerations in vv. 1–15 forms part of a satirical prologue to the assertive response of the three young men in vv. 16–18."[52] Indeed, when the king summons the many different kinds of important officials, the text continues by repeating the list by way of underlining the fact that each and every one of them responded. Each one came and assembled as an expression of obedience. But when Nebuchadnezzar summons the three Jews we read that they "were brought before the king" (v. 13). There is no hint of rebellion in this passivity, as though they had to be dragged into the king's presence against their wills. However, it does seem to be significant, for the literary purpose of distinguishing the three Jews, that whereas the obedience of all others was active their compliance was passive.

THE CHANGING OF NEBUCHADNEZZAR'S FACE

Verse 19 is crucial. It speaks of Nebuchadnezzar's face changing and uses *slm* ("and his *slm* towards them changed"), the very same word used to refer to the image of gold.[53] What is the relationship? Fewell proposes: "In Genesis 1 Elohim creates humanity in the divine image (*ṣelem*); in Daniel 3 Nebuchadnezzar creates, in his own (very human) image, an object to be worshipped. . . ."[54]

It is also interesting to compare the change in Nebuchadnezzar's face with the darkening of Cain's face in Genesis 4:5, which in context is arguably an indication of the results of image-perversion, the loss of the ability to reflect the glory of God (see 2 Cor 3:18). At any rate, as Fewell observes,

---

52. Avalos, "Comedic Function," 586.

53. See too Hebbard, *Reading Daniel*, 99. This linkage causes Meadowcroft and Irwin, *Book of Daniel*, 61, to speculate that the statue-image was intended to be a representation of Nebuchadnezzar himself.

54. Fewell, *Circle*, 51.

The changing of Nebuchadnezzar's "image," or expression, marks a turning point in the story. As the plot moves toward the seemingly certain execution, the narrator moves us away from the action.[55]

Quite apart from these broader allusions there is an immediate pun involved within the chapter itself. Longman explains, "The one who in his pride has created an image with the purpose of assuring uniform loyalty finds his own image provoked beyond his control."[56]

THE BINDING OF THE JEWS

The three Jews are bound before being cast into the furnace, dressed in their cloaks, their tunics, their hats, and other garments—all highly flammable.[57] Fewell sees here a recollection of the binding of Isaac for a holocaust on Mount Moriah (Gen 22), at which time, as here, divine intervention prevented destruction.[58] Fewell thinks this may indicate the sacrificial nature of the execution of the three Jews:

In order to be sovereign of the world, God must catch bigger fish than Israel. Israel becomes the sacrifice, the burnt offering without blemish, that is to secure the victory, the recognition of God's sovereignty by "all peoples, nations and languages."[59]

It is significant that the three men "fell" into the furnace, since the same word is used repeatedly of all who fell down to worship Nebuchadnezzar's statue. As Pace remarks: "The contrast is striking: here the young men lie prostrate as devoted servants to God, not as paragons of obeisance to an outrageous king and his idol."[60]

---

55. *Circle*, 51.

56. *Daniel*, 101.

57. Greidanus, *Preaching Christ from Daniel*, 90.

58. *Circle*, 52. The emphasis on the root *kpt* with reference to the king's command "to bind" them and on them being "bound" may conceivably involve an allusion to the binding of Isaac (Gen 22) and a suggestion of them being akin to bound sacrificial animals. But it may merely underscore the utter subordination of the three men. See Pace, *Daniel*, 104.

59. *Circle*, 60.

60. *Daniel*, 104.

THE PLACE OF INEVITABLE DESTRUCTION?

Remembering prior allusions to the Tower of Babel account and the mention there of burning bricks in the fire, it is interesting to speculate that the furnace may have been a brick kiln.[61] Daniel 3 is positive historical evidence that execution by burning in a furnace did take place during Nebuchadnezzar's reign.[62] Textual stress is laid upon the way in which the furnace is made so intolerably hot that it even kills those who approach it to throw in the three Jews.[63] This note together with the description of the binding of the men combines to indicate that there is no earthly hope for them.[64] But, in context, the increasing of the heat of the furnace is an expression of Nebuchadnezzar's rage. It does not indicate an underlying lurking suspicion on Nebuchadnezzar's part that God might in fact be able to save them.[65] He is not intensifying the heat of the furnace to ensure the impossibility of divine deliverance even though, of course, the record of what he did does serve to underscore that the fire is the place of absolutely certain destruction.

CERTAIN STRONG MEN AND CERTAIN JEWS

In this context we must note the telling interplay of the phrases "certain strong men" (v. 20) and "certain Jews" (v. 12) which parallels the similar

---

61. Greidanus, *Preaching Christ from Daniel*, 102.

62. Collins finds the closest parallel in 2 Maccabees 13:4–8 which records how Menelaus the high priest, on the orders of Antiochus V Eupator, was thrown from an execution tower into a pit of ashes, though this did not involve burning (Beaulieu, "Babylonian Background," 277). Jeremiah 29:21–23 provides corroboration, though the burning referred to here may not have been burning in a furnace. As Beaulieu shows, death by burning occurs a number of times in Babylonian sources from the eighth to third centuries BC. Indeed, Beaulieu identifies three instances in Mesopotamia where burning involves being thrown into an oven or furnace ("Babylonian Background," 282–85; cf. Holm's comments, *Courtiers*, 438–41). Holm (*Courtiers*, 437) finds the nearest parallels in Egyptian literature, "especially in Late Egyptian or Demotic tales with a court setting in which is courtiers who displease a king who are condemned to death by burning in a furnace." For a full consideration of existing evidence see Holm, "The Fiery Furnace in the Book of Daniel," 85–104. It needs to be added, contra Holm, that Daniel 3 itself needs to be accepted as *historical* evidence of Mesopotamian practice, even if it was a one-off.

63. There is irony here as well: "those who obey Nebuchadnezzar and comply with his commands are the ones who suffer loss of life." Hebbard, *Reading Daniel*, 100. Similarly, Goswell, *Daniel*, 25: "We discover that it is safer to defy Nebuchadnezzar than to serve him . . . "

64. Fewell, *Circle*, 53.

65. Contra Anderson, *Signs and Wonders*, 35.

offsetting of "certain Chaldeans" and "certain Jews" in verses 8–12. The irony of the situation is that it is those completely obedient to the king who end up dying. Fewell remarks, "The executioners die meaningless deaths in obedience to an unconcerned sovereign with limited power."[66] But, given our exegesis of Daniel 2, we see more intended here—the presence of "the rock," the representatives of the anti-idolatrous religion associated with "the mountain," Zion; a religion that is not constructed with human hands in contrast with the idolatrous hands of Nebuchadnezzar. The death of the executioners is a harbinger of the way in which God's people will bring about the destruction of the statue.

At this point in the LXX of Daniel, interposed between verses 23 and 24, appear The Prayer of Azariah (Azariah = Abednego) and The Song of the Three Young Men. But their absence from the MT and from the Qumran Daniel text 1QD clearly indicates that these passages are not original.[67]

FIRE AND THEOPHANY

Fire often accompanies theophany (Ex 3; 13:21–22; Num 16:35), so, remembering this theology, the oft-repeated "blazing fiery furnace" foreshadows the outcome, of God revealing himself in the fire.[68] Nebuchadnezzar sees an angel (v. 28), one "like a son of the gods" in the fire (v. 25)[69]— he could not be expected to recognize the figure as "the Son of God."[70] Further, a singular translation of the Aramaic plural *elahin* ("gods") is unlikely since the Aramaic singular form is used to describe the true God.[71] But "a son of the gods" is Semitic idiom for one who is to be classed among the gods. As Lucas points out, Nebuchadnezzar, as a polytheist, clearly regarded this figure as a member of the pantheon of deities.[72]

66. *Circle*, 53.

67. Towner, *Daniel*, 54.

68. Fewell, *Circle*, 54.

69. Beaulieu, "Babylonian Background," 287, noting the available examples of ancient Mesopotamian kilns and ovens, comments: "A furnace able to accommodate three walking men, with the addition of a fourth miraculous apparition, seems too large." But we need to remember that Nebuchadnezzar was famed for the grandiose nature of his constructions. There may also be an indication here of Nebuchadnezzar's sadism, in that he had come to watch the death of these men; so Harman, *Daniel*, 87.

70. Tertullian understood that Nebuchadnezzar saw Jesus with the three men in the fire. Gammie, "A Journey," 146. See Bucur for a discussion of early Christophanic exegesis: "Christophanic Exegesis," 227–44.

71. Walvoord, *Daniel*, 91.

72. *Daniel*, 92.

It is far-fetched to see the divine being as a substitute for the absent Daniel; rather he represents the presence of God with his people, in a manner which drives home all the further the fundamental disparity between humanistic Babylonian religion which worships ultimately transcendent, inaccessible gods, and the faith of the Jews who worship the real and living God who is with his people when they walk through the fire. Here then we have yet another implicit rebuttal of 2:11 (see too Isaiah 43:2)—a God who does "live among men." Since the God-sent angel is introduced initially as the "fourth man" (v. 25a) and since "looks like a son of the gods" evidently describes his glorious nature, it is not impossible that this fourth "man" is also to be identified with the glorious "one like a son of man" described in 7:13. Further, there is a contrasting correspondence between the "fourth" figure here and the "fourth" beast of Daniel 7. Here the fourth figure embodies divine protection, while in Daniel 7 the fourth beast represents ultimate destructive power, yet, ironically, is destroyed when thrown into "the burning fire."[73]

THE CULPABILITY OF SERVILE IDOLATERS

Verse 27 is of great importance. The abbreviated listing of important officials is by way of recalling verses 2–3 where we read of their complete obedience to Nebuchadnezzar's commands. It is these same people called to worship the image who now are the very ones to witness the miraculous survival of the three Jews.[74] This serves to accentuate the culpability of their obsequious, fear-motivated participation in idolatry.

QUALIFIED ACKNOWLEDGMENT OF GOD'S POWER

The miraculous deliverance of the three Jews is not *from* the fire, but *through* the fire.[75] This certainly inspires awe in Nebuchadnezzar at the power of the god who has delivered them. But though he recognizes the power of the Hebrew god, he doesn't even ask for an explanation as to the name or nature of this god. He is amazed and awe-struck, but he is not bowed.

Nebuchadnezzar acknowledges God as the one who delivered the three men who expressed their trust or faith in God (cf. 6:23) by "setting

---

73. Kim, *Biblical Interpretation*, 113. In effect, God acts in a manner analogous to Nebuchadnezzar, *Biblical Interpretation*, 114.

74. Fewell, *Circle*, 55.

75. Hebbard, *Reading Daniel*, 103.

aside" his command and by being willing to yield up their bodies rather than serve any other God. Significantly, the verb often translated "set aside" (NIV) or "disobey" is literally "change," and so stands in contrast with the way the king's face "changed" and also recalls the lack of "change" on their clothing and bodies.[76]

Fewell points out that Nebuchadnezzar does not concede that his own power should be subordinated to God's power and, indeed, the very issuing of a royal decree represents Nebuchadnezzar's attempt to exert some measure of control over this deity. Fewell observes too the irony of the parallel between this decree and the earlier decree regarding the image of gold. In both cases Nebuchadnezzar makes himself the one who demands and will enforce religious subservience. In both cases Nebuchadnezzar, in typical character, threatens death for disobedience.

As Fewell wryly observes, "Nebuchadnezzar is again in the business of controlling the religious attitudes of others by wielding his political power." All the indications are that despite witnessing this astounding miracle, Nebuchadnezzar's allegiance to this god, like his knowledge of this god, has its limitations. He, nevertheless, makes this god politically useful. Like the gold image, this god becomes a measurement of political fidelity: Whoever speaks against this god shall be "punished as culprits against the realm."[77]

THE ONLY SAVIOR

In verses 15 and 28 the verb *sezib* was used for the motif of deliverance. Earlier we suggested that the wording of verse 15c alluded to Deuteronomy 32:39 and it is therefore striking that v. 29 employs *nsl* as in *The Song of Moses*—"See now that I, even I, am he, and there is no god beside me; I kill and I make alive; I wound and I heal; and there is none that can deliver out of my hand."

By using this word the narrator is saying that while Nebuchadnezzar thinks of this god as the "highest god" he is in fact, though Nebuchadnezzar still does not recognize this, the only god.[78]

---

76. See Pace, *Daniel*, 107. "Their disobedience (lit. 'change' [*sannîw*]) of the king's order, which was tantamount to defiance, is contrasted with the king's 'change' of face (*'eštannî* [v19]) and the lack of 'change' on their clothing (*šĕnô* [v27]) or bodies."

77. Here Fewell cites Montgomery. *Circle*, 57.

78. Fewell, *Circle*, 58.

NEBUCHADNEZZAR CONTINUES TO ACT LIKE GOD

As Fewell points out, the royal decree shows also that Nebuchadnezzar still considers himself to be in control of life and death. In godlike fashion, he still decides the destinies of his subjects.[79]

This idea is reinforced in verse 30 which informs us that "the king made Shadrach, Meshach, and Abednego prosperous." There is assonance between the verb *haslah*, "he made prosper" and the infinitive in the preceding verse, *lehasalah*, "to rescue." Fewell believes an ironic connection is intended. Nebuchadnezzar's action reflects the action of God himself. The three Jews may be indebted to their God for their rescue. But now Nebuchadnezzar insinuates himself as the one to whom they are indebted for their prosperity.

This would probably be a fair conclusion if verse 30 had been included in the decree itself and, therefore, as a power claimed by Nebuchadnezzar. However, because it is presented in narrative summary form it is better to see a different irony intended. God is not only able to rescue his people from Nebuchadnezzar but even to cause such a king to be the means of their prosperity.

TOWARDS THE RECOGNITION OF GOD'S ABSOLUTE SOVEREIGNTY

Going beyond such insights we also see in verse 29 the direction in which God is steering history. Though Nebuchadnezzar is still trying to subsume what has happened under his own kingship, we find in his decree that progress has been made towards God's own objective—that all peoples fully acknowledge the absolute sovereignty of God. As we know, the text will continue to move this way[80] until Nebuchadnezzar is forced to acknowledge God's absolute sovereignty cannot be subsumed under his own kingship.

Meantime, Nebuchadnezzar pronounces dire consequences on any who would dare "say anything against," that is, "blaspheme[81] the God of Shadrach, Meshach, and Abednego."[82] There is also a probable pun in this

---

79. Fewell, *Circle*, 58.

80. The essential difference between written and oral text is that with respect to the former, knowledge of the whole can be assumed.

81. Paul, "Mesopotamian Background," 55–56. Paul cites other ancient examples employing equivalent terminology: "They utter grievous blasphemy against their goddesses" and "(Those Babylonians) who spoke gross blasphemy against Assur, my god, who has created me, I split their tongues and skinned them alive."

82. Goswell remarks, "Blasphemy against the God of the Jews is made a treasonable

verse. Nebuchadnezzar decrees that any who "say anything against the God of Shadrach, Meshach, and Abednego be cut into pieces." This answers to the way in which this whole situation arose; that is, when the Chaldeans approached the king and "ate pieces of" the Jews (v. 8).[83]

A METAPHOR OF EXILE?

Fewell sees the story as a metaphor of the exile where "fire" and "furnace" are metaphors of captivity—Deut 4:20; Isa 43:2.[84]

> Might it not be that this story that is too good to be true, this story that speaks of unequalled tyranny, unsullied faith, unflinching heroism, and unquestionable divine presence is but a small paradigm of a larger story of ambiguous politics, compromised faith, confused response, and an elusive god? This story is a metaphor for exilic experience.[85]

It is, of course, possible to read the record of this incident as also bearing a literary purpose without needing to jettison confidence in the essential historicity of the events concerned, as Fewell has done. Thus Fewell may well be right in seeing here a metaphor of the exile.[86] The persecution which occurred under Antiochus IV Epiphanes assumes considerable importance in the latter half of this book and serves as a powerful illustration of despotic opposition to faithful Jewish piety.[87] Certainly there is a merit in her final conclusion: "As a metaphor, the story communicates that, despite all attempts to make them conform, the Jews endure exile unchanged, identity secure, integrity intact, loyal to their god."[88]

---

offence. Is he still obsessed by his own power? Does he still think that he can legislate as to whom men worship and bow down? It is all very well to criticise this pagan king, but have we learned the lesson God is teaching us here? Here is a lesson for every believer involved in politics. There are definite limits to what can be achieved through political action. Both the Christian Right and the Christian Left need to learn that legislation cannot turn a country into a 'Christian nation.'" *Daniel*, 27.

83. Cf. "made mincemeat" of them. Greidanus, *Preaching Christ from Daniel*, 103.

84. *Circle*, 59.

85. *Circle*, 59.

86. Similarly Walvoord, *Daniel*, 92.

87. Kim makes much of this. *Biblical Interpretation*, 114–17.

88. *Circle*, 59.

SUMMARY

- As in previous chapters, Daniel 3 serves to reject Nebuchadnezzar's claims to absolute rule. Nebuchadnezzar's rule is a parody of Adamic rule and his exaltation of his image is perversion of the Image of God.

- His demand that all worship the image or suffer a horrible death serves to underscore the terrifying power possessed by this despot. Is there any future for those who would defy this king?

- Following on from the dream Nebuchadnezzar seeks to change the future, to secure his kingdom by ensuring all disunity is removed. Hence his determination to unite all in his empire around the worship of his idolatrous cult.

- It is the idolatrous nature of Nebuchadnezzar's kingship which ultimately explains the inherent weakness of his kingdom.

- The miraculous deliverance of the three Jews from a place of certain destruction proves Nebuchadnezzar does not hold the power of life and death in his hands.

- Through the series of events described in this chapter God secures the freedom of his people, the Jews, to remain distinctive in their worship of him alone.

- God's faithful people, as epitomized by these three Jews, are identifiable with the indestructible rule of God, the "rock" of Daniel 2. They constitute the reason why human rulers like Nebuchadnezzar are never able to achieve the full degree of unity which would safeguard their empires.

- Notwithstanding Nebuchadnezzar's forced acknowledgement of God he seeks to bring the worship of God under his own control by decreeing his own set of dire punishments for blaspheming God.

POINTS OF CONTACT WITH THE NEW TESTAMENT AND WITH LIFE

1. In Rev 13:15 John uses the language and imagery of Daniel 3 to depict "the image of the first beast." As in Daniel 3 all who refuse to worship the image are killed. As in Daniel 3 John proceeds to stress how all people are forced to be united in their worship of the image.

Each person has a mark showing them to be idolaters, albeit under compulsion.

2. In Daniel 3 Nebuchadnezzar erroneously believes himself to be the one who can destroy all who reject his rule by throwing them into the fiery furnace. In the New Testament it is God who truly will destroy all who reject his rule by throwing them into the fiery furnace. See Matthew 13:42, 50.

3. As Hebrews 11:34 indicates, Shadrach, Meshach, and Abednego are remembered as heroes of faith who by their faith "quenched the fury of the flames."

4. Many Christians suppose the fourth man in the fire was Jesus. It is possible to build a bridge, but along the lines wisely advised by Longman:

> It is impossible to be dogmatic unless one insists that every incarnate appearance of God must be the second person of the Trinity. It is safer to say that what we have here is a reflection of Immanuel, "God with us." God dwelt with the three friends in the midst of the flames to preserve them from harm. In this sense, the Christian cannot help but see a prefigurement of Jesus Christ, who came to earth to dwell in a chaotic world and who even experienced death, not so that we might escape the experience of death but that we might have victory over it.[89]

POSSIBLE SERMON OUTLINE

Title: Who holds the power of life and death?

1. *A King with an Image Problem.* Nebuchadnezzar does not appreciate that his setting up of the image involves problems at a number of levels. First, it expresses his own problem in that he grossly overestimates the extent of his own power and authority. Secondly, it is precisely this enforced idolatry which, far from securing his kingdom (his intention), will ultimately bring about its downfall.

2. *A King with a Temper Problem.* Once again, as in Daniel 2, the king is unable to control his rage when he senses his hold on absolute rule is threatened. It is the king's anger, coupled with his seemingly immense power to destroy, which makes him such a terrifying figure.

---

89. *Daniel*, 112.

3. *A King with a People Problem.* There are a people who will never bow the knee to a despotic king like Nebuchadnezzar no matter how horrific the consequences of refusal to obey; namely, the people of God as epitomized by Shadrach, Meshach, and Abednego. Nebuchadnezzar's problem is that these people are backed by a power far, far superior to his own.

4. *A King with a Failure Problem.* Though the miraculous rescue of the three Jews forces Nebuchadnezzar to acknowledge God's awesome power to save, nevertheless he is quick to secure damage control. His covers his own failure as a king by rationalizing the worship of Yahweh and making it a part of his own Babylonian cult complex.

Daniel 4

Cut Down to Size

God humbles a proud human ruler:
First demonstration of God's sovereignty
over all human kingdoms

LITERARY FEATURES

This chapter stands out in the Bible for two reasons: its first-person narration and the use of extensive flashback.[1] The first-person narration (vv. 1–18, 34–37) is interrupted by a third-person block (vv. 19–33). There are three main explanations for this, none of which excludes the others: (1) the result of the text's redactional history; (2) an issue of genre choices, combining a "natural" use of first person to report a dream and utter confessional praise, plus a "dramatically appropriate" insertion of third-person narrative; and (3) an alternation that serves the purposes of the story.[2]

With respect to purpose it is true that the use of first-person narration from none other than Nebuchadnezzar itself invests the text with an added

---

1. Fewell, *Circle*, 73.
2. See Widder, "Letting Nebuchadnezzar Speak," 198.

sense of authority.[3] The third-person narrative makes sense because we would hardly expect Nebuchadnezzar to narrate his own insanity.[4]

Ferguson likens the genre of Daniel 4 to a Babylonian document named *Ludlul Bēl Nēmeqi* ("I will praise the Lord of Wisdom," that is, Marduk) dated around 1200 BC.[5] This document is often called the "Babylonian Job," being the monologue of a highly placed literate Babylonian. It bears the following similarities with Daniel 4:

- It opens and closes with a doxology and confession.

- It contains affirmations of his god's universal kingship.

- The phrase "whose hands the heavens cannot hold back" correspond with Daniel 4:35: "He does as he pleases with the powers of heaven and the peoples of the earth. No one can hold back his hand or say to him, 'What have you done?'"

- The speaker announces his intention to provide people with instruction in worship and to present his situation as a public example of his god's ability to punish and restore.

- His situation is associated with a terrifying dream, as in Daniel 4:5.

- He repeatedly stresses that four classes of dream interpreters and omen experts could not help him (cf. Dan 4:6–7).

- He used to walk and talk arrogantly.

- He was put out of his house and had to wander outside like a recluse and an ox.

- He lost his position of authority and was replaced by someone else.

- He became like one who had gone insane. He was fettered and his fingernails grew out.

- The same god who struck him down raised him up.

- He wants to make known to all people what his god had done for him.

---

3. Lucas, *Daniel*, 103.

4. Widder notes Pace's observation that Nebuchadnezzar does not describe his humiliation. But he nevertheless admits that he experienced a period of insanity when he reports how his sanity was restored (v. 34). So Pace is wrong to think that Nebuchadnezzar's character was unchanged and, indeed, in the very next chapter Daniel will make it clear, in a way that shames Belshazzar, that a genuine transformation had occurred in Nebuchadnezzar's life (so Newsom). Widder, "Letting Nebuchadnezzar Speak," 199.

5. "Nebuchadnezzar, Gilgamesh, and the 'Babylonian Job,'" 329–30.

As Ferguson points out, Nebuchadnezzar was a well-informed worshiper of Marduk and so would have been familiar with various hymns written to Marduk.[6] Consequently, verses 2–3 and 34–35, 37 may well be based on "an old, time-honored pattern." Ferguson notes how in one of Nebuchadnezzar's inscriptions he describes himself as causing "to exist in the mouths of men the fear of the great gods."

STRUCTURE

The story of Daniel 4 diverges considerably from fairy tales as studied by Propp and it is precarious to seek a structure for the chapter that forces conformity with a supposed "tale" structure.[7] Again satire is pervasive. A chiastic structure of form and content has been identified by Shea[8]:

> *Prologue*
> vv. 1–3
> Post-fulfillment proclamation
> Poem I
>> A vv. 4–7 Dream reception
>>> X vv. 8–9 Dialogue I—King to Daniel
>>>> B vv. 10–17 Dream recital
>>>>> Y Dialogue II
>>>>> vv. 18–19a King to Daniel
>>>>> v. 19b Daniel to King
>>>> B' vv. 20–26 Dream interpretation
>>> Z v. 27 Dialogue III—Daniel to King
>> A' vv. 28–33 Dream fulfillment
> *Epilogue*
> vv. 34–38
> Post-fulfillment restoration
> Poem II

---

6. "Nebuchadnezzar," 330.

7. Milne, *Vladimir Propp*, 232–39, thoroughly evaluates Daniel 3:31–4:34 (MT) and concludes (238), "The reason that Propp's model has so little applicability to Daniel 4, lies, no doubt, in the fact that Daniel 4, because it is presented as an epistle or decree, is obviously set out in a different literary genre." The view of Humphreys and Collins that Daniel 4 is a tale of court contest similar in motif and pattern to the tales of Daniel 2 and 5 (see Milne, *Vladimir Propp*, 181) must be seriously questioned.

8. Fewell, *Circle*, 73.

Often the center of a chiasm (Y) marks a turning point in the story or a kind of plot climax. In this chapter, however, the plot climax occurs in verses 29–33. What significance, if any, should be accorded to Y? Fewell observes that at this point that "a major shift in narrative voice, or narrative point of view, occurs. It is at this place in the story (with verse 19a) where the first person narration of Nebuchadnezzar is taken over by a third person narrator."[9]

Fewell believes this indicates that the second half of the flashback (B', Z, A') presents a point of view that differs from that expressed by Nebuchadnezzar. However, this is a dubious conclusion. The transition reached in verses 18–19 is not merely a literary one. It is in fact a point of great tension in the relationship between Nebuchadnezzar and Daniel. Nebuchadnezzar recognizes that Daniel's wisdom is unique, differing from that of the Chaldeans because of the presence of "the spirit of the holy gods" in Daniel; "someone who is in a state of understanding with both God and man, and bridges the gap between the two."[10] As we shall see, however, this very use of language indicates that Nebuchadnezzar has still not learnt that Daniel's wisdom is different not merely in degree, but *in its essential nature*. Daniel, having heard the king's narration of the dream, does indeed perceive its meaning and is deeply disturbed. It is precisely at this point that we discover just how radically different Daniel's wisdom really is. For, at the king's insistence and despite his own great reluctance, Daniel proceeds to provide an interpretation of the dream that involves, in classical prophetic style, the pronouncement of judgment upon the king himself and a call upon him to repent. No other wise man in the kingdom would have dared to confront the mightiest king on earth in this manner. Daniel is not dealing with a pussycat here but with a man who has just shown himself to have all the savagery of a vicious lion.

The point needs to be firmly grasped. Daniel 4 represents a decided advance on Daniel 2 when it comes to driving a wedge between Daniel's wisdom and that of the Chaldeans. In chapter 2 the essential difference in this wisdom was expressed by the ability of Daniel to know what was impossible for the Chaldeans to know—the very precise details of Nebuchadnezzar's undisclosed dream. Notwithstanding the magnitude of this expression of God's unique sovereignty, Nebuchadnezzar has still failed to understand that he is dealing here with a wisdom that is utterly and completely unique in its essential nature. It is precisely at this point that God-given wisdom is differentiated,

9. *Circle*, 74.

10. Hebbard, *Reading Daniel*, 115. There is irony here because the application of the cosmic tree imagery to Nebuchadnezzar implies that he himself is the bridge between heaven and earth, which is clearly false.

not merely by its intelligence (access to otherwise inaccessible knowledge), but, more fundamentally still, by its moral fiber. It is the sheer courage and honesty of Daniel's interpretation, with all its confrontational moral force, that demands recognition of the absolute uniqueness of Daniel's wisdom.

COSMIC RULER?

In verse 1 Nebuchadnezzar assumes the role of world ruler. Young comments, "The Assyrian and Babylonian kings regarded themselves as kings of all the earth, and in their inscriptions were accustomed thus to speak of themselves." Nebuchadnezzar thinks of himself as king of the whole world.[11]

Fewell notes the possibility that the narrator intends the implied reader should see himself as included as an intended object of Nebuchadnezzar's speech.[12] This accentuates the utter foolishness and banality of Nebuchadnezzar's self-conception. To the implied reader, then, Nebuchadnezzar speaks as a voice from the grave: "we" are not his vassals, but then neither were all nations at the time Nebuchadnezzar speaks. Consequently, even in the context of his own times his statement assumes overweening arrogance.

In 3:30 Nebuchadnezzar has prospered Shadrach, Meshach, and Abednego. Now, apparently conceiving of himself as the source of prosperity, he issues his own supposedly efficacious word of blessing: "may you prosper greatly." It is important to recognize that this exaggerated opinion of his own greatness persists notwithstanding his sincere recognition of God's greatness.

THE GREATNESS OF GOD'S RULE ACKNOWLEDGED

On the positive side, in verses 2–3 we see a definite progression in Nebuchadnezzar's conception of God and the nature of his rule. Nebuchadnezzar speaks with pleasure of the miraculous signs and wonders "the Most High God" has performed for him. But we soon come to realize as the chapter continues, that this is not due, as we might have supposed, to the act of deliverance related in the preceding chapter but to the story about to be told.[13] This confirms our earlier reading of Daniel 3—that the deliverance

11. *Daniel*, 97. As Pace observes, "Despite this apparent sign of spiritual awareness. . . he remains preoccupied with his own power and never refers to God's intervention that punished his arrogance." *Daniel*, 125.

12. *Circle*, 62–63.

13. It would seem, therefore, that verses 1–3 are indeed best read along with the rest of Daniel 4 rather than as a conclusion to Daniel 3. In the Masoretic Text these verses do in fact are found at the close of Daniel 3.

had not been adequate. More was needed. Again note the way the text as a whole keeps moving to yet greater and greater perceptions on the part of Nebuchadnezzar as to the dimensions of the sovereignty of God.

In Daniel 1 Nebuchadnezzar was ignorant of God's sovereignty, despite the fact that it was being exercised under his nose. In Daniel 2 his mind apprehends the sovereignty of God in the realm of wisdom. In Daniel 3 the eyes of the king see the sovereignty of God displayed in an astounding miracle of deliverance. Now, the revelation of God's sovereignty in Nebuchadnezzar's life reaches its pinnacle. This time, not merely his mind and eyes, but his whole senses are involved as the sovereignty of God penetrates every aspect of his being. And it is the absolute and limitless nature of God's sovereignty he comes to acknowledge. At the same time, the third-person narration balances Nebuchadnezzar's own self-perception with the realization that in "humbling *this* king, the God of Israel demonstrated his sovereignty over *all* kings and kingdoms."[14] This is all the more so because, as verses 28–30 intimate, this occurred at the very peak of Nebuchadnezzar's reign.[15]

But subtleties in the text persist. Back in Daniel 2 only Daniel could "disclose" the knowledge of God. In this chapter Nebuchadnezzar implicitly claims the same power. It is now his avowed purpose to "disclose" the miraculous signs and wonders . . . (v. 2).[16]

Fewell observes that whenever the term "signs and wonders" is used in the Bible[17] it refers "to acts or events that embody a communication from God."[18] She notes seventeen occurrences of this term, observing that thirteen concern the signs and wonders performed by Yahweh when he brought his people out of bondage in Egypt. There are also three instances in the context of prophetic mediation. Fewell suggests,

> By appropriating this language, Nebuchadnezzar, whether consciously or not, elevates his role of mediator, one who imparts divine knowledge to his people. His authority is derived (apart from his kingship) from the experience he is about to relate, an experience that his language equates with Israel's exodus from Egypt.[19]

It is interesting to compare and contrast Nebuchadnezzar with Pharaoh. Both experienced humiliation following expressions of cruelty and

14. Widder, "Letting Nebuchadnezzar Speak," 211.

15. Widder, "Letting Nebuchadnezzar Speak," 212.

16. Fewell, *Circle,* 64.

17. See Exod 7:3; Deut 4:34; 6:22; 7:19; 13:1–2 [2–3]; 26:8; 28:46; 34:11; Neh 9:10; Ps 135:9; Isa 8:18; 20:3; Jer 32:20.

18. *Circle,* 64.

19. *Circle,* 64.

egomania.[20]God performed "miraculous signs and wonders" in the sight of both kings. But the context then was openly adversarial: God's might and power confronting the power of Pharaoh together with his magicians and gods. At that time Pharaoh knew that God, via Moses, was demanding that he let the Israelites go. But Israel had not been placed in Egypt because of the operation of covenant curses consequent upon covenant violation. However, this is the very reason why the Jews now find themselves captives in Babylon. It is not God's time as yet for them to return to the land of promise. There is no immediate pressure upon Nebuchadnezzar to let them go. And yet, as Nebuchadnezzar goes on to relate what had happened to him, we see that God's "miraculous signs and wonders" did involve Nebuchadnezzar's claims to absolute kingship being confronted with God's claims. When Israelites recalled these signs and wonders they were motivated to live lives of obedience and of exclusive devotion to Yahweh. But, as Pace observes, there is little to suggest that Nebuchadnezzar ever made the link between "signs and wonders" and divine justice.[21] Further, just as the mediatorial power of Moses exceeds that of his would-be Egyptian counterparts—the magicians—similarly the mediatorial role assumed by Daniel eclipses that of his Chaldean peers.

Nebuchadnezzar's acknowledgment that God's reign is an "everlasting" one, unwittingly but significantly touches base with 2:44. The fact that "miraculous signs and wonders" have been performed so as to reveal this reality to him in his experience confirms our earlier interpretation, that this eternal reign of God is set up by God "in the time of those kings," beginning with the period of Nebuchadnezzar's own rule. Just as in chapter 2 "the rock" threatens the entire statue, including the head (represented by Nebuchadnezzar), now, as related in Chapter 4, the eternal kingdom of God toppled the tree of the dream, that is, Nebuchadnezzar.

The wording of verse 3 corresponds very closely with that of Psalm 145:13. It is hard to believe that Nebuchadnezzar would have been conscious of these words as he composed the words of his edict. But perhaps, given his exalted position, Daniel himself helped to formulate the edict.[22] Or else the edict is recalled not in a verbatim fashion, but in a form that would cause a

20. See Pace, *Daniel*, 123.

21. *Daniel*, 124.

22. So Young, *Daniel*, 98; Harman, *Daniel*, 92–93. When we take into account the wider context of Psalm 145 we note that it is understood that God's people would be the ones to declare God's "mighty deeds." There may well then be some deliberate irony at play here in now casting a pagan ruler as the one who does this in Israel's stead: If God can't get his people to do it, he will find another way. Further the ultimate image of God as the one upon whom all creatures depend (vv. 14–19) may be compared with the analogous role God gives to Nebuchadnezzar (Daniel 4:11–12).

Jewish reader to marvel at the ways of God, in eliciting from the mouth of a pagan king the same words of worship used by God's own people.

NEBUCHADNEZZAR'S SECOND NIGHTMARE

Several cuneiform documents refer to the dreams of Nabonidus and one inscription, the Harran stela, speaks of him having a frightening dream which is followed by his return to Babylon.[23] It also confirms the authenticity of what we read in Daniel 4 because it likewise shows Nabonidus, like Nebuchadnezzar, seeking out dream interpreters and diviners to provide an interpretation of the dream.[24]

Here we have a description of a frightening dream experienced by Nebuchadnezzar while in his royal palace in Babylon. Indeed, in verses 4–5 we have what at first appears to be a re-run of chapter 2. Again stress is laid upon the disturbed state of Nebuchadnezzar's mind. This contrasts with his confessed sense of security. Nebuchadnezzar rejoices in his seeming invulnerability and the strength of his kingship. Therefore this dream, as the one before it, deeply distresses him because it presages loss of control; it implies that he is not the absolute ruler he fancies himself to be. Once more the issue concerns the control of the course of history.

Fewell reasons,

> Why must the king be shown the impending divine judgment again? Perhaps because he did not perceive it the first time. We know from his failure to display any signs of repentance that he does not understand the earlier dream to be a judgment against him personally.[25]

So far Nebuchadnezzar has refused to concede his inability to control the course of history despite the events depicted in chapters 2–3.

When Nebuchadnezzar speaks of himself as "flourishing" it would seem he chooses a word—"growing green"—which anticipates the description of the prosperous tree of the dream.[26] Ferguson cites one of Nebuchadnezzar's building inscriptions (Number 9) in which he says:

23. Bledsoe, "Identity," 748.

24. Bledsoe's presuppositions lead her to adopt the unnecessary conclusion that the experience of Nabonidus himself has been applied to Nebuchadnezzar ("Identity," 749). In my judgment the same evidence rather serves to confirm the text as it stands.

25. Fewell, Circle, 67.

26. Fewell, Circle, 66; Young, Daniel, 98; Harman, Daniel, 93.

The palace, the seat of my royal authority, a place of union of mighty peoples, abode of joy and happiness, the place where proud ones are compelled to submit, I rebuilt upon the bosom of the wide world. . . . My royal decisions, my imperial commands, I caused to go forth from it.[27]

POTENTIAL DREAM INTERPRETERS

If we did not read further we might suppose the words of verses 4–9 had been lifted out of chapter 2. The deliberately evocative language requires comparison. Just as in chapter 2, Nebuchadnezzar first summons the Chaldeans to interpret the dream for him. Only after they fail to interpret the dream—as in chapter 2—does Daniel do that which the Chaldeans cannot do or, possibly, what they were too scared to do.[28] Nebuchadnezzar's distance from knowledge of the true God who alone can reveal mysteries is accentuated by this repetition of the order of Daniel 2. Is Nebuchadnezzar's apparent unwillingness to directly and in the first instance summon Daniel an indication that he is trying to avoid the powers ("the holy gods") represented by Daniel? If so, is this because he perceives them as powers which augur the fall of his kingdom?[29] He wants an interpretation of the dream, but he wants to avoid an unfavorable one.

It is perhaps significant that the text does not speak of Nebuchadnezzar summoning Daniel, as he had in the case of his own Chaldeans. We read, "Finally, Daniel came into my presence." Notably this is the same pattern we have already met in Daniel 2 (v. 16). Daniel comes as one who is implicitly sent by God, not summoned by the king. First and foremost Daniel represents divine sovereignty.

When Nebuchadnezzar recollects how Daniel came into his presence he hastens to add his Babylonian name, Belteshazzar, with the explanation "after the name of my god," that is, Bel or Marduk. Though "Daniel" represents God the Ultimate King, Nebuchadnezzar still does not see him as

---

27. "Nebuchadnezzar," 324.

28. Thompson suggests that the movement from the tree to the fate of an individual could have had only one referent —Nebuchadnezzar. But his own wise men knew they could well be signing their own death warrant if they had told Nebuchadnezzar that dire things were about to happen to him. Indeed, from their perspective Daniel was acting very unwisely to explain the meaning of the dream to Nebuchadnezzar. "Who really rules in Babylon? "

29. So Calvin, "Daniel;" see Young, *Daniel,* 100.

such, but as someone who continues to represent "the holy gods,"[30] It has been argued by some scholars that the phrase should be rendered "the Spirit of the holy God."[31] But this is hard to defend given that in the very same breath Nebuchadnezzar speaks of "my god;" that is, he uses the singular.[32] It has been suggested that it was an accepted idiom for "very spiritual."[33] But this will not stand up to scrutiny, because in chapter 2 (which is clearly recalled) the "gods" are quite definitely deities who "do not live among men" (v. 11); that is, they are implicitly "holy," utterly separate, and transcendent.

THE KING ASKS DANIEL TO INTERPRET

Verse 9 is very revealing. Even before Daniel came to him Nebuchadnezzar was aware that he was able to interpret the dream. This underscores the importance of the sequence just described. Despite this knowledge Nebuchadnezzar had not begun by summoning Daniel.

This verse is also important because by calling Daniel by his Marduk-related name, and by classing him with the Chaldeans, albeit as the chief of them, Nebuchadnezzar reveals that prior events have still not convinced him that the wisdom represented by Daniel is not just different in degree but is also radically different in kind.

THE DREAM VISION DESCRIBED

The Initial Vision of the Prosperous Tree (vv. 10–12)

Apparently trees are not an unusual dream symbol[34], and furthermore the *axis mundi* or cosmic tree is a familiar mythological construct in the ancient

---

30. A Phoenician inscription, dated in the tenth century BC, was made for a temple built by Yehimilk, and refers to "the assembly of the holy gods of Byblos." Yet another Phoenician inscription, dated in the fifth century BC, is from the sarcophagus of Eshumunazar and refers to "the holy gods" and "these holy gods." Wooden, *Daniel and Manticism*, 231–32.

31. See Young, *Daniel*, 99; cf. Walvoord, *Daniel*, 100–101. This position is argued at length by Wooden, *Daniel and Manticism*, 226–49.

32. To the degree that ambiguity is involved in this phrase, it may well be the case that later Jewish readers would have recognized a double entendre (whether intended by the author or not), with the pagan king himself meaning "gods" literally, while, without realizing it, actually voicing recognition of the true and living God, the God of Daniel.

33. Baldwin, *Daniel*, 111.

34. Burkholder summarizes some ancient Near Eastern royal dream accounts noted by Walvoord: the dream of Astyages the Mede concerning a vine growing out of the

world.[35] It was used in various ways: world center; intersection of heaven and earth; "tree of life;" a representation of world history.[36] The tree visualized by Nebuchadnezzar stands "in the middle of the earth."

Ferguson summarizes long-standing traditions expressing the view that Babylon was the center of the world. A quarter of a millennium before Nebuchadnezzar the city had evidently been seen as the middle point of the cosmos with Babylon described as the "link of heaven and the underworld." Just a few generations before Nebuchadnezzar the only known Mesopotamian map of the world portrayed Babylon as a large rectangle near the center of the earth with all other kingdoms, depicted by small circles, revolving around it. Nebuchadnezzar's dream speaks of this tree being "visible to the ends of the earth" and the Mesopotamian map also has points (*nagû*) representing distant, remote parts of the earth identifiable with "the ends of the earth." Along with this, Ferguson observes that in his building inscriptions Nebuchadnezzar described his own kingdom as comprehending "all the lands, the entire inhabited world . . . kings of far-off mountains and remote *nagû*."[37]

Parpola's influential study of Mesopotamian iconography revealed how, in an Assyrian context, the cosmic tree represented the divine world order preserved by the king as the representative of the god Assur. In iconography the king was represented by a winged disk hovering above the tree. However, in some iconography the cosmic tree is the king.[38] That is, as Parpola explains:

> . . . in such scenes the king is portrayed as the human personification of the Tree. Thus if the Tree symbolized the divine world order, then the king himself represented the realization of that order in man, in other words, a true image of God, the Perfect Man.[39]

As Longman astutely concludes,

womb of his daughter Mandane and covering all of Asia, which Herodotus interpreted as a reference to Cyrus; Xerxes's dream of being crowned with a branch of an olive tree which spread over the world. "Literary Patterns," 47.

35. Baldwin, *Daniel*, 111. See too Geo Widengren, *The King and the Tree of Life*; Eliade, *Patterns*, 265–326. An Assyrian letter describes Ashurbanipal as a sheltering tree. Holm, *Courtiers*, 453.

36. Goldingay, *Daniel*, 87.

37. "Nebuchadnezzar," 323.

38. Burkholder draws attention to biblical references which use tree imagery to symbolize leadership, of which the following stand out: 2 Kings 14:9; Ezek 17; 31:2–18. "Literary Patterns," 48.

39. Summarized and cited by Longman, *Daniel*, 119.

The implications for Daniel 4 are clear: Nebuchadnezzar's dream shows that he identifies himself with the cosmic tree; he is the keeper of the cosmos, the true image of God, the Perfect Man.[40]

The application of exalted language in depicting Nebuchadnezzar in 2:37–38 (drawing on the Image of God tradition) indeed makes it probable that God is comparing Nebuchadnezzar with the cosmic tree in Daniel 4. This encourages us not to translate "in the middle of the land" as though the tree was merely located in the land of Babylon. The perspective is surely global as the very opening of the chapter indicates. In the dream God compares Nebuchadnezzar with the cosmic tree because this is precisely the grandiose nature of Nebuchadnezzar's self-conception. He sees himself as the world-center, something already clearly implicit in the statue he erected, but now mirrored in the portrayal of him as like a gigantic tree "visible to the ends of the earth." He sees himself as the one in whom the heavens and the earth meet, and so it is appropriate for him to be depicted as like the cosmic tree which grows so large that "its top touched the sky."

Ferguson refers to an inscription left by Nebuchadnezzar's father, Nabopolassar, which concerned the restoration of Etemenanki, "The House of the Foundation of the Heavens and the Earth." In this inscription Nabopolassar claims that he and his sons made the summit of Etemenanki "rival or equal to the heavens." Indeed, Nabopolassar "continually makes the claim that he build the palace and city from the abyss to the mountaintops."[41]

In his parable of the mustard seed (Mt 13:31–32 = Mk 4:30–32), Jesus apparently appropriates the language of 4:12, 21, using it as an image of the ultimate glory of God's kingdom, a kingdom in which all the birds of the air—presumably, all peoples (as in Daniel 4) —will find shelter. The tree in Nebuchadnezzar's dream is fruit-providing and provides shelter (v. 12), implying that Nebuchadnezzar (as per 2:37–38) unwittingly acts as God's agent, to provide protection and nourishment to all peoples of the world. In this respect this tree has Edenic connotations, as per the tree of Ezekiel 31, a connection we might expect given the allusion to Genesis 1 in 2:37–38.[42] Hartman and Di Lella comment that this tree "with its abundant fruit which provided nourishment for all (v. 9) is similar to Eden's tree of life; Nebuchadnezzar in his pride would take the place of God, who alone

---

40. *Daniel*, 119.

41. "Nebuchadnezzar," 324.

42. See Lucas, *Daniel*, 110. There are many points of correspondence between the association of both Pharaoh and Nebuchadnezzar with the cosmic tree in Ezekiel 31 and Daniel 4. It is possible that Daniel 4 reworks this same imagery. See Pace, *Daniel*, 128.

sustains man's life."[43] Indeed, while "God benevolently feeds the nonhuman creatures," Nebuchadnezzar "feeds humankind only to reign over it."[44]

Ferguson quotes from Nebuchadnezzar's Inscription Number 9:

> The produce of the lands, the product of mountains, the wealth of the sea I received in her. Under her everlasting shadow I gathered all men in peace. Vast heaps of grain beyond measure I stored up within her.[45]

There is also an ancient geographical treatise on the topography of Babylon which says the city "ensures the life of the land."

In the prophetic tradition the tree is used as a symbol of messianic rule (Isa 11:1–3,10; Ezek 17:22–24); an image of God's salvation and continuing protection (Hos 14:5–7); to represent judgment on the pride of political power: Isa 10:33–34; and with respect to the reign and fall of Pharaoh: Ezek 31:3, 6, 8b–9,10–12.

Given this identification of Nebuchadnezzar with the cosmic tree, the irony of the way in which Daniel 4 begins needs to be re-emphasized. For despite all that will happen in this chapter to humiliate Nebuchadnezzar he still acts as the world-center and as the one who can announce to the world the ultimate divine mystery. The irony of the chapter is that though the tree is toppled, the stump with its root remains. Indeed, not only is Nebuchadnezzar's kingdom restored to him, but he again conceives himself as being in effect the cosmic tree.

43. *Book of Daniel*, 176.

44. Kim, *Biblical Interpretation*, 151. "He misdirects dominion to other human beings that is originally supposed to be directed to nonhuman creatures," whom, I might add, he treats as if they were animals. Hence the poetic justice involved in the judgment which follows.

45. "Nebuchadnezzar," 323.

The representation of cosmic mountains, pillars and trees is common in the ancient world with cosmic trees being especially characteristic of Mesopotamian iconography. Notably, Egyptian and Hittite iconography can portray the king in the same way. In the ancient world, therefore, Daniel's identification of the cosmic tree with the king was not unprecedented. The mountain/pillar/tree/king characteristically rises in the center of the earth to support the heavens. Thus this Mesopotamian (Assyrian) representation shows the cosmic tree of life rising from the summit of the cosmic mountain with its "top touching the sky."

Ferguson provides an example from an "impressive array of data from the Mesopotamian world" which identifies the king as a tree, namely a Sumerian royal hymn which, addressing the king, says, "O chosen cedar . . . , for thy shadow the country may feel awe."[46]

The Vision of the Axed Tree (vv. 13–15a)

Verse 13 = 4:10 in MT: " . . . and lo, a watcher and a holy one descended from heaven."

This is the only occurrence in the Old Testament of the word "watcher" which refers to a "vigilant one," or "a wakeful one." Here the accompanying phrase, "the holy one," indicates we are dealing with an angel. The term "watchers" is used in 1 Enoch and Jubilees to refer to angels.[47] Here "the wakeful one" implies a contrast with a "sleeping" Nebuchadnezzar.[48] Indeed the very dream medium God uses to convey revelation to Nebuchadnezzar performs a vital function—it represents Nebuchadnezzar as the one who lies on his bed, and sleeps, in contrast to God whose is ever active in effecting his kingdom purposes.

It is likely (see below) that the reference to watchers is intended to echo the Epic of Gilgamesh, which would have been familiar to Nebuchadnezzar. In that epic there are watchers of the night, scorpion people who stand at the gate through which Gilgamesh must pass to find out about eternal life.[49] Ferguson also speaks of a Babylonian understanding of "personified night watchers who, alert and never sleeping, control destinies on the earth." They

46. "Nebuchadnezzar," 324.

47. Lucas, *Daniel*, 110. Lucas also notes the same usage in *T. Reuben* 5:6–7; *T. Naphtali* 3:5. The term can either mean fallen angels, as in these references and Jubilees 4:22; 7:21; and 10:5. Or it can refer to righteous angels as in Jubilees 4:15. Here it evidently represents an angel sent by Yahweh. See too Pace, *Daniel,* 129.

48. Fewell, *Circle,* 68.

49. See Ferguson, "Nebuchadnezzar," 326–27.

believed that while the great gods slept other deities were left in charge of watching the night.

"Heaven" is perhaps a circumlocution for "God" but if so this is the only such instance in the Old Testament.[50] But its use in Daniel is not startling given the prior designation of God as "the God of heaven," with the implication in the book of Daniel that it is in heaven that ultimate rule is effected (cf. Matt 5:34). That this is the correct way to understand "heaven" is explicitly confirmed by verse 26 when Daniel explains: "your kingdom will be restored to you when you acknowledge that Heaven rules."

God also causes Nebuchadnezzar to dream of a tree being chopped down so as to forge a connection with the Epic of Gilgamesh (see below).[51] In that epic Gilgamesh goes with Enkidu to the cedar mountain. There he kills the never-sleeping guardian of the sacred cedar, who had been appointed by Enlil, the high god, and then chops the tree down. It is said that prior to being chopped down the towering cedar "uplifted its fullness before the mountain; fair was its shade and full of delight."[52]

The fleeing of the beasts and birds from the tree concerns the inability of Nebuchadnezzar to personally act as the royal source of blessing and security for his subjects. However, the stump with its roots is still left and it is bound with a band of iron and bronze. This feature has mystified scholars. It has been difficult to find any evidence of such bands being used in the ancient Near East to protect trees, though this seems to be the function being exercised in Daniel 4.[53] Gowan considers the possibility that such bands were used to decorate sacred trees, and notes that the excavation of the Shamash temple at Khorsabad unearthed a tree trunk with two skillfully embossed bronze bands around it.[54] In Daniel 4, the bands, apart from perhaps underscoring that this tree remains a "sacred" tree, even in its reduced state, also serves to indicate that Nebuchadnezzar will not lose his rule altogether; that it will be restored. The use of an iron and bronze protective band may also be intended to recall the statue of Daniel 2. In that chapter human rule in all its devastating, crushing force is characterized by iron and bronze. God's use of iron and bronze, not to oppress, but to protect

50. See Anderson, *Signs and Wonders*, 46.

51. Ferguson shows how natural it would have been for Nebuchadnezzar to dream of such a tree given his own demonstrable obsession with chopping down cedars as an expression of his might. "Nebuchadnezzar," 328.

52. See Ferguson, "Nebuchadnezzar," 327–28.

53. Holm, *Courtiers*, 456, notes that Ashurbanipal's palace at Nimrud apparently possesses "an alabaster mural relief containing 'trees of life' with bands of some kind around them."

54. Gowan, *Daniel*, 78. See too Holm, *Courtiers*, 456.

the foundations of Nebuchadnezzar's reign highlights the contrast between human and divine rule.

The destruction of the tree though not complete and utter is so sudden "that the normal processes of withering and dying are precluded."[55] Nevertheless the lopping down of this cosmic tree now means that to the ancient mind nothing is left to stop the very sky from collapsing. When Nebuchadnezzar becomes incompetent to rule the result should be the disintegration of the entire created order and a reversion to chaos. But this is not the result. Therefore, there must be another rule, one greater than that of Nebuchadnezzar, which maintains the created order. It is only in Nebuchadnezzar's own personal life that the forces of chaos are expressed, as evidenced by his crossing of the creation order boundaries between himself and other creatures. The lopping down of the cosmic tree leaves Nebuchadnezzar himself without shelter and results in him being "drenched with the dew of heaven" (v. 15). He cannot even look to the continuing Babylonian empire for shelter but is fully dependent on God's rule to terminate his life of chaos and restore him to the God-ruled created order.[56]

The Vision of Animalization (vv. 15–17)

The lowering of Nebuchadnezzar to the status of an animal—a grotesque hybrid creature—is God's way of saying that he is unworthy of the divine image.[57] But it has additional significance in the fact that his human "mind" is exchanged for the "mind" of an animal. The man who exaggerates his own importance and thinks of himself as being like a god, possessing absolute control over all people and all creatures, will lose control over his own self and be driven by instinct like an animal. Even control over oneself lies in the hands of God. It is God who allows a man to think like a man, and an animal to think like an animal. It is his continued sovereignty that explains such phenomena. Therefore God alone can be described as the absolute sovereign.

55. Anderson, *Signs and Wonders,* 43.

56. Pace notes that dew can be a sign of blessing (e.g. Ps 133:3) or as a sign of the inevitable (e.g. 2 Sam 17:12) or as a sign of something transient or unfaithful (e.g. Hos 6:4): "As it is used of Nebuchadnezzar, the dew of heaven that bathes him is a sign of his animal-like state and his total dependence on God. Like the animals that have no permanent shelter, when Nebuchadnezzar is separated from the human community, he has no way to escape the nightly dewfall." *Daniel,* 130.

57. Kim, *Biblical Interpretation,* 153. Also compare the hybrid nature of Nebuchadnezzar's animal-like state with the similarly grotesque hybrid beasts of Daniel 7 and 8. Kim, *Biblical Interpretation,* 156.

The man who presumptuously thinks himself to be the absolute ruler of all the earth will be cut down to size. He must learn that only the Most High has such power and authority. The statement that he sets over the kingdoms of men "the lowliest of men" is a double-barreled statement. In the first instance it appears to be eschatological since true universal rule had not been exercised by any king to that point in human history. So the statement probably implies that God will place "the lowliest of men" over all the kingdoms of the earth—a purpose that is fulfilled only in Christ.

On the other hand, in the immediate context God does restore Nebuchadnezzar but only after he has become, in another sense, "the lowliest of men" by having been reduced to the status of an animal. To the extent it is valid to think of Nebuchadnezzar as being ruler over all the kingdoms of men, then it is true to say that God gives him this right of rule as "the lowliest of men." Of course, insofar as the phrase "lowliest of men" can be applied to Nebuchadnezzar, it does not imply that he had become a genuinely humble man. Indeed the irony of the passage, as we have previously observed, is that despite his humiliation Nebuchadnezzar continues to think of himself as the world-center and discloser of divine mysteries.

THE KING'S DEPENDENCE ON DANIEL
FOR INTERPRETATION

Fewell regards as significant the omission in this chapter of certain elements present in chapter 2. There is no disclaimer by Daniel, as per 2:27–28, that he lacks inherent wisdom to understand the dream that God alone can reveal. On the contrary, as verse 18 shows, Nebuchadnezzar thinks Daniel can interpret the dream "because the spirit of the holy gods is in you," which indicates that in Nebuchadnezzar's mind the boundary between divine and human ability is blurred. In chapter 4 there is no indication that Daniel sought to remove this misunderstanding from Nebuchadnezzar's mind. On this basis, Fewell mounts a spurious argument from silence that it suited Daniel's own political ambitions to allow the king to overestimate his abilities.[58]

Again arguing from silence, Fewell notes that whereas in chapter 2 Daniel, with his friends, prayed for divine revelation, there is no such prayer in chapter 4. Indeed Fewell goes so far as to claim that Daniel's variations in his interpretation—he doesn't press home the obvious meaning of certain

---

58. Fewell, *Circle,* 69.

aspects, e.g., stripping of foliage, scattering of fruit—constitute a softening of the divine decree, so that Daniel "tells the truth but not the whole truth."[59]

But if such omissions have significance at all it is quite possible to draw a quite different conclusion: that the mention of such matters would detract from the major emphasis of the passage which is upon Nebuchadnezzar's inability, despite all that has preceded, and despite Daniel's prior assurances, to appreciate the radical difference in kind between Daniel's wisdom and that of the Chaldeans. Even though he acknowledges that Daniel alone can interpret the dream, for him it is because he is "chief of the magicians" (that is, first among equals), and because the gods, conceived of in a Babylonian fashion, have chosen Daniel as the vehicle of their revelation. The fact that despite this Nebuchadnezzar does praise "the Most High" indicates that Daniel had in fact succeeded in communicating that there is one God in particular who is responsible for the dream and the revelation it involves.

Given the identification of the king with the cosmic tree, and remembering the Assyrian representation shown above, the inability of the wise men (magicians) to interpret the dream may have profound cosmological significance. The iconographic image of the cosmic tree shown earlier in the chapter has figures to the left and right of the tree—described by Keel as "conjuring priests."[60] That is, their magical incantations and gestures are also fundamental to the preservation of a created order, which centers on the role performed by the cosmic tree (in Daniel 4, Nebuchadnezzar). As Keel notes their role actually "[detracts] from the sovereignty of the sky god" and, more particularly in Daniel to the extent that the king takes his magicians seriously then their role detracts from the rule of Heaven, the rule of the Most High God, the God of Daniel. Therefore, it is essential to the purpose of what happens in Daniel 4 that the total incompetence and impotence of the Chaldeans also be fully exposed. The God-effected events of Daniel 4 effectively erase the two figures and the cosmic tree from the representation shown above and leave the entire creation order vulnerable to chaos. When the king and magicians are both removed from any involvement in controlling the created order, it becomes necessary to identify the ruler upon whom the created order really depends, the Most High.

Shea's analysis of the structure revealed a chiasm which has its apex in verses 18–19 and the change from first person address by Nebuchadnezzar to third person narration in verse 19 is suggestive that a turning point is achieved at this point in the chapter. This may amount to nothing more than that we have reached the point at which the interpretation of the dream

59. Fewell, *Circle*, 70.
60. *Symbolism*, 29.

begins. However, as noted above it indicates that the essential nature of the difference between Danielic and Chaldean wisdom consists in the prophetic, moral character of Daniel's wisdom.

THE TREE AND THE IMAGE OF GOLD

It is a strange but mysterious fact that most commentators do not think to note or make much of the connection between the tree and the statue. This is all the more necessary given our earlier observation that in the ancient world representations of cosmic trees and kings (including statues) are parallel conceptions of that which stands at the center of the earth and supports the sky, thus maintaining the created order.

There are many obvious points of correspondence between the tree, the statue of Nebuchadnezzar's dream in chapter 2, and the statue constructed by Nebuchadnezzar in chapter 3. Both the tree and the statue are colossal in their height. Both are prosperous and involve rule over the whole earth (note "birds of the air" and every creature corresponds to the comprehensive language drawn from Genesis 1 at 2:38). Both are toppled (cf. 2:34, 45). The scattering of the fruit recalls the chaff swept away by the wind (2:35).

Fewell suggests:

> Just as, in the Eden story, the tree of knowledge of good and evil represents the human desire to know all, that is, to be like God, so, too, the tree in the dream is representative of a human being wanting to be like a god. The dream implies that he considers himself above humanity, a tree of life nourishing the whole world. The existence of the entire world depends upon him. He acknowledges no other source of power besides himself. This is the sin for which he is to be punished.[61]

Since in verse 30 Nebuchadnezzar's boastful words probably recall the Tower of Babel episode (Genesis 11), it is likely that the very image of the tree having its heights in the heavens is connected with the city "with a tower which reaches to the heavens" (Gen 11:4). When God passes judgment on the tree, involving descent from heaven (vv. 13, 23 cf. Gen 11:5) the result is that the fruit is scattered: an evident echo of Genesis 11:8—"So the Lord scattered them over all the earth."[62]

61. Fewell, *Circle*, 67.

62. See Kim, *Biblical Interpretation*, 128. Kim finds the concept of the divine council also implicit in both contexts: "the watcher" cf. "Come, let us go down" (Gen 11:7), 133. Corresponding to the tree being "in the midst of the earth," Kim finds implicit in Genesis 11:1–9 the idea that humans considered Babylon to be the center of the earth,

DANIEL DISMAYED

The transition from first person to third person is natural given that Ne-buchadnezzar has just asked Daniel to interpret his dream. There is no need to adopt the cynicism of Collins who maintained that the change in voice signaled "the author's failure to maintain the fiction of the first person narrative."[63] The skillful alternation of first person—third person—first person enables us to compare and contrast the points of view of the author of the text and the main character in the text, Nebuchadnezzar.[64] This is in keeping with our earlier observation that at 2:4b the switch to Aramaic is an invitation to enter the Babylonian thought-world. The first person device used in chapter 4 is yet another indication of this intent. As Meadowcroft recognizes, while "Nebuchadnezzar is substantially responsible for the tell-ing of this particular story . . . he is not the observer through whose eyes the event is finally viewed."[65] Further, the switch to the third person also has the effect of showing that Daniel's input is not merely to provide an explana-tion of the dream, but that the interpretation itself is the divine word which brings about the very events that are now described. The final emphasis must fall not on Nebuchadnezzar's personal experience of divine rule but on the operation of divine rule itself.

Daniel, realizing that the dream will involve God's judgment falling upon Nebuchadnezzar, displays an extraordinary empathy for Nebuchad-nezzar and is "greatly perplexed for a time," while "his thoughts alarmed him" (v. 19). A window is opened here into Daniel's view of his own situa-tion. He clearly recognizes that he is in the service of Nebuchadnezzar by God's appointment. Therefore he is not bitter and resentful and he does not desire the downfall of Nebuchadnezzar. He is sincere about being a good

---

since it was "from there" that they were scattered in all directions; *Biblical Interpreta-tion,* 136–37.

63. Cited by Meadowcroft, "Point of View," 31. Meadowcroft notes Montgomery's view that the shift in person is due to "an unconscious dramatic sense."

64. Here Meadowcroft distinguishes between "point of view"—a term applying to texts—and "perspective"—the equivalent concept in visual media; "Point of View," 32. Others use different terms to describe the same basic distinction, e.g. Stanzel: the "at-titude" of the narrator vs. the "standpoint" of characters; Chatman: the "slant" put on the story by the narrator's point of view vs. the "filters" provided by characters within the narrative. To the extent that the attitude of the narrator is more "covert" than "overt" (Bar-Efrat), the narrator's attitude towards characters and events will not necessarily be self-evident. In Daniel 4, however, the surrounding strength of the characterisa-tion of Daniel and his friends and the narrator's clearly presented underlying theology makes it relatively easy to discern his attitude towards Nebuchadnezzar and the events described.

65. Meadowcroft, "Point of View," 35.

and faithful servant of the king, and genuinely seeks his welfare.[66] In this he is a fine model of the attitude and conduct Paul exhorts in Colossians 3:22.[67] He also serves as a template for diaspora Jews, showing "the possibility of peacefully coexisting with the pagan power structure while at the same time maintaining true Jewish piety and identity."[68]

From a purely literary standpoint this noting of Daniel's reaction highlights the fact that something terrible is about to happen to the king.[69]

THE INTERPRETATION OF THE DREAM (VV. 20–27)

In the preceding chapter the decree of Nebuchadnezzar was in fact undermined by the disobedience of Shadrach, Meshach, and Abednego. Following their miraculous deliverance by God, the question of them bowing down before the statue becomes otiose. But when God issues a decree against Nebuchadnezzar its enactment is inevitable and is totally irrevocable.

In verse 22 we meet with words— "You, O king, are that tree!"—which are strongly reminiscent of Nathan's words to David—"You are the man!" (2 Sam 12:7). In this connection it is also striking to compare the falling of Nebuchadnezzar into sin as he walks on the roof of the royal palace with the similar scenario concerning David's fall into adultery (2 Sam 12:2). Even the approach to both kings is similar insofar as the explicit and individualized indictment in each case is preceded by an allegorical "story." Daniel 4 stresses that Nebuchadnezzar's rule is a delegated rule, one he exercises by God's will. God has given him his kingdom and, therefore, Nebuchadnezzar is expected to rule righteously (4:27). Thus, in this new exilic situation Nebuchadnezzar now assumes a role which is roughly analogous to that which

66. As Hebbard puts it, "Daniel's service to the Babylonian king is exceptional because he serves as if he would for his heavenly King. . . Daniel does not serve this pagan king *despite* his devotion to Adonai, he serves the king *because* of his devotion to Adonai." *Reading Daniel*, 64.

67. In later rabbinic handling of Daniel 4, especially influenced by a negative experience of Roman imperial rule, it was common to read Daniel 4 in the light of Isaiah 14, to ignore Nebuchadnezzar's repentance and to be highly critical of Daniel for being so concerned for this tyrant's wellbeing. So David Satran as summarized by Wills, *Jewish Novel*, 48.

68. Wills taking up Humphreys's point. *Jewish Novel*, 49.

69. I have stressed the satirical nature of these early chapters. Nevertheless, the emphasis on Daniel's genuine distress does not encourage the conclusion reached by Wills (*Jewish Novel*, 49): "the coziness of Daniel with Nebuchadnezzar can be seen as part of the essentially comic worldview of the collection. There is a certain triumph over villainy in subordinating Nebuchadnezzar to Daniel, transforming the former into a comic foil, a *senex iratus* or 'blustering old man' of comic tradition." *Jewish Novel*, 49.

had previously been exercised by kings like David. But since "Heaven rules" (4:26) it is necessary, as before, when the king fundamentally oversteps the mark, that a representative from the heavenly court be sent to confront and rebuke the king and call upon him to repent. Collins observes,

> The difference between Daniel 4 and Daniel 2 lies neither in the portrayal of God nor in the role of the wise man, but in the presentation of the gentile king. Nebuchadnezzar in Daniel 2 was not subjected to criticism. In Daniel 4, however, Daniel confronts the king as Nathan confronted David in 2 Samuel 12, points out his sins, and exhorts him to repent.[70]

Thus Daniel is the new Nathan, and in chapter 4 he is unmistakeably cast as a prophet who even presses upon the king, to his face, his sinfulness and exhorts him to repent (4:27). The applying to Nebuchadnezzar of the image of a tree is especially interesting when we recall its prior use in describing the house of David (e.g., Isa 11:1–3, 10; cf. Ezek 17:22–24; Hos 14:5–7).[71]

The fact that the judgment is set for "seven times" implies that God is in complete control of the course of history, so much so that he can precisely determine when and for how long a particular set of events will occur. There may also be a hint of poetic justice here, recalling that in the previous chapter Nebuchadnezzar ordered the furnace to be heated "seven times" before throwing the three Jews into it. Further, in the prior narratives Nebuchadnezzar has sought to show his mastery over time and always in a manner that involves humiliating others. In the previous chapter he specified when all should worship his image. In Daniel 2 he refuses to let his astrologers gain more time and insists that they tell him the dream immediately. Now he learns to his chagrin that it is God who controls time and he himself is humiliated.[72]

It is often supposed by commentators that the period of Nebuchadnezzar's humiliation lasted for seven years. Against Hartman, who pontificated that it was impossible to fit such a period into what is known of Nebuchadnezzar's life, Ferguson points out that no time marker is used, so that the period may have been as little as seven days.[73] Besides, as Ferguson observes, following Montgomery: "royal families do not usually make such frailties public, records of the king's condition were probably never made."

70. *Apocalyptic Vision*, 48.

71. Reid, *Kingdoms*, 89.

72. Here I am developing further some seed ideas sown by Kim, *Biblical Interpretation*, 154–55.

73. "Nebuchadnezzar, Gilgamesh, and the 'Babylonian Job,'" 321–22.

In verse 27 clear indications are given that Nebuchadnezzar was guilty of oppression. Some commentators have missed the point here thinking that Daniel is exhorting a piety that will appease God through good works.[74] But the issue is not so much Nebuchadnezzar's private life but rather the issue of whether he is fit to rule the kingdom. God has already repeatedly revealed to Nebuchadnezzar that he is the Most High who "is sovereign over the kingdoms of men" and, knowing this (which is why the chapter begins with Nebuchadnezzar acknowledging this), it is all the more incumbent on Nebuchadnezzar to be a righteous king whose kingship is reflective of what he recognizes to be true.

A DREAM COMES TRUE (VV. 28–32)

"It is rather ironic that Daniel suggests to the king that the Most High will respond to a change in *behaviour* (. . .v27), whereas this episode implies that *words* trigger divine response."[75] So says Fewell, thinking Daniel advised Nebuchadnezzar that a righteous life and being kind to the oppressed would avoid judgment, whereas in fact it was Nebuchadnezzar's boastful words that brought about his humiliation. Fewell draws the strange conclusion from this that Daniel deliberately misadvised Nebuchadnezzar. Quite apart from this illegitimate cynicism (as verse 19 clearly shows), Fewell misreads verse 27, which does not promise that righteous living will result in the avoidance of judgment but, as Young recognizes, "merely speaks of a lengthening of a period of tranquility."[76] It is significant that any attempt that may have been made by the Chaldeans to use apotropaic rituals and magic spells to prevent the evil consequences portended have signally failed. Nothing short of repentance will do.[77]

In Inscription Number 9 Nebuchadnezzar claims concerning his palace that it was "bursting with splendor. Luxuriance, dread! Fulness, awe, gleaming majesty surrounded it." He also boasted that he had made Babylon into a fortress, as strong as a mountain, claiming, "I made the dwelling place of my lordship glorious."[78]

74. Towner, 63. Cyprian used Daniel's exhortation to Nebuchadnezzar to "practice righteousness" as grounds for the practice of almsgiving. Aquinas took 4:24 to mean that almsgiving is a work of justice and not of charity. Gammie, "A Journey," 149, 152.

75. *Circle*, 71.

76. *Daniel*, 109.

77. Wooden, *Daniel and Manticism*, 250–51.

78. Ferguson, "Nebuchadnezzar," 324.

Nebuchadnezzar's boastful words in Daniel 4 reveal that he built Babylon for his own glory, to make a name for himself.[79] This is reminiscent of Genesis 11.[80] It is of incidental interest that Babylonian records indicate that Nebuchadnezzar was more remembered as a builder than as a warrior.[81] Michael Roaf expresses well the stupendous grandeur of Babylon for much of which Nebuchadnezzar was personally responsible:

> Babylon contained two of the Seven Wonders of the Ancient World, the Hanging Gardens[82] and the city walls. The location of the Hanging Gardens is in doubt but the walls have been traced. The outer wall stretched for more than 8 kilometers and, according to Herodotus, had enough space on top to enable a four-horse chariot to turn around.[83]

We know of other impressive structures—temples to Marduk and at least fifty other gods, together with statues to over two hundred additional deities.[84] No wonder that as Nebuchadnezzar gazed upon his impressive achievements his heart swelled with pride at his own perceived greatness! Indeed, Ferguson eloquently describes the situation:

> Nebuchadnezzar stood on his palace roof, which had been made of cedar from the forests of Lebanon. Stacked all around

79. Mastin argues at length for the rendering "Surely this is great Babylon!" against the common understanding that this is a question requiring a "yes" answer, as per the NIV: "Is not this the great Babylon I have built . . ." Mastin, "Meaning," 234–47. But this technical question does not appear to change the essential meaning of the text.

80. The pride of Nabonidus is depicted in the Verse Account: "I am wise. I am knowledgeable. I have seen hid[den things]. (Although) I do not know the art of writing, I have seen se[cret things]. . . I surpass in all (kinds of) wisdom (even the series) *uskar-Anum-Enlilla*, which Adap[a] composed. . . ." Bledsoe, "Identity," 752. weakly proposes, despite Nebuchadnezzar's totally different basis for boasting at Daniel 4:30–31, that this is evidence for assuming that what is said of Nebuchadnezzar in Daniel 4 is really an application to him of traditions involving Nabonidus. But we have already seen inscriptional evidence of Nebuchadnezzar's own boasting and with relation to his building projects!

81. Young, *Daniel*, 109. Ferguson notes that in 1912 Stephen Langdon published fifty-two building inscriptions belonging to Nebuchadnezzar. "Nebuchadnezzar," 322.

82. Diodorus of Sicily describes how Nebuchadnezzar built the Hanging Gardens for his wife Amyitis, who pined for her home in Media. Reditt describes the gardens as covering "an area a hundred feet square, and built in ascending tiers. Each tier was sealed to prevent moisture from leaking through, packed with enough dirt to allow even the largest trees to take root, and planted with all kinds of vegetation. The tallest plants towered above the city wall, and, when viewed from the outside, looked like a garden suspended from above." *Daniel*, 7.

83. Cited by Longman, *Daniel*, 121.

84. Redditt, *Daniel*, 84, summarizing Wiseman.

were over fifteen million bricks, each containing his name and royal titles. He was surrounded by six walls and a 262-foot moat. Some of the buildings seemed to rival the heavens. The "contented one" swelled with pride and cried out, "Is not this Babylon, which I have built?" (Dan 4:30).

He had forgotten that all the bricks were made of mud. He had also forgotten the affirmation made at his accession that all he possessed came from one deity. He had not remembered that his father had represented himself on a monument as the "son of nobody," helpless without his god. He had failed to notice two streets below him called "Bow Down, Proud One" and "May the Arrogant Not Flourish." He did not even recall that one of the names of his palace was "The Place Where Proud Ones Are Compelled to Submit."[85]

NEBUCHADNEZZAR IS REDUCED TO AN ANIMAL STATE (V. 33)

The standard critical view is that what is described in Daniel 4 is an application and re-working of experiences which actually befell Nabonidus. But a reading of *The Verse Account of Nabonidus*, Cyrus Cylinder, *The Nabonidus Chronicle*, and *The Prayer of Nabonidus* shows the "evidence" to be very tenuous and far from compelling. There are good grounds to accept the biblical text as it stands. A different proposal is that it is not Nabonidus who is presupposed but Antiochus IV Epiphanes whom Jews insultingly called "epimanes," that is, "mad."[86] There is no solid basis for seeing the portrayal of Daniel in Daniel 4 as being influenced by the depiction of a Jewish exorcist in *The Nabonidus Chronicle*.

Verse 33 graphically portrays the abject humiliation of Nebuchadnezzar as the fulfillment[87] of what God portended in the nightmarish dream

---

85. "Nebuchadnezzar, Gilgamesh, and the 'Babylonian Job,'" 321.

86. Nelson, *Daniel*, 29.

87. Bledsoe, "Identity," 751 has to twist the use of the language of fulfillment here to force her argument that this constitutes evidence of *The Nabonidus Chronicle* being reworked to apply what had really happened to Nabonidus to Nebuchadnezzar. In that text, in referring to the time when Nabonidus returns to Babylon, "it is said that 'fulfilled was the year, the appointed time arrived.'" But this is an entirely different conception of fulfillment to that which we encounter in Daniel 4. Here fulfillment concerns that which was prophesied not time per se. Further, Bledsoe's reading of *The Nabonidus Chronicle* leads her to interpret such fulfillment in that text as evidence of moving away from a state in which Nabonidus was effectively cut off from society, which is the very opposite of what we have in Daniel 4!

Nebuchadnezzar had experienced. Sinclair Ferguson has an apt way of describing Nebuchadnezzar's fate in Daniel 4: "Superman has become Subman."[88] Paul Ferguson points out that in one of Esarhaddon's treaties, just a generation before the reign of Nabopolassar, Nebuchadnezzar's father, a Median king is warned about possible reduction to an animal-like state.[89] He also observes the close parallels between the Danielic portrayal of Nebuchadnezzar's humiliation and what happened to the primordial man in the Mesopotamian Gilgamesh epic.[90] Enkidu's whole body was covered with hair, with his locks sprouting like grain. He eats grass with the gazelles and with them drinks at the waterhole and ranges over the open country. After a seven-day period he becomes civilized, human, and then loses his kinship with the animals, which flee from him.[91]

It may well be that God brings this particular judgment on him because Nebuchadnezzar would have been familiar with the Epic of Gilgamesh, it having been noted by Wiseman that schools operating during Nebuchadnezzar's reign were still making copies of this epic, one of the most widely distributed pieces of Babylonian literature.[92]

Indeed, as Ferguson points out there are further parallels between Daniel 4 and the Epic of Gilgamesh:[93]

1. Both works have statements of the glorification of a king's building accomplishments.

2. Both are concerned about the mortality of a human king and the consequences of arrogance toward deity.

3. Both narratives tell of the chopping down of a very extraordinary tree which provided extensive shade.[94]

4. In both narratives "watchers" play a prominent part.[95]

5. Both narratives involve a troubling dream or dreams that must be interpreted.

---

88. Ferguson, *Daniel*, 102.

89. "Nebuchadnezzar," 326.

90. "Nebuchadnezzar," 325.

91. Cf. Lucas, *Daniel*, 113.

92. Ferguson, "Nebuchadnezzar," 326.

93. "Nebuchadnezzar," 326–27.

94. Gilgamesh takes pride in the way he killed the guardian and chopped down the sacred cedar on the cedar mountain.

95. In the Gilgamesh epic Huwawa, the guardian of the cedar tree, is a watcher who never sleeps.

Also the Gilgamesh epic is comparable with a Sumerian story that describes primordial people who "knew not the wearing of garments," who ate grass like sheep and drank water from ditches.

There is a tradition of reading this account of the humiliation of the arrogant Babylonian king together with Isaiah 14:13–16.[96] The 4th century Syrian saint, Ephrem, saw here an allusion to the Fall, a connection to be taken seriously given the prior likening of Nebuchadnezzar to Adam at 2:37–38.[97] Ephrem comments,

> David wept for Adam, at how he fell from that royal abode to the abode of wild animals (Ps 49:13). Because he went astray through a beast he became like the beasts: he ate, together with them as a result of the curse, grass and roots, and he died, becoming their peer. Blessed is He who set him apart from the wild animals again.[98]

He continues by drawing the correspondence:

> In that king [sc. Nebuchadnezzar] did God depict Adam; since he provoked God by his exercise of kingship, God stripped him of that kingship. The Just One was angry and cast him out into the region of wild beasts; he dwelt there with them in the wilderness, and only when he repented did he return to his former abode and kingship. Blessed is He who has thus taught us to repent so that we, too, may return to Paradise.[99]

Fewell comments on the significance of Nebuchadnezzar's reduction to an animal state:

> Rather than being like the great tree in the dream, Nebuchadnezzar takes on the characteristics of the dream's representations of his subjects—the birds and the beasts. He now acts like an ox and looks like a bird. This final repetition of the decree caps the

---

96. See Henze, "Nebuchadnezzar's Madness," 550–52. A Syriac Father, Aphrahat, does this in a work called *About Wars* (1st century CE). A tannaitic midrash, the *Mekilta de-Rabbi Ishmael*, also makes this connection in comments on Exodus 15:7.

97. Henze, "Nebuchadnezzar's Madness," 560. Ephrem has extensive comments on Nebuchadnezzar's madness emphasizing the significance of his repentance as a paradigm for all Christians. An Anchorite document, *Letter to the Mountaineers*, makes the same association of Nebuchadnezzar's reduction to an animal state with Adam's Fall ("Nebuchadnezzar's Madness," 565–66).

98. Henze, "Nebuchadnezzar's Madness," 560.

99. Henze, "Nebuchadnezzar's Madness," 560.

theme of poetic justice: A man who thinks he is like a god must become a beast to learn that he is only a human being.[100]

Kim finds here "trenchant satire" since for Jewish exiles they now read of this tyrant, as one "driven away from people," being exiled among animals.[101]

As might be expected, there has been no shortage of scholars who deny the historicity of this event. What is described in verse 33 may correspond with a kind of mental illness known as zooanthropy or lycanthropy. A person with this condition sees himself as a particular animal and wants to live like that animal. Monarchs George III of Britain and Otto of Bavaria suffered from this condition.[102] The most common form of this self-delusion is that of imagining oneself to be a wolf. In Nebuchadnezzar's case he saw himself as an ox.[103]

In 1946 Old Testament scholar R. K. Harrison observed a patient in a British mental institution whose condition closely corresponded with that described in verse 33. He wandered about the grounds of the institution eating grass as though he was a cow. His drank only water. Harrison stated: "the only physical abnormality noted consisted of a lengthening of the hair and a coarse, thickened condition of the fingernails."[104]

But in seeking comparable modes of appearance and behavior in human experience perhaps we will miss an essential aspect of what these descriptions would have meant to the first readers of the book of Daniel. As Hays observes, in ancient Near Eastern thought and mythology, the type of animal imagery employed in describing Nebuchadnezzar in verse 33 "frequently symbolized those who were afflicted by divine powers."[105] Hays shows that in Mesopotamia, the ancient Near East, and in the Bible, the

100. *Circle*, 72.

101. *Biblical Interpretation*, 139. Holm finds a parallel between Daniel 4 and the Egyptian court tale *Merib, the High Steward, and the Captive Pharaoh*. Both stories involve a king being forced into exile for a time where they live among animals. In both cases the king needs the help of a courtier with special relations with a deity and who urges the king to reverence that deity. *Courtiers*, 457–59.

102. Lucas, *Daniel*, 111.

103. There is also a relevant curse attached to Esarhaddon's vassal treaties: "Wander in the fields like a wild ass or a gazelle." Lucas, *Daniel*, 111–12. Pace observes that in the midrashim the eagle, ox and lion are respectively the "lords" of their own category: birds, beasts and wild beasts. She reasons, "Just as the ox, although superior to all beasts, acknowledges God as its master, so too must Nebuchadnezzar learn this lesson that it is God who determines his sovereignty." *Daniel*, 136.

104. The reference is from Stephen R. Miller's (1994) commentary on Daniel, cited by Robert C. Stone. http://www.hillcrestchapel.com/characters/nezzer.html

105. Hays, "Chirps," 305.

same complex of animal images was used to portray underworld figures—gods, demons and the spirits of the dead.[106] He finds that this imagery is transferred from such supernatural beings to those they afflict and that this occurs specifically in prayer texts. Hays argues that the first person address aspect of Daniel 4, together with a structure of affliction-restoration-praise presupposes awareness of prayer genres—thanksgiving and lament. He argues that "it is Nebuchadnezzar's *suffering* at the hand of God, rather than his madness, that this imagery should evoke."[107]

Hays identifies "a long tradition in Mesopotamia relating the dead to birds in particular,"[108] and observes the way ox imagery is attested in Sumerian spell texts to describe underworld demons. Hays, like Ferguson, also makes much of the *Epic of Gilagamesh* but now as providing a description of the underworld creature that dragged off Gilgamesh to the underworld[109]:

> His face was like that of Anzû;
> His hands were the paws of a lion,
> his claws were the claws of an eagle (are).
> He seized me by the hair, he was too strong for me,
> I hit him but he snapped back like a snare,
> He struck me and capsized me like a raft.
> Like a wild bull he trampled me.

Hays points out that this creature "looks like a composite beast comparable to a bird and a bull, among other things."[110] Hays cites from *The Netherworld Vision of an Assyrian Prince* in which the prince Kumma, who may represent Ashurbanipal, dreams of fifteen divine beings in the underworld. Most of them are described using animal imagery, as composite beings. We find the dragon, eagle, crocodile, lion, bird, ox, and goat. Of these only the lion, ox, and bird are referred to more than once.

Hays argues that in ancient Near Eastern thought the one who suffers an assault from such powers "can begin to look like the dead even before

106. Hays ("Chirps," 308) points out: "Ancient Mesopotamian portraits of the underworld (or world of the dead) made extensive use of animal imagery, even from Sumerian times." He clarifies that not "every appearance of these animals in a given period and culture indicates underworld imagery," but "a limited set of images became associated as a familiar complex representing the assault of supernatural powers and its effects—making it the best available interpretation of Daniel 4:30" (= v. 33).

107. "Chirps," 308.

108. Much of the evidence cited by Hays is based on the recognition by both ancient writers and modern scholars that demons and the dead are typically grouped together. "Chirps," 308–309.

109. "Chirps," 311.

110. "Chirps," 311.

he or she reaches the underworld."[111] So in the *Epic of Gilgamesh* Enkidu "begins to be portrayed as a bird as he is being taken to the netherworld."[112] In *Ludlul Bēl Nēmeqi* Shubshi-meshre-Shakkan's immense sufferings, described with death imagery, are attributed to malevolent powers. At different points in the poem he speaks of moaning like a dove and spending the night in his dung like an ox. Hays interprets the poem as illustrative of the way "ancient Mesopotamians expressed their suffering as a descent into hell or as a possession by demonic spirits of the underworld." He adds, "In the process, they are often portrayed as taking on the mythological physical characteristics of the dead."[113] He observes, using the story of Ahiqar as illustrative, that "eventually no explicit reference to demonic powers was necessary to evoke this association between animal characteristics and suffering or death."[114]

Hays sees the bull, eagle and songbird descriptors of verse 33 as presupposing an assault upon Nebuchadnezzar by demonic forces, with death breaking into his human life and beginning to take over. On the basis of such reflections Hays concludes that the description of Nebuchadnezzar at Daniel 4:33 is using "imagery of the underworld to convey to the reader the extreme affliction of its main character," with the mention of the restoration of reason in verses 34 and 36 merely serving to connote madness as "a further symptom of the divine affliction," as in some Mesopotamian apotropaic incantations.[115]

Hays has drawn attention to major Mesopotamian traditions which illuminate how ancients might have understood the judgment that befell Nebuchadnezzar. Avalos points out that there is a collection of magico-medical Mesopotamian texts, the dingir.šà.dib.ba incantations, which provide yet another perspective on Nebuchadnezzar's condition.[116] Contra Avalos, Hays's interpretation does not require that Nebuchadnezzar actually enter the netherworld.[117] So the lack of any explicit reference to this effect

111. "Chirps," 318.

112. The Enkidu tradition is a parallel in reverse, for it concerns humanising a primitive man and making him the king's companion, whereas Nebuchadnezzar is animalised. Holm, *Courtiers*, 455.

113. "Chirps," 322.

114. "Chirps," 323.

115. Hays cites one such text which describes the sufferer as being "like one who has lost his mind" ("Chirps," 324).

116. "Nebuchadnezzar's Affliction," 497–507.

117. Avalos notes the textual stress on Nebuchadnezzar's dwelling with the wild animals. "Nebuchadnezzar's Affliction," 500. While the text is clearly describing something Nebuchadnezzar experiences on earth rather than in the netherworld, it does

is not particularly significant. Still, the animals cited by Hays are not exclusively linked to the netherworld.[118] Indeed, the incantations to which Avalos refers plug into a tradition involving animal-like descriptions of those who become like a wild man due to divine curse.[119] Also to be found is an accent on loss of wisdom which accords well with the broader context in Daniel.[120]

NEBUCHADNEZZAR'S REGAINED SANITY AND GLORIFICATION OF GOD (VV. 34–37)

Hebbard observes the following chiasm:

A the time of insanity is fulfilled

   B Nebuchadnezzar looks to heaven

      C sanity is restored

         D Nebuchadnezzar's doxology to Adonai

      C' sanity is restored

   B' Nebuchadnezzar's advisers and nobles look for him

A' the time of royal restoration is fulfilled

As Hebbard observes, "The doxology that Nebuchadnezzar offers to Adonai is the turning point of his newly restored life, more so even than the restoration of his sanity, which is mentioned before and after the more lengthy doxology."[121] Further, the restoration of his "knowledge" ("reason") makes him the vehicle through which verse 17 is fulfilled: all living persons must come to "know" that the Most High rules supremely.[122]

---

not follow that netherworld imagery is irrelevant to the depiction of Nebuchadnezzar.

118. Avalos cites Jeremy Black and Anthony Green: "Even in the Assyrian period these iconographic elements were not confined to underworld denizens, since they are shared by beneficent and magically protective figures." "Nebuchadnezzar's Affliction," 500.

119. Here Avalos builds on Henze's proposal. Henze made much of Gilgamesh's friend, Enkidu. "Nebuchadnezzar's Affliction," 497. The fact that Nebuchadnezzar's entourage includes magico-medical consultants is significant (2:10, 27; 4:4; 5:7, 11, 15). Avalos observes a parallel between the reason for the beastlike condition being imposed by God and reasons for a similar condition being imposed by gods in the dingir.šà.dib. ha incantations. He cites a Mesopotamian patient who complains that his condition has "come upon me because of the raging of the wrath of my god and goddess. . . I repeated [what should not be uttered], improper things were on my lips. In innocence I went too far." "Nebuchadnezzar's Affliction," 504.

120. Avalos, "Nebuchadnezzar's Affliction," 503.

121. *Reading Daniel*, 122.

122. Hebbard, *Reading Daniel*, 122.

On verses 34–37 Fewell astutely observes,

> At last we know what has brought about the king's newfound piety. The power of the Most High has made its mark on him personally. The king has not witnessed the divine power in relation to someone else — that is, in Daniel's ability or in the deliverance of Shadrach, Meshach, and Abednego — he has experienced this power himself.[123]

When God's time of punishment has run its course Nebuchadnezzar indicates his readiness to acknowledge that God is indeed the supreme ruler by raising his eyes to heaven, the place where the Most High rules.[124] According to traditional biblical thought man, being created in God's image, is superior to the beasts. However, opposition to God is brutish and those who rebel against God are often depicted as beasts. Nebuchadnezzar's arrogant self-exaltation is an implicit denial of God's rule and it is for this reason that he becomes a beast. It is when Nebuchadnezzar acknowledges God's rule that he is restored to being a man once again.[125] This motif will be developed even more strongly in Daniel 7 with respect to the contrast between the four beasts and "the one like a son of man."

In verse 36 in describing his restoration Nebuchadnezzar reports: "my advisors and nobles sought me out." Bledsoe sees this as evidence that Nabonidus's return to Babylon is the event that really underlies this narrative.[126] In the Harran stela, as Bledsoe herself cites it, we read of Nabonidus being greeted by neighboring kings who came up to him and kissed his feet. Far from directly paralleling the Danielic narrative, as Bledsoe asserts, this is evidence rather that we are indeed dealing with a genuine tradition concerning Nebuchadnezzar himself, since it would have been simple to have elevated the text of Daniel 4 and to have had not merely counselors and nobles honoring Nebuchadnezzar but kings kissing his feet!

In verse 36 do we meet with merely an objective personal testimony? Fewell takes this to mean that the king is praising himself in the same terms as he praises God; that his self-praise has grown even more strident.[127] She thus sees Nebuchadnezzar's pious language as his "insurance" against getting pulled down again.[128] This conclusion is far too cynical. Fewell, not surprisingly, regards this whole chapter as all being a non-historical fable,

---

123. *Circle*, 72.

124. Towner, *Daniel*, 64.

125. See Casey, *Son of Man*, 25–26.

126. Bledsoe, "Identity," 755.

127. *Circle*, 77.

128. *Circle*, 79.

and regards as absurd the idea Nebuchadnezzar actually said these words, believing the narrator is playing a joke on the memory of Nebuchadnezzar. The integrity of the book requires we grant the essential historicity of the events here recorded, as unique as they undoubtedly are. After all Nebuchadnezzar is relating "miraculous signs and wonders." However, Fewell is probably not wrong in all respects. It is likely that Nebuchadnezzar's language, especially that concerning himself, still constitutes an exalted opinion of himself (note the stress on "my" in v. 36).[129] He refocuses on the power, status, and glory that have been restored to him.[130] Further, within the broader context of Daniel 1–4 it is indeed ironic to now see "the infamous ruler of the Babylonian captivity. . . portrayed as piously dependent upon the God of his captives. It is as if the king's song of praise puts the final touches on the author's portrait of the king as fool."[131]

SUMMARY

- Notwithstanding his prior experiences of God's might and rule, Nebuchadnezzar has not relinquished his own claims to absolute rule. The first nightmare has not shaken this arrogance. Nor did his experience of the miraculous deliverance of the three Jews. Now God combines dream and experience. But there is this change. The first dream and experience concern Nebuchadnezzar but stand at a step removed. The second dream and experience concern Nebuchadnezzar personally.

- Nebuchadnezzar is likened to the familiar cosmic tree of ancient thought. Ironically, even the experience of humiliation does not stop Nebuchadnezzar from conceiving of himself as being in effect the cosmic tree, the possessor of absolute rule. It is also ironic that, contrary to ancient thought, the lopping down of the supposed cosmic tree, that is, the reduction of Nebuchadnezzar to a beastlike state, does not in fact produce chaos except in the life of Nebuchadnezzar himself. For it is God who rules and preserves his creation.

- In true Nathan-like fashion Daniel is sent from the heavenly court to confront the king when he has fallen into sin and to call him to

---

129. Baldwin, *Daniel,* 116; Burkholder, "Literary Patterns," 53.

130. Valeta, *Lions,* 94.

131. Valeta, *Lions,* 89. Hebbard, *Reading Daniel,* 123, adopts a more positive view, speaking of Nebuchadnezzar's "conversion." There is a validity in his perspective that Nebuchadnezzar himself has become something of a hermeneut, in that he now has some understanding of the Yahwistic worldview.

repentance. At one level, the imminent humiliation of Nebuchadnezzar is designed to stop him from seeing Daniel as merely a vehicle of "the gods" and to see him as he really is, the representative of one God, "the Most High."

POINTS OF CONTACT WITH THE NEW TESTAMENT AND WITH LIFE

1. Nebuchadnezzar's ability to provide the kind of rule that will provide security and prosperity for his subjects is severely limited. It is the eternal kingdom of God which alone can fulfill these needs. Ironically, Nebuchadnezzar's reign begins with a great world rule which is cut down to the size of a stump whereas the kingdom of God begins with an insignificant mustard seed (Mt 13:31–32 = Mk 4:30–32) and yet becomes the most immense and enduring kingdom of all.

2. God will only place "the lowliest of men" over all the kingdoms of the earth something that is fulfilled in the Lord Jesus Christ. See especially Phil 2:5–11 noting how in this respect Christ models the mentality all God's people must share.

3. Lucas's comments are noteworthy:

> The allusions in this story to the story of the Garden of Eden remind us of the fundamental nature of the sin of pride: it can cut at the root of what it means to be truly human, to live in a proper creature–Creator relationship with God. Only when we are in that relationship are we able truly to 'image' God and so to be fully human. Since, like Adam and Eve, all of us do give in to the temptation to seek to be like God, the writer of the letter to the Hebrews sees that the only way in which humans can be enabled to reach their true destiny is through the grace of God expressed in the sacrificial death of Jesus (Heb 2:5–9). His cross is the true 'tree of life.' From it flows forgiveness and the establishing of a true relationship with God.[132]

4. Notwithstanding the essentially blasphemous nature of Nebuchadnezzar's rule Daniel provides a fine model of submission to God-instituted authority. See Rom 13:1–7 and 1 Pet 2:13–17.

---

132. *Daniel*, 117.

POSSIBLE SERMON OUTLINE

Title: "The Bigger They Come, the Harder They Fall!"

1. *Humiliating the Proud.* Nebuchadnezzar will be incapable of running his great empire until he comes to terms with the fact that the created order does not in fact depend upon his reign, despite the fact that the greatness of Nebuchadnezzar's kingship causes him to think of himself as the cosmic tree without which the world would be in chaos. Rather the preservation of the created world depends on God's rule. It is God who determines the limits of chaos which involves the disintegration of fundamental boundaries established at creation; for example, the boundary between being human and being animal. God's control over the created order is so comprehensive that the very distinction between the mind of a man and the mind of an animal is due to God, as God will demonstrate to Nebuchadnezzar.

2. *Exalting the Lowly.* God opposes the proud and is committed to setting over all kingdoms on earth the lowliest of men. The whole of history is a record of God's repudiation of arrogant human rule and moves to the words of the most humble of men: "All authority in heaven and on earth has been given to me" (Matt 28:18).

Daniel 5

The Writing's On the Wall

God Destroys a Blasphemous Human Ruler: Second Demonstration of God's Sovereignty over Human Kingdoms

STRUCTURE

Milne only finds six of the most important fairy-tale functions paralleled in Daniel 5 and notes that "the story as a whole does not closely resemble the heroic fairy tale in structure."[1] It is to content not form that we must look to identify the structure of this chapter and in so doing we cannot miss the cutting satirical tone that pervades the whole.

Lucas provides the following chiastic outline:[2]

A Introduction (1–4)

    B The omen appears (5–6)

        C The failure of the sages (7–9)

            D The queen's confidence that Daniel will interpret the omen (10–12)

1. *Vladimir Propp*, 230.
2. *Daniel*, 124.

E The king seeks Daniel's help (13–16)
E' Daniel rebukes the king (17–23)
D' Daniel interprets the omen (24–28)
C' The success of Daniel rewarded (29)
B' The omen fulfilled (30–31 [6:1])

Another way of structuring the chapter is as follows[3]:

A1 Description of the banquet (1–4)

A1' Interpretation of the banquet (22–23)

A2 Handwriting on the wall (5)

A2' Interpretation of the handwriting (24–28)

A3 Offer of honors for interpretation (6–7)

A3' Bestowal of honors for interpretation (29)

A4 Failure of the king's wise men (8–9)

A4' Fall of the Babylonian Empire (30–31)

B Recollection of Nebuchadnezzar's interpreter (10–12)

B' Nebuchadnezzar's interpreter recalls dream interpretation (18–21)

C Daniel arrives; king offers gifts (1–16)

C' Daniel declines gifts (17)

↓   ↑

→

Points of comparison and contrast between Daniel 5 and Daniel 3:[4]

Daniel 5	Daniel 3
Straight into the action: no opening temporal marker (v. 1)	Straight into the action: no opening temporal marker (v. 1)
"Belshazzar the king made . . ." (v. 1)	"Nebuchadnezzar the king made . . ." (v. 1)
A blasphemous banquet (vv. 3–4)	A blasphemous statue (vv. 5–6, etc.)
The greatness of the banquet (v. 1)	The greatness of the statue and dedication ceremony (vv. 1–7)
Belshazzar: center of attention (v. 1)	Nebuchadnezzar: center of attention (v. 3, 7, etc.)

3. Adapted from Redditt, *Daniel*, 88, who in turn has modified Shea.

4. See too, Fewell, *Circle*, 81–83, 93, 105–6.

Belshazzar's commands meet with compliance (vv. 2–3)	Nebuchadnezzar's commands meet with compliance (vv. 2–3, vv. 4–7, etc.)
Those assembled engage in idolatrous worship (v. 4)	Those assembled engage in idolatrous worship (v. 7)
Atmosphere of festivity and celebration	Atmosphere of festivity and celebration (v. 5, 7)
The manipulation of key political figures (vv. 1--2)	The manipulation of key political figures (vv. 2–3)
Belshazzar's egocentricity: "his wine," "his nobles," "his wives," "his concubines"	Nebuchadnezzar's egocentricity: "my sanity," "my honor," "my splendor," "my advisers," "my nobles"
The idolatrous use of the gold goblets (v. 3)	The idolatrous use of the gold statue (v. 5)
Belshazzar condemned because does worship images and because doesn't worship exiles' God	Three exiles condemned because they do not worship the image of gold
The controlling hands are not the hands of the king but of God	The king asks "what god will deliver you from my hands?"
An exile passes death sentence on the king	The king passes death sentence on the exiles

Gooding also points to ways in which chapters 4 and 5 answer to each other.[5] Both chapters are concerned with the discipline of a Gentile ruler, with Belshazzar, in comparison with Nebuchadnezzar, representing the movement (typical of the book as a whole) of increased defiance, unrepentance, and impiety. This is matched by progress "in the severity, summariness and finality of Belshazzar's punishment as compared with Nebuchadnezzar's."

THE KING THROWS A PARTY (VV. 1–4)

Straight into the Action

We will discover at the grand climax (v. 30) that we are dealing with very swift judgment. Indeed the very climax to the account supplies the temporal marker missing from the commencement of the story. But the reader must be immersed in the action from the outset. This is not a dated history but enacted history. The absence of dating prevents the reader from thinking that his own life is set in a different historical period for this would encourage the reader to stand at some distance from the action. Everything portrayed in this chapter happened within the space of a few hours. The

5. "Literary Structure," 62.

drama must be recaptured. There is not a moment to be lost, there is no time to mark time (contrast 1:1; 2:1; 4:29). And so it is that, as in Daniel 3, the opening of the scene is abrupt.

The Creation of the King

Again, as in Daniel 3, we meet the same opening grammatical structure:[6]

> 5:1 "Belshazzar the king made . . . "
> 3:1 "Nebuchadnezzar the king made . . . "

A Grandiose Creation

In short, as Fewell puts it: "One makes a great feast; the other makes a great image." Just as the immensity of the image, and the greatness of the dedication ceremony are stressed in chapter 3, so here stress is laid upon the greatness of Belshazzar's banquet, as indicated by the large numbers invited, their political importance, and the quality of the crockery and cutlery used. Belshazzar draws attention to his own importance and centrality by drinking wine "in the presence of the thousand."[7] He even seems to believe it is wise to do so.[8]

Wood speaks of personally standing in a room excavated by Koldeway, measuring 165 feet long by 55 feet wide, which may have served as the banquet room described in this chapter.[9] The holding of immense banquets by kings in the ancient world is well documented. From the Royal Archives of Assyria comes an account of a banquet held by King Ashurnasirpal (883–859 BC). He invited an extraordinary number of guests, which included 1500 "officials of all my palaces,"[10] perhaps comparable with Belshazzar's 1000 nobles.

There is speculation as to what motivated Belshazzar to stage such a "great feast." Proposals include:

---

6. Fewell, *Circle*, 81.

7. Fewell, *Circle*, 83.

8. We are told he "took counsel" in wine. Pace, *Daniel*, 62.

9. Wood, *Daniel*, 68.

10. "The Banquet of Ashurnasipal II," translated by A. Leo Oppenheim, in *Ancient Near Eastern Texts Relating to the Old Testament* (ed. James B. Pritchard; Princeton: Princeton University Press, 1969): 558–61.

1. A celebration of Belshazzar's coronation as sole ruler following the defeat of Nabonidus (Shea).[11] If correct this explanation underscores the appropriateness of referring to Belshazzar as "king" and squares with the absence of any mention of Nabonidus.[12] However, verse 16 may tell against this if Belshazzar's offer to make Daniel "the third highest ruler" implies Belshazzar is second to Nabonidus (but see exegesis below).

2. An *akitu* festival in honour of the Babylonian moon god, Sin (Wolters, following Beaulieu).[13]

3. With enemy armies amassing at the gate, as a foolish act of bravado to demonstrate he was still in control and unafraid.[14]

4. The banquet provided an opportunity to call on Marduk's protection against the threatening enemy forces.[15]

Given that Nabonidus tried to replace Marduk with Sin as head of the Babylonian pantheon, this second proposal is worthy of special consideration. There is no explicit mention of Sin in this chapter. The important word-play involving knots may involve an allusion to Sin, though an allusion to Marduk is perhaps more probable (see below).

Nabonidus did institute an *akitu* (New Year) festival in Harran, celebrated on the 17th of Tashritu. Beaulieu argues that Babylon was taken on the evening of the 17th of Tashritu.[16] If this is the case then "the great feast" may have been an *akitu* festival celebrated in Babylon by the supporters of Nabonidus. The *akitu* festival of Marduk was celebrated at a different time of the year, in Nisanu, the beginning of the Babylonian religious New Year.

Wolters makes the point that the 17th of Tashritu always falls

. . . in the days immediately following either the Harvest Moon or the Hunter's Moon, the only times during the year when

11. It was only a few days before this feast that the Persians had inflicted a great defeat on the Babylonians at the battle of Sippar, which was only c. 80 kilometers north of Babylon. Nabonidus fled in humiliation. Shea, "Nabonidus," 140–41.

12. Perhaps the demise of Nabonidus provides Belshazzar with the occasion to exalt himself as "king": Harman, *Daniel*, 111.

13. Wolters, "Belshazzar's Feast," 200.

14. So Thompson, "Judgment in Babylon." Somewhat similarly, Adeyemo sees Belshazzar as trying to boost morale in the face of the Persian threat. He adds, "Like Belshazzar, we in contemporary Africa often turn to wine, women and witchcraft when a crisis comes. These offer no solutions." "Daniel," 1024.

15. So De Bruyn, "Daniel 5," 634–35. This is pure speculation and there appears to be no explicit evidence in the text of Daniel 5 to support this view.

16. See Wolters, "Belshazzar's Feast," 200.

the moon for several days running rises right after sunset and shines throughout the night.[17]

It was the perception of people that the moon on the 17th of Tashritu was unusually large and luminous, making this an appropriate time to stage an *akitu* festival in honor of the moon deity. The dramatic words "that very night" (v. 30) may not mean "the night of the same day on which the feast was held" but rather indicate that the feast itself was nocturnal. If so, then this adds further weight to the real possibility that Belshazzar's feast honored the moon god. Babylonians believed this was the night when Sin showed himself in all his splendor. Instead, they are confronted with the terrifying self-revelation of Yahweh.

A Blasphemous Creation

In Daniel 3 the making of the image did not merely provide the setting of the story. It provided the first element in the conflict to be resolved. So it is here.[18] The nature of the feast "created" by Belshazzar is essentially blasphemous, as was the case with Nebuchadnezzar's statue.

A Kingly Creation

As can be seen from the comparative chart above 5:1–4 also mirrors Daniel 3 in the way it stresses compliance with the king's command, and in the way it involves the assembled persons in idolatrous worship. In both chapters 3 and 5, after those summoned by the king are assembled to participate in that which the king has "made," they are required to blasphemously commit an act of idolatry.

---

17. Wolters elaborates: "The phenomenon of Harvest Moon and Hunter's Moon has to do with the angle of the ecliptic relative to the horizon and is technically described in terms of the moon's "retardation" in different seasons of the year. Without going into the details of the celestial mechanics involved, we note that the full moon nearest the fall equinox (the Harvest Moon) introduces a period of several days when the moon rises right after the sunset, and that the same phenomenon, though less marked, can be observed after the next full moon (the Hunter's Moon). Although it is true at every full moon that sunset and moonrise are virtually simultaneous, it is only in the case of Harvest and Hunter's Moon that this near simultaneity holds for a longer period. The effect, of course, is that the moon has the whole night to itself for a number of successive nights." "Belshazzar's Feast," 202.

18. Fewell, *Circle*, 81.

An Aped Creation

Belshazzar must be understood with reference to Nebuchadnezzar. In this respect, Fewell draws attention to points of contact between chapters 3 and 5 which go well beyond broad plot parallels, noting that both chapters not merely share disjointed beginnings, but also duplicate grammar as well as vocabulary.[19]

Belshazzar is related to his "father" (v. 2). Actually, Nabonidus was Belshazzar's father in the flesh, but here "father" (this relationship is stressed; see v. 11, 18), is used in a loose sense to indicate that Belshazzar was Nebuchadnezzar's "grandson," or "descendant," even possibly "successor."[20] The portrayal of Belshazzar as Nebuchadnezzar's son is significant. Fewell explains, "One comes after the other. One knows of the other and imitates. A son models his father."[21] Belshazzar's aspiration to be as great as his "father" lies at the heart of all the thematic and grammatical interconnections between the narrative of Daniel 5 and that of Daniel 3.

We can only speculate as to the political motives that moved Belshazzar to "create" this banquet. In our study of Daniel 3 we noted that Nebuchadnezzar's manufacture of the image of gold aimed at securing his rule via imposed religious unity. Consequently, it was an act of self-deification that required all his subjects to completely submit themselves to his authority. Does Belshazzar's feast have a similar underlying motive?

The subsequent ease with which "Darius the Mede" took over the kingdom may itself be suggestive of complicity with the nobles, but the text does not openly indicate that undercurrents of political intrigue motivated Belshazzar to hold a magnificent banquet in order to shore up his position. The textual stress falls rather upon Belshazzar's attempt to ape Nebuchadnezzar.

In Daniel 3 the focus is upon the image, even if Nebuchadnezzar is also on front stage, but in Daniel 5 the focus is not so much on the banquet *per se*, the spotlight is upon Belshazzar directly as the one, for example, who "drinks wine in front of the thousand." The previous chapter has ended in an ironical fashion, with the "humbled" Nebuchadnezzar praising God and yet, as the masterful mental gymnast he proved to be, managing to simultaneously massage his own ego: "*my* sanity, *my* honour, *my* splendor" (4:36). It is significant that in this respect Daniel 5 carries on from where Daniel 4 leaves off. The egocentricity of the Babylonian ruler finds a successor in the

19. *Circle*, 81.

20. So Longman, *Daniel*, 136.

21. Fewell, *Circle*, 82.

aspirant Belshazzar, and hence the immediate stress on *his* lords, *his* wives, *his* concubines.[22]

A Pale Shadow of Nebuchadnezzar

And yet the indications of the text before us are that Belshazzar faces a very steep uphill battle to persuade anyone that he is as great as Nebuchadnezzar was. Though he apes Nebuchadnezzar's "making" of the image in his "making" of the banquet, it is not really comparable with the immensity and sheer scale of Nebuchadnezzar's achievement. We are not dealing with an impact upon all the peoples of the world here. There is no imagery here of Belshazzar being, as it were, the world center. In chapter 3 the completeness of Nebuchadnezzar's mastery was underscored by the constant reiteration of all the different types of distinguished political figures who unhesitatingly jump when Nebuchadnezzar commands, and do precisely and exactly what he demands. The long list of musical instruments cited there also indicates that the sheer scale of the celebration which attended the dedication of the image is out of all proportion to the relatively meagre attempt at greatness aspired to by Belshazzar.

Fewell contrasts the different ways in which Nebuchadnezzar and Belshazzar handle power:

> Nebuchadnezzar commands his officials' allegiance with the threat of death; Belshazzar cajoles his lords with wine and merriment. Nebuchadnezzar assumes power; Belshazzar still needs affirmation of power.[23]

Belshazzar bears a superficial likeness to David's son, Adonijah, as portrayed in 1 Kings 1. As Fewell points out, both have to deal with the reputation of their "fathers."[24] Further, neither has done anything to elicit respect and political support. Belshazzar, like Adonijah, seeks to buy such support with food, wine and entertainment.

22. Harman points out that the phrase "his wives and his concubines," while it fits the context well, can also be rendered "his concubines and his female servants." *Daniel*, 112.

23. Fewell, *Circle*, 83.

24. *Circle*, 83.

THE ACT OF BLASPHEMY (V. 4)

As they drank the wine, they praised the gods of gold and silver, of bronze, iron, wood, and stone.

An inclusio is formed by the references to "wine" in verses 1 and 4, with verses 2 and 3 clearly corresponding to each other. Yet the repetition is telling because of the slight but highly significant modification in wording. For in verse 3 we are reminded that it was not merely goblets from "the temple in Jerusalem" that Belshazzar used for drinking wine, but that it was from "the temple which is the house of God," underscoring the blasphemous defiance of Belshazzar's shameless act.[25]

There were plenty of temple vessels available for all of the thousand or so guests to use, for in Ezra 1:7–11 we read:

> Moreover, King Cyrus brought out the articles belonging to the temple of the Lord, which Nebuchadnezzar had carried away from Jerusalem and had placed in the temple of his god. Cyrus, king of Persia had them brought by Mithredath the treasurer, who counted them out to Sheshbazzar the prince of Judah. This was the inventory: 30 gold dishes, 1000 silver dishes, 29 silver pans, 30 gold bowls, 410 matching silver bowls, 1000 other articles. In all there were 5400 articles of gold and of silver. Sheshbazzar brought all of these along when the exiles came up from Babylon to Jerusalem.

It is significant, especially given the contextual parallels with Daniel 3, that the temple goblets were made of gold and silver. In Daniel 2 Nebuchadnezzar was identified as being the head of gold in the statue of his dream. In Daniel 3 Nebuchadnezzar seeks to take control of the reins of history by making a statue of pure gold; by seeking to make his own kingdom the entire statue; a kingdom which will exclude all weakness through totally removing the possibility of any disobedience in all the world. Effectively Nebuchadnezzar is not content with merely being the head of gold. The whole enterprise is thoroughly idolatrous and not merely because he demands that all worship the image, but because the image represents the fact that Nebuchadnezzar's understanding and exercise of kingship is a perversion of God-intended kingship as delegated to Adam (Dan 2:37–38). To sum: Nebuchadnezzar's *selem* is a corruption of the *Selem* of God (Gen 1:26).

This was the worst dimension of the kingship represented by Nebuchadnezzar. The best manifestation of his kingship came when, having been thoroughly humiliated, he acknowledged, though even then not with a

25. Arnold, "Wordplay," 481.

pure, unsullied heart, that "the Most High God" has an eternal kingdom and is absolutely sovereign (4:34–7). Now in the very next chapter Belshazzar apes Nebuchadnezzar, but tragically he seeks to emulate the worst aspects of Nebuchadnezzar's reign and to ignore the best aspect (vv. 22–23).

Belshazzar "sets himself against God" (v. 22) when he shows contempt for God's temple, the palace of God, the place associated with the acknowledgment of God's glorious kingship. For the purposes of the book of Daniel the statement of 1:1 introduces Nebuchadnezzar's reign, and thus alerts the reader as to how that reign was characterized at its outset. It was a reign that involved Nebuchadnezzar setting himself against God the Ultimate King. For the reader this is the significance of the opening statement when it records the articles which Nebuchadnezzar took from the temple and which he presumptuously, provocatively, and with blasphemous effrontery placed in the treasury of the temple of his own god, Bel.

Consequently, when Belshazzar lays his grasping fingers on the temple articles he is taking the reader back to the very beginning of the book. It is as though the significance of all that has intervened between the events described in 1:1 and now have passed Belshazzar by. He is ignorant of all that has transpired; he has no ability to learn from the past—for example, he evidently does not know much if anything about the pivotal role Daniel has played in that history. And so because of this grasper's distorted conception of history—he can only remember the greatness of Nebuchadnezzar's reign—he is condemned to repeat the tragic mistakes of the past. But if this is the path Belshazzar sets himself upon, if this is to be the nature of continuing Babylonian kingship, then it is pointless to keep on repeating the same process of correction which God brought into Nebuchadnezzar's personal life. If the Babylonian king cannot learn from the past then he has no future at all—a few hours at most!

Some qualification of the above is required. Daniel summarizes the period of Nebuchadnezzar's humiliation and the way he came to acknowledge "that the Most High God is sovereign over the kingdoms of men and sets over them anyone he wishes" (vv. 18–21). He then reproves Belshazzar for not humbling himself "though you knew all this" (v. 22). Is it possible then that Belshazzar's use of the temple articles was not merely a fatal mistake but an intended act of defiance? Had he been told that the God of the Jerusalem temple would end the Babylonian empire? If so, in the face of the Persian threat is Belshazzar wanting to say, through his blasphemous use of the temple articles, that he scoffs at such a notion?

It is important to recognize how pervasive references to the temple are in the book of Daniel. The temple motif is a major unifying feature of the entire work:

- Implicitly, in Daniel 1, the movement is from the desecration of the temple to the time when in the reign of Cyrus the temple will be restored (1:21).

- As the book began with an act of desecration of the temple, so it will end (12:11).

- Desecration of the temple sanctuary is often an explicit concern: 8:10–13; 9:16–19, 25–27; 11:31 (cf. vv. 36–37).

- In the next chapter, Daniel 6, the Babylonian rejection of devotion to the temple lies at the heart of the passage.

- In Daniel 9 Daniel's anguish centers on the tragic consequences associated with the desecration of the temple.

But the temple motif itself is a subset of a more encompassing theme: the supremacy and incomparability of divine rule. And so, the motif of desecration of the temple must be read together with the repeated descriptions of the way in which kings and Chaldeans engage in high-handed acts of defying the kingship of God, and especially this is done when, as in Daniel 5, a king operates with a blasphemous and grossly bloated conception of his own importance as king.

Fewell suggests that Belshazzar is trying to gain credibility in the eyes of his subjects. For this reason he tries to outdo Nebuchadnezzar. So he does not send for the temple vessels because they belong to the god of Jerusalem. Rather, he does this because they represent his father's greatest achievement. According to Fewell, he "belittles his father's achievement by using the vessels as if they were ordinary vessels."[26]

At this point Fewell's psycho-analysis falters because it is hard to imagine that either Nebuchadnezzar or Belshazzar would have seen the conquest of Judah and the appropriation of temple articles as a matter of any great import. Fewell further speculates that Belshazzar's act of drinking from vessels dedicated to a god was something Nebuchadnezzar would never have done and is intended to display Belshazzar's greater daring.[27] Fewell is on much stronger ground when she recalls that the temple vessels had been rededicated to Nebuchadnezzar's own god. It is on this basis, rather than on Fewell's speculative psychological projections, that we can indeed see an attempt on Belshazzar's part to outdo Nebuchadnezzar.

Perhaps Belshazzar's appropriation of the temple articles was not intended as a direct insult against God. Perhaps for him their significance

26. *Circle*, 85.
27. *Circle*, 85.

simply consisted in the fact that Nebuchadnezzar his father had taken them. His personal motives are not important, and for this reason are not indicated in the text. What matters is not so much the psychology of the man but his actions. He probably had little to no idea of how horrendous was his idolatrous misuse of the temple goblets. But his action was no less blasphemous for all that.

We are informed in verse 2 that Belshazzar sent for the vessels "*bitem hamra*," that is, "when he tasted the wine" or perhaps even "under the influence of the wine." If the latter, then this contributes to the overall portrayal of this blasphemous king as one who is not in control of himself.[28] But the phrase is ambiguous. Had he just tasted the wine, and therefore ordered the temple articles to be brought as a premeditated and deliberate act, or was the folly of his action partially attributable to the fact that he was intoxicated? Even if he was drunk it is still conceivable that the act was premeditated and that he drank the wine to give him the courage to do something he would fear to do normally. If this is the case then clearly his blasphemous act implies a rejection of what Nebuchadnezzar had come to conclude about the God associated with the temple articles concerned. Indeed Fewell goes so far as to draw a parallel between the way Absalom profaned his father's concubines to steel himself, and the manner in which Belshazzar profanes the vessels of his father's conquest.[29] However, I think this is to move from exegesis to surmise. As noted before, we have at best just tantalizing possibilities in the text as to Belshazzar's motives, and our stress therefore needs to be upon the blasphemous nature of the act as such.

When Belshazzar and those with him "praised the gods of gold and silver, of bronze, iron, wood, and stone," they did so as they drank from the gold goblets associated with God, and thus they were effectively exchanging the glory of the immortal God for images (Rom 1:23). The fact that they praised not only the gods of gold and silver—the metals represented by the temple goblets being used—would seem to imply a trivialization of the value of the temple goblets. The gods of gold and silver can be praised in the same breath as the gods of other metals and wood and stone. In context the point presumably is that what matters is the quality of the wine, not the container from which it is drunk.

28. Polaski observes that the word *tahem* (טְעֵם) elsewhere denotes a command given by the king, a report made to the king or a proper discretion needed at the king's court. He concludes, "Belshazzar follows the command (טְעֵם)) of wine, subtly raising the issue of Belshazzar's ability not just to hold his liquor but to hold political authority. Polaski, "*Mene, Mene, Tekel, Parsin*," 651–52.

29. *Circle*, 86.

Thus the history which lies behind the temple goblets is completely irrelevant to Belshazzar. As we have already seen, this seems typical of Belshazzar's attitude towards past history. All that matters is that now "we eat drink and be merry," though the irony is not that "tomorrow we die," for in this case Belshazzar will be slain that very night.

THE SUDDEN APPEARANCE OF THE MYSTERIOUS HAND (V. 5)

Suddenly the fingers of a human hand appeared and wrote on the plaster of the wall, near the lampstand in the royal palace. The king watched the hand as it wrote.

God is the ultimate gate-crasher. The "fingers" of a hand appear and write on the wall.[30] And they do so "at that hour," "instantly," a phrase which introduces disaster.[31] More particularly there is a "bringing forth" of these fingers that corresponds to the "bringing forth" of the vessels in verses 2–3.[32] As Valeta comments,

> This paronymous wordplay underlines the ironic contrast between the human insolence of the king and the divine response toward this rebellious behaviour. The king brings forth the vessels taken as booty by Nebuchadnezzar and these same vessels result in the bringing forth of the hand of judgment against him.[33]

Hilton speculates that by connecting this miracle with a lampstand the author has in mind the miracles associated with the Jewish menorah in the Maccabean period.[34] Needless to say there is not the slightest indication in the text of such an allusion. But Hilton does helpfully remind us of archaeological evidence showing that the walls of the sixth century BC palace and throne room were indeed covered with plaster.[35]

---

30. We are told Belshazzar saw "part of the hand" where some have understood "part" to refer to the palm of the hand, though Harman argues it is more likely to refer to the back of the hand or the whole hand below the wrist, *Daniel,* 114.

31. As Pace observes, *Daniel,* 165, this same phrase was used in Daniel 3 (vv. 6, 15) to state that refusal to obey Nebuchadnezzar's demands would be met by an instantaneous throwing of violators into the fiery furnace, but also in Daniel 4 to show how Nebuchadnezzar's arrogance was met with immediate punishment (v. 33).

32. Arnold, "Wordplay," 479–80; Pace, *Daniel,* 165.

33. *Lions,* 96.

34. Hilton, "Babel Reversed," 101–2.

35. "Babel," 103.

There has been much speculation about what form this writing took. One conjecture is that the following quadrilateral of letters was written on the wall, which transliterated were (1) a–n–m; (2) a–n–m; (3) l–q–t; (4) s–r–p. When reversed these become respectively, mene, mene, tekel, parsin.[36]

But this is only a guess. Hilton considers various rabbinic speculations, with the most common being Rabbi Hiyya's, which closely corresponds to the above explanation.[37] Rabbi Shimon ben Halafta proposed the letters were written in an *atbash* code, that is, the first letter of the alphabet was replaced by the last, the second by the penultimate, etc. More simply, Rabbi Meir suggested that everyone could read the words but only Daniel could understand their significance.

Alternatively, the description of verse 6 may suggest that the hand scratched the wall with its fingers and that these scratches were interpreted by Daniel as writing. Instone-Brewer observes,

> If a left hand were to scratch a surface with its fingers while it drew itself into a fist, it would leave a series of marks which could be interpreted in cuneiform as numbers. These numbers could be interpreted as '*Mina, Mina, Shekel* and a half.' The marks would be three vertical strokes of the small finger, ring finger and middle finger, followed by a cross made by the vertical of the forefinger being bisected by the horizontal of the thumb—i.e. '|||+'.[38]

It is not immediately apparent from this description whether all at the feast saw this phenomenon or whether it was only the king who did so. Certainly the stress of the account is on the king's own experience of the event. Yet the reference to the phenomenon occurring "near the lampstand" may indicate that all saw it.[39] Also, the fact that God's self-revelation occurs in the context of the artificial light of a lamp may constitute an implicit snub of a moonlight self-revelation of Sin.

Again divine revelation assumes a form that sharply distinguishes the book of Daniel from other apocalypses. In other apocalypses revelation is almost always highly transcendental. Indeed in many cases in order to receive the revelation at all the seer concerned has to leave earth itself as he goes on a heavenly journey. In fact he may have to pass through a series of heavens until he arrives at a heaven high enough to serve as a fit place for ultimate revelation to take place. By contrast in Daniel, over and over again,

36. Farrar, *Book of Daniel*, 212.

37. "Babel," 105–6.

38. Instone-Brewer, "MENE MENE TEQEL UPARSIN," 313.

39. So Hartman and Di Lella, *Book of Daniel*, 188.

the humanness of the revelation, and its occurrence within a precise historical context to which it is intrinsically and intimately related, distinguishes
Daniel not only from the "other-worldly" apocalypses just described, but
even from those which are set within works concerned with historical matters. For in the latter case such apocalypses merely review selected portions
of especially Old Testament history, while indulging in often outlandish em-
bellishments, but yet never (or rarely) relating the "revelation" of the apocalypse concerned to the precise historical context in which the seer is placed.
Indeed we are usually left almost totally ignorant of the particular historical
setting to which the revelation concerned belongs. By contrast again, Daniel
5:1–4 is at pains to provide a very concrete historical situation and this is in
fact crucial to the very nature of the revelation which otherwise is unintel-
ligible. The revelation has no autonomous meaning, but only in relation to
the very particular blasphemous act Belshazzar has performed.

The fact that this was a genuine act of divine revelation concerning
a definite historical situation does not in itself rule out the possibility that
God, through Daniel, is outplaying the Chaldeans at their own game; i.e.,
through a superior appropriation and mastery of Mesopotamian techniques
of mantic writing, as proposed by Broida.[40] It's all very well to point out,
as Broida does, such things as (1) the centrality of writing to the practice
of Mesopotamian divination; (2) a shared emphasis on secret knowledge;
(3) the use of lemmatic forms for dream interpretation in the ancient Near
East and in Mesopotamian scholarly commentaries, often explaining omen
texts; (4) the use of paronomasia in Mesopotamian written texts; and (5)
the exposure of exilic Jews to "the near-ubiquitous presence in Babylon of
divination and medicine." But let's be clear. What we have presented to us
in Daniel 5 is *not* an expression of Jewish "scribal interest in attributing
mantic writing to their deity." That view is sheer speculation. What we have
in Daniel 5 is the faithful recording of what actually happened, a divine act
of revelation. It has already been stressed in Daniel 1–4 that the wisdom of
Daniel and his friends is not merely superior to that of the Chaldeans, but
different in kind, precisely because it is grounded in actual divine revelation. In his interpretation of the writing on the wall, any conjectured use by
Daniel of Mesopotamian interpretative techniques is at best of secondary
importance.

The manifestation of the fingers of a human hand continues a theme
with which we are now familiar in Daniel. Back in Daniel 2 the Chaldeans
stated that it was impossible to receive ultimately genuine revelation because "the gods do not live among men." Even in Daniel 1, but unbeknown

40. See Broida, "Textualizing Divination," 1–13.

to either Nebuchadnezzar and the Chaldeans, God was present with Daniel and his three compatriots, and personally involving himself in their lives as they studied, imparting to them superior wisdom, and as they embarked on a distinctive diet, giving them superior health. This is all immanence not transcendence. And in chapter 2, when Daniel and his friends are given the dream and its interpretation, the whole point of this is to gainsay the conclusion reached by the Chaldeans. From one angle the Chaldeans are right: "the gods do not live among men." But in the sense that most matters they are completely and totally wrong, for "the Most High God" does live among men, and proves this by again involving himself in the lives of four men who are under the sentence of death, so that his revelation immediately impacts the concrete historical dilemma in which they have been placed by sparing them from death. Again this is immanence and not the transcendence typical of other apocalypses.

And what about chapter 3? After Nebuchadnezzar throws Shadrach, Meshach, and Abednego into the furnace, he expostulates in astonishment, "Look! I see four men walking around in the fire, unbound and unharmed, and the fourth looks like a son of the gods" (3:25). The fourth figure represents God, the God who "lives among men," but not only has God, via this angelic figure, entered a concrete human crisis situation, but he does so in the form of a man. There is that about the appearance of this figure that causes Nebuchadnezzar to think of the realm deemed utterly transcendental by the Chaldeans. But yet again we have here an immanence that is virtually unthinkable in the other apocalypses.

In chapter 4 when Nebuchadnezzar has yet another ominous dream, he recognizes that "the spirit of the holy gods" is located in Daniel. That is, he acknowledges that while the realm of the gods is transcendental to the Chaldeans, the gods are immanent in Daniel. Indeed in the ensuing context God's intervention in human history is not consigned to some remote end point but to the immediate historical situation, so precisely in fact that God's action comes as a specific response to specific words uttered by Nebuchadnezzar.

It is therefore of a piece with all that has gone before that God's unusual mode of revelation should not occur in some transcendental realm but in the very banquet chamber of the king, on the plaster of the very wall against which many doubtlessly had leaned their hands and backs on many occasions. Further, while the mode of manifestation is peculiar, it is nonetheless a human form that is assumed. While there is that about the revelation that speaks of a transcendental reality we are still left with an emphatic note of immanence.

THE HAND THAT GRASPS HISTORY

Valeta observes, "Fingers writing on stone walls bring to mind the stone hewn from the mountain without hands that destroyed Nebuchadnezzar's dream statue in Daniel 2."[41] Indeed, it may be doubly significant that the fall of the Babylonian empire is signaled by the appearance of the mysterious hand. In Daniel 2:45 it is said that the stone that will cause the statue to topple will be cut of "no human hand." I argued that the statue of Daniel 2 is a representation of the Babylonian empire, though as epitomizing all human rule through to the "end," that conclusive point in history that will see blasphemous anti-God rule replaced for evermore by divine rule. In Daniel 5 the very appearance of the hand of God, in human form for reasons just explained, is highly suggestive. That which is written by the hand underscores the fact that God has measured Belshazzar and his reign and has decided to end the Babylonian Empire that very night. It is the hand of God that truly grasps history.[42]

But allusions may extend back to the Exodus. When the Egyptian magicians were incapable of matching the power of God, they expostulated, "This is the finger of God" (Exod 8:19). From a narrative point of view, it is from this point on that the catastrophic judgment of Egypt becomes inevitable, for the magicians of Egypt cannot summon up a power to turn back God's hand of judgment. Similarly, in Daniel 5, immediately after the fingers of God do their work, the king (cf. Pharaoh) summons his "enchanters, astrologers, and diviners" (v. 7). The inability of the king's "magicians" to match the power of God through interpretation of the writing signals the inevitability of judgment on Babylon.

Yet there is still more! For as Hilton points out, the Tower of Babel story of Genesis 11:1–9 (which we have already noted to be of influence in Daniel) marks the fact that Babylonia begins with a confusion of language.[43] Fittingly now, the end of Babylon is associated with the confusion of language.[44] Indeed, Daniel 5 forms an inclusio with Daniel 1 in one important respect. For, in a context alluding to the Tower of Babel incident, Daniel 1 speaks of Nebuchadnezzar's intent to teach Daniel and his friends "the language and literature" of the Babylonians. This was part of

---

41. Valeta, *Lions*, 96. Because the abuse of temple articles, the desecration of the temple, is foundational to what transpires, the motif of "judgment from the sanctuary" recurs here. See Vogel, "Cultic Motifs," 35.

42. Cf. Lucas, *Daniel*, 139.

43. "Here of all places it should be realized that God alone is the master of all languages!" "Babel," 106.

44. Longman, *Daniel*, 142.

the Babylonian monarch's intent to show that he was the absolute ruler who controlled the destinies of God's people. In Daniel 5 it is Daniel who teaches the Babylonian ruler the language and writing of God. It is God's intent to show that he is the absolute ruler who controls the destiny of Babylon. How additionally ironic it is that God uses a representative of his people ("one of the exiles" (v. 13—an allusion to 1:3) to bring down the Babylonian empire with one irrevocable sweep of the prophetic sword!

THE KING IN DISTRESS (V. 6)

The portrayal of the king's distress is not only to be expected because of the frightening spectacle he witnesses, but also because before this, whenever God had moved to counter Nebuchadnezzar's gross over-estimation of his greatness through the imparting of dreams, Nebuchadnezzar too was cast into a state of great distress. Indeed recollection of those prior contexts seems to be intended because the same words are used here to depict Belshazzar's consternation as those used in Daniel 2 and Daniel 4. Yet alongside this there is also an implicit contrast between Belshazzar who fears (vv. 6, 9, 10) and Nebuchadnezzar who was feared (v. 19).

On past occasions Nebuchadnezzar's distress indicated his anxiety at having lost control of the situation, and involved a premonition of impending disaster with respect to his own rule. Similarly here Belshazzar's distress signals to the now intelligent reader that Belshazzar's kingship is in crisis.

Perhaps a humorous suggestion lies in the story that it is precisely while he is carousing that Belshazzar sees the appearance of the human hand. Given that verse 2 may intend us to understand that Belshazzar was already intoxicated, maybe his first thoughts were that he had had too much to drink. First though, his face goes white.[45] His mind is filled with terror. But it is the next expression which is particularly intriguing.

In verse 6 we read: "the knots/joints of his loins were loosened."[46] We are dealing here with an instance of satirical toilet humor.[47] Belshazzar has

45. See Paul, "Mesopotamian Background," 60. Literally, "his colors changed." Meadowcroft and Irwin, Book of Daniel, 103.

46. Paul, "Mesopotamian Background," 60–61, considers Akkadian equivalents. He cites the example of the goddess Anat's terrified reaction to ill tidings: "Her feet wobble. Behind, her tendons break; above her face sweats. Bent are the joints of her sinews; weakened are [the tendons] of her back." Also: "If a. . .baby's sinews are loosened from its neck to its backbone, it will die."

47. See Wolters, "Untying," 119. Pace, following Brenner, sees also an attack on the king's virility. She cites Brenner: "He is hit exactly in the organs he has employed in his orgiastic drinking feast; instead of having sexual intercourse with his concubines,

lost control of his bodily functions. In his terror, either his bowels evacuated filling his "pants"[48] or else his bladder, filled with too much wine, left a puddle at his feet. Some have taken this expression to merely mean his "knees knocked together and his legs gave way" (NIV), or that "the joints and muscles of his hips and back gave way and his knees smote together" (Amplified, similarly RV), or "he became limp in every limb and his knees knocked together" (NEB), or "his hip joints went slack, and his knees began knocking together" (NASB), or something of the kind. But such diluted understandings do not fit well with the overall satirical thrust of Daniel 1–6.

Fewell expresses it, "The king who would appear powerful shows himself to be weak."[49] His father Nebuchadnezzar imperiously commands sages to be called, and issues a decree that they be brought. Belshazzaar, by contrast, responds in panic—he cries loudly for the sages to be brought. In his terror he does not behave in a regal and dignified manner. He has lost control of himself. Valeta notes that more is added to Belshazzar's misery:

> This loosening of his loins is not only highly embarrassing for
> the king, but it also implies impotence. The king's sexual prowess
> and power is inferred by the presence of many wives and concu-
> bines as related in v.3 stands in sharp contrast to a king who has
> had the contents of his bowels frightened right out of him.[50]

THE KING LOOKS FOR ANSWERS (VV. 7–16)

The King is Desperate (v. 7)

So imperative is it that the writing be interpreted and the king thus be enabled to regain control that the king is prepared to make the solver of the mystery a very important political figure, perhaps even next in power to himself. On the other hand his very promises reveal the limits of his own kingship. He can bestow glorious purple[51] garments, a gold chain[52], and ex-

---

he becomes impotent; instead of eating and drinking, he loses control and becomes incontinent." Pace, *Daniel*, 171.

48. So Valeta, *Lions*, 97.

49. *Circle*, 87.

50. *Lions*, 97.

51. Purple was the royal color and a mark of royal favor. Compare Esth 8:15; 1 Esdras 3:5–7; 1 Macc 10:20, 62–65. Lucas, *Daniel*, 129.

52. Xenophon maintained such a gold chain could be worn by Persians of rank only if presented to them by the king (Lucas, *Daniel*, 129). Of course, this incident predates Persian rule. Presumably, as in many other societies a gold chain or collar was merely

alted positions, but he is unable to read the writing. God is able to unsettle him in the core of his being.

The Summoning of the Chaldeans (vv. 8–9)

The summoning of the Chaldeans has almost become a pat sequence, as though the mention of this is necessary to maintain consistency with earlier accounts. But, of course, the repetition drives home afresh the immense distance between the Chaldeans and Daniel. Daniel can do what is utterly and completely impossible for the Chaldeans.[53] The writing, as per the dreams given to Nebuchadnezzar, ultimately is involved with a revelation of God as the one who exercises complete control over the course of history, as he will demonstrate in exceedingly swift judgment upon Belshazzar. The inability of the Chaldeans to interpret the writing is thus expressive of their inability to understand the times in which they are living.[54] The result of their impotence is to leave the king even more terrified, because he now seems to have nowhere to turn to relieve his terror. He gave a banquet for his nobles, but they are no help to him now, for they are just as baffled as he is. He strikes a pathetic figure, utterly alone and gripped by stark terror.

The Significance of the Queen's Involvement (vv. 10–12)

It is important to note that the queen comes onto the scene having heard the commotion. She is not summoned. It is not as though Belshazzar as a last resort appeals to her. We are still left with the picture of a Belshazzar who has nowhere to turn.

Evidently the queen had not been invited to the banquet, or else she deliberately distances herself from it. At any rate her speech indicates that she sees herself linked to Nebuchadnezzar over and above Belshazzar.[55] If Belshazzar has neglected her then this is consistent with the way he has

---

a mark of high rank.

53. ". . .both the king and the wise men had no means of transcending the natural and the human and therefore the writing on the wall escaped them altogether, according to Calvin. . . God's order spreads beyond time and space." Mol, *Calvin,* 19.

54. On the basis of the LXX translation, Harman suggests that the Aramaic verb rendered in the NIV as "were perplexed," has the idea of "throw into confusion," *Daniel,* 116–17. This may well involve an allusion to the aftermath of the Tower of Babel episode (Gen 11:7, 9).

55. Hebbard following Fewell sees the queen as the voice of the dead Nebuchadnezzar, *Reading Daniel,* 33. Similarly, Goswell, identifying her as Nebuchadnezzar's widow. *Daniel,* 34.

ignored vital historical lessons of the very recent past. Insofar as the queen is identified with Nebuchadnezzar it appears that just as those who threaten Adonijah's power were not invited to his banquet (1 Kings 1), so too here Belshazzar avoids all who were intimately associated with the rule of his father. He wants to create for himself his own greatness commensurate with that of Nebuchadnezzar.

The identity of "the queen" is unclear (v. 10). Beginning with Josephus most commentators have thought her to be the queen mother.[56] In favor of this is the fact that we have already been told that his wives and concubines were present, so it seems unlikely that she was Belshazzar's wife. Further she displays an intimate knowledge of past events. The freedom she felt to come into the banquet hall may also indicate she had a higher station than being merely the wife of Belshazzar. It was common in the ancient Near East for the queen mother to be treated as a key political figure.[57] Possibly she is the wife or daughter of Nebuchadnezzar or the wife of Nabonidus.[58]

In Daniel 2 Arioch recommended Daniel to the king, and in this respect the queen now performs an analogous role. A close look at what the queen says is instructive. Fewell summarizes:

> Her language. . .is double-edged. While on the one hand, her words *speak* a message of comfort, on the other hand, her words *function* to bring attention to the king's discomfort. If any of those present have missed the king's display of fear, she makes sure that they now take note of it.[59]

The queen begins by hailing the king with the words, "O king, live forever!" (cf. 6:21). In context this heightens the biting satire of the chapter because in reality Belshazzar's reign and indeed his life will run out that very night. The queen then tells him of Daniel as one who has the ability "to solve problems." The expression used is very interesting—"to loosen knots" (v. 12). This is a common enough form of words to use with respect to resolving a mystery such as this. But in this particular context the language is highly suggestive. For the identical phrase used to describe the king's panic

56. Towner, *Daniel,* 69–70. Various ones have speculated as to her identity, with proposals including Nitocris, wife of Nebuchadnezzar; the wife of Nabonidus and grandmother of Belshazzar; Adadguppi, wife of Nabonidus and mother of Belshazzar. Hebbard, *Reading Daniel,* 130–31. See too, Holm, *Courtiers,* 461.

57. Lucas, *Daniel,* 130.

58. Herodotus tells the story of Nitocris, a wise and powerful queen who fortified Babylon with a canal system. Herodotus believed her to be Nebuchadnezzar's wife and Nabonidus's mother (Towner, *Daniel,* 70).

59. *Circle,* 88.

now reappears.[60] Has the queen upon entering noticed that Belshazzar's hip joints have gone slack, or even seen a puddle of urine at his feet?[61] Certainly, this is a satirical pun that would have caused many a Jewish reader to burst into laughter.[62]

In addition, given earlier parallels between Daniel and Joseph, we must not miss the parallel implicit here with Exodus 1:8: "Now there arose over Egypt a new king who did not know Joseph."[63] History repeats itself.

In Nebuchadnezzar's Shadow

We have already noted in the first four verses how Belshazzar's attempts to "play the great man" (sc. Nebuchadnezzar) seem pathetic by comparison. In this light it is striking to see how the queen—and Daniel will reinforce this when he speaks—keeps referring back to Nebuchadnezzar. She pointedly refers to him as King Nebuchadnezzar, and as "your father the king" (v. 11), as though implicitly she was denying Belshazzar's right, at least by comparison, to fully own such a title. She speaks of Nebuchadnezzar's attitude towards Daniel—the most crucial part of the history of Nebuchadnezzar, which Belshazzar has completely missed in his attempt at recapitulation. Indeed Belshazzar's ignorance of Daniel and his consequent "desecration of the temple" (at least symbolically) is somewhat reminiscent of Pharaoh's ignorance of Joseph and his similarly blasphemous disdain for God's people; a parallel encouraged by the commonality of the unknown hero idea in both contexts.

In stressing that Daniel was called Belteshazzar by Nebuchadnezzar, the queen may be drawing attention via the almost identical names to the contrast between Belshazzar and Daniel. It is the wisest of men who is most fit to exercise rule over the kingdom, and recognition of this is implicit in Belshazzar's readiness to give the problem-solver political power of this order. Certainly in the outworking of God's kingdom purposes it is Belteshazzar who is central at this time and Belshazzar of absolutely no use whatsoever.

---

60. See Paul, "Mesopotamian Background," 61.

61. So suggested by Fewell, *Circle*, 89.

62. Wolters, "Untying," 121.

63. Hebbard, *Reading Daniel*, 134. Hebbard argues that it is insinuated in the text that Belshazzar's ignorance of Daniel is a case of willful avoidance. It is not simply that he doesn't know Daniel but that he does not *want* to know him.

DANIEL, THE UNTIER OF KNOTS

The Symbolism of Knots

In verse 12 Daniel is introduced as one who "unties knots" (NIV: "solves difficult problems").[64] Those present have experienced divine power at work—a power that has "tied knots."

Eliade[65] has demonstrated that the concept of gods who bind is very common in the ancient world. Indo-European mythologies differentiate between warrior gods who fight by military means and those who wield a different kind of weapon: magic. So, for example, in contrast to the thunderbolt weapon of the warrior god Indra, the weapon of the most invincible of the gods, Varuna, is depicted in the form of a noose or knot. Indeed sometimes Indra is represented as rescuing victims who have been "bound" by Varuna and "unloosing" them. In ancient India, Yama and Nirrti, divinities of death, also make use of the same magic weapon. Similarly in Greek mythology while Zeus fights wars Ouranus "binds" his eventual rivals in hell. In Roman mythology, Romulus "binds with all-powerful bonds." Iranian mythology especially recognizes gods who bind: the demon Astovidhotush and the gods Fredun, Tistrya, Verethragna, and Ahriman. Along the same lines Pauhi is the ancient Chinese god of the wind and the net. Eliade also notes various Island peoples who believe in gods who bind.

More relevant still to Daniel 5 is Eliade's observation that "in the Semitic world...magic bonds of every kind are a divine (and demonic) power that is almost universal."[66] By way of illustration Eliade refers to Enlil and his wife Ninkhursay (Ninlil) and En-zu, that is, Sin (the god preferred by Nabonidus). Perhaps it is significant that Sin, like these other Semitic deities, is represented as having a net with which he catches those guilty of perjury. Other Semitic gods who bind include Shamash, Nisaba, Tammuz and again, most significantly, Marduk. Bel (Enlil) is addressed in this way: "Father Bel, who dost hurl thy noose, and every noose is a hostile noose." Marduk, like Indra, uses the noose and cords as a divine champion. In *Enuma Elish* Ea "binds" the primordial monsters Apsu and Mummu with magical incantations, prior to killing them. In his fight with the sea monster, Tiamat, Marduk's chief weapon is the "net." Marduk "binds" Tiamat, "shackles" him and

---

64. Wooden's view is that all that is in mind by the image of "knots" is enigmas, knotty matters (*Daniel and Manticism*, 260–61). But this fails to take seriously the widespread use of such imagery in the ancient Near East and in Mesopotamia itself.

65. Eliade, *Images*, 92–124.

66. *Images*, 108.

then kills him. He then chains up all the gods and demons who aligned themselves with Tiamat.

In the ancient world, magical bonds were used against human enemies and also to provide protection against wild animals and against disease, witchcraft, demons, and death. Eliade cites scattered examples: the cord buried near the house of an enemy; the cord hidden in a ship to make it capsize; and the use of knots to bring about all sorts of ills. The use of knots, strings and cords for protection against disaster during the time of child-birth is especially common.

Depending on the context, the act of binding or tying can be either positive or negative. Eliade observes that illness and death are the "two elements of the magico-religious complex of 'binding' which have had the widest currency almost all over the world."[67] It is against this background that much biblical language takes on a new edge. Consider, for example, the psalmist who cries out: "the cords of Sheol entangled me, the snares of death confronted me" (Ps 18:5). Or, again: "I will spread my net for him, and he will be caught in my snare; I will bring him to Babylonia . . . " (Ezek 12:13). In such instances the context is not that of magic. However, in the rest of the ancient world magical connotations predominate. Eliade contends that the "Babylonian word *markasu*, 'link, cord,' means, in the mythology, 'the cosmic principle that unites all things,' and also 'the support, the power and the divine law' that hold the universe together."[68]

With regard to the context of Daniel 5 it is important to recognize that it is in the sphere of knowledge and wisdom that we encounter the language of "tearing away" the veils of unreality, and "untying" the "knots" of existence.[69] Given all of the above background, the image of Daniel as the untier of knots takes on added significance. The worldview of Belshazzar and his entourage would lead them to see the mysterious writing or etching on the wall as an ominous divine act of magical binding. The extreme terror experienced by Belshazzar may well be attributable to his automatic, and now comprehensible association of such "binding" with a sense of imminent death and disaster. But the great untier of knots, Daniel, does not meet magic with magic. Daniel only unravels the cords of mystery.[70] The cords of death remain tightly fastened around Belshazzar's gasping throat.

67. *Images*, 101.

68. *Images*, 115–16.

69. Eliade, *Images*, 116.

70. Paul, Mesopotamian Background," 61–62, suggests, "And, as so often happens, it may very well serve as a clever double entendre, whereby the king desired to have the enigmatic code 'spelled' out, so that his 'charmed' existence would remain unharmed."

Daniel is Summoned

When Belshazzar addresses Daniel he again ignores the status given to him by his father.[71] He has a strangely selective approach to understanding the significance of the history associated with Nebuchadnezzar!

Belshazzar identifies him as an exile whom his father had brought from Judah. Has he learnt this in the meantime, or, did he know this already but decided to shun Daniel as a symbol of his father's regime, given his desire to carve his own greatness?[72] Whatever the answer to this question might be, in describing Daniel as one "brought from Judah" he is, wittingly or (probably) unwittingly, identifying Daniel with the temple articles "that had been taken from the temple of God in Jerusalem" (v. 3).[73] Having blasphemed the God of the temple of Jerusalem, it is most fitting that his God-sent nemesis should be a man devoted to the temple of Jerusalem, a man from Judah.

Whereas Nebuchadnezzar had come to be fully confident of Daniel's ability to interpret mysteries (chapter 4; cf. 5:11–12), Belshazzar, whether through lack of familiarity with the facts or for other reasons, appears to lack such assurance: "I have heard about you, that you are able . . . if you are able." He speaks of hearing that the spirit of the holy gods is in Daniel and this stands in contrast with Nebuchadnezzar who "knew" such was the case.[74] From the start he has probably been expressing a level of disdain or condescension for Daniel, relegating him to being but an exile from Judah, rather than recognizing his high credentials as an interpreter. He adds to this by explicitly expressing his doubts in Daniel's competence: "Now *if* you can read . . ."[75]

Fewell provides the following analysis of Belshazzar's speech to Daniel:

> A You are that Daniel, one of the exiles from Judah whom the king my father brought from Judah
>
> > B *I have heard of you*, that the spirit of the gods is in you and light and insight and excellent wisdom have been found in you.
> >
> > > C The sages . . . were not able to disclose the interpretation of the matter.

---

71. Fewell, *Circle*, 91.

72. So Lacocque, supported by Fewell, *Circle*, 91: "Belshazzar has overtly shunned Daniel because Daniel is a symbol of his father's regime."

73. Similarly, Wooden: "Like the vessels from the temple in Jerusalem (5:2), Daniel is one of the items brought from Judaea (5:13) by Nebuchadnezzar and belittled by Belshazzar." *Daniel and Manticism*, 265.

74. Hebbard, *Reading Daniel*, 136.

75. See Hebbard, *Reading Daniel*, 135–36.

B' *I have heard of you*, that you are able to give interpretations and to solve problems.

A' Now, if you are able . . . you will rule as third in the kingdom.[76]

Fewell sees this talk as effectively being a challenge to Daniel to prove that the things heard of him are true:

> In chapter 3, accusation brings the three men before the king. In chapter 5, recommendation brings Daniel before the king. In chapter 3 the king questions the truth of the accusation. In chapter 5, it would seem, the king is questioning the truth of the recommendation. In chapter 3 the king is forced, on account of his earlier ultimatum, to threaten Shadrach, Meshach, and Abednego with death for their failure to obey. In chapter 5 the king is forced, on account of his earlier promise, to offer Daniel a reward for his success. Just as Nebuchadnezzar is surely not anxious to learn that his top officials, whom he himself appointed, have been disobedient to his command, so Belshazzar is not anxious to see his father's chief sage succeed (particularly if the writing is an ill-omen) where his own sages have failed.[77]

At the least, Belshazzar's initial failure to call upon Daniel underscores the extent to which he has lost control, or the ability to know to whom he should turn to regain control. Wolters captures the satirical force in the way Belshazzar alludes to Daniel's supposed ability:

> After the pagan wise men have failed to interpret the riddle, the queen mother recommends the Israelite prophet Daniel, whom she describes as particularly competent to 'untie knots' for him. The unwitting double entendre evokes more derisive laughter. Finally the king himself comes face to face with Daniel—the pagan king Belshazzar before the Israelite prophet Belteshazzar—and says, in effect, 'I understand that you can untie my knots for me.' Again we can imagine the audience's uproarious laughter as the hapless pagan king unwittingly makes a fool of himself before the prophet of the Lord. We see how the story uses burlesque humor to underscore the sovereignty of the Israelite God, before whom the great kings of the earth can at a moment's notice be reduced to figures of fun, preparatory to being brought to justice.[78]

---

76. Fewell, *Circle*, 93.

77. *Circle*, 93.

78. Cited by Valeta, *Lions*, 100.

Daniel Puts Belshazzar in his Place

There is an immediate contrast with the preceding chapter in that Daniel was deeply distressed when he perceived the dream spelled dire consequences for Nebuchadnezzar. Not so now.[79]

Fewell follows Porteous in regarding the refusal of rewards as out of character for Daniel whom, it is argued, showed no such aversion back in Daniel 2. Indeed Fewell goes so far as to malign Daniel's character: "Daniel's refusal is designed to offend. His refusal is motivated not by his humility, but by his pride."[80] This is pure cynicism.

Daniel's response addresses Belshazzar as king but in the same breath ascribes to him no power and authority. It was to his father, Nebuchadnezzar, that God gave such sovereignty (v. 18). As Fewell comments, this "stings Belshazzar in his most sensitive spot."[81]

In fact Daniel's words:

1. Recall Nebuchadnezzar's own failure to see that God had given him his kingdom.

2. Taunt Belshazzar by describing the immense extent of his father's power, with Daniel employing language which normally would only be ascribed to God. This includes the exercise of sovereignty over people of every language. Belshazzar's inability to deal with the language inscribed on the wall underscores Belshazzar's lack of true imperial authority.[82]

3. Teach that God never gave Belshazzar power; he has tried to grasp what will never be his.

In drawing Belshazzar's attention to the way in which God humbled Nebuchadnezzar, Daniel speaks of "*when* his heart became arrogant and hardened with pride" (v. 20). Fewell reasons that Daniel is implying: "Because the power given to Nebuchadnezzar was so great . . . the overextension of his pride was inevitable. Daniel speaks as though, given such power, it was only a matter of *when* his heart would be lifted up in pride" (v. 20). Indeed, the word "when" leads us to expect that we will keep on running into this same problem whenever a man occupies the throne of a human kingdom.[83]

79. Hebbard, *Reading Daniel*, 136.
80. *Circle*, 94.
81. *Circle*, 95.
82. So Polaski, "*Mene, Mene, Tekel, Parsin*," 656.
83. *Circle*, 96.

It is interesting to note the role adopted by Daniel in responding to the king. In the past the contrast between the Chaldeans and Daniel has always resulted in Daniel being presented as the Wise Man par excellence. But now, for the first time, Daniel begins not as a sage but as a prophet. Fewell is again unreasonably cynical: When Daniel is chief sage then he is discrete, but when spurned aggressive, confrontational. Belshazzar's "desecration of the temple" is a covenantal offence, and now Daniel speaks as God's prophet,[84] the royal messenger, and covenant mediator who indicts Belshazzar for this unconscionable offence which has grievously offended the Ultimate Ruler.[85]

THE INTERPRETATION OF THE WRITING

The Worthlessness of Belshazzar

Ferguson eloquently captures the essential significance of the writing on the wall:

> Palace walls often speak with mute eloquence, covered as they often are with paintings and artifacts of an entire lineage of rulers and their achievements. Such walls characteristically display the royal family's estimation of itself and its judgment of its dynasty. Here, however, an artist who neither possessed nor required any royal patronage depicted His estimation of the king's rule.[86]

There are many interpretations which mistakenly presuppose that *mene, tekel,* and *parsin* are coins. Instone-Brewer takes all three terms to describe coinage with "tekel" being the Aramaic spelling of "shekel" and "parsin" probably, though by no means certainly,[87] representing a half "mena."[88] So understood, the proportions of the coins are 60:1:30. Reid[89] comments, "A modern equivalent would be a hand on the wall writing something like, 'A dollar, a dollar, two cents, fifty cents.'"

84. So too Anderson, *Signs and Wonders,* 59.

85. *Circle,* 97.

86. *Daniel,* 112.

87. "MENE MENE TEQEL UPARSIN," 312.

88. Babylonian weights in the British Museum carried the inscription *prs.* In 1887 Clermont-Ganneau argued this meant half a mena/mina. In the Elephantine papyri *tql* stands for shekel. In Babylon there were 60 shekels in a mina, though in Assyria and Ugarit a 50 shekel mina may have been used. Lucas, *Daniel,* 133.

89. *Kingdoms,* 101–2.

Lucas finds the use of coinage to measure the worth of people in a Talmud reference, which esteems a certain man as "a mina son of a half-mina," that is, much more worthy than his father.[90]

Polaski sees the entire mode of revelation as employing key elements associated with the exercise of imperial authority: the importance of inscriptions; the hand being "sent" like an ambassador; and the listing of coins as an allusion to the royal treasury. He believes that the following meaning is communicated: "An empire that neither comprehends inscriptions nor attends to careful accounting is no empire at all."[91] Fewell remarks,

> The image of coinage and the verbs themselves. . .both suggest that the issue is one of *value*. And, indeed, the problem of value has been the crux of the story. Belshazzar has not valued his father's example. He has not valued the captured vessels. He has not valued his father's chief sage. He has not valued his father's God. Instead, he has valued the services of incapable sages. He has valued gods who do not see, who do not hear, and who do not know.[92]

Wolters points out that treating *mene, teqel,* and *peres* as coins is mistaken for the simple reason that there was no such thing as coinage in Mesopotamia in Belshazzar's period of history. Even later there were never coins either in Babylonia or Palestine that weighed as much as a mina or half-mina.[93] *Mene, teqel,* and *peres* are rather units of weight.[94]

A common way of understanding the interpretation of verses 25–28 is to see each word functioning as a pun. For example, a common rendering, as expressed in the NIV, is as follows:

> MENE is related to the verb MNH, meaning "numbered" (cf. "teach us to *count* [*mnh*] our days," Ps 90:12);[95]
> TEKEL is related to the verb TQL, meaning "weighed,"[96]

---

90. *Daniel*, 133.

91. "*Mene, Mene, Tekel, Parsin*," 657–59.

92. *Circle*, 100.

93. "Mene," 162.

94. Wolters, "Mene," 160; cf. Nelson, *Daniel*, 154.

95. Harman suggests the verb may also involve the connotation "finished," as in "his days are numbered," *Daniel*, 122.

96. The Babylonian kingdom has been weighed and found "wanting," that is, "deficient in the qualities of righteousness and justice that God requires." Harman, *Daniel*, 122–23.

and PARSIN is related to the verb PRS, meaning "divided" or "broken."[97] The significance of each pun is explicitly set out in verses 26–28.

However, in his article Wolters has persuasively argued that Daniel's interpretation involves dividing the nine consonants into three units of three letters each. Different ways of vocalizing the combinations of these consonants explains how it is possible to apply a different level of meaning to each unit.

> Level 1: scale weights (not coins) vocalized as *mĕnē, tĕqēl, pĕrēs*: "mina," "shekel," "half-mina."
> Level 2: God's acts of evaluation vocalized as *mĕnāh, tĕqal, pĕras*: "he has reckoned," "he has weighed," "he has assessed (not "divided")."
> Level 3: the outcome of God's evaluation vocalized as *mĕnāh, tiqqal, pāras*: "he has paid out," "you are too light;" "Persia!"

Wolters argues that the vocalization involved in all of these three levels always presupposes the image of a pair of scales, representing God's judgment. It is additionally significant that the annual rise of Libra—symbolized by scales—occurred on the very eve of Babylon's fall to the Persians. When God enables Daniel to decode an otherwise undecodable series of consonants, he reveals that it is he, not the Babylonian astrologers, who knows the future and, indeed, he even controls it.

Some, for example Kraeling, Ginsberg, and Freedman,[98] have sought to identify each term with a particular Babylonian king. Kraeling regards Evil-Merodach and Neriglissar as the two minas, the eight-month rule of the boy king Labashi-Marduk as the shekel and Nabonidus with his co-regent Belshazzar as two pereshin. Ginsberg suggests Nebuchadnezzar (mina), Evil-Merodach (shekel) and Belshazzar (peresh). Freedman and Cross go for Nebuchadnezzar, Nabonidus, and Belshazzar. But this is highly speculative and there is no indication from the text that this is warranted.[99]

Notwithstanding that the underlying imagery is of weights rather than coins, it remains the case that God in judgment is assessing the value of Belshazzar and of the Babylonian empire. Fewell explains,

---

97. This doesn't imply that the Babylonian kingdom will be split into two parts with one part going to the Medes and the other to the Persians, but merely that the kingdom will be split up and come to an end. Harman, *Daniel*, 123.

98. See Hartman and Di Lella, *Book of Daniel*, 190.

99. Instone-Brewer, "MENE MENE TEQEL UPARSIN," 312.

The portrayal of Belshazzar as a weak king communicates also the irony that the man of inappropriate values is himself of little value. He is of little value to Daniel; he is of little value to God. Thus the images of weights and balances fit comfortably with the images of lifting and lowering: the weak king of little value has tried to lift himself, that is, to make himself valuable, but to no avail. 'You have been weighed in the balances and have been found wanting,' says Daniel. Weighed against whom? According to this reading—Nebuchadnezzar. If Nebuchadnezzar is a minah, Belshazzar is only a shekel (a ratio of 60 to 1) and while the Medes and Persians (half-minahs) may be less valuable than Nebuchadnezzar, they are a good deal better than Belshazzar.[100]

Instone-Brewer suggests that if they had been able to read the words they may have attempted to provide interpretations, e.g., the monetary value of a sacrifice to be offered to Nabu, or the weight of gold soldiers would capture in battle, or numbered and weighed are the Persians.[101]

Calvin interprets verse 8 to mean that God blinded the Chaldeans.[102] Lacocque proposed that the words were Aramaic, which had been translated into cuneiform characters.[103] Along similar lines Instone-Brewer suggests that the original writing was cuneiform numerals, which Daniel translated into Aramaic.[104] However, God gave the interpretation to Daniel. If Instone-Brewer's proposal is correct Daniel interpreted a sequence of three vertical strokes and a cross as numbers and then converted them into the names of the weights the numbers represented. Segal notes that Jewish scholars have proposed differing ways in which these words were coded, but remarks, "It is unclear why any of these solutions would pose an insurmountable challenge for the wise men to solve."[105] Indeed, Segal goes on to argue on the basis of verse 8 that the problem was not that the wise men were unable to interpret the words but that they were not able to read them, implying that only the king actually saw the vision of the hand and the inscription. Since the lamp should have made such a vision and writing visible to all, everybody else, including the Chaldeans, are left bewildered as to what the Belshazzar experienced. They are thus placed in a position parallel to the

100. *Circle*, 100.

101. "MENE MENE TEQEL UPARSIN," 312.

102. "Commentary," 316. Also Instone-Brewer, "MENE MENE TEQEL UPARSIN," 313.

103. As cited by Instone-Brewer, "MENE MENE TEQEL UPARSIN," 313.

104. "MENE MENE TEQEL UPARSIN," 313.

105. "Rereading the writing on the wall," 162.

Chaldeans of Daniel 2, who were unable to interpret Nebuchadnezzar's dream because they had no access to it, no experience of it.

Segal's reading, as outlined above, is ingenious but I doubt he is correct. Wolters reasons that it is reasonable to expect that Aramaic words were written on the wall, both without vocalization and also without word-division. Consequently, given the lack of a literary context,

> . . . it was indeed impossible to 'read' the inscription, that is, to know what vocalization and word-division should be supplied for the nine-letter series of consonants written on the wall. The wise men are being asked to 'read out' (qĕrāʾ) the inscription, which could only be done by dividing into words and then vocalizing the consonants of the inscription.[106]

Daniel, in prophet-like style, indicts Belshazzar: "you did not honor the God who holds in his hand your life and all your ways" (v. 23), which, he adds, immediately explains why God chose to reveal his hand, writing that which demonstrated precisely this reality.[107] Fewell disagrees with Lacocque's view that Belshazzar was deliberately issuing a direct challenge to God. She finds no evidence that Belshazzar even recognized the existence of God.[108] However, it is more likely that Belshazzar simply trivializes this God whom he knows had come to mean a great deal to Nebuchadnezzar.

Fewell goes beyond the evidence in supposing that the value of a king consisted in whether he was a strong king or not: "Nebuchadnezzar . . . was valuable enough to God to have been spared in spite of his presumption. His redeeming quality was his strength. Strong kings can be successful agents." Consequently she sees Belshazzar as being of no use to God, because he is a weak king, and this serves to magnify his presumption.[109] But the reason supplied by the text for his demise is simply his failure to acknowledge that God is sovereign, and this indeed has been the consistent contextual stress (e.g., 4:32).

---

106. Wolters, "The Riddle of the Scales." 158. Wolters persuasively shows that the Chaldeans were confronted with a highly ambiguous consonantal text, by giving many examples of different ways the nine letters have been construed by modern scholars. Indeed, if word-division was not indicated then they "did not necessarily represent three words of three letters each," allowing for divisions yielding many different possible readings: "she has counted the voice of Persia," "what shall I weight, a half-mina?," "who has caused Persia to stumble?," "whoever you are, Persia is insignificant," "crush whoever has been peeled," "he has crushed by a sign of a scale."

107. Cf. Greidanus, *Preaching Christ from Daniel*, 152. It is the same hand that wrote on the wall which determines Belshazzar's destiny.

108. *Circle*, 100–101.

109. *Circle*, 101.

Fewell censures Daniel because he "never bothers to distinguish between his words and those of God." She speaks of Daniel's arrogance and
resentment: "How ironic that Daniel grows ever more like his friend Nebuchadnezzar. He wields the words of life and death as easily as this king
wields power over life and death (5:19)."[110] Such cynicism is unwarranted.
In Daniel 4 we noted how Nebuchadnezzar was comparable in some respects with David, and Daniel with Nathan. Thus what we find in Daniel 5
is the same boldness of a prophet. Revelation is implied rather than explicit.
Indeed, as Wooden points out, the visions of both Daniel 7 and 8 predate
this climactic event, so that it has already been made plain to Daniel both
that the Babylonian empire will come to an end and that the Persian empire
would rise to take its place.[111] Wooden reasons,

> Thus, through the dating given to these visionary experiences,
> Daniel is given the necessary revelations—his own visions and
> guided interpretation—so that by the last day of Belshazzar, the
> interpreter had sufficient revealed information to make sense of
> the writing on the wall; with those revelations and his superior
> intellect (1:17) and ability to solve riddles (5:12, 16), he knows
> what to make of the words through the use of word plays.[112]

Returning to the words used in the revelatory event, it seems clear that
the climactic word *peres* (v. 28) plays upon "Persian," and ominously points
ahead to the impending disaster at the hands of the Persians.[113]

The Worthlessness of Babylon's gods

Daniel rebukes Belshazzar for praising the gods of silver and gold, bronze,
iron, wood, and stone, since these gods "cannot see or hear or understand"
(v. 23). It may be significant that "silver" precedes "gold." Is this an allusion
to the dream-image of Daniel 2, implying that Belshazzar's reign is inferior
to that of Nebuchadnezzar?[114] Lederach observes, "The sacrilegious actions

110. *Circle*, 102.

111. Wooden, "Changing Perceptions," 22.

112. "Changing Perceptions," 22. There is no way of knowing to what extent God's
Spirit gives Daniel immediate insight and to what extent God is merely using Daniel's
long-developed abilities.

113. As de Guglielmo argues there is every reason to suppose that a double meaning
is intended: "Prs—your kingdom has been divided (*perisath*) and has been given to the
Medes and Persians (*prs*)." "Daniel 5:25," 205. As noted above, however, Wolters would
argue for "assessed" not "divided."

114. So Meadowcroft and Irwin, *Book of Daniel*, 110.

of Belshazzar set the stage for a confrontation between the Most High God and the gods of the Babylonians, which recalls that of Elijah and the prophets of Baal (1 Kings 18:20–40)."[115] Such gods cannot save Babylon from its impending disaster. Lederach recalls from the Babylonian Chronicle how Nabonidus assembled the nation's gods in the city of Babylon for their protection. All of the gods supposedly present at Belshazzar's state banquet are not able to deliver Babylon from the judgment decreed by God.

THE HISTORICAL SEQUEL

Daniel's Rise to Pre-eminence

Niditch and Doran's study of folktales has led them to identify a particular type they find in Daniel 2, Genesis 41 and Ahiqar 5–7. Daniel 5 has some affinities with the pattern belonging to this genre. The king is faced with a problem and offers a reward to anyone who can solve it. This results in a contest between sages. But only one sage is able to solve the conundrum and this is the one who is greatly rewarded.

But the book as a whole repeatedly draws attention to the gulf between Babylonian wisdom and the wisdom which is given by God to Daniel, while at the same time, and in closely interrelated fashion, sharply discriminating between the bloated claims of the Babylonian kings and the reality of God's absolute kingship. This theological frame is adequate to account for the pattern of problem solving presented in this chapter. Correspondences with folktale patterns are therefore presumably coincidental, and, if intended, constitute merely a use of a familiar story-telling form without buying into the typical set of presuppositions concerning non-historicity which underlie folktales.

Belshazzar had promised Daniel that success in solving the problem at hand will result in his political exaltation. When Belshazzar says he will make Daniel the "third highest ruler" (v. 16), this may mean second only to Belshazzar, it being presupposed that Nabonidus, Belshazzar's father, is the supreme ruler of Babylon with Belshazzar the executor of that rule. Alternatively, following Montgomery, it may be that the term *talti* is simply a high official title meaning "Thirdling" or "Triumvir."[116]

115. Lederach, *Daniel*, 113.

116. Lucas (*Daniel*, 130) notes that the Hebrew term originally denoted the third man on a chariot (Ex 14:7). Later, it could be used for a high military officer or attendant at court (2 Kgs 7:2, 17, 19; 9:25; 15:25). Harman, (*Daniel*, 115–16) similarly questions whether *talti* implies "third," recognizing the problem of identifying who might be the two superior officials. He suggests that a customary official title, such as *shalshu*

Fewell remarks, "As many commentators have noticed, it is rather odd that Daniel now accepts what previously he had refused."[117] Fewell finds Daniel's motives bad. I can't see any problem myself. The text is simply saying that Daniel was not looking for a reward to do what was asked of him.

Belshazzar's Immediate Demise

Hilton makes much of a Masoretic note placed at the end of the book which states that the death of Belshazzar occurs at the very center of the book.[118] Along with this he notes a midrashic interpretation according to which Belshazzar miscalculated, thinking that the end of the seventy-year exile prophesied by Jeremiah had already elapsed. So, expressing his contempt for Jeremiah's words, Belshazzar decides to desecrate the temple vessels—and thus seals his fate.

Herodotus and Xenophon also describe the fall of Babylon in strikingly similar terms: that "when Babylon was captured in a surprise attack by the Medes and Persians, the Babylonian king and his nobles were carousing at a nocturnal banquet."[119] At the time of the attack Nabonidus, the king, may well have been in Tema.

Other sources add to our understanding of how Babylon fell. The Cyrus Cylinder depicts Cyrus as entering Babylon unopposed and states that he captured Nabonidus. The Babylonian Chronicle ties together Cyrus's capture of Sippar with an internal revolt against Nabonidus. According to this source, Nabonidus was captured when he returned to Babylon. As per the Cyrus Cylinder, the Babylonian Chronicle also speaks of Cyrus entering Babylon without a battle.[120] The Dynastic Prophecy appears to represent Cyrus sending Nabonidus into exile. According to Berossus, it was while Nabonidus was under siege in Borsippus that Cyrus took Babylon. Cyrus then exiled Nabonidus to Carmenia.[121]

The humiliation of Belshazzar is accentuated by the fact that he, a young king, is defeated by an old king. In verse 31 the word for "took over"

("adjutant"), might be in mind.

117. *Circle*, 103.

118. "Babel Reversed," 100.

119. Hartman and Di Lella, *Daniel*, 187.

120. Apparently, the Euphrates flowed under parts of Babylon. By diverting its waters, the Medo-Persian troops were able to access the city through the underground tunnels. Harman, *Daniel*, 125.

121. Lucas, *Daniel*, 127. Prior to this, Nabonidus had the citizens of Opis massacred for revolting when Cyrus attacked the city. Redditt, *Daniel*, 7.

is *qabel*, which also means "to receive." There is ambiguity here. Is the kingdom a result of conquest or does it come as a gift?[122] Certainly the wider context stresses the sovereignty of God in effecting the transference of the kingdom.

SUMMARY

- Nebuchadnezzar's unshakeable egocentricity now finds its successor in one who deliberately seeks to ape him, namely, Belshazzar.

- Belshazzar demonstrates the incorrigibility of idolatrous, God-defying Babylonian rule. Hence the imminent doom not only of Belshazzar but of the Babylonian empire.

- When the probably drunken Belshazzar sees the mysterious handwriting on the wall he evidently wets or soils himself in his terror. The king who so pathetically seeks to be great and powerful like "his father," is utterly shamed before all his guests.

- Belteshazzar (Daniel) is the nemesis of Belshazzar, once more the vehicle of a prophetic word which effects that which it proclaims.

POINTS OF CONTACT WITH THE
NEW TESTAMENT AND LIFE

1. The doom of Belshazzar is sealed by his failure to humble himself before God and his God-defying worship of "the gods of silver and gold, of bronze, iron, wood, and stone which cannot see or hear or understand" (5:23). In Revelation 9:20 John applies this same language to "the rest of mankind that were not killed by these plagues." They share this in common with Belshazzar: both are incapable of learning from the lessons of the past.

2. A somewhat analogous humiliating demise befalls Herod, the God-defying ruler who so lusted for self-aggrandizement that his failure to glorify God resulted in him being struck down by God and being eaten by worms (Acts 12:21–22).

---

122. Fewell, *Daniel*, 103–4.

POSSIBLE SERMON OUTLINE

Title: *"The Writing's on the Wall"*

1. Belshazzar, the Pathetic King
2. God, the Terrifying King
3. Daniel, the Untier of Knots

Daniel 6

Two Decrees

Ultimate Commitment to Distinctiveness:
God's Sovereignty Revealed in Rescuing his
Servant from the Place of Certain Destruction

STRUCTURE

Chiastic structures for the chapter are proposed by Towner and Goldingay
respectively:

(1) Towner[1]

    Daniel emerges as best satrap
      His enemies plot
        The king makes a fatal decree
          Devout Daniel is arrested and sentenced to death
            DANIEL DELIVERED—GOD WINS!
          Daniel released
        The king makes a saving decree
      The enemies are destroyed
    Daniel confirmed as best satrap

1. *Daniel*, 79.

(2) Goldingay[2]

2–4 Introduction: Daniel's success

5–11 Darius signs an injunction, but Daniel takes his stand (of obedience to God)

12–16 Daniel's colleagues plan his death

17–19 Darius hopes for Daniel's deliverance

20–24 Darius witnesses Daniel's deliverance

25 Daniel's colleagues meet with their death

26–28 Darius signs a decree and takes his stand

29 Conclusion: Daniel's success

Relooking at Daniel 6 with these two proposals in mind it is possible to identify a more thoroughgoing chiasm:

1–3 Daniel's success: faithful to both king and God

4–9 Darius's Irrevocable Decree: rooted in the rejection of Daniel's faithfulness to his God

10 Daniel remains faithful to God despite the decree

11–15 Daniel's enemies "faithful" to the decree maneuver Daniel's demise

16–20 Darius approves Daniel's faithfulness to his God and hopes God will vindicate him through deliverance

21–22 Daniel's faithfulness vindicated by God's deliverance

23 Darius is delighted and witnesses Daniel's vindication

24 Daniel's enemies destroyed for their faithlessness

25–27 Darius's Irrevocable Decree: recognizing Daniel's God as King, Savior, and Vindicator of Daniel

28 Daniel's success

As the above outlines indicate, Anderson is correct to reject the popular title "Daniel in the Lions' Pit" and prefer "Darius and the Two Decrees."[3] However, the above outline also indicates the central importance of Daniel's faithfulness to both king and God. Hence an even better title is something like "Daniel's Faithfulness Vindicated and Darius's Two Decrees."

Note that my outline serves to draw attention to two isolated elements: verses 21–22 at the center of the chiasm, stressing God's vindication of Daniel as both faithful to God and the king; and verse 10—the description of

2. *Daniel*, 125.

3. *Signs and Wonders*, 64.

what Daniel's faithfulness consisted in. The latter verse is especially significant because it reveals Daniel's devotion to Jerusalem, pre-empting Daniel 9.
Given the focal importance of this statement within the structure of Daniel
6, the closing reference to "Cyrus the Persian" should be construed as being
more than an historical marker: Daniel sets his heart on Jerusalem, unfail-
ingly praying for the return of his people to Jerusalem, and God honours his
faithfulness, prospering Daniel till he sees that very day dawn.

DANIEL'S EXALTED POSITION (VV. 1-2)

It is significant that under Persian rule there is no longer any mention of
astrologers, magicians, diviners, etc. as if to underscore an emphasis of the
prior narrative that they were of no use whatsoever. Now there are only
political offices mentioned.[4]

Daniel is one of three administrators chosen by Darius to ensure that
Darius's interests are protected. Ensuring the king "suffers no loss" presumably implies putting the lid on potential uprisings and ensuring taxes are
fully collected.[5] Daniel had not only distinguished himself as an interpreter
of dreams, but had ruled "over the entire province of Babylon" during Nebuchadnezzar's reign (2:48). Nebuchadnezzar died in 562 BC. In the years that
followed Daniel ceased to have the same political prominence so that some
twenty-three years later Belshazzar knows Daniel as but "one of the exiles"
brought by Nebuchadnezzar from Judah (5:13).

Following the interpretation of the writing on the wall Belshazzar fulfilled his promise by proclaiming Daniel to be the "third highest ruler in
the kingdom" (5:7, 29), that is, occupying the position of supreme control
next to Nabonidus and Belshazzar. Daniel had no interest in using the situation provided by God's intervention to advance his political career (5:17).
There is perhaps implicit in Daniel's refusal an implication that such largesse
is worthless. Certainly any claim of Belshazzar to be able to give political
power to another proves to be but a balloon which bursts even before the
party begins. For Belshazzar was slain on the same night that he gave Daniel
such "power." Although Daniel only enjoyed such authority for a few hours
nevertheless he is given a position of considerable importance.

---

4. See Hebbard, *Reading Daniel*, 144.
5. Baldwin, *Daniel*, 128.

THE DISTINCTIVENESS OF DANIEL (V. 3)

We now return to a familiar theme—the distinctiveness of Daniel. In chapter 1 Daniel (and his three Jewish friends) maintained their distinctiveness from their Chaldean peers by refusing to be obsequious, servile lackeys to the king. They did this not through open defiance, but by adopting a different diet. They were distinguished from their Chaldean peers by the superior health God gave them, and also by their distinctively superior grasp of Babylonian wisdom, as recognized by Nebuchadnezzar himself.

Central to the thought of Daniel 2 is that the distinctiveness of the wisdom of Daniel and his friends is not simply a difference of degree, but of kind. Their wisdom is poles apart from the magic-oriented and elitist wisdom of their Chaldean peers—a wisdom that has strict limits and does not enable man to know the mind of "the gods." By contrast the wisdom of Daniel and his friends is one that is rooted in the fact that God is personally involved in their lives. In a relatively undramatic way he had already shown this by nourishing their bodies and enhancing their natural intelligence. But now God demonstrates that while "the gods" do not live among the Chaldeans, he himself does live among his people, as represented by Daniel and his friends.

Of course, it is only the implied reader who understands this. Ironically even the proof that Daniel's wisdom is radically different in nature is assimilated to Babylonian conceptions of deity so that Nebuchadnezzar takes it for granted that Daniel's wisdom is due to the fact that "the spirit of the holy gods" is in him. God then takes him through a set of experiences which result in Nebuchadnezzar acknowledging the distinctiveness of "the Most High God" with whom Daniel is associated, though a close study of the text demonstrates that Nebuchadnezzar never succeeds in completely casting off the moorings of Babylonian religion.

The preceding chapter has continued to beat the drum of Daniel's distinctiveness. When Belshazzar seeks an explanation of the meaning of the writing on the wall he calls first for the Chaldeans to interpret it. We are now familiar with this pattern of leaving Daniel till last. Emphasis on this point in the text suggests much concerning the state of mind of the king in each case. But it is also a skillful literary device used repeatedly in order to keep before the mind of the reader the distinctiveness of Daniel. So now again at the beginning of yet another reign it is time for Daniel's distinctiveness to be demonstrated afresh.

This time Daniel's distinctiveness consists in "his exceptional qualities" which are such as to make him stand out before Darius. He is distinguished among the administrators and satraps to such a degree that the king plans to entrust all political power and authority to him. Again we must remember that Belshazzar had actually had this proclaimed. But in Daniel 5 it is imperative to recognize that "the Most High God is sovereign over the kingdoms of men and sets over them anyone he wishes" (v. 21). Because Belshazzar had not humbled himself like his father, his kingdom was given to another and as a consequence Belshazzar did not actually have the ability to give Daniel supreme political authority. Thus it follows that the authority Darius wants to give Daniel is due to the sovereignty of the Most High.

THE CONSPIRACY AGAINST DANIEL (VV. 4-5)

In Daniel 3 "certain Chaldeans" denounced "certain Jews," namely Shadrach, Meshach, and Abednego, seeking their destruction. Now again jealous Babylonian political leaders seek Daniel's demise. But, according to the KJV: "neither was there any error or fault found in him." Paul proposes that the two nouns "error" and "fault" are the cognate equivalents of an Akkadian expression, *arnu u sillatu*, meaning "crime and/or improper speech." Consequently, the conspirators were unable to discover any "improper speech" or "corruption" against him.[6] That is, "in both speech and deed Daniel remained a loyal and trustworthy servant to his king." Daniel's political behavior is impeccable. Here is a man of complete moral integrity: a man who kept his promises, a man who could not be bribed, a man who fulfilled his obligations.

In this chapter there is significant play on the words "seek" and "find."[7] Daniel's enemies "tried to find grounds for charges against Daniel" (v. 4) but "could find no corruption in him," concluding, "We will never find any basis for charges against this man Daniel unless . . . " (v. 5). Their trap involves securing the execution of any who "make petition"—the same root is used (*bea*). After manipulating Darius we read how "these men went as a group and found Daniel praying" (v. 11). By contrast we have the image of Daniel seeking God's help (v. 11). After Daniel has been thrown in the lions' den Darius is addressed by Daniel who declares: "I have been found innocent in his sight" (v. 22). When Daniel was lifted from the den we are informed that "no wound was found on him, because he had trusted in his God" (v. 23). Ironically, that which is apparently Daniel's greatest point of

---

6. "Mesopotamian Background," 56–57. Paul provides the following example of the use of this expression: "If she [sc. a slave woman] commits any offence or insult (the buyer may sell her)."

7. See Arnold, "Wordplay," 483–85.

vulnerability—his greatness weakness—is his praying to God. But it turns out that this is actually his greatest strength.[8]

Daniel's enemies are aware of the fact that "the law of his God," or perhaps here "religion of his God,"[9] is of immense importance to Daniel. In fact we immediately are left with the impression that it is precisely Daniel's devotion to the law that explains his blamelessness.

DARIUS MOVED TO ISSUE A DECREE (VV. 6–9)

Daniel's enemies have identified the fact that Daniel's supreme authority is "the law of his God," but they fatally presuppose that his disciplined prayer life is because of his adherence to religious law and fail to see that it is expressive of devotion to his living and almighty God.[10] Their inability to properly interpret the situation makes them actors who are analogous to the hermeneutically incapable Chaldeans of the earlier chapters. At any rate, they deliberately try to set up a situation where Daniel will be forced to choose between the authority of his God and the authority of the king. Indeed, the setting of the law of God against the law of the Medes and Persians is part and parcel of the satire against blasphemous and human rule. Exposed in this chapter is the absurdity of a ruler being prevented by his own laws from doing what is right.

The Source of Enmity

Verse 7 employs language that takes us back to Daniel 3. The listing of Babylonian officials recalls the similar listing of Daniel 3, and in both cases the listing stresses that all Babylonian political leaders recognize the authority of the king, but in a backboneless, servile manner.

Hostility against Daniel emanates from Babylonian enemies,[11] and not from a Persian context. Indeed the ensuing context will stress Darius's chagrin at having allowed himself to be placed in the position of being Daniel's executioner. We are informed that Daniel's political peers "went as a group;"

---

8. See Valeta, *Lions*, 104; Arnold, "Wordplay," 485.

9. So Anderson pointing to Ezra 7:12, 14. (*Signs and Wonders*, 67).

10. See Hebbard, *Reading Daniel*, 146. What they don't appear to realize is that there is in fact no law that requires Daniel to pray in such a disciplined manner.

11. Van der Toorn ("Scholars," 40–41) studies the correspondence of scholars in the Assyrian court. He discovers "many allusions to, and descriptions of, the reversal of fortune of individual sages." This dependence on the favor of the king led to competition for jobs and best positions and to sometimes quite vicious court intrigues.

that they "acted in concert, harmony."[12] This is consistent with the constant emphasis upon the unbridgeable gulf between Daniel and his three friends on the one hand, and their Babylonian peers on the other.

To effect their plot the Babylonian politicians resort to deceit. When they say that "the royal administrators, prefects, satraps, advisers and governors have all agreed that the king should issue an edict . . . ," they are lying because, of course, Daniel is one of the three administrators and he has not agreed to this at all.[13] But they are concerned to make sure that there is no way out for Daniel, so they maneuver Darius to not merely publish a royal edict but also to make it legally binding.[14] The idea is to "establish" (*qum*) that which will reverse Darius's plan to "establish" (*qum*) Daniel as the governor over the whole kingdom (cf. v. 3). Although Darius at one level is a more positive ruler than Nebuchadnezzar and Belshazzar the portrayal of him as easily duped and manipulated by his toadies is very much part of the penetrating satire against blasphemous and idolatrous human rule that we have seen to be so pervasive in chapters 1–5.

Praying Only to Darius

What was the force and nature of Darius's decree?[15] If he was deifying himself then we might reason that this served to establish Darius's kingly authority, on the assumption that in the ancient world the veneration of a king as a divine figure made subjects more unwilling to risk divine wrath by opposing such a person.[16] However, most commentators will not accept that a Persian king could ever have declared himself to be the only god who could be worshiped for a period of thirty days.[17] Presumably, the monotheistic worship of Ahura Mazda in pure Zoroastrianism would run counter to

---

12. Young, *Daniel*, 133.

13. Fewell, *Circle*, 109.

14. Paul ("Mesopotamian Background," 57–58) argues that the expression rendered "make a firm decree" (KJV) is the cognate equivalent of the Akkadian *dunnunu* which, in legal contexts, means "to make valid and binding." He cites two examples using this term: "Let him make his tablets binding" and "He made the treaty binding."

15. The next few paragraphs are substantially a summary of Walton's arguments. See Walton, "Decree," 279–286.

16. Cf. Baldwin, *Daniel*, 128.

17. The reference to a 30-day period may indicate that the book of Daniel belongs to a context in which dates and times are calculated according to a solar calendar. Alternatively, as Boccaccini observes, the 30-day period may have no relationship at all with the month. Then again, it may simply refer to the Mesopotamian calendar used at the king's court. Boccaccini, "Solar Calendars," 312.

self-deification on the part of a king. Even if pure Zoroastrianism was not practiced at this time there is no indication that Achaemenid kings had any tendency toward self-deification. Indeed, many, assuming Daniel was written during the second century BC, believe that a ruler such as Antiochus Epiphanes is in mind. According to this view the portrayal of Darius here is anachronistic and a piece of historical fiction.

Petitionary prayer was a required and regular aspect of Iranian worship and was an essential element of pure Zoroastrianism. Darius the Great prayed not only to Ahura Mazda but to all the gods to keep enemy hordes, famine, and the "Lie" away from the empire. Prayer was deemed essential for evil forces to be held at bay. Walton comments, "It was a requirement in the practice of even a syncretized Zoroastrianism that, even if not practiced by Darius the Mede, would have been practiced by a large majority of Medes and Persians."[18] Indeed, Daniel's practice of praying three times a day accorded with pagan Iranian custom. Zoroastrianism involved praying five times a day to Ahura Mazda. Consequently, Walton reasons that "for Darius the Mede to decree even a temporary end to prayer would be unenforceable and politically suicidal, for he would be prohibiting the religious practice of every Iranian."[19]

Further it was recognized that all deities had some degree of power. Therefore, tolerance of other religions was typical. It follows, as Walton observes, that: "to deprive all other gods of the prayer of their followers was to risk the wrath of all deities, again making it unlikely that that was the intention."[20]

A number of commentators do not understand verse 8 as meaning that Darius saw himself as a god. Rather, for the period of thirty days, Darius acts as the only legitimate representative of the gods. Keil and Delitzsch, following Klieforth, believe,

> The object of the law was only to bring about the general recognition of the principle that the king was the living manifestation of all the gods, not only of the Median and Persian, but also of the Babylonian and Lydian, and all the gods of the conquered nations. . ..All the nations subjected to the Medo-Persian kingdom were required not to abandon their own special worship rendered to their gods, but in fact to acknowledge that the Medo-Persian world-ruler Darius was also the son and representative of their national gods. For this purpose they must for

18. "Decree," 281–82.
19. "Decree," 282.
20. "Decree," 282.

the space of thirty days present their petitions to their national gods only in him as their manifestation.[21]

In third-century AD Persian theology the king was seen as the representative of deity and could even assume the title "god" (*bagh*). As such he acted as a mediator. In Daniel 2:8 it may be that the king is banning priestly mediation for a month while he himself acts as the sole mediator for prayers to all deities.

The developing syncretism of Zarathuštra's teaching may help explain Darius's decree. Walton notes that during the time of Xerxes I (486–465) the worship of the *daivas* (deities unacceptable to Zarathuštra) was prohibited. As a consequence certain temples of the *daivas* were destroyed as Xerxes acted to suppress syncretism. Walton reasons that a decree forbidding the worship of the *daivas* could well have taken the same kind of form as the decree of Darius in Daniel 6. However, we know of no such injunctions prior to Xerxes.

Walton ponders the possibility that Darius was acting to counter the development of the kind of Zoroastrian calendar-based worship that arose during the reign of Xerxes's successor, Artaxerxes I (465–425). At that time the Magi replaced the civil and religious calendars previously employed. In this syncretistic calendar each of the thirty days of the month was associated with the name of particular deities called *yazatas*. Against this we have no evidence that there was such a calendar issue in the sixth century BC.

Assuming such a background, Walton proposes that Darius was approached by the conspirators "with the suggestion that by setting himself up as the only legitimate mediator for prayers for a period of thirty days a stand could be made for the worship of Ahura Mazda according to the pure teachings of Zarathuštra."[22] He comments,

> While it would certainly not eliminate syncretism nor depose the Magi from their powerful position, it would make a statement concerning the stand of the king, throwing his support to orthodox Zoroastrianism.[23]

Walton notes that all Persian kings were committed to the public performance of prayers each day. Cyrus established an elevated stand for fire (the most sacred element in Zoroastrianism) for the performance of the king's daily ritual. The intention may have been to exclude the use of images in public worship. Therefore, Darius's action was possibly aimed at publicly

---

21. "Daniel," 211.

22. "Decree," 285.

23. "Decree," 285.

expressing his opposition to syncretism and providing a royal model of orthodoxy. For the month concerned as "each individual directed his daily prayers to the king as mediator, the king in his public ritual would direct those prayers to Ahura Mazda."[24]

THE PUNISHMENT FOR DISOBEYING THE DECREE

It is not clear whether the casting of infractors into a lions' pit[25] was a standard means of execution or not.[26] Van der Toorn believes that the author of Daniel 6, in trying to create a Mesopotamian setting for his stories, has misunderstood a Mesopotamian metaphor for depicting one's enemies as "a lion's den," and, therefore, has taken this literally.[27] Van Deventer takes a different tack, and argues that the metaphor of "teeth" is so used in the book of Psalms as to indicate "a literary connection between the malicious accusations of the 'presidents and satraps' (in Dan 6) and Daniel's eventual fate among the lions."[28] In casting doubt upon the idea of an actual lion's pit being used by the king, Van der Toorn and Van Deventer assume that

24. "Decree," 285.

25. Van der Toorn points out that the Aramaic term refers to a pit rather than a den, "Scholars," 42.

26. Van der Toorn believes that the text does imply that confinement in a pit of lions was a generally practiced punitive measure among the Medes and Persians. He observes that there is no extra-biblical evidence to verify this. "Scholars," 42.

27. "Scholars," 43–53. Van der Toorn makes far too much of a metaphorical reference to lions in *Ludlul Bēl Nēmeqi* ("I shall praise the Lord of Wisdom"), over-emphasizing its very slender correspondence to the book of Daniel insofar as it too deals with "the tale of a the vindicated courtier." In that text the protagonist, Subsi-mesre-Sakkan says, "Marduk put a muzzle on the mouth of the lion that was devouring me." Van der Toorn shows that here "the lion" is the protagonist's enemy, "the hostile courtiers whose allegations eroded the confidence of the king." "Scholars," 46. Against this specious reasoning, there is no reason why the actual use of lions to execute people, as in Daniel 6, should not have given rise to metaphorical uses such as this and the other case van der Toorn cites (47–50), namely that of Urad-Gula who does speak of praying day and night to the king "in front of the lion's pit." The Bible itself is full of such metaphorical uses of lions.

28. Van Deventer, "Literary Lions," 832. In this article, all Van Deventer succeeds in doing is showing that in the Psalms there is a tradition of likening malicious verbal attacks with the threat posed by savage lions. It's one thing to emphasize the metaphorical "lions" of the Psalter and quite another, on this basis, to suggest that the "lions" of Daniel 6 are non-historical, merely concocting a narrative to match a theme found in the Psalms. However, as Daniel 7:4 indicates, it is quite possible to take the historical event of Daniel being thrown into the lions' den and then apply this and develop this in a metaphorical manner.

Daniel 6 itself cannot be regarded as a reliable historical source.[29] But there is nothing implausible about an ancient king agreeing to use a lions' pit to execute infractors either as a one-off or standard means of punishment.

Verse 8 sets up another basic contrast: the contrast between the law of Daniel's God and the law of the Medes and Persians. Darius is a strong supporter of Daniel and has immense respect for him. Daniel's enemies observe that in each man's life the fulcrum is provided by their respective law codes. Daniel is devoted to God's law and can be expected to refuse to shift in any way from this position. Similarly Darius is devoted to the law of the Medes and Persians and most certainly will not change it. Thus Daniel's enemies create a situation that will drive a wedge between the two men by placing loyalty to their respective law codes in hiatus.

FAITHFULNESS IN PRAYER

Of all the contrasts forged in this chapter, one of the greatest is the contrast between praying to king Darius and praying to God, the ultimate king.[30]

Daniel's practice of praying three times a day does not represent compliance with any particular command, though it follows David's example as set forth in Psalm 55:16–10. But it does represent, as has already been indicated in verse 5, Daniel's devotion to "the law of his God." We read in 2 Chronicles 6:36–39:

> When they sin against you—for there is no one who does not sin—and you become angry with them and give them over to the enemy, who takes them captive to a land far away or near; and if they have a change of heart in the land where they are held captive, and repent and plead with you in the land of their captivity and say, "We have sinned, we have done wrong and acted wickedly"; and if they turn back to you with all their heart and soul in the land of their captivity where they were taken, and pray toward the land you gave their fathers, toward the city you have chosen and toward the temple I have built for your Name;

29. "Scholars," 42. Van der Toorn's conclusions are based on his research into Assyrian court life. He concedes, "Things many have been slightly different at the Babylonian court, but the only evidence that might be adduced to this effect is the very Book of Daniel." Now comes his bias: "It seems more prudent to assume that the biblical author drew upon his imperfect knowledge of the Babylonian court to throw his protagonist into sharper relief . . . ." Van der Toorn's presuppositions concerning the dating of Daniel preclude him from being able to accept that the author had firsthand knowledge of Mesopotamian court life.

30. So Thompson, "The Rescuer in Babylon."

then from heaven, your dwelling place, hear their prayer and their pleas, and uphold their cause. And forgive your people, who have sinned against you.

It is to this "law" that Daniel is devoted. In the upstairs room where he prays three times a day the windows are open toward Jerusalem, that is, toward the place where Solomon had built the temple now five hundred miles away to the west. Gandhi found consolation in what he saw as a fine example of *satyagraha*, believing that Daniel, though without ill-will, defiantly threw open the windows.[31] As Smith-Christopher observes, the passive voice of the Aramaic verb implies the windows were always in this state.[32] It is pointless arguing from the use of the active voice in the Old Greek translation that Daniel was indeed acting defiantly. Much depends on what agenda is being served when interpreters use this word "defiant" in this connection. Of course, there is an inescapable level of "defiance" insofar as Daniel's faithfulness to his God sets him against Darius's decree. But there is no encouragement from the context of any deliberate intent to express defiance. It is precarious on the basis of such a reading of 6:10 to find support for the view that the court tales of chapters 1 to 6 are examples of resistance literature.[33] Daniel has no desire or intent to be in a state of resisting the king he so faithfully and wholeheartedly serves. While his enemies seek security by finding fault in Daniel, he "is seeking God, where he will find security as a by-product."[34]

As Daniel faces Jerusalem through those open windows, he is "seeking first the kingdom of God," yearning and praying for the day when God's kingly rule will be re-established in a restored Jerusalem. He has never reconciled himself completely to life in Babylon. It is impossible for him to be at home in Babylon. In the core of his being Daniel identifies himself not with the Babylonians—and the immediately preceding context has drawn attention to his "loneliness"—but with the people of God.

Daniel knows that he is placing his life in jeopardy by continuing to pray as he does, nevertheless his devotion to God's law is such that, in his own mind, he has no choice but to maintain his practice. Daniel could have said to himself, "It won't matter if I stop praying for thirty days. I can resume again once the crisis is over." But Daniel lives every day for Jerusalem; he breathes Jerusalem. Jerusalem is at the heart of what God's kingship means

---

31. See Smith-Christopher, "Gandhi," 326. *Satyagraha* means "insistence on truth" and is the term used to describe the philosophy of nonviolent resistance.

32. "Gandhi," 328.

33. Contra Smith-Christopher, "Gandhi," 331.

34. Arnold, "Wordplay," 485.

for Daniel. To stop praying even for a day would be to undermine God's kingship in Daniel's life. Arguably back in Daniel 1 Daniel's decision not to defile himself with the king's food was not so much a matter of being scrupulous to avoid cultic defilement, but more a case of avoiding being Nebuchadnezzar's lackey (in contrast to the standard portrayal of Babylonian political officials as servile), and expressing his distinctive and ultimate allegiance to God. Now Daniel sees the situation as much the same. Again he must choose between God the King, as symbolized by Jerusalem, and the Persian ruler. He must choose between the law of his God and the law of the Medes and Persians.[35]

It is important to take to heart the fact that Daniel's prayer life is an expression of his devotion to seeing the fulfillment of God's sovereign purposes. There are many who overlook this and simply recommend the practice of a disciplined prayer life which involves the setting aside of particular times for prayer. Discipline is important but the application becomes legalistic if greater emphasis is not placed on the need for the formation of convictions concerning God's kingship, convictions one is ready to die for if called upon to do so.

Daniel gives thanks "to his God," that is, he consciously violates the law of the Medes and Persians which stipulated the execution, via the decree, of "anyone who prays to any god . . . " (v. 7).

Although Daniel's faithful praying "toward Jerusalem" implies his persistent plea that God's people return to their land, nevertheless Daniel's praying is not morose and baleful. The chief characteristic of his praying mentioned here is that he "gave thanks to God." Daniel recognizes God's hand in all that has happened, and his thanksgiving points to a conviction that God is still very much in control and has wonderful purposes for his people. Daniel's praying toward Jerusalem does not imply despair and pessimism, but as his habit of thanksgiving clearly indicates, he is a man of great hope.

THE CONSPIRATORS INCRIMINATE DANIEL (VV. 11-15)

The diabolical plan of Daniel's enemies has succeeded. They have succeeded in creating a situation in which Darius must order the execution of Daniel.

35. Gooding, "Literary Structure," 63–64, sees Daniel 1 and 6 as intended pairs within the total structure of the book and makes much of the contrast between Daniel refusing to participate in a practice imposed by the king which he believes would defile him (chapter 1) and refusing to abstain from a practice that expresses his devotion to the Lord (chapter 6).

When Daniel's colleagues go to the king it as those who have baited the fish and now take delight in reeling it in.

To implement their evil plan these enemies "discover" Daniel at prayer. Once again special attention is given to the fact that they "came together" in order to accomplish their purpose—an emphasis we have already encountered in verse 7. The chasm between Daniel and his political peers is unbridgeable. Significantly Daniel is asking God for help. What kind of help? Daniel knows that the decree has been published, and therefore he knows his life to be at peril. Presumably he asks God for help in this predicament.

This prayer for help is not merely presented as being a natural prayer given the circumstances. It anticipates all that will happen in this chapter. It therefore serves to underline the fact that when Daniel prays to his God it is not just to "any god" (v. 7); that Daniel's prayers are not simply the mark of a religious devotee. Daniel really and truly is in relationship with his God, remembering that the Chaldean belief is that the gods "do not live among men;" that the gods belong to a transcendent realm. By contrast, in this book, Daniel's God repeatedly demonstrates that he is vitally involved in the continuing historical process, and it cannot be overstated that this is a major point of difference between Daniel and the apocalypses. This contrast is not merely with so-called otherworldly apocalypses which often have little connection with history, but also there is a decided hiatus between the God–History relationship depicted in Daniel and the God–History relationship depicted in the so-called historical apocalypses. For while these latter apocalypses indicate that God predetermines aeons in world history there is little to nothing which corresponds with the book of Daniel's stress on the way God constantly intervenes in concrete historical situations and into the personal lives and circumstances of specific individuals.

Once again in this passage the distance between the Babylonians and Daniel is accentuated. This time it is the way in which Daniel's enemies refer to him as being "one of the exiles from Judah." This is clearly not just a haphazard mode of identification. Nor do these words merely reflect the Babylonians rejection of Daniel as a foreigner who as such should not rule over them.[36] This is not a simple case of racism. The insinuation is not merely: "what else can you expect from an exile." The words are loaded having been carefully applied before in the book on a number of occasions.

Of course, the identity of Daniel and his three friends is emphasized at the very outset of the book (1:1–3), when they are described as "some from Judah" (1:6). When Daniel is first introduced to Nebuchadnezzar it is as "a

---

36. Young emphasizes the implication that he is unfaithful to the king because he is a foreigner; *Daniel*, 36.

man among the exiles from Judah" (2:25). When Chaldeans denounce Daniel's friends it is as "certain Jews" (3:12) who are to be sharply discriminated from "certain Chaldeans" (3:8). Belshazzar asked Daniel, "Are you Daniel, one of the exiles my father the king brought from Judah?"(5:13).

Now yet again our attention is drawn to the essential identity of Daniel—and the Chaldeans have proved to be remarkably perceptive in this respect, as evidenced by their ability to see how foundational God's law was to Daniel's life (v. 5). Daniel is an exile, and the preceding context has made it apparent that this is precisely how Daniel sees himself. It is so essential to Daniel's self-identity that he think of himself as an exile, that he will court seemingly certain death rather than deny what it means to him to be an exile, namely to be one who lives for the hope of eventual return to Jerusalem.

DARIUS RELUCTANTLY THROWS DANIEL TO THE LIONS (V. 16)

The first time Daniel's life is in danger in this book is when he is comes face to face with Nebuchadnezzar's executioner whose name, Arioch, ironically means "lion." Now at the end of the narrative section we send Daniel's life in danger yet again and once more he comes face to face with lions. Darius has Daniel thrown into the lions' pit. In sharp contrast with the Nebuchadnezzar of Daniel 3, Darius is not in the slightest offended by Daniel's devotion to his God. Darius never intended that the decree he issued be applied in this way.

Darius summarizes for us the meaning of what we have already been told concerning Daniel's devotion to the law of his God, and his habitual practice of praying toward Jerusalem three times every day without fail. He speaks of it as Daniel's "continual service" of God. Daniel is thus understood to be the faithful servant of God.

There is great irony here. Consistently in the book of Daniel the Babylonian officials act as though they were the king's lackeys and their toady language and tactics are expressive of servility and obsequiousness. Yet Daniel and his friends stand head and shoulders above these fawning boot-lickers in terms of their devotion to the king, whoever he might be. The irony is that their service of God actually makes them better, not worse servants of the king.

This was a point stressed in Daniel 1. Daniel and his friends preserved in their private lives a commitment to God that overrode their loyalty to Nebuchadnezzar. But it was a private ordering of priorities and not an act of open and resentful defiance. In all other respects they fully acquiesce with Nebuchadnezzar's requirements and in the end he finds them to be vastly superior to their peers. The whole point of the training program devised by Nebuchadnezzar was that it equip all trainees to serve in his presence. Daniel and his friends end up being the very best servants of Nebuchadnezzar in the entire kingdom.

In Daniel 2 the Chaldeans were of absolutely no use to the king. The king's perception of them as being essentially boot-lickers who in fear will tell him what he wants to hear is indicated by his refusal to divulge details of the dream. Only Daniel (and his friends) is able to serve the king by providing the interpretation he demands. The same contrast is implicit in Daniel 4.

In Daniel 3 again the abject obsequiousness of the Babylonians is stressed as never before. Shadrach, Meshach, and Abednego answer Nebuchadnezzar's demand that they worship his image of gold with the language of service: "we want you to know, O king, that we will not serve your gods or worship the image of gold you have set up" (v. 18). When Nebuchadnezzar sees them walking around in the fire unscathed he calls them out saying, "Shadrach, Meshach, and Abednego, servants of the Most High God, come out! Come here!" (v. 26), and later praises God "who has sent his angel and rescued his servants!" (v. 28). Following this whole incident which has involved these men placing loyalty to their God above loyalty to the king, Nebuchadnezzar's response is to promote them (v. 30), to acknowledge that they are in fact even better suited to serve him.

In Daniel 4 the depth of Daniel's devotion to king Nebuchadnezzar is revealed when the meaning of the dream dawns upon Daniel and in great distress he cries out, "My lord, if only the dream applied to your enemies and its meaning to your adversaries" (4:19). Daniel's underlying primary devotion to God was not seditious in any sense. In all sincerity he was simultaneously the servant of God and the servant of the king.

The tragedy of Daniel 5 is that Belshazzar aspires to the greatness enjoyed by Nebuchadnezzar but this is all he appears to remember of that history. He is ignorant of how crucial Daniel's service was to Nebuchadnezzar, and treats him accordingly, neglecting him until events force him to identify Daniel with the Mister X he had decided to place in the position of supreme power next to himself. Belshazzar was desperately seeking a servant who would deal with his extreme distress.

Now in Daniel 6 we see once again that service of God and service of the king need not be in conflict. When this happens in the book it is because of foolish decisions made by the kings concerned. But Darius himself greatly esteems Daniel's service and never for a moment thinks that Daniel's primary allegiance to God undermines his ability to serve him better than any other in the kingdom. And so he even longs that this man who serves his God continually be rescued, and thus be enabled to serve him too.

The irony of the entire situation is indicated by another extraordinary development. The edict had stated that "anyone who prays to any god of man during the next thirty days, except to the king shall be thrown into the lions' den" (6:7). The king alone stands outside this law. But it is no use Daniel praying to King Darius to rescue him from the lions' pit. The edict, at least ostensibly, presupposes that the king has absolute control and power. But ensuing events prove this is far from being the case and the king himself is bewildered by his inability to exercise his power and authority to rescue Daniel. He himself is a prisoner of the law that issued from his own mouth, of his own actions. And the supreme irony of this is that, placed in this predicament, the king himself prays to God: "May your God . . . rescue you!"

THE KING'S ANXIETIES AND HOPES
CONCERNING DANIEL (VV. 17–20)

The above points are underscored by this next unit which stresses the king's extreme distress at the thought of losing his most highly valued servant who, ironically, is again honored as one who serves his God continually. Once again we strike the motif of the sleeplessness of the king. Darius "spent the night without eating and without any entertainment being brought to him." The word "entertainment" could refer to "musicians" or "dancing girls" or it could simply be added to reinforce the fact that he did not eat, that is, "no table was brought to him."[37]

The king's lack of absolute control is now a well-established emphasis in the book. Here it is highlighted by mention not only of the stone being placed over the mouth of the pit, but also by the fact that the king, most unwillingly, is forced to seal the stone with his own signet ring and with the rings of his nobles. The seal tells everyone that Daniel has been thrown into the lions' den on the king's authority and that anyone who tried to rescue him would be committing a treasonable act.[38] The king is forced to side with his nobles, the very ones who have manipulated him into acting as he has. The king is not only doing what he does not want to do—not only compelled to follow his own law's demands to "the bitter end"—but also finds himself forced to do what his nobles wanted him to do.

But there is irony in what happens:

> As Darius has sealed the mouth of the pit, so God has shut the mouths of the lions. During the night, Darius has not been able to

37. Anderson, *Signs and Wonders*, 70–71.
38. Olyott, *Dare to Stand*, 82.

eat; likewise, neither have the lions. The lions are not allowed to harm Daniel because Daniel has done nothing to harm the king.[39]

The sleeplessness of the king has become a familiar motif, and each time such a state is described in the book, or the distress of the king is mentioned, we see that the king feels he has lost control of the situation concerned; that he is at a loss to know what to do; that he is dependent on God stepping into the situation and resolving it for him. So it is here.

In contrast to Nebuchadnezzar who claimed no god could deliver from his hand we see Darius asking whether Daniel's god has been able to deliver him.[40] The fact that the king goes to the pit at dawn and on finding Daniel still alive, gives orders for him to be lifted from the pit, may involve another irony. The conspirators, knowing the irrevocable nature of the law of the Medes and Persians, urge the king to prescribe the punishment of throwing violators into the lions' den. However, their proposed edict does not stipulate that this punishment should be a mode of execution. Therefore, at this point the law works in the king's favor. For now he is enabled to interpret the language of his edict as a trial by ordeal. If this had been an execution then there would be no limit on how long Daniel should stay in the pit. But Daniel is able to regard his deliverance as indeed a trial by ordeal, which has proved his innocence (v. 22).[41] By contrast, the instant destruction of the conspirators is not merely fitting retribution but also proof of their guilt.

THE DELIVERANCE OF DANIEL AND THE EXECUTION OF THE CONSPIRATORS (VV. 21–24)

What follows bears remarkably close correspondence to the description of the deliverance of the three Jews in Daniel 3. Just as God sent an angel into the place of destruction to rescue Shadrach, Meshach, and Abednego (3:28), so now he sends an angel into the place of destruction to rescue Daniel. In both cases the context in differing ways emphasizes the point that the victims concerned are thrown into a place where, humanly speaking, destruction is most assured and inevitable. In Daniel 3 this is conveyed by reference to the fact that those who threw in the three Jews were themselves burnt to death by the flames into which they threw them. In Daniel 6 the same point is made by noting that when the enemies were thrown into the pit they were

---

39. Fewell, *Circle*, 115.
40. Hebbard, *Reading Daniel*, 151.
41. Cf. Longman, *Daniel*, 162–63.

killed before they even reached the floor of the pit (cf. those killed in Daniel 3 who had not "reached" the furnace).

When Daniel answers Darius he does so as one whose devotion to the king has never been in question. The use of the words "O king" have a completely different ring on Daniel's lips to the hollow fawning tones of his political peers and enemies (cf. vv. 6–8). Daniel's first words match theirs: "O king, live for ever!" But the deceit of Daniel's enemies makes their similar acclamation spurious. Daniel's devotion is unquestionable and corresponds to the devotion he expressed for Nebuchadnezzar in 4:19.

Although technically Daniel has broken the law issued by the king, after emerging from the pit Daniel can declare with a clear conscience, "I have never done anything wrong before you, O king."[42] This is clearly a statement of considerable importance in coming to terms with the nature of biblical ethics. It is in fact possible to break the law of the governing authority without wronging the authority concerned. This conclusion is at odds with those who espouse a strict hierarchical ethic and who would often argue those placed in analogous situations are required to choose the lesser of two evils. This is not how Daniel views the choice he has made. Daniel's innocence is understood to be the reason for his rescue in 1 Maccabees 2:60. Further, as Hebbard puts it, "If Daniel is found innocent before the supreme power, then he should be found innocent before a power who receives his authority from the superior power."[43] There's more. Daniel lives up to the meaning of his name, "God is my judge," for he is claiming innocence despite his technical breach of the law. As Hebbard recognizes, "The act of judicial interpretation implies that only a judge or someone who claims the duties of a judge can be responsible for an interpretation of law."[44]

God's deliverance of Daniel is not simply his way of "thumbing his nose against Darius" and showing him who is really the boss. It is an act that vindicates Daniel and this corresponds to the conclusion reached by Nebuchadnezzar following the deliverance of the three Jews. For then Nebuchadnezzar acknowledged that they had been right to defy his command and to faithfully serve their God. For this reason he decrees the death penalty for any who would speak ill of God.

---

42. Daniel's prayer has not been "a violation of the spirit of the law that seeks to protect the kingdom against conspiracy. . .his prayer complies with the spirit of the law and works neither to conspire nor to destabilize security. Therefore, we can justify Daniel's claim to innocence according to his judicial interpretation." Hebbard, *Reading Daniel*, 154.

43. *Reading Daniel*, 153.

44. *Reading Daniel*, 153.

The theme of vindication in Daniel is an important one, which emphasizes that even in captivity God has a righteous people; those who are innocent in his sight; those he blesses because of their faithfulness to him. It is not necessary for God's people to be in the promised land in order to live a righteous life. Here biblical thought contradicts all ideologies which believe that character and identity are largely or even completely determined by societal conditions and the environment in which one lives. Daniel and his friends are proof positive that it is possible to live a righteous life in the most adverse and hostile of situations. Although this anticipates the New Testament conception of righteousness, which is not dependent on the enjoyment of particularly Jewish privileges, nevertheless it would be wrong at this point to think that the promised land had now become irrelevant to the righteousness of Daniel and his friends. What makes Daniel a righteous man in this passage is precisely the fact that he is devoted to Jerusalem—the very reason why he was thrown into the lions' pit.

When Daniel is lifted from the den we are told: "no wound was found on him, because he had trusted in his God." This clearly echoes Daniel 3 where the faith of Shadrach, Meshach, and Abednego is also stressed (v. 28; cf. vv. 17–18), along with the note that "the fire had not harmed their bodies, nor was a hair of their heads singed; their robes were not scorched, and there was no smell of fire on them" (v. 27b).

In addition to this the word "found" is used in a climactic way. For beginning at 5:11 there has been a continuing stress on this word. Alluding back to the earlier part of the book (1:19, 20; 2:25), the queen (mother?) tells Belshazzar of Daniel, the man who "was found to have insight and intelligence and wisdom like that of the gods" (5:11). This same basic sentiment is repeated in 5:12 and 5:14. By contrast, Belshazzar is "found wanting" (5:27). In Daniel 6, as we have already observed, there is a continuing play on this word with exclusive reference to Daniel. All prior uses serve to emphasize that Daniel is invested with godlike wisdom (Daniel 5) and wholehearted, unswerving devotion to his God (Daniel 6). The reason why the lions did not hurt Daniel was because he was "found" innocent in God's sight (6:22); no wound was "found" on him, because he had trusted in his God (6:23). Thus the use of this word in the account of Daniel's deliverance highlights all the more that Daniel is approved by God.

When Daniel's enemies, together with their families, are thrown into the lions' pit, they are immediately overpowered and crushed by the lions.[45] The word "overpowered" is the same term associated with sovereignty in the

45. The execution of wives and children along with the condemned prevented immediate family members from exacting revenge, while also serving as a terrible deterrent. Harman, *Daniel*, 146–147.

Aramaic portion of Daniel and here, given God's control over savage beasts (anticipating the beastly imagery of Daniel 7–12), insinuates the subordination of human rule to God's transcendent rule.[46] At this point also the contexts of Daniel 3 and Daniel 6 interlock, for Daniel 3 concluded with Nebuchadnezzar's decree that any who speak "anything against the God of Shadrach, Meshach, and Abednego be cut into pieces and their houses be turned into piles of rubble" (3:29). The fate of Daniel's enemies represents a fulfillment of this decree. This is highly ironic. Daniel's enemies, in seeking Daniel's destruction, depended fully on the inviolability of the law of the Medes and Persians, but are undone by the irrevocability of Nebuchadnezzar's God-approved decree. It is also possible that in executing Daniel's accusers Darius was acting on an unstated claim of false suit. As Valeta puts it: "Because they have falsely accused Daniel of acting against the king's interests, they are subject to the same penalties to which Daniel would have been subject if proven guilty—death in the lions' den."[47]

DARIUS'S SECOND DECREE (VV. 25–27)

Darius writes to everybody in the kingdom and decrees that all fear and reverence God. This is ironic because the supposedly irrevocable law of the Medes of Persians, the first decree that put Daniel in the lions' den, has been rescinded.[48]

Prinsloo[49] considers the poetic form of Darius's communication, noting how, as in 2:20–23, this achieves foregrounding, underscoring that something out of the ordinary is being said. Also, just as at 2:20–23, it is through this poetic form that fundamental theological truth is communicated. This is the first time in the book that a Gentile ruler commands his subjects to relate to God in a positive manner. It is emphasized in the chapter how positively Darius's heart was disposed toward Daniel. Not only was the king in great anguish when Daniel's doom seemed inevitable, but also when Daniel was found to be safe "the king was overjoyed." The warmth of Darius's feelings for Daniel are matched by his warmth

46. Valeta, *Lions*, 109.

47. *Lions*, 109. Hebbard identifies four things that are confirmed in the destruction of Daniel's malicious adversaries: (1) the very legislators of this law were themselves guilty of conspiracy against Darius (I would add, that to undermine Darius's way of organizing his rule with Daniel in charge is to conspire against Darius); (2) the unquestionable innocence of Daniel in the eyes of Adonai; (3) the effectiveness and sincerity of Daniel's prayer; (4) the limitless, saving power of Adonai. *Reading Daniel*, 154.

48. See Hebbard, *Reading Daniel*, 155.

49. "Two Poems," 101–6.

for Daniel's God. In his decree Darius clearly expresses his admiration for Daniel's God. However, the fact that he refers to God as "the God of Daniel" indicates that there is still a measure of distance between Darius and this God he extols. Consequently, we are not to think that Darius has been converted.

It is a mark of the immense respect in which Darius holds Daniel that Darius calls God "the God of Daniel." In chapters 3 and 4 Nebuchadnezzar also praises God and identifies him in relation to the three Jews calling him "the God of Shadrach, Meshach, and Abednego." These two designations of God are striking not merely because of their formal correspondence to each other. Both effectively are shorthand for the thought "the God who saved his servant(s)." Thus the identification of God with the names of these particular Jews is really an acknowledgment of God as the only God who can save.

Theologically this is a most important point of conclusion given the wider historical context in which the book is set. It is probably not too far-fetched to see in the fiery furnace and the lions' pit not only the recording of actual historical events but also enacted parables of the condition of Israel at that time. In this respect it is important to remind ourselves that the book of Daniel shows no interest in Shadrach, Meshach, and Abednego as individuals, but only as a group. This, plus the repeated emphasis on their identity and that of Daniel as "exiles from Judah," indicates that Daniel and his friends are representative of all Jews in captivity.

The fact that the events of Daniel 3 are paralleled in Daniel 6 also indicates that the event has a wider application than in the lives of the particular persons God delivers. Had not Israel as a captive people been thrown, as it were, into the "fiery furnace" and into "the lions' pit?" Is not the situation in which Israel was then embroiled one from which there can be no escape? Does not realism force all to acknowledge that the extinction of Israel as God's people was imminent? Is it possible for God's people to live in a corrupt and idolatrous society which involves a rule inimical to that of God's and remain unscathed and pure?

DANIEL PROSPERS (V. 28)

Just as Daniel prospered during the reigns of the Babylonian rulers, now he continues to prosper during the rule of the Persian kings. I have already drawn attention to the significance of verse 10. It is Daniel's devotion to Jerusalem and longing for the return of his people to Jerusalem which occasioned all that has happened in Daniel 6. It is therefore most fitting, in God's wonderful providence, that Daniel should prosper until the very time when, under Cyrus, the great decree was issued occasioning Israel's return to Jerusalem. Thus verse 28 forms a fitting parallel with 1:21 which is also set in a chapter which has emphasized the tragedy of God's people being uprooted from Jerusalem. There the mention of Cyrus insinuates that Daniel outlasts Nebuchadnezzar and indeed the entire Babylonian kingdom.

But Daniel 1 also begins with insistence on the reality of God's rule notwithstanding external appearances and begins to trace the outworkings of this in an exilic setting. Therefore, Daniel 1:21 indicates that God's rule outlasts and transcends Babylonian rule. Similarly, Daniel 6:28 immediately follows Darius's declaration concerning "the God of Daniel," as one whose kingdom is everlasting and indestructible.

In addition to the theological interests served by the mention of Cyrus, it is important to note that this helps to link Daniel 1–6 with Daniel 7–10, given that the vision of Daniel 10–12 is set in "the third year of Cyrus, king of Persia" (10:1).[50]

COMPARISONS AND CONTRASTS IN DANIEL 6

Daniel the most excellent servant of the king.	The implicit inferiority of Daniel's Babylonian counterparts.
Daniel's devotion to "the law of his God."	Darius's devotion to "the laws of the Medes and Persians."
Daniel's irrevocable compliance with the law.	Darius's irrevocable compliance with the law.
Daniel's law exalts his God.	Darius's law is idolatrous.
Darius has sealed the mouth of the pit.	God shut the mouths of the lions.
During the night, Darius not able to eat.	During the night the lions not able to eat.
The lions do not harm Daniel.	Daniel has not harmed the king.
Darius's inability to rescue Daniel, despite his earnest desire to do so.	God alone is able to rescue Daniel.
Daniel is the most highly prized servant of the king.	Daniel is the faithful servant of God.

We have already noted many points of comparison between Daniel 5 and Daniel 3. Daniel 6 also parallels Daniel 3 in a remarkable manner:

50. Towner, *Daniel*, 88.

Daniel 6	Daniel 3
SIMILARITIES	
Jealous Babylonians denounce Daniel before the king.	Jealous Babylonians denounce the three Jews before the king.
The professed servility of the Babylonians is expressed in their labored emphasis on Darius being king (note esp. the repeated "O king!").	The professed servility of the Babylonians is expressed in their labored emphasis on Nebuchadnezzar being king (note esp. the repeated "O king!").
The professed servility of Babylonian political leaders is comprehensive: "royal administrators, prefects, satraps, advisers, and governors."	The professed servility of Babylonian political leaders is comprehensive: "satraps, prefects, governors, advisers, treasurers, judges, magistrates, and all other provincial officials."
Darius issues a decree which violates devotion to God.	Nebuchadnezzar issues a decree which violates devotion to God.
The king's decree requires the king be treated as the supreme god.	The king's decree requires the king be treated as the supreme god.
Even if he should die Daniel will continue to obey his God.	Even if they should die the three Jews will continue to obey God.
Daniel places obedience to God above obedience to the king.	The three Jews place obedience to God above obedience to the king.
Daniel is thrown into the lions' pit.	The three Jews are thrown into the fiery furnace.
The lions' pit is a place of inevitable destruction: the rapacious lions destroy Daniel's enemies.	The fiery furnace is a place of inevitable destruction: the rapacious flames destroy the three Jews' executioners.
The enemies are destroyed before they reach the ground.	The executioners are destroyed before they reach the furnace.
God sends his angel into the lions' pit to be with Daniel and deliver him..	God sends his angel into the fiery furnace to be with the three Jews and deliver them.
Daniel remains unscathed while amidst the rapacious lions.	The three Jews remain unscathed while amidst the rapacious flames.
Daniel's body is unsuccessfully examined for injury when he emerges from the lion's pit.	The bodies of the three Jews are examined when they emerge from the fiery furnace.
Daniel is vindicated as innocent and as not having wronged the king.	Nebuchadnezzar vindicates the three Jews, passing the death sentence on any who would speak against them.
The king honors Daniel as a faithful servant of God (before the "execution").	The king honors the three Jews as faithful servants of God (after the "execution").

Daniel is delivered because he trusted in his God.	The three Jews are delivered because they trusted in God.
The king issues a decree.	The king issues a decree.
The deliverance causes the king to praise God.	The deliverance causes the king to praise God.
The king praises God as Savior.	The king praises God as Savior.
The decree is addressed to "all the peoples, nations, and men of every language throughout the land."	Nebuchadnezzar's decree is binding on "the people of any nation or language."
The king orders everyone to reverence Daniel's God.	The king promises the death penalty for any who treat God with irreverence.
The king causes Daniel to prosper.	The king promotes the three Jews.
CONTRASTS	
The initiative for the idolatrous decree comes from the Babylonians not the king.	The initiative for the idolatrous decree comes from the king.
The decree is only effective for a thirty-day period.	No time frame is provided.
The enemies are political figures.	The enemies are Chaldeans.
God's servant is tested in the area of private worship.	God's servants are tested in the area of public worship.
The king is distressed and is determined to rescue Daniel.	The king is enraged and becomes more intensely committed to destroying the three Jews, ordering that the heat of the furnace be increased.
The king accepts Daniel's devotion to God.	The king demands the three Jews repudiate their devotion to God.
Darius accepts the possibility that God may deliver Daniel.	It is unthinkable to Nebuchadnezzar that God be able to deliver the three Jews from his hand.
The king is under the authority of his own law.	The king is his own law.
The king does not see the angel in the place of destruction with God's servant.	The king sees the angel in the place of destruction with God's servants.
The king's decree is positive, telling his subjects how they should relate to God.	The king's decree is negative, telling his subjects how not to relate to God.

There are also points of correspondence between Daniel 6 and Daniel 4 that have especially been recognized by Fewell.[51]

51. In her 1988 edition, Fewell sets out the following points of correspondence between Daniel 6 and Daniel 4.

Daniel 4	Daniel 6
Decree of "the holy ones" causes problems for Nebuchadnezzar.	Darius's decree causes problems for Daniel.
After learning of the decree, Nebuchadnezzar goes up on to the roof of his palace and it is there that he does something which brings the sentence of the decree upon him.	After learning of the decree, Daniel goes up to his upper room and his action brings the sentence of Darius's decree upon him.
A voice from heaven interrupts Nebuchadnezzar and the decree is fulfilled.	The officials interrupt Daniel and the decree is enforced.
Nebuchadnezzar suffers a temporary loss of political position and an association with beasts.	Daniel suffers a temporary loss of political position and an association with beasts.
Nebuchadnezzar is driven from society.	Daniel is thrown into the lions' pit.
Nebuchadnezzar is restored to his position and prospers.	Daniel is restored to his position and prospers.

There are also similarities between the way Nebuchadnezzar and Darius address their subjects:

A common vocabulary shared by the two stories broadens the analogous narrative contexts. The language that Nebuchadnezzar uses in his first doxology in 3:31–33 is echoed by Darius at the end of chapter. 6. Both kings address their messages to "all peoples, nations, and languages who dwell in all the earth." Both use the common expression "May your peace be multiplied" to greet their subjects. Both praise God's signs and wonders. Both speak of the endurance of God's kingdom and rule.

SUMMARY

- Nothing can budge Daniel from his prayerful dependence upon God to preserve his people and effect their return to Jerusalem. The Chaldeans rightly perceive Daniel to be an exile and indeed this identity is central to Daniel's whole life as evidenced by his praying towards Jerusalem.

- God is totally committed to establishing the utter distinctiveness of Daniel from his Chaldean peers in the mind of the king and the reader.

- Daniel's supreme authority is "the law of his God" not the supposedly irrevocable law of the Medes and Persians. Ironically, as the king himself is well aware, this makes him a far better servant of the king than the Chaldean peers who orchestrate and submit to the king's decree only because it suits their ends.

- Further irony is found in the fact that the king makes a decree expressive of absolute control and then is bewildered by the way in which as a result he totally loses control of the situation. Once again the contrast between the limited control of the ruler and the absolute control of God is stressed.

- God's identity as King is yet again closely associated with his identity as Savior. The most powerful king on earth is unable to deliver Daniel from the place of certain destruction, much as he longs to do so. Only God can save from the place of certain destruction.

- Daniel proves yet again that it is possible to live a righteous life in the most adverse and hostile of situations.

POINTS OF CONTACT WITH THE
NEW TESTAMENT AND LIFE

1. There are some loose, largely insubstantial parallels that can be and have been drawn between Daniel's experience in Daniel 6 and Jesus' experience in the Passion events.[52] Very roughly the following pattern is common to both: betrayal; entrapment on the basis of faithfulness being anti-state; God's servant prays before his arrest; the authority figure is forced to act against his will and sympathizes with the victim whose innocence he recognizes; both are consigned to the place of irrevocable destruction; the place of death is closed with a stone and sealed; the person presumed dead miraculously re-emerges from the place of irrevocable destruction. A closer look at these parallels reveals they are often considerably different and there are other points at which the experience of Daniel, as recounted in Daniel 6, bears no correspondence with Jesus, e.g., "no wound was found on him" —though "where there's a will there's a way" and those who are intent on spiritualizing Daniel 6 will have little difficulty in even assimilating this disparity. In my judgment it is precarious to use the language of type and anti-type. Certainly, it is proper to note the analogy for Christ's passion that is afforded by Daniel's experience and to use Daniel 6 as an illustration of the sufferings of Christ and indeed of all the righteous. With respect to

---

52. See Towner, *Daniel*, 84–5.

the Passion Narratives perhaps the most substantial point of contact is provided in Matthew 27:66 where the description of the stone placed over Christ's tomb may well be intended to recall Daniel 6.[53] Jesus, like Daniel, is put in a place from which the dead cannot return.

2. Hebrews 11:34 alludes to the faith of Daniel which enabled him to "shut the mouths of lions."[54] Within the context of Daniel 6 itself we see that there is little to discriminate between "faith" and "faithfulness." In Hebrews also faith translates into faithfulness.

3. In 2 Timothy 4:17[55] Paul compares his own experience of a malicious attack and God's deliverance with Daniel's experience when he remarks, "And I was delivered from the lion's mouth." This deliverance was effected by God for the sake of the broadcasting of his message to all Gentiles. In a similar manner in Daniel 6 the deliverance of Daniel provides a platform for a global declaration of God's greatness. Paul goes on to say, "The Lord will rescue me from every evil attack and will bring me safely to his heavenly kingdom." These words could equally have been uttered by Daniel and it may even be that Paul deliberately "takes the words right out of his mouth."

4. Daniel's faithful prayers, directed at Jerusalem, are an expression of his "seeking first the kingdom of God" (Matt 6:33). This cannot be put on hold, even for a month. God's rule is far more important to him than any human rule, no matter how dire the consequences may be of violating human rule.

POSSIBLE SERMON OUTLINE

Title: "*The Lion Tamer*"

1. Daniel's Faithfulness

2. Darius's Decrees

3. The Only King and Savior

---

53. See Van Henten, "Daniel 3 and 6," 158–60.
54. See Van Henten, "Daniel 3 and 6," 163–66.
55. See Van Henten, "Daniel 3 and 6," 160–62.

Study Questions

I have provided the following leading questions to fulfill three purposes:

1. For use in personal Bible Study and devotions.
2. For use in Bible Study groups.
3. For Bible College and Seminary students to use to orient themselves before being lectured on Daniel or before getting lost in the forest of details that characterize most commentaries (including this one!) and to enable them to interact intelligently with the lecturer/lecture material/commentary, etc.

For each chapter a rather long list of possible questions is provided. Bible Study leaders should feel free to select just a few questions for each study and reword them according to their requirements.

DANIEL 1

Exegetical

- What particular emphases emerge from an analysis of the structure of the chapter?
- Is God presented as a defeated God in Daniel 1? Give reasons for your answer.
- What significance do the events of 1:1–2 hold for understanding the book of Daniel?
- How is Nebuchadnezzar presented in Daniel 1?

- What kind of defilement did Daniel seek to avoid?
- In what ways does the wisdom of Daniel and his friends differ from that of the Chaldeans?
- How (if at all) do Daniel and his friends represent God's people?
- What parallels are there between Daniel's career and that of Joseph?
- What other allusions are there to earlier biblical material?

New Testament Development

- What does avoidance of defilement mean and entail in New Testament thought?
- How does God's Reign ("Kingdom of God") in the New Testament parallel the presentation of God's Rule in Daniel 1? Association with apparent defeat? Hidden providential hand?
- What is the relationship between God's Rule and Temple in the New Testament?
- What are the counterparts to Nebuchadnezzar and Babylon in the New Testament?
- How is the contrast between God-given wisdom and the world's wisdom developed in the New Testament?
- In what ways does the world put God's people to the test in similar ways in the New Testament world?
- How is the Christian relationship to magical practices elaborated in the New Testament?
- What does the New Testament teach about the basis of personal identity?
- What does the New Testament teach about resistance to human authority? When is it appropriate? What are appropriate and inappropriate expressions of resistance?
- In what does the distinctiveness of God's people consist in New Testament thought? How does Daniel 1 fit in with such perspectives?
- How does Revelation 2:10 develop Daniel 1:12–14?
- What analogies can be drawn between the historical disaster described in verses 1–2 and the cross of Christ?

Personal Relevance and Application

(Caution: do not seek to answer these questions in isolation from the text of Daniel 1)

- In what ways is this chapter relevant for modern Christians as they seek to live godly lives in a God-denying world?

- As you live your life in the world, what things are you and your fellow Christians constantly exposed to that are antithetical to Christian faith? Is it possible or wise to cut yourself off from such influences altogether? If not, what are you and your fellow Christians doing to protect yourself from defilement?

- In which situations (e.g., the work-place, as a citizen) do you and your fellow Christians find yourselves to be subject to the authority of non-Christians? What attitude and behavior should you and your fellow Christians adopt when relating to non-Christians who have authority over you in various spheres of life?

- How should you and your fellow Christians regard literature, videos, etc., which have been written and produced by non-Christians? At what point should you and your fellow Christians draw the line?

- How can you and your fellow Christians emulate Daniel and his friends in your quest to be wise? What will it mean for you to be wise in this world?

- What things are fellow Christians and you yourself required or pressured to do?

- How should you and fellow Christians respond to the occult and to the superstitious thinking and practices of non-Christians (and perhaps even Christians) around you?

- What is your personal identity and the personal identity of your fellow Christians rooted in?

DANIEL 2

Exegetical

- What particular emphases emerge from an analysis of the structure of the chapter?
- Why was Nebuchadnezzar so deeply disturbed by his dream?
- What is significant about God using the dream-vision medium to reveal his message?
- Why did Nebuchadnezzar refuse to disclose the dream to the Chaldeans (wise men/astrologers)?
- What do we learn about the wisdom of the Chaldeans?
- How is Daniel distinguished from the Chaldeans? How does Daniel 2 go beyond Daniel 1 in establishing this distinctiveness?
- What is revealed about Babylonian religion?
- What did the failure of the Chaldeans to interpret the king's dream reveal about the king himself?
- How does God demonstrate his sovereignty? Does he do this fully?
- How does Daniel's God differ from the Babylonian gods?
- What do we learn about Daniel's character and limitations?
- What did Daniel learn about God?
- What is the significance of the different materials which make up the statue?
- What is the meaning of feet being composed partly of iron and partly of clay?
- Can the different materials be identified with particular reigns, empires, and periods of history?
- What does it mean to identify Nebuchadnezzar with "the head of gold?"
- When are the reigns described destroyed?
- What do you think is meant by "the rock" which strikes and shatters the statue?
- To what extent does Nebuchadnezzar respond appropriately to the interpretation Daniel gives him?

- Why is the exaltation of Daniel and his friends significant in this particular context?

- What do we learn about the eschatological reign of God from this dream-vision?

- Do you think that Daniel and his friends might be associated with the rock in any way?

- How does Daniel 2 extend the parallelism between the careers of Daniel and Joseph?

- Why does Daniel change from Hebrew to Aramaic from verse 4 onwards?

New Testament Development

- Does the New Testament give any indications as to how the vision will find its fulfillment? (e.g., see Matt 21:44; Luke 20:18; 1 Cor 15:24; Rev 11:15)

- How do Romans 13:1–7, 1 Peter 2:13–14, and Titus 3:1 develop the theology implicit in Dan 2:37?

- What is the essence of "the mystery" in Daniel 2? Does the New Testament conception of "the mystery" represent a development of this at all? (cf. Matt 13:11; Rom 16:25–27; Col 1:27; Eph 2:3–10)

Personal Relevance and Application

(Caution: do not seek to answer these questions in isolation from the text of Daniel 2)

- How can you and your fellow Christians emulate Daniel?

- Is your wisdom as a Christian and the wisdom of your fellow Christians something which transcends human capabilities? In what respects?

- Do you and your fellow Christians know God as the one who lives and moves among his people? Are "the gods" of non-Christians always ultimately gods which "do not live among men?"

- How does Daniel 2 help us to develop a God-honoring view of history?

DANIEL 3

Exegetical

- What particular emphases emerge from an analysis of the structure of the chapter?

- What is the relationship (if any) between Nebuchadnezzar's image of gold and the statue of Nebuchadnezzar's dream in Daniel 2? For example, why is the use of gold significant?

- How is an understanding of the essential nature of Nebuchadnezzar's kingship advanced by this chapter?

- Why is there so much repetition in the literary narrative (vv. 2–3, 5, 7,10)?

- In what ways do the events and language of this chapter touch base with prior historical experience?

- How are the Chaldeans described in this chapter? What is the significance of this portrayal?

- What are the implications of committing idolatry?

- Why do the three Jews refuse to commit idolatry? To what extent was this due to their confidence in God's ability to save them?

- What does the death of the soldiers who put the three Jews in the fire serve to indicate?

- Who is the fourth "man" in the fire?

- Why is it stressed that the fire caused no damage to the clothing or persons of the three Jews?

- To what unprecedented point is Nebuchadnezzar brought by the events described in this chapter? Does he now appreciate the implications of God's sovereignty in a full manner?

- Is it significant or merely stylistic that the chapter should begin and end by referring to what happens "in the province of Babylon?" If the former, what significant movement has taken place in this chapter?

- How are the three Jews portrayed in this chapter? Is there any continuity between this portrayal and the material of Daniel 2 (e.g., "the rock")?

- Who denounces the three Jews? What further parallels to this phenomenon are provided by the book of Daniel and what is the significance of this?

New Testament Development

- Noting Revelation 13:18 what is the significance of the dimensions of the image (60 by 6 cubits)?
- How does the book of Revelation associate Babylon with idolatry?
- How do the words "no other god can save in this way" find even greater fulfillment in the New Testament?
- Compare the stand taken by the three Jews in this chapter with the stand taken by various ones in the New Testament (e.g., Stephen).

Personal Relevance and Application

(Caution: do not seek to answer these questions in isolation from the text of Daniel 3)

- Given our understanding of what idolatry means and involves in this chapter, what constitutes idolatry for us as God's people?
- How should and how can we emulate the three Jews?
- What does the deliverance of the three Jews mean? For example, does it imply that we as God's people can always expect him to miraculously deliver us from extreme peril?
- How does the presence of the "fourth man" with the three friends provide encouragement for God's people today?
- Is cultural pluralism a safeguard against idolatry?
- How did the three Jews get into such trouble? How does this parallel the ways in which Christians today are persecuted?

DANIEL 4

Exegetical

- What particular emphases emerge from an analysis of the structure of the chapter?

- How did Nebuchadnezzar view his own rule?

- How is Nebuchadnezzar's understanding of God advanced in this chapter? Does Nebuchadnezzar attain to a full and proper understanding of God or are there still discernible deficiencies? What change (if any) occurred in Nebuchadnezzar's understanding of other gods?

- Why didn't Nebuchadnezzar summon Daniel?

- What was Nebuchadnezzar's understanding of Daniel's relationship to deity?

- What effect did immense power have upon Nebuchadnezzar's personal life?

- What is the purpose of "the miraculous signs and wonders" of God in this chapter and in the book as a whole? In what way is God's miraculous intervention in this chapter unprecedented?

- What themes in this chapter involve continuity with Daniel 1–3? What effect is achieved by repeating past motifs, e.g., the interpretive incompetence of the Chaldeans?

- What relationship (if any) does the tree of Nebuchadnezzar's dream-visions bear towards the image of God in Daniel 3 and the statue of the dream-vision in Daniel 2?

- What is the significance of the tree described in the dream-vision in ancient thought?

- Given ancient perspectives is the identification of this tree with Nebuchadnezzar surprising? How do ancient worldviews compare and contrast with the reality revealed in this chapter?

- What was Nebuchadnezzar's role in the world of his day? Was this a God-given role? Why did God take this away from him?

- What is the continuation of Nebuchadnezzar's own rule dependent upon?

- What particular significance is there in the fact that God makes Nebuchadnezzar like an animal?

- What does this chapter reveal about Daniel's relationship with and attitude towards Nebuchadnezzar? How does this build on what has already been indicated in Daniel 1–3?

- What parallels are there (if any) between Daniel and the prophets? (e.g., compare this chapter with Nathan's confrontation of David in 2 Samuel 12)

- What connections (if any) are there between the material of this chapter and the doctrine of the Image of God?

New Testament Development

- Compare this event with Acts 12: 19b–23. What similarities and differences do you note?

- Who is "the lowliest of all men" according to New Testament understanding? What has God given to him? How does this impact on our lives?

- Does Matthew 3:10 presuppose Daniel 4:14? If so, what might be the significance of such an allusion?

- How is an understanding of the Parable of the Mustard Seed (Matthew 13:31–32) helped by this Danielic background (see esp. v. 12)?

- How does the New Testament develop our understanding as to the relationship between God's kingdom and human kingdoms?

- How does the New Testament underscore and develop the view of God presented in this chapter? For example, note Romans 9:20.

- How is this chapter's understanding of "Heaven" (e.g., v. 26) developed in the New Testament?

Personal Relevance and Application

(Caution: do not seek to answer these questions in isolation from the text of Daniel 4)

- In what ways does Daniel's attitude towards Nebuchadnezzar, as presented in this chapter, serve as a model for God's people?

- Nebuchadnezzar begins this chapter by presenting himself as the source of prosperity. What does this chapter reveal about prosperity and what is the significance of this for understanding our own lives?

- What are the roots of pride and why is it so reprehensible? How can we protect ourselves against a spirit of pride?

- What is humility? Why is it so important? How do we learn humility?

DANIEL 5

Exegetical

- What particular emphases emerge from an analysis of the structure of the chapter?

- How does Daniel 5 develop the motifs of Daniel 1–4?

- What is the significance of Belshazzar's great banquet? Does it echo earlier events in Daniel? Are there any indications as to why Belshazzar staged this banquet?

- What was Belshazzar's concept of God? What did he fail to understand about God?

- What is the point of distinction in this chapter between God and other gods?

- What did Belshazzar's act of blasphemy reveal about Babylonian rule?

- What would you say is the overall purpose of this chapter?

- How does God's treatment of Belshazzar advance our understanding of God's rule beyond what we have already discovered in Daniel 1–4?

- In what ways does this chapter compare and contrast Belshazzar with Nebuchadnezzar?

- To what extent (if at all) can Nebuchadnezzar be viewed as the creator of the situation described in this chapter?

- Why does God deal with Belshazzar more harshly than he dealt with Nebuchadnezzar?

- What was so heinous about Belshazzar's sin?

- What is significant about the way Belshazzar used the temple articles? How does this line up with the Temple motif in Daniel?

- How did Daniel come to be summoned? What is the significance of this?
- How is Daniel portrayed in this chapter?
- What effect did the writing on the wall have on Belshazzar?
- What role does Daniel assume in this chapter with respect to Belshazzar?
- What do we know about and what can we conclude about Darius the Mede?

New Testament Development

- From whom is the kingdom taken in the New Testament? Compare and contrast the respective situations.
- How is Daniel 5:4, 23 taken up and developed in Revelation 9:20?
- Compare Acts 17:28 with Daniel 5:23b. What common reality is expressed? How is this applied in Acts 17 and elsewhere in the New Testament?

Personal Relevance and Application

(Caution: do not seek to answer these questions in isolation from the text of Daniel 5)

- Especially recalling Belshazzar's concept of God, what commensurate acts of blasphemy are perpetrated in our world today? Why do you see these as analogous to Belshazzar's act?
- What appears to have been Belshazzar's underlying motivation in acting as he did? In what ways does a similar motivation express itself in our lives?
- Critique Belshazzar as a leader and consider how a similar leadership style might be expressed in Christian circles.
- What do you learn about God from this chapter? What implications does this have for the way you and your fellow Christians should live?
- What is the relationship between knowledge and humility (v. 22)? What warning does this send to us?

DANIEL 6

Exegetical

- What particular emphases emerge from an analysis of the structure of the chapter?

- What motifs in Daniel 1–5 are developed in this chapter?

- What parallels are there between this chapter and Daniel 3? In what respects does Daniel 6 go beyond Daniel 3?

- Why did Darius so greatly exalt Daniel?

- Why did the other officials seek Daniel's demise? How does this accord with material already presented in Daniel 1–5?

- How is Daniel portrayed in this chapter? How was he viewed by his enemies? By Darius? By God?

- What was at the center of Daniel's devotion? In the minds of his enemies? In his own mind and heart?

- How is the theme of decrees developed in this chapter?

- What does the first decree reveal about the essential nature of human rule? How does this line up with the general representation of human rule in Daniel?

- In what respects does Darius's rule represent a departure from Babylonian rule and in what respects is it continuous with it?

- What is revealed in this chapter about Daniel's relationship with human rule? What corresponding things have already been presented in Daniel 1–5?

- What kind of person makes the best kind of servant for the king?

- How did God effect Daniel's deliverance?

- What role do angels have in this chapter and elsewhere in Daniel?

- Does this chapter advance or merely repeat the understanding of God's rule?

New Testament Development

- Compare and contrast Acts 12 with Daniel 6.
- Compare Matthew 27:66 with Daniel 6:17 and comment on the points of contact between these respective contexts.
- In what ways does Daniel remind us of Jesus?

Personal Relevance and Application

(Caution: do not seek to answer these questions in isolation from the text of Daniel 6)

- In what ways does Daniel serve as a model for God's people today?
- Compare verse 10 with Matthew 6:6 and consider the implications of this for your prayer life.
- What caused Darius to set in motion a situation he deeply regretted but was helpless to change? What practical lessons can we learn from this?

Bibliography

Adeyemo, Tokunboh. "Daniel." In *Africa Bible Commentary,* edited by Tokunboh Adeyemo, 1015–38. Nairobi: Word Alive Publishers/Zondervan, 2010.

Allison, D. C., Jr. "Apocalyptic." In *Dictionary of Jesus and the Gospels,* edited by J.B. Green, S. McKnight and I. H. Marshall, 17–20. Downers Grove, IL: InterVarsity, 1992.

Albertz, Rainer, "The Social Setting of the Aramaic and Hebrew Book of Daniel." In *The Book of Daniel: Composition and Reception* 2 vols, edited by John J. Collins and Peter W. Flint, 1:171–204. Leiden: Brill, 2002.

Alter, R. *The Art of Biblical Narrative.* New York, NY: Basic Books, 1981.

Anderson, R. A. *Signs and Wonders: A Commentary on the Book of Daniel.* International Theological Commentary. Grand Rapids, MI: Eerdmans, 1984.

Archer, Gleason L., Jr. "Modern Rationalism and the Book of Daniel." *Bibliotheca Sacra* 136:542 (April–June 1979) 129–47.

Arnold, Bill T. "Wordplay and Narrative Techniques in Daniel 5 and 6." *Journal of Biblical Literature* 112/3 (1993) 479–85.

Avalos, Hector I. "The Comedic Function of the Enumerations of Officials and Instruments in Daniel 3." *Catholic Biblical Quarterly* 53 (1991) 580–88.

———. "Nebuchadnezzar's Affliction: New Mesopotamian Parallels for Daniel 4." *Journal of Biblical Literature* 133/3 (Fall 2014) 497–507.

Baldwin, Dalton D. "Free Will and Conditionality in Daniel." In *To Understand the Scriptures: Essays in Honor of William H. Shea,* edited by David Merling, 163–72. Berrien Springs, MI: Andrews University Institute of Archeology, 1997.

Baldwin, J. G. *Daniel.* Tyndale Old Testament Commentary. Leicester: InterVarsity, 1978.

Batstone, David B. "Jesus, Apocalyptic and World Transformation." *Theology Today* 49/3 (Oct 1992) 383–97.

Beaulieu, Paul Alain. "The Babylonian Background of the Motif of the Fiery Furnace in Daniel 3." *Journal of Biblical Literature* 128/2 (2009) 273–90.

———. Babylonian Collection. Yale University. http://www.achemenet.com

Berquist, Jon L. "Postcolonialism and Imperial Motives for Canonization." *Semeia* 75 (1996) 15–35.

Bledsoe, Amanda M. Davis. "The Identity of the 'Mad King' of Daniel 4 in the Light of Ancient Near Eastern Sources." *Cristianesimo Nella Storia* 33 (2012) 743–58.

Boccaccini, Gabriele. "The Solar Calendars of Daniel and Enoch." In *The Book of Daniel: Composition and Reception* 2 vols, edited by John J. Collins and Peter W. Flint, 2:311–28. Leiden: Brill, 2002.

Boutflower, C. *In and Around the Book of Daniel*. Grand Rapids, MI: Zondervan, 1963.

Breed, Brennan W. "Daniel's four Kingdom Schema: A History of Re-Writing World History." *Interpretation* 71/2 (2017) 178–89.

———. "A Divided Tongue: The Moral Taste Buds of the Book of Daniel." *Journal for the Study of the Old Testament* 40/1 (2015) 113–30.

Bright, John. *A History of Israel*. London: SCM, 1960.

Broida, Marian. "Textualizing Divination: The Writing on the Wall in Daniel 5:25." *Vetus Testamentum* 62 (2012) 1–13.

Bucur, Bogdan G. "Christophanic Exegesis and the Problem of Symbolization: Daniel 3 (the Fiery Furnace) as a Test Case." *Journal of Theological Interpretation* 10/2 (2016) 227–44.

Burkholder, Byron. "Literary Patterns and God's Sovereignty in Daniel 4." *Direction* 16/2 (Fall 1987) 45–54.

Calvin, John. "Commentary on Daniel—Volume 1." *Christian Classics Ethereal Library*. Available at: https://www.ccel.org/ccel/calvin/calcom24.html Accessed: 25 September, 2019.

Casey, Maurice. *Son of Man. The Interpretation and Influence of Daniel 7*. London: SPCK, 1979.

Charles, R. H. *Daniel*. The Century Bible. Edinburgh: T. C. & E. C. Jack, 1913.

Chappell, Bryan. *The Gospel According to Daniel. A Christ-Centered Approach*. Grand Rapids, MI: Baker, 2014.

Charlesworth, J. H., ed. *The Old Testament Pseudepigrapha*, vols 1–2. Garden City, NJ: Doubleday, 1983.

Collins, John J. "Apocalypse: An Overview." In *The Encyclopedia of Religion*, edited by M. Eliade, 334–6. New York, NY: Macmillan, 1978.

———. "Apocalyptic Eschatology as the Transcendence of Death." In *Visionaries and Their Apocalypses*. Issues in Religion and Theology 2, edited by P. D. Hanson, 61–84. Philadelphia, PA: Fortress, 1983.

———. *The Apocalyptic Imagination*. New York, NY: Crossroad, 1984.

———. *The Apocalyptic Vision of the Book of Daniel*. Harvard Semitic Monographs, 16. Harvard, MA: Scholars Press, 1977.

———. "Current Issues in the Study of Daniel." In *The Book of Daniel: Composition and Reception* 2 vols, edited by John J. Collins and Peter W. Flint, 1:1–15. Leiden: Brill, 2002.

———. "The Court Tales in Daniel and the Development of Apocalyptic." *Journal of Biblical Literature* (1975) 218–34.

———. *Daniel*. Hermeneia. Minneapolis, MN: Fortress, 1993.

———. "Daniel and His Social World." *Interpretation* 39 (April 1985) 131–43.

———. *Daniel with an Introduction to Apocalyptic Literature*. Grand Rapids, MI: Eerdmans, 1989.

———, ed. "Apocalypse: The Morphology of a Genre." *Semeia* 14. Missoula, MT: Society of Biblical Literature, 1979.

Cook, Edward M. "'In the Plain of the Wall' (Dan 3:1)." *Journal of Biblical Literature* 108/1 (Spring 1989) 115–6.

Cook, Stephen L. *Prophecy & Apocalypticism: The Postexilic Social Setting.* Minneapolis, MN: Fortress, 1995.

Culver, Robert Duncan. *Daniel and the Latter Days.* Chicago, IL: Moody, 1977.

Davies, P. R. *Daniel.* Old Testament Guides. Sheffield: JSOT Press, 1988.

de Bruyn, J. Jacobus. "A clash of gods—Conceptualising space in Daniel 1." *HTS Teologiese Studies/Theological Studies* 70/3 (2014). http://dx.doi.org/10.4102/hts.v70i3.1956 Downloaded 11/8/18

de Guglielmo, Antonine. "Daniel 5:25: An Example of a Double Literal Sense." *Catholic Biblical Quarterly* 11/2 (April 1949) 202–6.

———. "Daniel 5, Elohim and Marduk: The Final Battle." *Old Testament Essays* 26/3 (2013) 623–41.

Dillard, Raymond B., and Tremper Longman III. *An Introduction to the Old Testament.* Grand Rapids, MI: Zondervan, 1994.

Dorsey, David A. *The Literary Structure of the Old Testament. A Commentary on Genesis-Malachi.* Grand Rapids, MI: Baker, 1999.

Doukhan, Jacques B. *The Vision of the End: Daniel.* Berrien Springs, MI: Andrews University Press, 1987.

Dumbrell, W. J. *The Faith of Israel: Its Expression in the Books of the Old Testament.* Grand Rapids, MI: Baker, 1988.

Dunn, James D. G. "The Danielic Son of Man in the New Testament." In *The Book of Daniel: Composition and Reception* 2 vols, edited by John J. Collins and Peter W. Flint, 2:528–49. Leiden: Brill, 2002.

Dyer, Charles H. "The Musical Instruments in Daniel 3." *Bibliotheca Sacra* (October–December 1990) 426–36.

Ecklebarger, Kermit A. "Dreams." In *Baker Encyclopedia of the Bible* 4 vols, edited by Walter A. Elwell, 2:641–3. Grand Rapids, MI: Baker, 1997.

Edlin, Jim. *Daniel. A Commentary in the Wesleyan Tradition.* New Beacon Bible Commentary. Kansas City, KS: Beacon Hill, 2009.

Eliade, Mircea. *Images and Symbols: Studies in Religious Symbolism.* Translated by Philip Mairet. Princeton, NJ: Princeton University Press, 1991.

———. *Patterns in Comparative Religion.* Translated by Rosemary Sheed. New York, NY: World Publishing, 1972.

Evans, Craig A. "Daniel in the New Testament: Visions of God's Kingdom." In *The Book of Daniel: Composition and Reception* 2 vols, edited by John J. Collins and Peter W. Flint, 2:490–527. Leiden: Brill, 2002.

Farrar, F. W. *The Book of Daniel.* The Expositor's Bible. London: Hodder & Stoughton, 1895.

Ferguson, Paul. "Nebuchadnezzar, Gilgamesh, and the 'Babylonian Job.'" *Journal of the Evangelical Theological Society* 37/3 (Sept 1994) 321–31.

Ferguson, Sinclair. *Daniel.* Mastering the Old Testament. Dallas, TX: Word, 1988.

Fernando, Ajith. *Spiritual Living in a Secular World. Applying the Book of Daniel Today.* London: Monarch, 2002.

Fewell, Danna Nolan. *Circle of Sovereignty: Plotting Politics in the Book of Daniel.* Nashville, TN: Abingdon, 1991.

Flint, Peter W. "The Daniel Tradition at Qumran." In *The Book of Daniel: Composition and Reception* 2 vols, edited by John J. Collins and Peter W. Flint, 2:329–67. Leiden: Brill, 2002.

Flusser, D. "Biblical Literature: Intertestamental Literature." In *Encyclopaedia Britannica* (15th edn) 32 vols. 14:953–61. Chicago, IL: Merriam-Webster, 2010.

Ford, Desmond. *Daniel.* Nashville, TN: Southern Publishing Association, 1978.

Frost, S. B. *Old Testament Apocalyptic.* Ann Arbor, MI: Epworth, 1952.

Fyall, Robert. *Daniel.* Focus on the Bible. Ross-shire, UK: Christian Focus Publications, 1998.

Gager, J. G. *Kingdom and Community.* Englewood Cliffs, NJ: Prentice Hall, 1975.

Gammie, John G. "The Classification, Stages of Growth, and Changing Intentions in the Book of Daniel." *Journal of Biblical Literature* 95 191–204.

———. "A Journey Through Danielic Spaces, The Book of Daniel in the Theology and Piety Of the Christian Community." *Interpretation* 39 (Apr. 1985) 144–56.

Gane, Roy. "Genre Awareness and Interpretation of the Book of Daniel." In *To Understand the Scriptures: Essays in Honor of William H. Shea,* edited by David Merling, 137–48. Berrien Springs, MI: Andrews University Institute of Archeology, 1997.

Gangel, Kenneth O. *Daniel.* Holman Old Testament Commentary. Nashville, TN: Holman Reference, 2001.

Gardner, Anne E. "Daniel 7, 2–14: Another Look at its Mythic Pattern." *Biblica* 82 (2001) 244–252.

Ginsberg, H. L. "The Composition of the Book of Daniel." *Vetus Testamentum* 4 (1954) 246–75.

Goldingay, J. E. *Daniel.* Word Biblical Commentaries, 30. Milton Keynes: Word, 1991.

Gooding, David W. "The Literary Structure of the Book of Daniel and its Implications." *Tyndale Bulletin* 32 (1981) 43–80.

Goswell, Greg. *Daniel. A Kingdom That Cannot Be Destroyed.* An Onesimus Bible Study Guide. Box Hill North: PTC Media, 2005.

———. "The Temple Theme in the Book of Daniel." *Journal of the Evangelical Theological Society* 55/3 (2012) 509–20.

Gowan, Donald E. *Daniel.* Abingdon Old Testament Commentaries. Nashville, TN: Abingdon, 2001.

Gruenwald, I. "Jewish Apocalypticism in the Rabbinic Period." In *The Encyclopedia of Religion,* edited by M. Eliade, 336–42. New York, NY: Macmillan, 1978.

Greidanus, Sidney. *Preaching Christ from Daniel: Foundations for Expository Sermons.* Grand Rapids, MI: Eerdmans, 2012.

Grillo, Jennie. "'From a Far Country': Daniel in Isaiah's Babylon." *Journal of Biblical Literature* 2 (2017) 363–80.

Gurney, Robert. "The Four Kingdoms of Daniel 2 and 7." *Themelios* 2/2 (Jan 1977) 39–45.

———. *God in Control: An Exposition of the Prophecies of Daniel.* Worthing, West Sussex: H.E. Walter, 1980.

Guthrie, Donald. "Pseudepigrapha." In *The New Bible Dictionary,* edited by J. D. Douglas et al., 1059–62. London: InterVarsity, 1968.

Hamilton, James M., Jr. *With the Clouds of Heaven: The Book of Daniel in Biblical Theology.* New Studies in Biblical Theology. Downers Grove, IL: InterVarsity, 2014.

Hammer, Raymond. *The Book of Daniel.* Cambridge Bible Commentary on the NEB. Cambridge: Cambridge University Press, 1976.

Hanson, P. D. "Introduction." In *Visionaries and Their Apocalypses*. Issues in Religion and Theology 2, edited by P. D. Hanson, 1–15. Philadelphia, PA: Fortress, 1983.

———. "Old Testament Apocalyptic Reexamined." In *Visionaries and Their Apocalypses*. Issues in Religion and Theology 2, edited by P. D. Hanson, 37–60. Philadelphia, PA: Fortress, 1983.

Harman, Allan M. *Daniel*. Evangelical Press Study Commentary. Darlington, UK: Evangelical Press, 2007.

Harrison, R. K. "Daniel, Book of." In *International Standard Bible Encyclopedia* 4 vols, edited by Geoffrey W. Bromiley, 1:859–66. Grand Rapids, MI: Eerdmans, 1979.

Hartman, L. E., and A. A. Di Lella. *The Book of Daniel*. The Anchor Bible, 23. Garden City, NY: Doubleday, 1977.

Hasel, Gerhard F. "The Four World Empires of Daniel 2 Against its Near Eastern Environment." *Journal for the Study of the Old Testament* 12 (1979) 17–30.

Hays, Christopher B. "Chirps from the Dust: The Affliction of Nebuchadnezzar in Daniel 4:30 in Its Ancient Near Eastern Context." *Journal of Biblical Literature* 126/2 (2007) 305–25.

Heaton, E. W. *The Book of Daniel*. Torch Bible Commentaries. London: SCM, 1964.

Hebbard, Aaron B. *Reading Daniel as a Text in Theological Hermeneutics*. Princeton Theological Monograph Series. Eugene, OR: Pickwick, 2009.

Hellholm, D., ed. *Apocalypticism in the Mediterranean World and the Near East*. Tübingen: Mohr-Siebeck, 1983.

Henze, Matthias. "Nebuchadnezzar's Madness (Daniel 4) in Syrian Literature." In *The Book of Daniel: Composition and Reception* 2 vols, edited by John J. Collins and Peter W. Flint, 2:550–71. Leiden: Brill, 2002.

Hilton, Michael. "Babel Reversed—Daniel Chapter 5." *Journal for the Study of the Old Testament* 66 (1995) 99–112.

Holm, Tawny L. "The Fiery Furnace in the Book of Daniel and the Ancient Near East." *Journal of the American Oriental Society* 128/1 (Jan-Mar 2008) 85–104.

———. *Of Courtiers and Kings. The Biblical Daniel Narratives and Ancient Story-Collections*. Explorations in Ancient Near Eastern Civilizations. Winona Lake, IN: Eisenbrauns, 2013.

Instone-Brewer, David. "MENE MENE TEQEL UPARSIN: Daniel 5:25 in Cuneiform." *Tyndale Bulletin* 42/2 (1991) 310–16.

Jeffcoat, W. D. *The Linguistic Argument for the Date of Daniel* Montgomery, AL: Apologetics Press. http://www.apologeticspress.org/rr/reprints/Linguistic-Argument-for-the-Dat.pdf Downloaded 22/2/07

Jerome. *Jerome's Commentary on Daniel*. Translated by Gleason L. Archer Jr. Grand Rapids, MI: Baker, 1958.

Johnson, E. Elizabeth. "The Function of Apocalyptic and Wisdom Traditions in Romans 9–11: Rethinking the Questions." *Seminar Papers 1995*, 352–61. Atlanta, GA: Scholars Press, 1995.

Kasemann, E. "The Beginnings of Christian Theology." *New Testament Questions of Today*. Philadelphia, PA: Fortress, 1969.

———. "What is Apocalyptic? An Attempt at a Preliminary Definition (1972)." In *Visionaries and Their Apocalypses*. Issues in Religion and Theology 2, edited by P. D. Hanson, 16–36. Philadelphia, PA: Fortress, 1983.

Keel, Othmar. *The Symbolism of the Biblical World: Ancient Near Eastern Iconography and the Book of Psalms*. Translated by T. J. Hallett. London: SPCK, 1978.

Keil, C. F., and F. Delitzsch. "Daniel" in *Commentary on the Old Testament. Ezekiel, Daniel*, 10 vols, vol 9. Translated by M.G. Easton. Grand Rapids, MI: Eerdmans, 1982.

Kik, J. Marcellus. *An Eschatology of Victory.* Phillipsburg, NJ: Presbyterian & Reformed, 1978.

Kim, Daewoong. "Biblical Interpretation in the Book of Daniel: Literary Allusions in Daniel to Genesis and Ezekiel." PhD diss., Rice University, 2013.

Kitchen, K. A. "The Aramaic of Daniel." In *Notes on Some Problems in the Book of Daniel*, edited by D. J. Wiseman, et al., 31–79. London: Tyndale, 1965.

Knibb, Michael A. "The Book of Daniel in its Context." In *The Book of Daniel: Composition and Reception* 2 vols, edited by John J. Collins and Peter W. Flint, 1:16–35. Leiden: Brill, 2002.

Koch, Klaus. "Is Daniel Also Among the Prophets?" *Interpretation* 39 (1985) 117–30.

———. *The Rediscovery of Apocalyptic.* London: SCM, 1972.

Kruschwitz, Robert B., and Paul L. Redditt. "Nebuchadnezzar as the Head of Gold: Politics and History in the Theology of the Book of Daniel." *Perspectives in Religious Studies* 24/4 (Winter 1997) 399–416.

Ladd, George Eldon. "Apocalyptic." In *The New Bible Dictionary*, edited by J. D. Douglas, 43–44. London: Inter-Varsity, 1968.

———. "The Origin of Apocalyptic in Biblical Religion." *The Evangelical Quarterly* 30/3 (1958) 140–46.

Lawson, Jack N. "'The God Who Reveals Secrets': The Mesopotamian Background to Daniel 2.47." *Journal for the Study of the Old Testament* 74 (1997) 61–76.

Leatherman, Donn W. "Apparent Indicators of Textual Discontinuity in the Book of Daniel." In *To Understand the Scriptures: Essays in Honor of William H. Shea*, edited by David Merling, 149–61. Berrien Springs, MI: Andrews University Institute of Archeology, 1997.

Lederach, Paul M. *Daniel.* Believers Church Bible Commentary. Scottdale, PA: Herald, 1994.

Lenzi, Alan. "Secrecy, Textual Legitimation, and Intercultural Problems in the Book of Daniel." *Catholic Biblical Quarterly* 71 (2009) 330–48.

Longman, Tremper, III. *Daniel.* NIV Application Commentary. Grand Rapids, MI: Eerdmans, 1999.

Lucas, Ernest C. *Daniel.* Apollos Old Testament Commentary, 20. Leicester, UK: Apollos, 2002.

Lucas, Ernest C. "The Origin of Daniel's Four Empires Scheme Re-examined." *Tyndale Bulletin* 40 (1989) 185–202.

———. "The Source of Daniel's Animal Imagery." *Tyndale Bulletin* 41.2 (1990) 161–85.

MacArthur, John, Jr. *An Uncompromising Life: Daniel 1, 3, and 6.* John MacArthur's Bible Studies. Chicago, IL: Moody, 1988.

Martin, W. J. "The Hebrew of Daniel." In *Notes on Some Problems in the Book of Daniel*, edited by D. J. Wiseman, et al., 28–30. London: Tyndale, 1965.

Mastin, B. A. "The Meaning of H^{a}LA ' at Daniel IV 27." *Vetus Testamentum* XLII/2 (1992) 234–47.

Matthews, Victor H., and Don C. Benjamin. "Annals of Mesha." In *Old Testament Parallels. Laws and Stories from the Ancient Near East*, 167–9. New York, NY: Paulist, 2006.

Meade, David G. *Pseudonymity and Canon. An Investigation into the Relationship of Authorship and Authority in Jewish and Earliest Christian Tradition.* Grand Rapids, MI: Eerdmans, 1987.

Meadowcroft, Tim. "Point of View in Storytelling. An Experiment in Narrative Criticism in Daniel 4." *Didaskalia* 8/2 (Spring 1997) 30–34.

Meadowcroft, Tim, and Nate Irwin. *The Book of Daniel.* Asia Bible Commentary Series. Singapore: Asia Theological Association, 2004.

Mendelsohn, I. "Dream." In *The Interpreter's Dictionary of the Bible* 5 vols, edited by George A. Buttrick, 1: 868–9. Nashville, TN: Abingdon, 1980.

Mendez, Hugo. *The Hellenistic World as the Fourth Kingdom of Daniel 2: An Intratextual Defense of the Greek View.* http://sda2rc.blogspot.com/2010/09/catholic-blog-on-daniel-2.html Viewed 15/8/11.

Millard, A. R. "Daniel 1–6 and History." *Evangelical Quarterly* 49.2 (April-June 1977) 67–73.

Miller, Stephen R. *Daniel.* The New American Commentary, 18. Nashville, TN: Broadman and Holman, 1994.

Milne, Pamela J. *Vladimir Propp and the Study of Structure in Hebrew Biblical Narrative.* Bible and Literature Series, 13. Sheffield: Almond Press, 1988.

Mitchell, T. C., and R. Joyce. "The Musical Instruments in Nebuchadrezzar's Orchestra." In *Notes on Some Problems in the Book of Daniel,* edited by D. J. Wiseman, et al., 19–27. London: Tyndale, 1965.

Mol, Hans. *Calvin for the Third Millenium.* ANU Press, 2008.

Montgomery, James A. *A Critical and Exegetical Commentary on the Book of Daniel.* International Critical Commentary. Edinburgh: T & T Clark, 1964.

Nel, Marius. "Function of space in Daniel 1." *Die Skriflig* (48) /*In Luce Verbi,* S.l., (June 2014) 1–7. https://indieskriflig.org.za/index.php/skriflig/article/view/1778/2466 Downloaded 12/8/18.

Nelson, William B. *Daniel.* Understanding the Bible Commentary Series. Grand Rapids, MI: Baker, 2012.

Olojede (Unisa), Funlola. "Daniel 'More than a Prophet'? Images, Imagery, Imagination, and the *Mashal* in Daniel 2." *Old Testament Essays* 27/3 (2014) 945–59.

Olyott, Stuart. *Dare to Stand Alone. Read and enjoy the Book of Daniel.* Welwyn Commentaries. Darlington, UK: Evangelical Press, 1982.

Oppenheim, A. Leo. *Ancient Mesopotamia: Portrait of a Dead Civilization.* Chicago, IL: University of Chicago Press, 1964.

————, trans. "The Banquet of Ashurnasipal II." In *Ancient Near Eastern Texts Relating to the Old Testament,* edited by James B. Pritchard, 558–61. Princeton, NJ: Princeton University Press, 1969.

Pace, Sharon. *Daniel.* Smyth and Helwys Bible Commentary. Macon, GA: Smyth and Helwys, 2008.

Patterson, Richard D. "The Key Role of Daniel." *Grace Theological Journal* 12.2 (1991) 245–61.

————. "Wonders In The Heavens And On The Earth: Apocalyptic Imagery In The Old Testament." *Journal of the Evangelical Theological Society* 43:3 (March 2000) 385–403.

Paul, Shalom M. "The Mesopotamian Background of Daniel 1–6." In *The Book of Daniel: Composition and Reception* 2 vols, edited by John J. Collins and Peter W. Flint, 1:55–68. Leiden: Brill, 2002.

Péter-Contesse, René, and John Ellington. *A Handbook on the Book of Daniel*. New York, NY: United Bible Societies, 1994.

Perrin, N. "Apocalyptic Christianity." In *Visionaries and Their Apocalypses*. Issues in Religion and Theology 2, edited by P. D. Hanson, 121–45. Philadelphia, PA: Fortress, 1983.

Philpot, Joshua M. "Review of Hamilton, James M, Jr. With the Clouds of Heaven: The Book of Daniel in Biblical Theology." *Journal of the Evangelical Theological Society* 57/4 (2014) 811–4.

Polaski, Donald C. "*Mene, Mene, Tekel, Parsin*: Writing and Resistance in Daniel 5 and 6." *Journal of Biblical Literature* 123/4 (2004) 649–69.

Porteous, N. *Daniel*. Old Testament Library. London: SCM, 1974.

Prinsloo, G. T. M. "Two Poems in a Sea of Prose: The Content and Context of Daniel 2.20–23 and 6.27–28." *Journal for the Study of the Old Testament* 59 (1993) 93–108.

Pritchard, James B., ed. *Ancient Near Eastern Texts Relating to the Old Testament*. Princeton, NJ: Princeton University Press, 1969.

Redditt, Paul L. *Daniel*. New Century Bible Commentary. Sheffield: Sheffield Academic Press, 1999.

Reid, A. *Kingdoms in Conflict: Reading Daniel Today*. Sydney: Anglican Information Office Press, 1993.

Reid, Stephen Breck. *Enoch and Daniel. A Form Critical Analysis and Sociological Study of Historical Apocalypses*. BIBAL Monograph Series 2. Berkeley, CA: BIBAL Press, 1989.

Reynolds, Bennie H., III. "Between Symbolism and Realism: The Use of Symbolic and Non-Symbolic Language in Ancient Jewish Apocalypses 333–63 BCE." Doctoral diss., University of North Carolina, Chapel Hill, 2009.

Retief, F. P., J. F. G. Cilliers, and S. P. J. K. Riekert. "Eunuchs in the Bible." *Acta Theologica Supplementum* 7 (2005) 247–58. https://www.ajol.info/index.php/actat/article/view/52578 Downloaded 13/8/18

Rindge, Matthew S. "Jewish Identity under Foreign Rule: Daniel 2 as a Reconfiguration of Genesis 41." *Journal of Biblical Literature* 129/1 (2010) 85–104.

Rist, M. "Apocalypticism." In *The Interpreter's Dictionary of the Bible,* 5 vols, edited by George A. Buttrick, 1: 157–61. Nashville, TN: Abingdon, 1980.

Rowland, C. *The Open Heaven*. New York, NY: Crossroad, 1982.

Russell, D. S. *Daniel*. Daily Study Bible. Edinburgh: St Andrew Press, 1981.

Schwab, George M. *Hope in the Midst of a Hostile World. The Gospel According to Daniel*. The Gospel According to the Old Testament. Phillipsburg, NJ: P & R, 2006.

Segal, M. "From Joseph to Daniel: The Literary Development of the Narrative in Daniel 2." *Vetus Testamentum* 59/1 (2009) 123–49.

———. "Rereading the writing on the wall (Daniel 5)." *Zeitschrift für die alttestamentliche Wissenschaft.* 125/1 (2013) 161–76.

Shea, William H. "Nabonidus, Belshazzar, and the Book of Daniel: an Update." *Andrews University Seminary Studies* 20/2 (Summer 1982) 133–49.

Sherriffs, Deryck C. T. "Nebuchadnezzar's Theology and Ours." In *Mission and Meaning. Essays presented to Peter Cotterell,* edited by Anthony Billington, Tony Lane, and Max Turner, 12–30. Exeter: Paternoster, 1965.

Siegman, Edward F. "The Stone Hewn From the Mountain (Daniel 2)." *Catholic Biblical Quarterly* 18/4 (October 1956) 364–79.

Sims, James H. "Daniel." In *A Complete Literary Guide to the Bible,* edited by Leland Ryken and Tremper Longman III, 324–36. Academic and Professional Books. Grand Rapids, MI: Zondervan, 1993.

Smith, J. Z. "Wisdom and Apocalyptic." In *Visionaries and Their Apocalypses.* Issues in Religion and Theology 2, edited by P. D. Hanson, 101–20. Philadelphia, PA: Fortress, 1983.

Smith-Christopher, Daniel L. "Gandhi on Daniel 6: Some Thoughts on a 'Cultural Exegesis' of the Bible." *Biblical Interpretation* 1/3 (1993) 321–38.

———. "Prayers and Dreams: Power and Diaspora Identities in the Social Setting of the Daniel Tales." In *The Book of Daniel: Composition and Reception* 2 vols, edited by John J. Collins and Peter W. Flint, 1:266–90. Leiden: Brill, 2002.

Stone, M.E. "A Note on Daniel 1.3." *Australian Biblical Review* 7 (December 1959) 69–71.

———. "Enoch and Apocalyptic Origins." In *Visionaries and Their Apocalypses.* Issues in Religion and Theology 2, edited by P. D. Hanson, 92–100. Philadelphia, PA: Fortress, 1983.

———. "New Light on the Third Century." In *Visionaries and Their Apocalypses.* Issues in Religion and Theology 2, edited by P. D. Hanson, 85–91. Philadelphia, PA: Fortress, 1983.

———. *Scriptures, Sects and Visions.* Philadelphia, PA: Fortress, 1980.

Strom, Mark. *Days Are Coming: Exploring Biblical Patterns.* Sydney: Hodder and Stoughton, 1992.

Thompson, Mark. "Faith in Babylon—Daniel 3" 2015. Sound recording. Moore Theological College, heard 13 September, 2019. https://moore.edu.au/resources/faith-in-babylon-daniel-3-mark-thompson/

———. "Judgment in Babylon—Daniel 5" 2015. Sound recording. Moore Theological College, heard 14 September, 2019. https://moore.edu.au/resources/judgment-in-babylon-daniel-5-mark-thompson/

———. "Living in Babylon—Daniel 1" 2015. Sound recording. Moore Theological College, heard 13 September, 2019. https://moore.edu.au/resources/living-in-babylon-daniel-1-mark-thompson/

———. "The Rescuer in Babylon—Daniel 6" 2015. Sound recording. Moore Theological College, heard 14 September, 2019. https://moore.edu.au/resources/the-rescuer-in-babylon-daniel-6-mark-thompson/

———. "Who really rules in Babylon?—Daniel 4" 2015. Sound recording. Moore Theological College, heard 14 September, 2019. https://moore.edu.au/resources/who-really-rules-in-babylon-daniel-4-mark-thompson/

———. "Wisdom in Babylon—Daniel 2" 2015. Sound recording. Moore Theological College, heard 13 September, 2019. https://moore.edu.au/resources/wisdom-in-babylon-daniel-2-mark-thompson/

Towner, W. Sibley. *Daniel.* Interpretation. Atlanta, GA: John Knox, 1984.

———. "The Poetic Passages of Daniel 1–6." *Catholic Biblical Quarterly* 31 (1969) 317–26.

Ulrich, Eugene. "The Text of Daniel in the Qumran Scrolls." In *The Book of Daniel: Composition and Reception* 2 vols, edited by John J. Collins and Peter W. Flint, 2:573–85. Leiden: Brill, 2002.

Valeta, David M. *Lions and Ovens and Visions. A Satirical Reading of Daniel 1–6.* Hebrew Bible Monographs, 12. Sheffield: Phoenix Press 2008.

Vanderkam, James C. "Recent Studies in 'Apocalyptic.'" *Word and World* 4/1 (1984) 70–77.

Van der Toorn, Karel. "Scholars at the Oriental Court: The Figure of Daniel against its Mesopotamian Background." In *The Book of Daniel: Composition and Reception* 2 vols, edited by John J. Collins and Peter W. Flint, 1:38–54. Leiden: Brill, 2002.

Van Deventer, H. J. M. (Hans). "Literary Lions with Real Bite: Re-examining the Intertextual Rhetoric in Daniel 6." *Old Testament Essays* 28/3 (2105) 832–46.

Van Henten, Jan Willem. "Daniel 3 and 6 in Early Christian Literature." In *The Book of Daniel: Composition and Reception* 2 vols, edited by John J. Collins and Peter W. Flint, 1:149–69. Leiden: Brill, 2002.

Veiss, Suzana Dobric. *Ideological Texture Analysis of Daniel 1 and Diaspora*. Emerging Leadership Journeys. https://www.regent.edu/acad/global/publications/elj/vol9iss1/3ELJ-Veiss.pdf Accessed: 26 September, 2019.

Venter, Pieter M. "Space in Daniel 1." *Old Testament Essays*. 19/3 (2006) 993–1004.

Vogel, Winfried. "Cultic Motifs and Themes in the Book of Daniel." *Journal of the Adventist Theological Society* 7/1 (Spring 1996) 21–50.

Von Rad, Gerhard. *Old Testament Theology. The Theology of Israel's Historical Traditions* 2 vols. Translated by D. M. G. Stalker. London: SCM, 1977.

Walker, William O. "Daniel 7:13–14." *Interpretation* 39 (Apr. 1985) 176–81.

Walton, John H. "The *Anzu* Myth as Relevant Background for Daniel 7?" In *The Book of Daniel: Composition and Reception* 2 vols, edited by John J. Collins and Peter W. Flint, 1:69–89. Leiden: Brill, 2002.

———. "The Decree of Darius the Mede in Daniel 6." *Journal of the Evangelical Theological Society* 31/3 (September 1988) 279–86.

———. "The Four Kingdoms of Daniel." *Journal of the Evangelical Theological Society* 29/1 (March 1986) 25–36.

Walvoord, John F. *Daniel: The Key to Prophetic Revelation* (Chicago, IL: Moody, 1991.

Waterhouse, S. Douglas. "Why was Darius the Mede Expunged from History?" In *To Understand the Scriptures: Essays in Honor of William H. Shea*, edited by David Merling, 173–89. Berrien Springs, MI: Andrews University Institute of Archeology, 1997.

Wesselius, Jan-Wim. "The Writing of Daniel." In *The Book of Daniel: Composition and Reception* 2 vols, edited by John J. Collins and Peter W. Flint, 2:291–310. Leiden: Brill, 2002.

Wharton, James A. "Daniel 3:16–18." *Interpretation* 39 (Apr. 1985) 170–76.

Widder, Wendy L. "The Court Stories of Joseph (Gen 41) and Daniel (Dan 2) in Canonical Context: A Theological Paradigm for God's Work among the Nations." *Old Testament Essays* 27/3 (2014) 1112–28.

———. "Letting Nebuchadnezzar Speak: The Purpose of the First-Person Narrative in Daniel 4." *Old Testament Essays* 32/1 (2019) 197–214.

Widengren, Geo. *The King and the Tree of Life in Ancient Near Eastern Religion*. Uppsala: Lundequistaka, 1951.

Wills, Lawrence M. *The Jew in the Court of the Foreign King. Ancient Jewish Court Legends*. Harvard Dissertations in Religion, 26. Minneapolis, MN: Fortress, 1990.

———. *The Jewish Novel in the Ancient World*. Eugene, OR: Wipf and Stock, 2015.

Wiseman, D. J. "Some Historical Problems in the Book of Daniel." In *Notes on Some Problems in the Book of Daniel*, edited by D. J. Wiseman, et al., 9–18. London: Tyndale, 1965.

Wolters, Al. "Belshazzar's Feast and the Cult of the Moon God Sin." *Bulletin for Biblical Research* 5 (1995) 199–206.

————. "The Riddle of the Scales in Daniel 5." *Hebrew Union College Annual* 62 (1951) 155–77.

————. "Untying the King's Knots: Physiology and Wordplay in Daniel 5." *Journal of Biblical Literature* 110/1 (1991) 117–8.

Wood, Leon J. *Daniel.* Study Guide Commentary. Grand Rapids, MI: Zondervan, 1975.

Wooden, R. Glenn. "The Book of Daniel and Manticism: A Critical Assessment of the View that the Book of Daniel Derives from a Mantic Tradition." PhD diss., University of St. Andrews, 2000.

————. "Changing Perceptions of Daniel: Reading Daniel 4 and 5 in Context." In *From Biblical Criticism to Biblical Faith: Essays in Honor of Lee Martin McDonald*, edited by William H. Brackney and Craig A. Evans, 9–23. Macon, GA: Mercer University Press, 2007.

Young, E. J. *Daniel.* London: Banner of Truth, 1972.

www.ingramcontent.com/pod-product-compliance
Lightning Source LLC
Chambersburg PA
CBHW070910100426
42814CB00003B/121